1943

The World's Great Catholic Literature

THE MACMILLAN COMPANY
NEW YORK · BOSTON · CHICAGO
DALLAS · ATLANTA · SAN FRANCISCO

MACMILLAN AND CO., LIMITED
LONDON · BOMBAY · CALCUTTA
MADRAS · MELBOURNE

THE MACMILLAN COMPANY
OF CANADA, LIMITED
TORONTO

The World's Great Catholic Literature

EDITED BY

GEORGE N. SHUSTER
President of Hunter College

WITH AN INTRODUCTION BY

WILLIAM LYON PHELPS

NEW YORK
The Macmillan Company
1942

Set up and electrotyped

First Printing

: Printed in the United States of America :

ACKNOWLEDGMENTS

THANKS are due to the following publishers for the use of quoted material:

To the Allerton Book Company for "De Soto at the Mississippi" from *A Narrative of De Soto's Expedition* by Gonzalo de Oviedo.

To Burns Oates & Washbourne for "The Divine Goodness" and "Courtesy" from *On the Love of God* by Saint Francis de Sales; also for "Hope in the Mercy of God" from the *Autobiography* of Saint Teresa of Avila.

To Chatto and Windus for "The Abbot" and "The Cellarer" from *The Rule of Saint Benedict* translated by Cardinal Gasquet; also for "Of the Blessed Man Paul the Simple" and "Of the Blessed Woman Thais" from *The Paradise of the Fathers* edited by E. A. W. Budge.

To the *Commonweal* for "Fallen among the Iroquois" by Henry Longan Stuart and for "The Stage Director" by Richard Dana Skinner.

To Devin-Adair for "My Convent School" from *Twenty-five Years: Reminiscences* by Katharine Tynan Hinkson.

To Doubleday Doran for "Hunting a Hair Shirt" from *Hunting a Hair Shirt and Other Spiritual Adventures* by Aline Kilmer; for "The Art of Christmas Giving" from *Joyce Kilmer: Poems, Essays and Letters,* edited by R. C. Holliday; and for "Thick Weather" from *Rulers of the East and West* by Joseph Conrad.

To E. P. Dutton for "King Otto Is Victorious" from *The Works of Luitprand of Cremona* translated by F. A. Wright; for "Letter to Pope Gregory XI" from *Saint Catherine as Seen in Her Letters* translated by Vida D. Scudder; and for "The Mystery of Pain" from *Essays and Addresses on the Philosophy of Religion* by Friedrich von Hügel.

To Frank-Maurice, Inc. for "Paradise" and "The Charity Children" from *The Romance of the Rabbit* by Francis Jammes, translated by Gladys Edgerton.

To Gotham House for "Testimony of St. Jeanne d'Arc" from *The Trial of Jeanne d'Arc* translated by W. P. Barrett.

To Harcourt Brace for "The Hand of Herod" from *The Collected Edition of Heywood Broun* edited by Heywood Broun.

To Harper & Brothers for "An Accident" from *Ten Tales by Francois Coppee* translated by Walter Learned.

To the Harvard University Press for "In Memory of Nepotian" from *Selected Letters* by Saint Jerome translated by F. A. Wright; for "The Martyrdom of St. Polycarp" by Eusebius from *Ecclesiastical History* translated by Kirsopp Lake; for "To the Romans" by Saint Ignatius from *The Apostolic Fathers* edited by Kirsopp Lake; and for "The Presbyters" by Saint Polycarp from the same volume.

To B. Herder Book Company for "When the Popes Left Rome" from *The History of the Popes* by Ludwig Pastor, translated by F. I. Antrobus.

To Henry Holt for "Wisdom and the Church of God" by King Alfred from *English Prose and Verse* edited by H. Pancoast; for "King Canute Passes" by Thomas of Ely from the same volume; and for "Maria Visits Her Brother" from *Jesse and Maria* by Enrica von Handel-Mazzetti.

To Houghton Mifflin for "Madame Celestin" from *Bayou Folk* by Kate Chopin.

To P. J. Kenedy for "In the Reign of Charles I" from *Oddsfish* by Robert Hugh Benson; and for "Charge to the Priesthood" from *Literary Life and Other Essays* by Patrick Sheehan.

To Alfred Knopf for "Remorse" from *The Promised Land* by Ladislas Reymont translated by M. H. Dziewicki.

To John Lane and to Dodd Mead for "Joy and the Christian" from *Orthodoxy* by G. K. Chesterton.

To John Lane for "The Mamma of Sampietro from *In His Image* by Frederick, Baron Corvo; and for "Children in Midwinter" from *The Children* by Alice Meynell.

To Little Brown for "Pan Michael at Kamenyets" from *Pan Michael* by Henryk Sienkiewicz, translated by Jeremiah Curtin; and for "A Jesuit Missionary" from *The Jesuits in North America* by Francis Parkman.

To Longmans Green for "A Catholic's Faith" and "The Gentleman" from *Apologia* and for "Farewell to Oxford" from *The Idea of a University,* all by Cardinal Newman; also for "Saint Martin," "Saint Elizabeth" and "Saint Marcellinus" from *The Golden Legend* by Jacobus de Voragine translated by Granger Ryan and Helmut Ripperger; for "Thou Dost Smile" from *Job the Man Speaks with God* by Peter Lippert; and for "The Cross" from *Selected Works of Richard Rolle* edited by G. C. Heseltine.

To Macmillan and Company, London, for "The Catholic Idea of the State" from *The History of Freedom and Other Essays* by Lord Acton; and for "The Challenge of Divine Truth" from *Essays Chiefly on Poetry* by Aubrey de Vere.

To The Society for Promoting Christian Knowledge and The Macmillan Company, New York, for "Christian Humanism" from *A Literary History of Religious Thought in France* by Henri Bremond, translated by K. L. Montgomery; and for "Address to the Beloved" and "Questions" from *The Book of the Lover and the Beloved* by Ramon Lull, translated by E. Allison Peers.

To The Macmillan Company for "Conversion" from *The Catholic Church and Conversion* by G. K. Chesterton.

To Robert McBride for "Mary, Queen of Scots" by Pierre de Bourdeille, translated by Barrett H. Clark, from *Great Short Biographies of the World.*

To Methuen for "Portrait of Hurrell Froude" from *Hurrell Froude* by Louise Imogen Guiney.

To John Murphy for "Liberty and Law" from *A Retrospect of Fifty Years* by Cardinal Gibbons.

To the Oxford University Press for "The Conversion of Abelard" by Peter the Venerable from *Monastic Life at Cluny* by Joan Edwards; for "Two Days" by Gerard Manley Hopkins and for "On the Fall of Eutropius" by St. John Chrysostom both from *The Notebooks and Papers of Gerard Manley Hopkins.*

To Kegan Paul for "Brother Simeon" from *En Route* by Joris-Karl Huysmans.

To Peaslee, Brigham and Albrecht, agents, for "Marzio's Crucifix" from the book of the same name by F. Marion Crawford.

To Charles Scribner's Sons for "Man in Need" from *Monica* by Paul Bourget, translated by William Marchant; and for "Image and Reality" from *The Courtier* by Count Castiglione, translated by Leonard E. Opdycke.

To Sheed & Ward for "Action" from *Essays in Order* edited by Christopher Dawson and J. F. Burns; and for "St. Joan at Orleans" by Marshal Foch, from *Joan of Arc; An Act of Homage* edited by Gabriel Hanotaux.

INTRODUCTION

By William Lyon Phelps

In this anthology of the World's Great Catholic Literature, President Shuster has produced a volume that will interest all lovers of good reading. The book admirably fulfills a triple purpose. It supplies Catholics with well-chosen selections from authors indispensable to their daily devotions: it gives Protestants and others extracts from the range of Catholic literature, beginning with the First Century, the martyrs and Church Fathers, and coming down to our own day with G. K. Chesterton and contemporaries; it presents to mature minds, to men and women who are bearing the burden and heat of the day, literature that combines artistic excellence with spiritual beauty. It is a library extended over nearly two thousand years.

The contents are divided into seven parts—The Early Church, The Middle Ages, The Early Renaissance, Religious Humanism, An Expanding Faith, The Nineteenth Century and After, Modern Creative and Critical Writing.

In the third quarter of the nineteenth century many false prophets went out into the world. The approaching death not only of the Catholic Church but of Christianity was by many learned men confidently asserted. I remember when I was a graduate student at Yale, and was studying the work of Eduard von Hartmann, *Philosophy of the Unconscious* (1869), the author said that Christianity was already dead, having passed through all its phases. At about the turn of the century, I tried to find out whether von Hartmann was dead. Naturally the man in the street had never heard of him; but I asked a number of professors of philosophy and they did not know. It is perhaps better to be dead than not to have anyone know whether or not you are alive. Merely for the record, he died in 1906, and failed to be included in the eleventh edition of the Encyclopaedia Britannica in 1910. About the year 1899 a learned professor (not in New England) told me that the Cathedral of St. John the Divine in New York would never be completed. To my question if he meant that sufficient money could not be raised, he said, "Oh, no; but before the time comes for its completion, Christianity will be dead." *He* is now dead.

The difficulty with many men is that they imagine their world of thought is the thought of the world. Thomas Hardy, for whose literary art and for whose character I have great admiration, wrote in the introduction to *The Dynasts,* "The abandonment of the masculine pronoun in allusions to the First or Fundamental Energy seemed a necessary and logical consequence of the long abandonment by thinkers of the anthropomorphic conception of the same."

On the other hand, Browning was the greatest secular ally of Christianity in modern times. In the Pope's speech (Innocent XII) in *The Ring and the Book* we find a line

I must survive a thing ere know it dead.

So many things pronounced dead survive the diagnosticians.

In Browning's amazing dialectic, *Bishop Blougram's Apology,* not intended to be a statement of the grounds of Christian belief, but merely an unanswerable argument against those who choose with their own weapons to attack Christian believers, the Bishop *ironically* assumes that by 1920 no prelate will believe in Catholic dogma. And Thomas Carlyle, looking at a roadside crucifix, said, "Poor fellow! Your day is over!"

How amazed the imaginary agnostic talking with Blougram and how amazed Carlyle would have been could they have foreseen the tremendous rise in numbers and in prestige of the Catholic Church in English-speaking countries in the twentieth century. I am not a Catholic; but I regard this increase as one of the most noteworthy features of British and American life, both religious and social. I think it may partly be accounted for by the fact that Catholics teach Christianity as a real religion; whereas many Protestant churches have substituted social reforms for spiritual regeneration. The hungry sheep look up and are not fed.

A Catholic priest was called to the bedside of a sick man; and the sufferer angrily remonstrated, "Why are you trying to force your religion on me?" And the priest replied, "I am not trying to force my religion on you; I am trying to help you to have a religion of your own." For without religious belief life has no meaning; Shakespeare and Beethoven were merely doing tricks, and self-sacrificing love is reduced to the chemistry of the brain.

It is infinitely better to have some definite faith than merely a sentimental vagueness. St. Thomas Aquinas said the faith of an adult was better than the faith of children, because it was founded on reason, and with a knowledge of what could be urged against it. One man said that religious exercises should be held daily in every college because there is a great field of the unknown which should be recognised. Religious exercises would be a tribute to this X. I agree with him; it is X, only my X is a Cross.

No one can be or should be compelled to believe in any religious doctrine; but this admirable anthology gives the *testimony* of a long line of great writers to the reality of faith. These men of genius are not advocates, they are witnesses; and we know that the words of an intelligent witness are more valuable than the eloquence of an advocate.

I am glad that President Shuster has admitted such a vast variety of writers. He says some of them were saints and some of them were poor sinners. No living saints or sinners are included, the former, I surmise, because of the difficulty in finding any, the latter because they are so multitudinous. But we have those who have only recently gone to their reward—Chesterton, Francis Thompson, Heywood Broun, Richard Dana Skinner, Hermann Bahr, Louise Guiney, Wilfrid Ward, Katharine Tynan, Gerard Hopkins, Joyce Kilmer, and many others. Here, as Dryden said, is God's plenty. We range from Justin Martyr and the fiery Tertullian to the joyous humour of G. K. C. For Chesterton and his contemporary, Samuel Butler, unlike in everything else, agreed that the Chief Duty of a

Christian is to be happy. Every Christian and many others who read these pages will be the happier for this experience. As Mr. Santayana says of Dickens, those who read "will love winter, and one another, and God the better for it."

Yale University
Easter, 1942

PREFACE

This book is a collection of passages from many writers. It will in a measure illustrate the impact of Catholic thought and feeling upon world literature since the days of the Apostles. I have said "in a measure"; for the achievement is so vast in extent and so diversified in character that a book twice the size of the present volume would illustrate it far from adequately. Of course the Church is not concerned, in any fundamental sense, with the writings of men. It is, rather, a community of faithful souls of whom Christ is the king, given to charity, prayer and the healing of the spirit unto eternal life. But, according to the noble thought of St. Thomas, the grace that comes to humanity through the Church not only clarifies but also builds upon nature; and nothing is more natural than human self-expression. On the drama of man's love and anguish there is erected, as a consequence, the divine comedy of the struggling soul.

It is with such convictions in mind that this book has been formed. Some of the writers are saints, and some were poor sinners. There are those among them who worked all their days with the materials of the natural order, content to be artists and poets, to see man and beast and field as these things are. Others manifested a passionate dissatisfaction with earthly experience and sought to find the road to the land where the mystic dwells. Still others were historians of events which had a bearing on the progress and fortunes of Christianity. I have tried to give each group fair representation, and to include always some less well-known persons in the hope that they might symbolize the large number whom it was not possible to include. In order that there might be room enough, all living writers have been omitted. Serviceable anthologies of contemporary prose literature already exist.

A word may be in order concerning the manner in which the editor thinks the book could be read profitably. Of course the selections speak for themselves, and can be understood without the help of notes of any kind other than the biographical sketches supplied. One object of the volume is, however, very definitely to encourage further reading. And so, if those interested will first read through the volume and gain from it some sort of impression of the development of Catholic literary expression through the ages, they may then feel impelled to choose a segment or a trend of particular interest and importance to themselves. There have been three great periods of creative prose. The first came just before the fall of Rome, and is associated with St. Augustine, St. Jerome, and others who formed the outlines of Catholic thought and feeling. The second began, roughly speaking, with Dante and came to a close with what is termed the Renaissance. The third was inaugurated after the middle years of the nineteenth century and has not yet ended. Then there are subsidiary periods of great importance in some of the national literatures, as witness the flowering of Christian Humanism in France during the seventeenth century.

I have sought to preserve the contour of each period, although the arrangement is not chronological. Pieces which seem to belong together have been grouped within the broad framework of the time of their origin. Thus the historians have their several sections, and the creative writers have a goodly number of pages to themselves. Most of the writing is grave and concerned with matters not of this earth, but place has been found for humor and even for satire. The reader will no doubt miss passages which are dear to him. Many things have been omitted with regret; but I had to consider the book as a whole, and also to find prose which could be read separately without too much difficulty. Finally, a few selections by non-Catholic authors have been included. These are famous passages, and it seemed to me the reader would relish having them at hand.

The notes are designed to guide the reader a little farther in his quest for information and inspiration. Often a selection will indicate a great book; and such other titles are listed as seem to the editor likely to promote knowledge of the literature in its essentials.

I must add some sincere words of gratitude addressed to all those who have helped me, either with suggestions or with the actual making of the book. Publishers of copyright volumes are named in the biographical notes concerning authors whose work they have issued, and I have in each instance indicated my thanks for permissions given. Here I should like to underscore my indebtedness to them for courtesy and coöperation.

In conclusion, let me say that while the task here brought to completion has been no easy one, it can none the less be termed a burden borne lightly and with pleasure. To the tradition which it in a feeble measure illustrates I am more than ever attached now that the blood of martyrs loyal to it is being shed in so many dark places in the world. Where shall we look for peace or for a reason justifying hope, if not to Christ and His Church?

George N. Shuster

CONTENTS

III. THE EARLY RENAISSANCE

IV. RELIGIOUS HUMANISM

V. AN EXPANDING FAITH

VI. THE NINETEENTH CENTURY AND AFTER

VII. MODERN CREATIVE AND CRITICAL WRITING

I

THE EARLY CHURCH

THE NATIVITY

And it came to pass, that in those days there went out a decree from Caesar Augustus, that the whole world should be enrolled.

This enrolling was first made by Cyrinus, the governor of Syria.

And all went to be enrolled, every one into his own city.

And Joseph also went up from Galilee, out of the city of Nazareth into Judea, to the city of David, which is called Bethlehem: because he was of the house and family of David.

To be enrolled with Mary his espoused wife, who was with child.

And it came to pass, that when they were there, her days were accomplished, that she should be delivered.

And she brought forth her first-born son, and wrapped him up in swaddling clothes, and laid him in a manger; because there was no room for them in the inn.

And there were in the same country shepherds watching, and keeping the night watches over their flock.

And behold an angel of the Lord stood by them, and the brightness of God shone round about them; and they feared with a great fear.

And the angel said to them: Fear not; for, behold, I bring you good tidings of great joy, that shall be to all the people:

For, this day, is born to you a Saviour, who is Christ the Lord, in the city of David.

And this shall be a sign unto you. You shall find the infant wrapped in swaddling clothes, and laid in a manger.

And suddenly there was with the angel a multitude of the heavenly army, praising God, and saying:

Glory to God in the highest; and on earth peace to men of good will.

And it came to pass, after the angels departed from them into heaven, the shepherds said one to another: Let us go over to Bethlehem, and let us see this word that is come to pass, which the Lord hath shewed to us.

And they came with haste: and they found Mary and Joseph, and the infant lying in the manger.

ST. LUKE

THE EIGHT BEATITUDES

And seeing the multitudes, he went up into a mountain, and when he was set down, his disciples came unto him.

And opening his mouth, he taught them, saying:

Blessed are the poor in spirit: for theirs is the kingdom of heaven.

Blessed are the meek: for they shall possess the land.

Blessed are they that mourn: for they shall be comforted.

Blessed are they that hunger and thirst after justice: for they shall have their fill.

Blessed are the merciful: for they shall obtain mercy.

Blessed are the clean of heart: for they shall see God.

Blessed are the peacemakers: for they shall be called the children of God.

Blessed are they that suffer persecution for justice' sake: for theirs is the kingdom of heaven.

Blessed ye when they shall revile you, and persecute you, and speak all that is evil against you, untruly, for my sake.

Be glad and rejoice, for your reward is very great in heaven. For so they persecuted the prophets that were before you.

You are the salt of the earth. But if the salt lose its savour, wherewith shall it be salted? It is good for nothing any more but to be cast out, and to be trodden on by men.

You are the light of the world. A city seated on a mountain cannot be hid.

Neither do men light a candle and put it under a bushel, but upon a candlestick, that it may shine to all that are in the house.

So let your light shine before men, that they may see your good works, and glorify your Father who is in heaven.

ST. MATTHEW

I AM THE TRUE VINE

I am the true vine: and my Father is the husbandman.

Every branch in me, that beareth not fruit, he will take away: and every one that beareth fruit, he will purge it, that it may bring forth more fruit.

Now you are clean by reason of the word, which I have spoken to you.

Abide in me, and I in you. As the branch cannot bear fruit of itself, unless it abide in the vine, so neither can you, unless you abide in me.

I am the vine; you the branches: he that abideth in me, and I in him, the same beareth much fruit: for without me you can do nothing.

If any one abide not in me, he shall be cast forth as a branch, and shall wither, and they shall gather him up, and cast him into the fire, and he burneth.

If you abide in me, and my words abide in you, you shall ask whatever you will, and it shall be done unto you.

In this is my Father glorified; that you bring forth very much fruit, and become my disciples.

As the Father hath loved me, I also have loved you. Abide in my love.

If you keep my commandments, you shall abide in my love; as I also have kept my Father's commandments, and do abide in his love.

These things I have spoken to you that my joy may be in you, and your joy may be filled.

This is my commandment, that you love one another, as I have loved you.

Greater love than this no man hath, that a man lay down his life for his friends.

ST. JOHN

THE CRUCIFIXION

And when the sixth hour was come, there was darkness over the whole earth until the ninth hour.

And at the ninth hour, Jesus cried out with a loud voice, saying: Eloi, Eloi, lamma sabacthani? Which is, being interpreted, My God, my God, why hast thou forsaken me?

And some of the standers by hearing, said: Behold he calleth Elias.

And one running and filling a sponge with vinegar, and putting it upon a reed, gave him to drink, saying: Stay, let us see if Elias come to take him down.

And Jesus having cried out with a loud voice, gave up the ghost.

And the veil of the temple was rent in two, from the top to the bottom.

And the centurion who stood over against him, seeing that crying out in this manner he had given up the ghost, said: Indeed this man was the son of God.

And there were also women looking on afar off: among whom was Mary Magdalen, and Mary the mother of James the less and of Joseph, and Salome:

Who also when he was in Galilee followed him, and ministered to him, and many other women that came up with him to Jerusalem.

And when evening was now come (because it was the Parasceve, that is, the day before the sabbath,)

Joseph of Arimathea, a noble counsellor, who was also himself looking for the kingdom of God, came and went in boldly to Pilate, and begged the body of Jesus.

But Pilate wondered that he should be already dead. And sending for the centurion he asked him if he were already dead.

And when he had understood it by the centurion, he gave the body to Joseph.

And Joseph buying fine linen, and taking him down, wrapped him up in the fine linen, and laid him in a sepulchre which was hewed out of a rock. And he rolled a stone to the door of the sepulchre.

ST. MARK

THE MISSION OF SAINT PAUL

Then Agrippa said to Paul: Thou art permitted to speak for thyself. Then Paul stretching forth his hand, began to make his answer.

I think myself happy, O king Agrippa, that I am to answer for myself this day before thee, touching all the things whereof I am accused by the Jews.

Especially as thou knowest all, both customs and questions that are among the Jews: Wherefore I beseech thee to hear me patiently.

And my life indeed from my youth, which was from the beginning among my own nation in Jerusalem, all the Jews do know:

Having known me from the beginning (if they will give testimony) that according to the most sure sect of our religion I lived a Pharisee.

And now for the hope of the promise that was made by God to the fathers, do I stand subject to judgment:

Unto which, our twelve tribes, serving night and day, hope to come. For which hope, O king, I am accused by the Jews.

Why should it be thought a thing incredible, that God should raise the dead?

And I indeed, did formerly think, that I ought to do many things contrary to the name of Jesus of Nazareth.

Which also I did at Jerusalem, and many of the saints did I shut up in prison, having received authority of the chief priests: and when they were put to death, I brought the sentence.

And oftentimes punishing them, in every synagogue, I compelled them to blaspheme: and being yet more mad against them, I persecuted them even unto foreign cities.

Whereupon when I was going to Damascus with authority and permission of the chief priest,

At midday, O king, I saw in the way a light from heaven above the brightness of the sun, shining round about me, and them that were in company with me.

And when we were all fallen down on the ground, I heard a voice speaking to me in the Hebrew tongue: Saul, Saul, why persecutest thou me? It is hard for thee to kick against the goad.

And I said: Who art thou, Lord? And the Lord answered: I am Jesus whom thou persecutest.

But rise up, and stand upon thy feet: for to this end have I appeared to thee, that I may make thee a minister, and a witness of those things wherein I will appear to thee.

Delivering thee from the people, and from the nations, unto which now I send thee:

To open their eyes, that they may be converted from darkness to light, and from power of Satan to God, that they may receive forgiveness of sins, and a lot among the saints, by the faith that is in me.

Whereupon, O king Agrippa, I was not incredulous to the heavenly vision:

But to them first that are at Damascus, and at Jerusalem, and unto all the country of Judea, and to the Gentiles did I preach, that they should do penance, and turn to God, doing works worthy of penance.

ACTS OF THE APOSTLES

THE GREATEST OF THESE

If I speak with the tongues of men, and of angels, and have not charity, I am become as sounding brass, or a tinkling cymbal.

And if I should have prophecy and should know all mysteries, and all knowledge, and if I should have all faith, so that I could remove mountains, and have not charity, I am nothing.

And if I should distribute all my goods to feed the poor, and if I should deliver my body to be burned, and have not charity, it profiteth me nothing.

Charity is patient, is kind: charity envieth not, dealeth not perversely: is not puffed up:

Is not ambitious, seeketh not her own, is not provoked to anger, thinketh no evil:

Rejoiceth not in iniquity, but rejoiceth with the truth;

Beareth all things, believeth all things, hopeth all things, endureth all things.

Charity never falleth away: whether prophecies shall be made void, or tongues shall cease, or knowledge shall be destroyed.

For we know in part, and we prophesy in part.

But when that which is perfect is come, that which is in part shall be done away.

When I was a child, I spoke as a child, I understood as a child, I thought as a child. But, when I became a man, I put away the things of a child.

We see now through a glass in a dark manner; but then face to face. Now I know in part; but then I shall know even as I am known.

And now there remain faith, hope, and charity, these three: but the greatest of these is charity.

ST. PAUL

BEFORE THE THRONE

After these things, I saw four angels standing on the four corners of the earth, holding the four winds of the earth, that they should not blow upon the earth, nor upon the sea, nor on any tree.

And I saw another angel ascending from the rising of the sun, having the sign of the living God; and he cried with a loud voice to the four angels, to whom it was given to hurt the earth and the sea.

Saying: Hurt not the earth, nor the sea, nor the trees, till we sign the servants of our God in their foreheads.

And I heard the number of them that were signed, an hundred and forty-four thousand were signed, of every tribe of the children of Israel.

Of the tribe of Juda *were* twelve thousand signed: Of the tribe of Ruben, twelve thousand signed: Of the tribe of Gad, twelve thousand signed:

Of the tribe of Aser, twelve thousand signed: Of the tribe of

Nephthali, twelve thousand signed: Of the tribe of Manasses, twelve thousand signed:

Of the tribe of Simeon, twelve thousand signed: Of the tribe of Levi, twelve thousand signed: Of the tribe of Issachar, twelve thousand signed:

Of the tribe of Zabulon, twelve thousand signed: Of the tribe of Joseph, twelve thousand signed: Of the tribe of Benjamin, twelve thousand signed.

After this I saw a great multitude, which no man could number, of all nations, and tribes, and peoples, and tongues, standing before the throne, and in the sight of the Lamb, clothed with white robes, and palms in their hands:

And they cried with a loud voice, saying: Salvation to our God, who sitteth upon the throne, and to the Lamb.

And all the angels stood round about the throne, and the ancients, and the four living creatures; and they fell down before the throne upon their faces, and adored God.

Saying: Amen. Benediction, and glory, and wisdom, and thanksgiving, honour, and power, and strength to our God for ever and ever. Amen.

And one of the ancients answered, and said to me: These that are clad in white robes, who are they? and whence came they?

And I said to him: My Lord, thou knowest. And he said to me: These are they who are come out of great tribulation, and have washed their robes, and have made them white in the blood of the Lamb.

Therefore they are before the throne of God, and they serve him day and night in his temple: and he, that sitteth on the throne, shall dwell over them.

They shall no more hunger nor thirst, neither shall the sun fall on them, nor any heat.

For the Lamb, which is in the midst of the throne, shall rule them, and shall lead them to the fountains of the waters of life, and God shall wipe away all tears from their eyes.

THE APOCALYPSE

FROM THE CANON OF THE MASS

Wherefore, O Lord, being mindful of the blessed passion of the same Jesus Christ, Thy Son and Our Lord, of His resurrection likewise from the grave, and His glorious ascension into Heaven, we, Thy servants but also Thine Holy people, offer unto Thy illustrious Majesty from among the things Thou hast given us and showered upon us a Victim pure, a Victim sacred, a Victim stainless,—the Holy Bread of life everlasting, and the Chalice of eternal salvation.

Do Thou vouchsafe to look upon this with a kindly and untroubled countenance and to accept it, even as Thou wert pleased to accept the offerings of Abel, the just, who was Thy servant, the sacrifice of Abraham our patriarch, and that which Melchisedech Thy high-priest offered unto Thee, which was a holy sacrifice, a victim without blemish.

We humbly beseech Thee, almighty God, to give order that by the hands of Thine holy angel this our sacrifice be lifted up to Thine altar which is on high, into the very presence of Thy divine Majesty, so that as many of us as shall, by partaking at this altar, receive the most sacred body and blood of Thy Son may be filled with every heavenly blessing and grace. Through the same Jesus Christ, our Lord.

Be mindful likewise, O Lord, of Thy servants and handmaidens, N. and N., who have passed on ahead of us bearing the sign of the faith, and who now sleep in the sleep of peace. To these and to all who rest in Christ, do Thou assign, we pray Thee, a place of coolness, of sunshine, and of quiet. We ask it in the same Christ, Our Lord. Amen.

Vouchsafe, also, to grant unto us sinners, Thy servants relying on Thy tender mercies, some part and fellowship with Thy holy apostles and martyrs—with John, Stephen, Matthew, Barnabas, Ignatius, Alexander, Marcellinus, Peter, Felicitas, Perpetua, Agatha, Lucy, Agnes, Cecilia, Anastasia—and with all Thy saints, into whose company we beseech Thee to admit us, not weighing our deserts but pardoning our offenses. Through Christ our Lord.

By whom, O Lord, Thou dost always create, make holy, quicken, bless all these good things and bestow them upon us.

MISSALE ROMANUM

PETITION TO THE GOD OF SAINTS

O God, whose nature it is to have mercy always and to forgive: deign to hear our petition that we and all Thy children whom the chains of ill-doing keep in bondage may, in mercy, be released through the kindness of Thine affectionate hand.

Hear, we beseech Thee, the prayers of those who ask a boon of Thee, and forgive the faults of those who place their trust in Thee, so that out of Thy goodness all of us alike may have good fare and peace.

Out of Thy consideration, Lord, show unto us Thine incomparable mercy, so that at one and the same time Thou be found to free us from all sins and to remit to us the punishments which we should endure by reason of those sins.

O God, who art offended by our offenses and appeased by our works of penitence, look with indulgence upon the prayers of Thy people clamoring unto Thee, and turn aside the scourges of Thy wrath, which we deserve by reason of our sins.

Almighty, everlasting God, have mercy upon Thy son, our Sovereign Pontiff, and guide him according to Thy good will in the way of eternal well-being, so that as Thou desirest, he may seek whatever is pleasing unto Thee and be resplendent in every virtue.

O God, from whom there derive all holy wishes, all right counsels and all good works, give unto Thy servants the peace which this world cannot give, so that our hearts may be attuned to Thine edicts and given times which Thou makest peaceful with Thy protection, having dispelled the menace of armies.

Set on fire with Thy Sacred Spirit our bowels and our hearts, O Lord, so that we may serve Thee with pure bodies and unsullied hearts.

O God, the creator and redeemer of all who are faithful unto Thee, grant unto the souls of all Thy sons and daughters forgiveness of all their sins, so that the indulgence which they have always craved may be the answer to their reverent prayers.

We beseech Thee, O Lord, that Thou wouldst come before our actions with Thine inspiration and wouldst see them through with Thine assistance, so that every prayer and every undertaking of ours may always have its beginning in Thee and, thus begun, find its completion in Thee.

Almighty, everlasting God, who rulest over the living and the dead alike and dealest mercifully with all whom Thou foreknowest Thine in faith and works, we reverently petition Thee that those for whom it is our intention to kneel in prayer, whether they are still detained in the flesh by the present time or have already been received out of their bodies into the world to come, may through all the saints interceding for them, through the loving-kindness of Thy goodness, obtain the forgiveness of their every sin, Through Our Lord Jesus Christ. Amen.

THE LITANY OF THE SAINTS

PROPHECY

For even until the present time gifts of prophecy exist among us, from which fact you yourselves ought to understand that what was of old in your nation has been transferred to us. For just as there were also false prophets in the time of the holy prophets that were among you, so there are among us also many false teachers, of whom our Lord bade us beware beforehand, so that we should never be at a loss, being aware that He foreknew what would happen to us after His resurrection from the dead, and His ascent to heaven. For He said that we must be slain and hated for His name's sake, and that many false prophets and false Christs would come forward in His name, and would lead many astray. And this is the case. For many have taught what is godless and blasphemous and wicked, falsely stamping their teaching with His name, and have taught what has been put in their minds by the unclean spirit of the devil, and teach it until now. And we strive to persuade them, as well as you, not to be led astray, knowing, as we do, that everyone who can say what is true and saith it not shall be judged by God, as God solemnly testified by Ezekiel, saying: I have set thee to be a watchman for the house of Judah. If the sinner sin, and thou dost not solemnly testify to him, he indeed shall perish by his sin, but from thee will I require his blood. But if thou solemnly testifiest to him, thou shalt be innocent. So it is that out of fear we endeavor for our part to discourse in accordance with the Scriptures, not from love of money, or of vainglory, or of pleasure. For no one can bring any charge of this kind against our life. For we do not at all wish to live like the rulers of your people, with whom God finds fault, saying: Your rulers are partners with thieves, loving bribes, following after a reward. But if you do know any such even among us, yet at least do not blaspheme, or try to misinterpret, the Scriptures and Christ because of such men.

JUSTIN, MARTYR

THE FIRE OF LOVE

God loved mankind, for whose sake he made the world, to whom he subjected all things which are in the earth, to whom he gave reason, to whom he gave mind, on whom alone he enjoined that they should look upward to him, whom he made in his own image, to whom he sent his only-begotten Son, to whom he promised the kingdom in heaven—and he will give it to them who loved him. And when you have this full knowledge, with what joy do you think that you will be filled, or how greatly will you love him who thus first loved you? But by your love you will imitate the example of his goodness. And do not wonder that it is possible for man to be the imitator of God; it is possible when he will. For happiness consists not in domination over neighbors, nor in wishing to have more than the weak, nor in wealth, and power to compel those who are poorer, nor can anyone be an imitator of God in doing these things, for these things are outside of his majesty. But whosoever takes up the burden of his neighbor, and wishes to help another who is worse off in those respects in which one is the stronger, and ministers unto those in need out of the abundance of things he has received and keeps out of God's bounty —this man becomes a god to those who receive from him, and this man is an imitator of God. Then, even though your lot be that of this earthly life, you will know that God lives in Heaven, you will commence to speak of God's mysteries, you will love and admire those who suffer because they will not deny God. Then will you condemn the treachery and error of the world when you know what the true life of Heaven is, when you despise the manifest death of this world, when you fear that death which is real and is in store for those who shall be condemned unto everlasting fire, which shall punish endlessly them that are delivered into it. Then will you wonder at those who endure for righteousness's sake a fire which burns for a time only, and you will deem them blessed who have been aware of that other fire.

EPISTLE TO DIOGNETUS

TO THE ROMANS

From Syria to Rome I am doing battle with wild beasts by land and sea, by night and day, bound to ten "leopards" (namely a company of soldiers) whom kind treatment only makes worse. By reason of their misdeeds I become all the more a disciple, "but not by this am I justified." I long for the beasts which are made ready for me, and I pray that they may be found prompt in so far as I am concerned. I shall even entice them into devouring me with despatch, lest it may happen to me as it has happened to others whom they have not touched through fear. Even if they themselves be unwilling, I will compel them to it. Grant me this favor. I know what is a good thing for me—I am now commencing to earn my spurs as a disciple. May there be no envy in things seen or unseen of my attaining unto Jesus Christ. Let fire, cross, encounters with wild beasts, stabbing, tearing asunder, the racking of bones, the mangling of limbs, the crushing of my whole body, the cruel torments of the devil, come upon me. But may I attain unto Christ Jesus.

ST. IGNATIUS

THE PRESBYTERS

May the presbyters be compassionate, too, and merciful to all, bringing home those who have gone astray, caring for all who are weak, neglecting neither widow nor orphan nor the victim of poverty, and always "providing for that which is good before God and man," abstaining from every trace of wrath, of respect for persons, of unjust judgment. May they be far above any covetousness of money, nor quickly believing evil of anyone, nor being hasty in judgment, realizing that we all owe a debt of sin. If then we ask the Lord to give us forgiveness, we ourselves ought also to forgive. For we stand in the presence of the eye of the Lord, and must appear before the judgment seat of Christ, each to give an account of himself. Wherefore let us serve Him with fear and all reverence, as He Himself has commanded us to do, and as the Apostles likewise did—they who brought us the Gospel—and the Prophets of old, who foretold the coming of our Lord. Let us be zealous to do good, avoiding the giving of offense and keeping aloof from false brethren and from those who, using the name of the Lord hypocritically, deceive empty-minded men.

ST. POLYCARP

THE MARTYRDOM OF ST. POLYCARP

After this the document concerning Polycarp continues as follows: "Now when he had at last finished his prayer, remembering all who had ever even come his way, both small and great, high and low, and the whole Catholic Church throughout the world, the hour came for departure, and they set him on an ass, and led him into the city, on a 'great Sabbath day.' And the police captain Herod and his father Niketas met him and removed him into the wagon, and sat by his side trying to persuade him and saying: 'But what harm is it to say, "Lord Caesar," and to offer sacrifice and to be saved?' But he at first did not answer them, but when they continued he said, 'I am not going to do what you counsel me.' And they gave up the attempt to persuade him, and began to speak fiercely, and turned him out in such a hurry that in getting down from the wagon he scraped his shin; and without turning round, as though he had suffered nothing, he walked on promptly and quickly, and was taken to the arena, while the uproar in the arena was so great that no one could even be heard. Now when Polycarp entered into the arena there came a voice from heaven: 'Be strong, Polycarp, and play the man.' And no one saw the speaker, but many of our friends who were there heard the voice. And when he was brought forward, there was a great uproar of those who heard that Polycarp had been arrested. Next when he approached the proconsul asked him if he were Polycarp, and when he admitted it he tried to persuade him to deny, saying: 'Respect your age,' and so forth, as they are accustomed to say. 'Swear by the genius of Caesar, repent, say, "Away with the Atheists."' But Polycarp, with a stern countenance looked on all the crowd in the arena, and waving his hand at them, he groaned and looked up to heaven and said: 'Away with the Atheists.' But when the Governor pressed him and said, 'Take the oath and I will let you go, revile Christ,' Polycarp said, 'For eighty and six years have I been his servant, and He has done me no wrong, and how can I blaspheme my King who saved me?' But when he persisted again, and said, 'Swear by the genius of Caesar,' he said, 'If you vainly suppose that I will swear by the genius of Caesar, as you say, and pretend that you are ignorant who I am, listen plainly—I am a Christian. And if you wish to learn the doctrine of Christianity fix a day and listen.' The Proconsul said, 'Persuade the people.' And Polycarp said, 'You I should have held worthy of discussion, for we have been taught to render honor, as is meet, if it hurt us not, to princes and authorities appointed by God; but as for those, I do not count them worthy that a defence should be made to them.' And the proconsul said, 'I have wild beasts, I will deliver you to them, unless you change your mind.'

And he said, 'Call for them, for change of mind from better to worse is a change we may not make; but it is good to change from evil to righteousness.' And he said again to him, 'I will cause you to be consumed by fire, if you despise the beasts, unless you repent.' But Polycarp said, 'You threaten with the fire that burns for a time, and is quickly quenched, for you do not know the fire which awaits the wicked in the judgment to come and in everlasting punishment. But why are you waiting? Come, do what you will.'"

EUSEBIUS

THE TESTIMONY OF THE CHRISTIAN SOUL

Stand forth, O soul, whether thou art a divine and eternal substance, as most philosophers believe—if it is so, thou wilt be the less likely to lie,—or whether thou art the very opposite of divine, because indeed a mortal thing, as Epicurus alone thinks—in that case there will be the less temptation for thee to speak falsely in this case: whether thou art received from heaven, or sprung from earth; whether thou art formed of numbers, or of atoms; whether thine existence begins with that of the body, or thou art put into it at a later stage; from whatever source, and in whatever way, thou makest man a rational being, in the highest degree capable of thought and knowledge,—stand forth and give thy witness. But I call thee not as when, fashioned in schools, trained in libraries, fed up in Attic academies and porticoes, thou belchest forth thy wisdom. I address thee, simple and rude, and uncultured and untaught, such as they have thee who have thee only, that very thing pure and entire, of the road, the street, the workshop. I want thine inexperience, since in thy small experience no one feels any confidence. I demand of thee the things thou bringest with thee into man, which thou knowest either from thyself, or from thine author, whoever he may be. Thou art not, as I well know, Christian; for a man becomes a Christian, he is not born one. Yet Christians earnestly press thee for a testimony; they press thee, though an alien, to bear witness against thy friends, that they may be put to shame before thee, for hating and mocking us on account of things which convict thee as an accessory.

We give offence by proclaiming that there is one God, to whom the name of God alone belongs, from whom all things come, and who is Lord of the whole universe. Bear thy testimony, if thou knowest this to be truth; for openly and with a perfect liberty, such as we do not possess, we hear thee both in private and in public exclaim, "Which may God grant," and, "If God so will." By expressions such as these thou declarest that there is one who is distinctively God, and thou confessest that all power belongs to Him to whose will as Sovereign thou dost look. At the same time, too, thou deniest any others to be truly gods, in calling them by their own names of Saturn, Jupiter, Mars, Minerva; for thou affirmest Him to be God alone to whom thou givest no other name than God; and though thou sometimes callest these other gods, thou plainly usest the designation as one which does not really belong to them, but is, so to speak, a borrowed one. Nor is the nature of the God we declare unknown to thee: "God is good, God does good," thou art wont to say; plainly suggesting further, "But man is evil." In asserting an antithetic proposition, thou in a sort of indirect and figurative way reproachest man with his wickedness in departing from a God so good. So, again, as among us, as belonging to the God of benignity and goodness, "Blessing" is a most sacred thing in our religion and our life, thou too sayest as readily as a Christian needs, "God bless thee"; and when thou turnest the blessing of God into a curse, in like manner thy very words confess with us that His power over us is absolute and entire. There are some who, though they do not deny the existence of God, hold withal that He is neither Searcher, nor Ruler, nor Judge; treating with especial disdain those of us who go over to Christ out of fear of a coming judgment, as they think, honouring God in freeing Him from the cares of keeping watch, and the trouble of taking note,—not even regarding Him as capable of anger. For if God, they say gets angry, then He is susceptible of corruption and passion; but that of which passion and corruption can be affirmed may also perish, which

God cannot do. But these very persons elsewhere, confessing that the soul is divine, and bestowed on us by God, stumble against a testimony of the soul itself, which affords an answer to these views: for if either divine or God-given, it doubtless knows its giver; and if it knows Him, it undoubtedly fears Him too, and especially as having been by Him endowed so amply. Has it no fear of Him whose favour it is so desirous to possess, and whose anger it is so anxious to avoid? Whence, then, the soul's natural fear of God, if God cannot be angry? How is there any dread of Him whom nothing offends? What is feared but anger? Whence comes anger, but from observing what is done? What leads to watchful oversight, but judgment in prospect? Whence is judgment, but from power? To whom does supreme authority and power belong, but to God alone? So thou art always ready, O soul, from thine own knowledge, nobody casting scorn upon thee, and no one preventing, to exclaim, "God sees all," and "I commend thee to God," and "May God repay," and "God shall judge between us." How happens this, since thou art not Christian? How is it that, even with the garland of Ceres on the brow, wrapped in the purple cloak of Saturn, wearing the white robe of the goddess Isis, thou invokest God as judge? Standing under the statue of Aesculapius, adorning the brazen image of Juno, arraying the helmet of Minerva with dusky figures, thou never thinkest of appealing to any of these deities. In thine own forum thou appealest to a God who is elsewhere; thou permittest honour to be rendered in thy temples to a foreign god. Oh, striking testimony to truth, which in the very midst of demons obtains a witness for us Christians!

TERTULLIAN

IN MEMORY OF NEPOTIAN

Nepotian regarded the clerical office not as an honor but as a burden. He made it his first care to silence envy by humility, his second to give no ground for scandal against him and by continence to dumfound those who railed against his youth. He helped the poor, visited the sick, challenged others to acts of hospitality, soothed men's anger with soft words, "rejoiced with those who rejoiced, and wept with those who wept." He was a staff to the blind, food to the hungry, hope to the wretched, a consolation to the sorrowful. Each single virtue was as conspicuous in him as if he had possessed no others. Among his fellow-presbyters and equals in age, he was first in industry, last in rank. Any good that he did he ascribed to his uncle; if the result was different from what he had expected, he would say that his uncle knew nothing of the matter and that it was his own mistake. In public he recognized him as a bishop, at home he treated him as a father. The gravity of his character was tempered by the cheerfulness of his looks. A smile, not a guffaw, was the sign that he felt happy. Widows and Christ's virgins he honored as mothers, and exhorted as sisters, with all chastity. On his return home he left the clergyman outside, and submitted himself to the hard rule of a monk. Frequent in supplication, wakeful in prayer, he offered his tears not to men but to God. His fasts he regulated, as a charioteer does his pace, by the weariness or the vigor of his body. He would sit at his uncle's table and just taste the dishes set before him, thus both avoiding superstition and yet keeping to his rule of self-restraint. His chief topic of conversation and his favorite form of entertainment was to bring forward some passage from the Scriptures for discussion; then he would listen modestly, answer diffidently, support the right, and mildly refute the wrong, instructing his opponent rather than vanquishing him. With the ingenuous modesty which was one of his youthful charms he would frankly confess the source of each argument he used, and in this way by disclaiming any reputation for learning he gradually came to be considered the most learned of us all. "This," he would say, "is Tertullian's view and that is Cyprian's; this is the opinion of Lactantius and this of Hilary; such is the doctrine of Minucius Felix, so Victorinus teaches, in this fashion Arnobius speaks." Myself too he sometimes quoted, for he loved me because of my association with his uncle. Indeed, by constant reading and daily meditation he had made his breast a library of Christ.

How often did he beg me in his letters from across the sea to write something for him! How often did he remind me of the man in the Gospel who sought help by night, and of the widow who importuned the harsh judge! When he found that I did not write and saw himself checked by my silence, the modesty of his request being matched by the modesty of my refusal, he made another move. He got his uncle to ask on his behalf, knowing that a request for another could be more freely made and that my respect for a bishop would ensure him an easier success. Accordingly I did what he wished, and in a short treatise dedicated our friendships to eternal remembrance, while he on receiving it boasted that he surpassed the wealth of Croesus and the treasures of Darius. He would always hold my book in his hands, devour it with his eyes, fondle it in his breast, and repeat it with his lips. In bed he would frequently undo the roll and fall asleep with the dear page upon his heart. If a stranger or a friend came in, he rejoiced to show him the evidence of my regard; and anything lacking in my poor work was compensated for by careful modulation and varied emphasis, so that, when it was read aloud, it was he, not I, who seemed to please or displease. Whence could this fervor come save from love of God? Whence this tireless meditation on the law of Christ save from longing for Him who gave that law? Let others add coin to coin, fastening their claws on married ladies' purses and hunting for death-bed legacies; let them be richer as monks than they were as men of the world; let them possess wealth in the service of a poor Christ such as they had never had in the service of a rich devil; let the Church sigh over the opulence of men who in the world were beggars. Our dear Nepotian tramples gold under foot, books are the only things he desires. But while he despises himself in the flesh and walks abroad in splendid poverty, he yet seeks out everything that may adorn his church.

In comparison with what I have said the following details are trivial; but even in small things the same spirit is revealed. We admire the Creator, not only as the framer of heaven and earth, of sin and ocean, of elephants, camels, horses, oxen, leopards, bears and lions, but also as the maker of tiny creatures, ants, gnats, flies, worms, and the like, things whose shapes we know better than their names.

And as in all creation we reverence His skill, so the mind that is given to Christ is equally earnest in small things as in great, knowing that an account must be given even for an idle word. Nepotian therefore took anxious pains to keep the altar bright, to have the walls free from soot and the pavement duly swept. He saw to it that the door-keeper was constantly at his post, that the curtains were hanging at the entrance, that the sanctuary was neat, and the church-vessels brightly polished. His careful reverence extended to every form of ceremonial, and no duty, small or great, was neglected. Whenever you looked for him in his church, there you found him. . . . He adorned the church buildings and the halls of the martyrs with different kinds of flowers and with the foliage of trees and clusters of vine leaves. Indeed, everything in his church that pleased by its arrangement or its appearance bore witness to the labor and the zeal of its presbyter.

ST. JEROME

ST. AUGUSTINE AND HIS MOTHER

As the day now approached on which she was to depart this life (which day Thou knewst, we did not), it fell out—Thou, as I believe, by Thy secret ways arranging it—that she and I stood alone, leaning in a certain window, from which the garden of the house we occupied at Ostia could be seen; at which place, removed from the crowd, we were resting ourselves for the voyage, after the fatigues of a long journey. We then were conversing alone very pleasantly; and, "forgetting those things which are behind, and reaching forth unto those things which are before," we were seeking between ourselves in the presence of the Truth, which Thou art, of what nature the eternal life of the saints would be, which eye hath not seen, nor ear heard, neither hath it entered into the heart of man. But yet we opened wide the mouth of our heart, after those supernal streams of Thy fountain, "the fountain of life," which is "with Thee;" that being sprinkled with it according to our capacity, we might in some measure weigh so high a mystery.

And when our conversation had arrived at that point, that the very highest pleasure of the carnal senses, and that in the very brightest material light, seemed by reason of the sweetness of that life, not only not worthy of comparison, but not even of mention, we, lifting ourselves with a more ardent affection towards "the self-same," did gradually pass through all corporeal things, and even the heaven itself, whence sun, and moon, and stars shine upon the earth; yea, we soared higher yet by inward musing, and discoursing, and admiring Thy works; and we came to our own minds, and went beyond them, that we might advance as high as that region of unfailing plenty, where Thou feedst Israel for ever with the food of truth, and where life is that Wisdom by whom all these things are made, both which have been, and which are to come; and she is not made, but is as she hath been, and so shall ever be; yea, rather, to "have been," and "to be hereafter," are not in her, but only "to be," seeing she is eternal, for to "have been" and "to be hereafter" are not eternal. And while we were thus speaking, and straining after her, we slightly touched her with the whole effort of our heart; and we sighed, and there left bound "the first-fruits of the Spirit;" and returned to the noise of our own mouth, where the word uttered has both beginning and end. And what is like unto Thy word, our Lord, who remaineth in Himself without becoming old, and "maketh all things new"?

We were saying, then, if to any man the tumult of the flesh were silenced,—silenced the phantasies of earth, waters, and air,—silenced, too, the poles; yea, the very soul be silenced to herself, and go beyond herself by not thinking of herself,—silenced fancies and imaginary revelations, every tongue, and every sign, and whatsoever exists by passing away, since, if any could hearken, all these say, "We created not ourselves, but were created by Him who abideth for ever:" If, having uttered this, they now should be silenced, having only quickened our ears to Him who created them, and He alone speak not by them, but by Himself, that we may hear His word, not by fleshly tongue, nor angelic voice, nor sound of thunder, nor the obscurity of a similitude, but might hear Him—Him whom in these we love—without these, like as we two now strained ourselves, and with rapid thought touched on that Eternal Wisdom which remaineth over all. If this could be sustained, and other visions of a far different kind be withdrawn, and this one ravish, and absorb, and envelop its beholder amid these inward joys, so that his life might be eternally like that one moment of knowledge which we now sighed after, were not this "Enter thou into the joy of Thy Lord"? And when shall that be? When we shall all rise again; but all shall not be changed.

Such things was I saying; and if not after this manner, and in these words, yet, Lord, Thou knowest, that in that day when we were talking thus, this world with all its delights grew contemptible to us, even while we spake. Then said my mother, "Son, for myself, I have no longer any pleasure in aught in this life. What I want here further, and why I am here, I know not, now that my hopes in this world are satisfied. There was indeed one thing for which I wished to tarry a little in this life, and that was that I might see thee a Catholic Christian before I died. My God has exceeded this abundantly, so that I see thee despising all earthly felicity, made His servant,—what do I here?"

* * *

What reply I made unto her to these things I do not well remember. However, scarcely five days after, or not much more, she was prostrated by fever; and while she was sick, she one day sank into a swoon, and was for a short time unconscious of visible things. We hurried up to her; but she soon regained her senses, and gazing on me and my brother as we stood by her, she said to us inquiringly, "Where was I?" Then looking intently at us stupefied with grief, "Here," saith she, "shall you bury your mother." I was silent, and refrained from weeping; but my brother said something, wishing her, as the happier lot, to die in her own country and not abroad. She, when she heard this, with anxious countenance arrested him with her eye, as savouring of such things, and then gazing at me, "Behold," saith she, "what he saith"; and soon after to us both she saith, "Lay this body anywhere, let not the care for it trouble you at all. This only I ask, that you will remember me at the Lord's altar, wherever you be." And when she had given forth this opinion in such words as she could, she was silent, being in pain with her increasing sickness.

But, as I reflected on Thy gifts, O thou invisible God, which Thou instillest into the hearts of Thy faithful ones, whence such marvellous fruits do spring, I did rejoice and give thanks unto Thee, calling to mind what I knew before, how she had ever burned with anxiety respecting her burial-place, which she had provided and prepared for herself by the body of her husband. For as they had lived very peacefully together, her desire had also been (so little is the human mind capable of grasping things divine) that this should be added to that happiness, and be talked of among men, that after her wandering beyond the sea, it had been granted her that they both, so united on earth, should lie in the same grave. But when this uselessness had, through the bounty of Thy goodness, begun to be no longer in her heart, I knew not, and I was full of joy admiring what she had thus disclosed to me; though indeed in that our conversation in the window also, when she said, "What do I here any longer?" she appeared not to desire to die in her own country. I heard afterwards, too, that at the time we were at Ostia, with a maternal confidence she one day, when I was absent, was speaking with certain of my friends on the contemning of this life, and the blessing of death; and when they—amazed at the courage which Thou hadst given to her, a woman—asked her whether she did not dread leaving her body at such a distance from her own city, she replied, "Nothing is far to God; nor need I fear lest He should be ignorant at the end of the world of the place whence He is to raise me up." On the ninth day, then, of her sickness, the fifty-sixth year of her age, and the thirty-third of mine, was that religious and devout soul set free from the body.

* * *

I closed her eyes; and there flowed a great sadness into my heart, and it was passing into tears, when mine eyes at the same time, by the violent control of my mind, sucked back the fountain dry, and woe was me in such a struggle! But, as soon as she breathed her last, the boy Adeodatus burst out into wailing, but, being checked by us all, he became quiet. In like manner also my own childish feeling, which was, through the youthful voice of my heart, finding escape in tears, was restrained and silenced. For we did not consider it fitting to celebrate that funeral with tearful plaints and groanings; for on such wise are they who die unhappy, or are altogether dead, wont to be mourned. But she neither died unhappy, nor did she altogether die. For of this were we assured by the witness of her good conversation, her "faith unfeigned," and other sufficient grounds.

What, then, was that which did grievously pain me within, but the newly-made wound, from having that most sweet and dear habit of living together suddenly broken off? I was full of joy indeed in her testimony, when, in that her last illness, flattering my dutifulness, she called me "kind," and recalled, with great affection of love, that she had never heard any harsh or reproachful sound come out of my mouth against her. But yet, O my God, who madest us, how can the honour which I paid to her be compared with her slavery for me? As, then, I was left destitute of so great comfort in her, my soul was stricken, and that life torn apart as it were, which, of hers and mine together, had been made but one.

The boy then being restrained from weeping, Evodius took up the Psalter, and began to sing—the whole house responding—the Psalm, "I will sing of mercy and judgment: unto Thee, O Lord." But when they heard what we were doing, many brethren and religious women came together; and whilst they whose office it was were, according to custom, making ready for the funeral, I, in a part of the house where I conveniently could, together with those who thought that I ought not to be left alone, discoursed on what was suited to the occasion; and by this alleviation of truth mitigated the anguish known unto Thee—they being unconscious of it, listened intently, and thought me to be devoid of any sense of sorrow. But in Thine ears, where none of them heard, did I blame the softness of my feelings, and restrained the flow of my grief, which yielded a little unto me; but the paroxysm returned again, though not so as to burst forth into tears, nor to a change of countenance, though I knew what I repressed in my heart. And as I was exceedingly annoyed that these human things had such power over me, which in the due order and destiny of our natural condition must of necessity come to pass, with a new sorrow I sorrowed for my sorrow, and was wasted by a twofold sadness.

So when the body was carried forth, we both went and returned without tears. For neither in those prayers which we poured forth unto Thee when the sacrifice of our redemption was offered up unto Thee for her,—the dead body being now placed by the side of the grave, as the custom there is, prior to its being laid therein,—neither in their prayers did I shed tears; yet was I most grievously sad in secret all the day, and with a troubled mind entreated Thee, as I was able, to heal my sorrow, but Thou didst not; fixing, I believe, in my memory by this one lesson the power of the bonds of all habit, even upon a mind which now feeds not upon a fallacious word. It appeared to me also a good thing to go and bathe, I having heard that the bath (balneum) took its name from the Greek, because it drives trouble from the mind. Lo, this also I confess unto Thy mercy, "Father of the fatherless," that I bathed, and felt the same as before I had done so. For the bitterness of my grief exuded not from my heart. Then I slept, and on waking found my grief not a little mitigated; and as I lay alone upon my bed, there came into my mind those true verses of Thy Ambrose, for Thou art—

Deus creator omnium,
Polique rector, vestiens
Diem decoro lumine,
Noctem sopora gratia;
Artus solutos ut quies
Reddat laboris usui,
Mentesque fessas allevet,
Luctusque solvat anxios.

And then little by little did I bring back my former thoughts of Thine handmaid, her devout conversation towards Thee, her holy tenderness and attentiveness towards us, which was suddenly taken away from me; and it was pleasant to me to weep in Thy sight, for her and for me, concerning her and concerning myself. And I set free the tears which before I repressed, that they might flow at their will, spreading them beneath my heart; and it rested in them, for Thy ears were nigh me,—not those of man, who would have put a scornful interpretation on my weeping. But now in writing I confess it unto Thee, O Lord! Read it who will, and interpret how he will; and if he finds me to have sinned in weeping for my mother during so small a part of an hour,—that mother who was for a while dead to mine eyes, who had for many years wept for me, that I might live in Thine eyes,—let him not laugh at me, but rather, if he be a man of noble charity, let him weep for my sins against Thee, the Father of all the brethren of Thy Christ.

ST. AUGUSTINE

THE SHADOW OF THINGS TO COME

When one's thoughts turn to the prevailing beauty and usefulness of the creation which man, albeit adrift in a sea of sorrows, has been graciously permitted to gaze upon and enjoy, how shall one find words adequate to set forth the beauty so manifold and diverse of the sea and the land, or the marvelous radiance and brimming fulness of the light, of sun and moon and stars, or the colors and perfumes of the flowers, or the shade that is amid the woods, or the variousness and number of the birds noticeable for either plumage or song, or the countless kinds of beasts that are so numberless and so huge, or those minute forms of bees and ants that are still more marvelous than the mighty-bodied whale, or the awesome panorama of the sea, altering again and again its hue, being now green, now a blaze of many colors, now purple, now green? How pleasant is the sight of the sea to the eye, even when its mood is one of fury; and how much more charming still is it when it soothes the soul of him who looks out upon it, watching the churning waves and yet not in peril of being tossed upon their mounting crests of foam!

What will not He who has lavished such boons on those He has predestined to die give to those He has fore-ordained unto life? Can we glimpse the blessings He will bestow in yonder realm upon those in whose behalf He has willed that His only-begotten Son should die? Will He not give us all things when we are with Him? What shall our life and our nature not be when His promise unto us shall have been fulfilled! What will the spirit of man be like when it is placed above every vice that masters and subdues—when, its warfare ended, it is wholly at peace?

ST. AUGUSTINE

TO THE MOTHER OF GOD

Glory be to thee, O holy mother of God, masterpiece of the universe, shining star, lustre of virginity, sceptre of faith, indestructible temple, in whom He dwelt whom immensity cannot contain. Virgin mother of Him who, blessed forever, comes to us in the name of the Lord, by thee is the Trinity glorified, the holy cross praised and adored throughout the world, the heavens are made joyful and the angels to tremble with joy, the devils put to flight, and man enabled to pass from slavery to the freedom of Heaven. Through thee idolatrous creatures have known incarnate truth, the faithful have received baptism, churches have been erected in all parts of the earth. By thine assistance the Gentiles have been brought to repentance. And finally, through thee, the only Son of God, source of all light, has shone upon the eyes of the blind, who were sitting in the shadow of death. O virgin mother, who can speak thy praises? But let us make our laud of them according to such powers as are given us, at the same time adoring God thy Son, the chaste spouse of the Church, to whom are due all honor and glory now and forever.

ST. CYRIL

II

THE MIDDLE AGES

THE ABBOT

Let him who has been created abbot ever reflect upon the weighty burden he has taken up and remember unto Whom he shall give an account of his stewardship. Let him know also that it is better for him to profit others than to rule over them. He must therefore be learned in the Divine Law that he may know when to bring forth new things and old. He must be chaste, sober, merciful, and always exalt mercy above justice, that he may obtain mercy. He shall hate vice and love the brethren. Even in his correction he shall act with prudence and not try too much, lest whilst too violently scouring off the rust the vessel itself be broken. Let him always bear in mind his own frailty, and remember that the bruised reed must not be broken.

In saying this we do not propose that he should allow vices to spring up, but, as we have declared before, seek to root them up prudently and with charity, in the way he shall think proper in each case. Let him aim at being loved rather than feared. He must not be worried nor anxious, neither should he be too exacting or obstinate, or jealous, or oversuspicious, for then he will never be at rest. Even in what he orders, whether it relates to God or to worldly matters, let him be prudent and considerate. In all that he enjoins he should be discreet and moderate, meditating on the prudence of holy Jacob, who says, If I shall cause my flocks to be over-driven, they will all die in one day. Wherefore adopting these and like principles of discretion, the mother of virtues, let him so temper all things that the strong may have their scope and the weak be not scared. And especially let him keep the present Rule in all things, so that when he shall have well administered it he may hear from our Lord what the good servant heard who gave corn to his fellow-servants in due season: Amen; I say to you, over all his goods will he place him.

THE RULE OF ST. BENEDICT

THE CELLARER

Let one of the community be chosen as cellarer of the monastery, who is wise, mature in character, temperate, not a great eater, not arrogant nor quarrelsome, nor insolent, and not a dawdler, nor wasteful, but one who fears God and is as a Father to the community. Let him have the charge of everything; do nothing without the abbot's order; see to what is commanded, and not make the brethren sad. If any of them shall perchance ask something unreasonable he must not vex him by contemptuously rejecting his request, but humbly and reasonably refuse what he wrongly asks.

Let him look after his own soul, mindful of the Apostolic principle, that they that ministered well, shall purchase to themselves a good degree. Let him take every care of the sick, of children, of guests, and of the poor, knowing that without doubt he shall have to render an account of all these on the judgment day.

Let him look upon all the vessels and goods of the monastery as if they were consecrated chalices of the altar. He must not think anything can be neglected; he must not be covetous, nor a prodigal wasting the goods of the monastery; but let him do everything with forethought and according to the direction of his abbot.

Above all things let him have humility and give a gentle answer to those to whom he can give nothing else, for it is written, A good word is above the best gift. Let him take charge of all the abbot shall commit to him, but let him not meddle with anything which is forbidden him. Let him provide the brethren with their appointed allowance of food without impatience or delay, so that they be not driven to offend, being mindful of the divine word which declares the punishment he deserves Who shall scandalize one of these little ones. It were better for him that a millstone should be hanged about his neck, and that he should be drowned in the depth of the sea. If the community be large let him be given helpers, by whose aid he may without worry perform the office committed to him. What is given let it be given, and what is asked for let it be asked at suitable times, so that no one be troubled or distressed in the House of God.

THE RULE OF ST. BENEDICT

PRAYER TO THE VIRGIN MARY

Remember, O most loyal Virgin Mary: never since the beginning of time has it been heard that any one who sought refuge with thee, asked thy help, or implored thine intercession, was turned away. Therefore it is with complete confidence that I run unto thee, Virgin amongst all virgins, my Mother. I come up to where thou art; I stand before thee, a grieving sinner. Do not, O Mother of the Word made flesh, frown upon my requests, but graciously hear me and have pity on my need. Amen.

ST. BERNARD

THE GLORY OF THE BODY

Bereft of their bodies, the souls of the blessed ones have neither the wish nor the power to reach their ultimate end. Therefore, until such time as their bodies are restored to them, souls cannot be absorbed into God with that fulness which is their loftiest, their perfect, state. Neither would the spirit yearn once more for the fellowship of the flesh were it possible to reach the perfect condition of human nature in aught other way. In all verity, the taking up and laying down of the body is not without purpose unto the soul. For precious in the sight of the Lord is the death of His saints.

But if death be precious, how dear must be life, above all the life to come? One cannot wonder that the body transfigured will be of use to the soul, since even now, in its frailness and mortality, there is much help that is given by the body, manifestly. He spoke well, indeed, who said, to them that love God, all things work together unto good. Whether in this life, or in death, or in the final resurrection, the body availeth much to the soul that loveth the Lord. In the first case, it produces the fruit of penitence; in the second, the boon of rest; and in the third, the last condition of beatitude. The soul is right in deeming that since the body is of service to her in every state, it too should have a part in perfection.

ST. BERNARD

CONSOLATRIX AFFLICTORUM

O thou who findest thyself tossed by the tempests in the midst of the shoals of this world, turn not away thine eyes from the star of the sea if thou wouldst avoid shipwreck. If the winds of temptation blow, if tribulations rise up like rocks before thee, a look at the star, a sigh to Mary, will be thy aid. If waves of pride, ambition, calumny, jealousy threaten to swallow up thy soul, look towards the star, pray to Mary. If anger, avarice, or love of pleasure shiver thy frail vessel, seek the eyes of Mary. If horror of thy sins, trouble of conscience, dread of the judgments of God, commence to plunge thee into the gulf of sadness and the abyss of despair, attach thy heart to Mary. In thy perils, thy anguish, thy doubts, think of Mary, call on Mary. Let the name of Mary be on thy lips, in thy heart; and in taking refuge with her in petition lose not sight of the example of her virtues. Following her thou canst not wander. Whilst thou prayest to her thou canst not be without hope. As long as thou thinkest of her thou wilt be in the right path. Thou canst not fall while she sustains thee; thou hast nothing to fear while she protects thee. If she favor thy voyage, thou shalt reach the port of safety without weariness.

ST. BERNARD

THE CONVERSION OF ABELARD

I do not remember to have known a man whose appearance and bearing manifested such humility. Saint Germain cannot have seemed humbler or Saint Martin poorer. I set him among the first of this great flock of brethren; but by the carelessness of his apparel he seemed the least of all. When in our processions he walked before me with the community I have often marveled and been amazed that a man of so great and so famous a name should be able thus to despise himself and thus to abase himself. There are some who profess religion, who when they don the religious habit, do not find it splendid enough; but instead he was so sparing in his wants that, contented with a plain habit, he demanded nothing further. He maintained the same simplicity in his food and drink, and in every need of his body; and by word and deed condemned in himself and all men, I do not say only superfluities, but everything not absolutely necessary. He was continually reading, frequently at his prayers, and almost always silent; unless obliged to speak by friendly conversation with his brethren or by some discourse on holy things to the community. He offered the holy sacrifice of the immortal Lamb to God as often as might be, and after by my letters and labor he had been reinstated in the graces of the Holy See, he hardly missed a day. What more can I say? His mind, his speech, his actions, were ever meditated, and taught and bore witness to holiness, philosophy and learning. Such among us was this man, simple and righteous, fearing God and shunning evil; such among us for a little while, consecrating the last days of his life to God. For the sake of rest—for he was more than usually troubled with the itch and other weaknesses of the body—I sent him to Chalon, for the mildness of the climate, which is the best in our part of Burgundy; and to a home well fitted for him, near the town but yet with the Saône flowing between. There, as much as his infirmities permitted, returning to his former studies, he was ever bent over his books, nor (as we read of Gregory the Great) did he ever allow a moment to pass in which he was not either praying or reading, or writing or dictating. In the midst of such labors Death, the bearer of good tidings, found him—not like so many asleep, but awake.

PETER THE VENERABLE

ST. BERNARD

His body was marked by a certain grace rather spiritual than bodily; his face was radiant with a light not of earth but of heaven; his eyes shone with angelic purity and dovelike simplicity. Such was the beauty of the inner man, that it broke forth by manifest tokens to the sight, and even the outer man seemed bedewed with the abundance of his inward purity and grace. His whole body was meagre and emaciated. His skin itself was of the finest texture, with a slight flush of red on the cheeks, seeing that all the natural heat of his frame had been drawn thither by constant meditation and the zeal of his holy compunction. His hair was of a yellow inclining to white; his beard was auburn, sprinkled towards the end of his life with grey. His stature was of an honourable middle size, yet inclining to tallness. Nevertheless, whereas his flesh (first by the gift of preventing grace, then by the help of nature, and lastly by the holy use of spiritual discipline) scarce dared to lust now against the spirit, yet the spirit lusted so sore against the flesh, beyond the man's strength and above the power of flesh and blood, that the frail beast fell beneath the load and could not rise again.

ALAN, OF AUXERRE

CHARLEMAGNE

Charles was temperate in eating, and particularly so in drinking, for he abominated drunkenness in anybody, much more in himself and those of his household; but he could not easily abstain from food, and often complained that fasts injured his health. He very rarely gave entertainments, only on great feast-days, and then to large numbers of people. His meals ordinarily consisted of four courses, not counting the roast, which his huntsmen used to bring in on the spit; he was more fond of this than of any other dish. While at table, he listened to reading or music. The subjects of the readings were the stories and deeds of olden time: he was fond, too, of St. Augustine's books, and especially of the one entitled "The City of God." He was so moderate in the use of wine and all sorts of drink that he rarely allowed himself more than three cups in the course of a meal. In summer, after the midday meal, he would eat some fruit, drain a single cup, put off his clothes and shoes, just as he did for the night, and rest for two or three hours. He was in the habit of awaking and rising from bed four or five times during the night. While he was dressing and putting on his shoes, he not only gave audience to his friends, but if the Count of the Palace told him of any suit in which his judgment was necessary, he had the parties brought before him forthwith, took cognizance of the case, and gave his decision, just as if he were sitting on the judgment-seat. This was not the only business that he transacted at this time, but he performed any duty of the day whatever, whether he had to attend to the matter himself, or to give commands concerning it to his officers.

Charles had the gift of ready and fluent speech, and could express whatever he had to say with the utmost clearness. He was not satisfied with command of his native language merely, but gave attention to the study of foreign ones, and in particular was such a master of Latin that he could speak it as well as his native tongue; but he could understand Greek better than he could speak it. He was so eloquent, indeed, that he might have passed for a teacher of eloquence. He most zealously cultivated the liberal arts, held those who taught them in great esteem, and conferred great honours upon them. He took lessons in grammar of the deacon Peter of Pisa, at that time an aged man. Another deacon, Albin of Britain, surnamed Alcuin, a man of Saxon extraction, who was the greatest scholar of the day, was his teacher in other branches of learning. The King spent much time and labour with him studying rhetoric, dialectics, and especially astronomy; he learned to reckon, and used to investigate the motions of the heavenly bodies most curiously, with an intelligent scrutiny. He also tried to write, and used to keep tablets and blanks in bed under his pillow, that at leisure hours he might accustom his hand to form the letters; however, as he did not begin his efforts in due season, but late in life, they met with ill success.

He cherished with the greatest fervour and devotion the principles of the Christian religion, which had been instilled into him from infancy. Hence it was that he built the beautiful basilica at Aix-la-Chapelle, which he adorned with gold and silver and lamps, and with rails and doors of solid brass. He had the columns and marbles for this structure brought from Rome and Ravenna, for he could not find such as were suitable elsewhere. He was a constant worshipper at this church as long as his health permitted, going morning and evening, even after nightfall, besides attending mass; and he took care that all the services there conducted should be administered with the utmost possible propriety, very often warning the sextons not to let any improper or unclean thing be brought into the building, or remain in it. He provided it with a great number of sacred vessels of gold and silver, and with such a quantity of clerical robes that not even the door-keepers, who fill the humblest office in the church, were obliged to wear their everyday clothes when in the exercise of their duties. He was at great pains to improve the church reading and psalmody, for he was well skilled in both, although he neither read in public nor sang, except in a low tone and with others.

He was very forward in succouring the poor, and in that gratuitous generosity which the Greeks call alms, so much so that he not only made a point of giving in his own country and his own kingdom, but when he discovered that there were Christians living in poverty in Syria, Egypt, and Africa, at Jerusalem, Alexandria, and Carthage, he had compassion on their wants, and used to send money over the seas to them. The reason that he zealously strove to make friends with the kings beyond seas was that he might get help and relief to the Christians living under their rule. He cherished the Church of St. Peter the Apostle at Rome above all other old and sacred places, and heaped its treasury with a vast wealth of gold, silver, and precious stones. He sent great and countless gifts to the popes; and throughout his whole reign the wish that he had nearest at heart was to re-establish the ancient authority of the city of Rome under his care and by his influence, and to defend and protect the Church of St. Peter, and to beautify and enrich it out of his own store above all other churches. Although he held it in such veneration, he only repaired to Rome to pay his vows and make his supplications four times during the whole forty-seven years that he reigned.

EGINHARD

KING OTTO IS VICTORIOUS

That you may know how easy it is for God to conquer a host with a handful of men, and how "no one shall be saved by the abundance of his own valor," hear the way in which Our Lord repeated a miracle of the past. The king's soldiers had reached the Rhine at a place called Birten, and had already begun to cross the river, unaware that Henry with his aforesaid confederates was in the near neighborhood. A few men had landed from the boats and were just able to mount their horses and put on their armor, when with their own eyes they saw the enemies' forces advancing to the attack before they had received any warning of their approach. They therefore addressed one another with these mutual exhortations: "The size of this river, as you see, prevents our comrades from coming to our help, and also bars our retreat, even if we wished to retire. We know also full well how ridiculous it would seem, especially among nations of our character, for brave men to surrender to the enemy, escaping death indeed by non-resistance but only winning life at the price of eternal ignominy. The fact that we have no hope of retreat—which is rather a disadvantage to the enemy—and the everlasting shame that we should earn by surrender, both inspire us with confidence; and there is a further motive which urges us to fight, namely the truth and justice of our cause. Even if our earthly habitation be destroyed in resisting unrighteousness, we shall gain in heaven a home not made by hands." Fired by these words they advanced at full speed and fell upon the ranks of their foes.

The king for his part, thinking that his men were not without divine inspiration in showing this courage, since the intervening stream prevented him from helping them with his bodily presence, remembered how the Lord's people had overcome the Amalekites' attack by the prayers of Moses, the servant of God. Accordingly he leaped down from his horse and with all his army burst into tearful prayer, kneeling before the victory-bringing nails that had once pierced the hands of Our Lord and Saviour Jesus Christ and were then fixed upon his spear. What strength the prayers of a righteous man possess, according to Saint James's words, was then plainly revealed. As he prayed, before a single man on his side had fallen, the enemy all turned in flight, some of them not knowing in the least why they were retreating, since their pursuers were so few that they could not see them. Many of them were killed and Henry was struck heavily on the arm. The triple mail of his cuirass prevented the sword from piercing his flesh, but the cruel force of the blow turned the skin completely black.

LUITPRAND OF CREMONA

ST. LOUIS

The government of his land was so arranged that every day he heard the hours sung, and a Requiem mass without song; and then, if it was convenient, the mass of the day, or of the saint, with song. Every day he rested in his bed after having eaten, and when he had slept and rested, he said, privily in his chamber—he and one of his chaplains together—the (office for the) dead; and afterwards he heard vespers. At night he heard compline.

A gray-friar (Franciscan) came to him at the castle of Hyeres, where we disembarked; and said in his sermon, for the king's instruction, that he had read the Bible, and the books pertaining to misbelieving princes, and that he had never found, either among believers or misbelievers, that a kingdom had been lost, or had changed lords, save there had first been failure of justice. "Therefore, let the king, who is going into France, take good heed," said he, "that he do justice well and speedily among his people, so that our Lord suffer his kingdom to remain in peace all the days of his life." It is said that the right worthy man who thus instructed the king, lies buried at Marseilles, where our Lord, for his sake, performs many a fine miracle. He would never consent to remain with the king, however much the king might urge it, for more than a single day.

The king forgot not the teaching of the friar, but ruled his land very loyally and godly, as you shall hear. He had so arranged that my Lord of Nesle, and the good Count of Soissons, and all of us who were about him, should go, after we had heard our masses, and hear the pleadings at the gate which is now called the Requests.

And when he came back from church, he would send for us and sit at the foot of his bed, and make us all sit round him, and ask if there were any whose cases could not be settled save by himself in person. And we named the litigants; and he would then send for such and ask: "Why do you not accept what our people offer?" And they would make reply, "Sire, because they offer us very little." Then would he say, "You would do well to accept what is proposed, as our people desire." And the holy man endeavoured thus, with all his power, to bring them into a straight path and a reasonable.

Ofttimes it happened that he would go, after his mass, and seat himself in the wood of Vincennes, and lean against an oak, and make us sit round him. And all those who had any cause in hand came and spoke to him, without hindrance of usher, or of any other person. Then he would ask, out of his own mouth, "Is there any one who has cause in hand?" And those who had a cause in hand stood up. Then would he say, "Keep silence all, and you shall be heard in turn, one after the other." Then he would call my Lord Peter of Fontaines and my Lord Geoffrey of Villette, and say to one of them, "Settle me this cause."

And when he saw that there was anything to amend in the words of those who spoke on his behalf, or in the word of those who spoke on behalf of any other person, he would himself, out of his own mouth, amend what they had said. Sometimes have I seen him, in summer, go to do justice among his people in the garden of Paris, clothed in a tunic of camlet, a surcoat of tartan without sleeves, and a mantle of black taffeta about his neck, his hair well combed, no cap, and a hat of white peacock's feathers upon his head. And he would cause a carpet to be laid down, so that we might sit round him, and all the people who had any cause to bring before him stood around. And then would he have their causes settled, as I have told you previously he was wont to do in the wood of Vincennes.

JOINVILLE

OF THE BLESSED MAN PAUL THE SIMPLE

Now there was a certain husbandman whose name was Paul, who was more simple and innocent in nature than are usually the children of men; and he had a wife who was beautiful in her appearance, and wicked in her deeds and actions, and she had wandered from him and had been committing adultery for a long time. And one day, suddenly Paul went into his house from the field, and he found her and another working impurity together; now this took place so that Divine Grace might incite Paul to follow that which was more excellent. And having gone in and seen them, he laughed chastely, and answered and said, "It is good, it is good, truly she is not accounted mine by me. By Jesus, henceforth I will not take her again. Get thee gone, and behold she is thine, she and her children: and as for me, I will go and become a monk."

And saying nothing to any man he went away a journey of eight stages, and he arrived at the cell of Mâr Anthony the Great. And having knocked at the door, the blessed man Mâr Anthony went out, and he said unto Paul, "What dost thou seek?" Paul said unto him, "I seek to become a monk." Mâr Anthony answered and said unto him, "Thou art an old man eighty years old, and it is impossible for thee to become a monk here; but depart to the village, and work in the fields for thy living, and give thanks unto God at the same time that thou art not able to endure the afflictions of the desert." And again Paul answered and said unto him, "Whatsoever thou wilt teach me, that will I do." Anthony said unto him, "I have told thee that thou art an old man, and thou canst not do it; but if thou wishest to become a monk, get thee gone to some monastic house and abide where the brethren are many, and where they will be able to bear with thy sickness. As for me, I live by myself alone here, and

I only eat once in five days, and even then I do not eat a full meal." With these and suchlike words did Anthony frighten Paul. And as he would not be persuaded to depart, Anthony went into his cell, and shut the door upon himself for three days, and because of him he did not go outside his cell for three whole days, not even for his need's sake. Nevertheless Paul did not go away; and on the fourth day, when his need compelled him, Anthony opened the door and went forth. And again he said unto Paul, "Get thee gone, O old man, why dost thou trouble me? It is impossible for thee to stay here." Paul said unto him, "It is impossible for me to die in any other place except this."

And the blessed Anthony, having looked carefully and seen that he was carrying no food with him, and no bread and no water, and that he had fasted during the four days which he had remained, said within himself, "Peradventure he will escape and die, and will plunge my soul into tribulation": so he accepted him and brought him into his cell. And because of Paul during those days Anthony performed exceedingly severe ascetic labours, the like of which, even in his early manhood, he had never performed. And he soaked palm leaves in water, and gave them unto Paul, and said unto him, "Take these palm leaves, and weave a mat therefrom even as I do myself." And the old man Paul took them, and wove them into a mat fifteen cubits long, until at the ninth hour he was exhausted. And Anthony, seeing what he had woven, was angry with him, and said unto him, "Thou hast woven the leaves loosely, unweave them, and weave them over again neatly and closely." And Paul unwove what he had woven, and wove the leaves over again, but still he wove too loosely, because the leaves had become twisted through the former weaving and unweaving. Meanwhile Paul was fasting all these days, and Anthony laid these hard labours upon him while his soul was vexed with hunger, so that he might become disgusted and depart from him.

Now when Anthony saw that Paul was neither angry nor wrathful, and that he made no complaint, his mercy made itself manifest; and behold when Paul had lived there another day, he said unto him,

"Dost thou wish to eat a piece of bread?" The old man Paul said unto him, "As it pleaseth thee, father." And this also especially shamed Mâr Anthony, that he did not hasten in his desire to the promise of food, but that he cast all his desire upon him. Thereupon Anthony said unto him, "Set the table and bring bread." And Anthony placed on the table four loaves, each of which was of the weight of about six ounces, and he dipped them in water because they were dry, and he placed one before himself and three before Paul. And having placed them there he sang a psalm which he knew twelve times, and he recited twelve prayers that he might try Paul, but Paul prayed with him in gladness; and after the twelve prayers they sat down to eat in the late evening. Having eaten one loaf Anthony did not touch another, but the old man Paul ate slowly, and when Anthony had finished he had still some of his loaf to eat, and Anthony was waiting for him to finish it. And having finished it, he answered and said unto him, "Little father, wilt thou eat another loaf?" And Paul said unto him, "If thou wilt eat another I will also; but if thou wilt not, I will not." Anthony saith unto him, "I have had enough, for I am a monk." And Paul said unto him, "I also have had enough, for I also seek to become a monk." And after these things Anthony again stood up, and made twelve prayers, and when they had said together the psalms twelve times they slept for a little during the night, and then they sang and prayed until the morning.

And when Anthony saw that the old man was carrying out with gladness a rule of life similar unto his own in every respect, he said unto him, "If thou art able to bear every day passed in this wise, then stay with me." Paul said unto him, "Although I know nothing else, yet the things which I do know I can perform easily"; and on another day Anthony said unto him, "Behold, thou hast become a monk." And a few months afterward when Anthony saw that his soul was perfect before God, and that he was simple beyond measure, and that Divine Grace was helping him, he built him a cell at a distance of about three or four miles away, and said unto him, "Behold, thou art a monk, and henceforth thou must live by thyself so that thou mayest receive the temptation of devils." Now when Paul had lived by himself a year, the gift of healing and of casting out devils was given unto him.

And in those times they brought unto Anthony a certain man who was vexed by a fierce devil, and that devil was one of the princes of the devils, and he was so fierce that he would even revile and blaspheme the heavens. And when Anthony saw the man he said, "I cannot heal this man, for over this race of princes neither the gift nor the power of healing hath been given unto me; unto Paul it belongeth to heal this man."

THE PARADISE OF THE FATHERS

OF THE BLESSED WOMAN THAIS

And now I desire to narrate unto you the excellent history and the great repentance of the blessed woman Thais or Thaisis, for speech concerning her is most excellent, and it is full of encouragement and penitence of soul unto those who love God. Now this woman had a mother who, because her daughter was beautiful of face, made her to take up a position in the market, and the rumour of her beauty travelled unto every place, and those who were living afar off desired greatly to see her; and no man who looked upon her was satisfied with the sight of her face, because she burned like a flame of fire into the hearts of those who saw her, and many by reason of their mad love for her sold whatever property they had to her parents that they might have commerce with her. Now when Bessarion, the servant of God, heard these things concerning this woman and that through her beauty she was dragging many to destruction, he arrayed himself in the apparel of a man who was in the world, and took with him one *dînâr* and went unto her, and when he saw her he brought forth the *dînâr* and gave it to her; and having taken the *dînâr* she said unto him, "Let us go into a room," and he said unto her, "Yea, let us go in." And having gone in, the blessed man Bessarion saw the couch which was laid out, now it was a very high one, and the woman said unto the old man, "Come, get up on this couch"; and he said unto her, "Hast thou not inside this chamber another room?" and she said unto him, "Yea." Then he said unto her, "Let us then go in there." And Thais answered and said unto him, "If it be that thou art ashamed of men seeing thee, know that no man can see us in this chamber; but if it be God of Whom thou art afraid He can see us in whatsoever place we enter." And the blessed man Bessarion hearing these words, said unto her, "My daughter, dost thou know that God existeth?" And she said unto him, "Yea, I know that God existeth, and that there will be kingdom, and judgment." Then the old man said unto her, "If thou knowest that God is, and that there will be kingdom and judgment, why dost thou destroy men in this manner?" And straightway the woman cast herself at his feet, and said unto him, "I know that there is repentance for those who sin. But I beseech thee, master, to tarry with me for three hours, and whatsoever thou wishest to do unto me that do because of all the evil things which have been wrought by me"; and having told her in what place he would await her he left her and went away.

Then in that same hour the woman took everything which she had gained by fornication and burnt it with fire in the midst of the city, and she said, "Come, O all ye who have had commerce with me, and see that I am burning before your eyes every possession which I have gathered together by means of sin"; and the things which were burned were worth three hundred pounds of gold, and there were there also goods and apparel of all kinds; and after she had burned up everything she went to the blessed man Bessarion. And when Bessarion saw her he took her by the hand and led her along and brought her to a religious house of sisters, and he shut her in a little cell, leaving her only one small window in the wall through which a woman passed in food to her. And the blessed Bessarion said unto the head of the house, "Give her a pound of dry bread each day, and water according to her need." Then the blessed woman Thais said unto the venerable Bessarion, "With what petition dost thou command me to pray unto God? That He should forgive me my sins?" The blessed Bessarion said unto her, "Thou art neither worthy to pray unto God, nor to make mention of His Name with thy lips, nor to stretch out thy hands unto Him; for thy lips are unclean and polluted, and thy hands are contaminated with impurity; thou shalt only sit down and gaze towards the East, and thou shalt say nothing except, 'O Thou who didst create me, have mercy upon me.' And having dwelt in that cell for a space of about three years, the blessed Bessarion had mercy upon her, and the blessed man went to Abbâ Anthony that he might learn from him whether God had forgiven her her sins or not. Then having spoken concerning her unto Anthony that blessed man called unto his disciples, and said unto them, "Let each of you shut himself in his cell all night, and pray ye unto God that we may see unto whom shall be revealed the matter concerning which the blessed Bessarion hath come unto us this day."

And when they all had done as they had been commanded and when a long time had elapsed, the blessed Paul, the chief of the disciples of Mâr Anthony, looked into the heavens and saw a couch which had been spread with great splendour, and three angels who were carrying three lamps were standing before that couch, and a crown of glory was laid thereupon. And having seen all this glorious sight, he said, "This couch can only be for my father Anthony." Then a voice came unto him from heaven, saying, "This couch is not for Anthony, thy father, but for Thais the harlot"; and the blessed Paul rose up early in the morning and related the vision which he had seen. And the blessed Mâr Bessarion came back from Abbâ Anthony in great joy, and he went to the religious house of the sisterhood, and he opened the door that he might bring the woman out from the cell wherein she was secluded; but she made entreaty unto him, saying, "Leave me here until my death, for my sins are many." Then the blessed man said unto her, "Behold the merciful God hath had compassion upon thee, and He hath accepted thy repentance;" and then she wished to go forth from her cell. "Believe me, O Father, from the day wherein I entered this cell I have made all my sins a mighty burden and I have set it before my eyes, in such wise that as the breath of my nostrils hath not separated itself from me, so my sins have not separated themselves from me until this hour."

And the blessed Bessarion answered and said unto her, "God hath not forgiven thee thy sins because of thy repentance, but because of the thought which thou hadst—that thou wouldst deliver thyself over unto Christ." Now this blessed woman Thais lived after her repentance fifteen days, and she departed unto our Lord in peace. Thus was the crowning of the blessed Thais, who was lost and was found, and was dead and who came to life by the grace of Christ, unto Whom belong mercy, and compassion, and glory, and honour, for ever and ever. Amen.

THE PARADISE OF THE FATHERS

ON THE FALL OF EUTROPIUS

Note: Eutropius, minister of the Emperor Arcadius, fell from power in the year 399, as a result of intrigues involving the Empress Eudoxia and leading to a rebellion headed by Tribigild the Ostrogoth. He found refuge in the Church, though he had apparently been serving the worldly ruler rather than God.

It is always in season but now more than ever is it seasonable to say: Vanity of vanities and all is vanity. . . . Where is the gay torch-light now? Where are the clapping hands and the dances and the assemblies and the festivals? Where the green garlands and the curtains floating? Where the cry of the town and the cheers of the hippodrome, and the noisy flattering lungs of the spectators there? All that is gone: a wind blew and on the sudden cast the leaves and shewed us the tree bare and all that was left of it from the root upwards shaking—the gale that struck it was so fearfully strong and threatened, indeed, to tear it up root-whole, or shatter it this way and that, even to the rending of the grain of the timber. Where now are the friends, the make-believes, followers of the fashion? Where the suppers and feasts? Where the swarm of hangers-on? The strong wine decanting all day long, the cooks and the daintily dressed table, the attendants on greatness and all the words and ways they have to please? They were all night and dreaming: now it is day and they are vanished. They were spring flowers, and, spring over, they all are faded together. They were a shadow, and it has travelled on beyond. They were smoke, and it has gone out in the air. They were bubbles, and are broken. They were cobweb, and are swept away. And so this spiritual refrain is left us to sing, coming in again and again with: Vanity of vanities and all is vanity. O this is the verse that should be written on walls, and in clothing and at markets and at home and by waysides and on doors and over entries and above all in the conscience of each, written wherever we look that we may read it whatever we do. While this swindle of the business of life and this wearing of masks and playing of characters is taken for truth by the many, this is the verse that every day, at dinner and supper, and every meeting between men I wish that each one of you could be bringing to his neighbour's ear and hearing from his neighbour's tongue: Vanity of vanities, all is vanity.

ST. JOHN CHRYSOSTOM

A MOTHER'S DEMAND

One more instance of the loving-kindness of the glorious Virgin I found in an ancient sermon, and certainly it should not be despised. A certain poor woman loved the Blessed Virgin, decking her image with roses and lilies and such ornaments as she could find. It befell that her son was taken and hanged. The woman, in the bitterness of her soul, went to the image of the Blessed Virgin and besought her to restore her son; and, seeing that she recovered not her son as soon as she wished, she said: "Is this then the price of service to thee, that thou succourest me not in my need?" Then, as though maddened by the excess of her grief, she said: "If thou restore me not my son, I will take away thy Son." And, as she reached out her hand impetuously to bear away the image of the little Babe, behold! her son stood by her and seized her cloak and cried: "What dost thou, Mother?

Hast thou lost thy senses? Behold, the Mother of God hath restored me to thee." So the mother rejoiced to recover her son.

LIBER EXEMPLORUM

THE JACKDAW OF RHEIMS

Albeit all who call themselves Christians are as it were naturally persuaded, by that Faith wherewith they have been imbued, that the sentence of excommunication is no less than a separation from God and an estrangement from eternal life; yet, for that hearts benumbed with negligence are sometimes more easily moved by examples than by preaching, I have thought it necessary to show how terrible is this peremptory sentence to a rational creature, when even a brute beast is thereby sometimes subjected either to death or to some most grievous calamity. . . . This monastery (of Corvey) in the time of the last Emperor Frederick was ruled by one Conrad, who, according to the pompous custom of prince-abbots, among other gauds of worldly glory, wore gold rings—in a spirit far different from that of the truly poor and humble-minded abbot-founder of Clairvaux, who (we find it written) delighted more in rake and hoe than in mitre and ring. Now it came to pass one day when he sat at meat and, in courtly fashion, had laid down a precious golden ring for the sake of washing his hands, that some trifle or some serious matter intervened, and the ring was left, somewhat too negligently, on the table. Meanwhile a tame raven, whom the abbot's courtiers kept as a pet, watching an unguarded moment, caught the ring in his beak and flew away swiftly to his nest without conscience of his own guilty theft. When, therefore, the feasters' hunger was satisfied, and the meats removed, and the guests arisen from the table, then the abbot learned his loss, blamed his servants' negligence, and bade them seek the ring forthwith in every corner: which, however, could nowhere be found, nor could the thief be discovered. Whereupon the abbot, suspecting both guests and servants, and stirred to fervent indignation, sent word to the parish priests of the great and wealthy town which was situated hard by the abbey and subjected to its rule, bidding them publicly launch the most grievous sentence of excommunication upon him who had not feared to defile himself with this crime. The sentence was proclaimed; and, as all rational beings in those parts found in their guiltless conscience a crown of innocence, so the irrational creature itself could not escape the temporal penalties of that curse, whereof the eternal pains could take no hold upon his fragile and shortlived condition. For this thief, guilty yet unaware of his own guilt, began to sicken little by little, to loathe his food, to cease more and more from his droll croakings and other irrational follies whereby he was wont to delight the minds of fools who neglect the fear of God; then he began even to droop his wings; and at last his very feathers fled from the corruption of his decaying flesh, exposing him as a miserable and marvellous spectacle to all beholders. It came to pass one day that, as the abbot's household disputed one with the other, in his presence, concerning this portentous change in the bird, and concluded that so great a marvel must have some cause, one of them said half in jest to the abbot: "Ye ought to consider, my lord, whether by chance this be the thief whom ye seek, and whether this loathsome plague which ye behold be not the token of that curse wherein he is involved." At which word all were astonished; and the abbot bade one of his servants straightway to climb the tree wherein this bird had his nest, and to turn over diligently his couch of straw and plaited twigs. The servant climbed, found the ring forthwith, cleansed it from the filth that disfigured it, and laid it within the abbot's hands, to the amazement of all that stood by. Wherefore, since the wretched thief, who suffered these horrible pains for his crime and yet had no guilty conscience thereof—when he, as we must believe, had been discovered by the finger of God, then the lord abbot, by the advice of prudent men, sent word to the priests who had pronounced this sentence of excommunication, to proclaim that the ring was now restored, and the curse of none effect. Whereupon, even as at first the aforesaid bird had sickened by slow degrees, and visibly languished from day to day under that insidious disease, even so he now began slowly to revive and recover his former strength; until at last, by a plain miracle of God, he was wholly restored to his first health and beauty.

PATROLOGIA LATINA

A STORM AT MATINS

Not more than a few weeks afterwards it was the vigil of the martyrs, Gervase and Prothasius, when there was a little thunder and occasional lightning with thick clouds and tempestuous winds. Now in the morning when we rose, the bell for the first hour had just sounded; we assembled in the church with unusual quickness and after a very short prayer we had said, "O God, come to my assistance"; but when we were about to begin what follows, with thunder-clap a bolt from heaven broke into the church with the following results. The cock over the tower, the cross and the staff were either shattered or burnt; the beam on which these stood, was weakened. Then after half-burning and tearing up the shingles fixed to them by nails, the bolt passed through the western window of the tower. The image of the crucified Lord standing beneath was broken, the head being shattered to pieces and the right side pierced, but not scorched, whilst the right arms both of the cross and of the figure were so burnt and maimed that with the exception of the thumb no one could find a single piece of the whole arm.

As therefore, when the shepherd is smitten, the sheep are scattered abroad with blows and death, the bolt passing to the right through the arch under which stood the stricken image, descended the stone of the arch in a two-forked black furrow and entering the choir struck dead in a moment two monks standing on either side of the arch. Then sweeping to the left on one side it stripped off the colouring from the surface of the stone not continuously, but stepwise as if a stone had been rolled over it, and crushed a monk standing there, although neither in the case of the two others nor of this one, was there any mark of injury to be seen on them, except that on the upturned eyes of the last one there appeared a little dust fallen from the arch. This indeed was remarkable, that the dead men remained sitting. But we, who, stupefied by the shock of the bolt, were half-dead, fell headlong on one another. Moreover, some of us who fell down, lost all feeling in the body below the girdle; some were so hurt that, fearing their death, we hastily anointed them with holy oil. Darting into the breasts of some, the flame burnt off the hair and scorched the growth of hair under the armpits; and boring through the soles and sandals passed out by the extremities.

It is impossible to describe how with judgment the punishment of heaven raged, by what bends and turns it ran about, what it damaged, what it burned, what it broke. Nobody has heard anything like it as happening in France in our generation. I saw, I call God to witness, an hour after these things had happened, the image of the Blessed Mother of God, which stood below the crucifix, having such a disturbed look, so changed from her usual calm, that she seemed quite another person. Not trusting my own eyes I found out that the same thing had been noticed by others. When we had recovered from the amazement which had fallen on us through this event, after making confession, we began to reflect why we had suffered for our sins beyond human expression, and being brought by God face to face with ourselves, by looking into our consciences, we discovered how justly we had been punished. Thereupon we saw the face of the Holy Mother changed to a tranquil expression. Verily the grief and the shame which for some time we felt, passes all belief.

GUIBERT, ABBOT OF NOGENT SOUS COUCY

GIVE THAT YE MAY RECEIVE

I have heard from an abbot of our Order that another abbot—I think of the Order of Black Monks—was very hospitable and most merciful to the poor. And, being himself fervent in all works of mercy, he took care to ordain as stewards of the house men who would not hinder his fervour, but rather kindle it. The more guests he received, and the more charity he showed to the poor, the more bountifully did the Lord bless him and his house. But after his death his successor, urged by avarice, removed these merciful officials and set others in their room whom he knew to be more parsimonious, saying: "My predecessor was too lavish and indiscreet; his officials were too prodigal: we must so order and temper the expenses of our monastery that, if by chance our crops were smitten by hail, or if times of dearth were to come, we might yet have wherewithal to succour the poor." Cloaking his avarice with such words, he shut hospitality away altogether, and withdrew the accustomed alms from the poor. When these charities had been cut off, the monastery could not profit in worldly goods; nay, within a little while it fell to such a depth of poverty that the brethren had scarce enough to eat. One day a gray-haired, venerable man came to the porter and sought hospitality; the man took him in secretly and fearfully, and, rendering him such offices of hospitality as at that time he could, added these words: "Let it not scandalize thee, good man, that I minister so scantily to thy needs; for our necessities are cause thereof. In old days I have seen this monastery in such prosperity that, if a Bishop had come, he would have been harboured with great charity and abundance." To which the old man answered: "Two brethren have been expelled from this your monastery: nor will it ever prosper until their return: the name of the one is Date, and of the other Dabitur." And so saying, he vanished from the porter's eyes. I think that he was some angel, through whom the Lord wished to recall the first charity of these brethren. The porter, being a lay-brother, kept those names in his heart, and told the abbot and brethren all that he had heard. They returned to their former hospitality, and soon the Lord began to bless them as before.

CAESARIUS OF HEISTERBACH

THE VIRGIN OF CHARTRES

Who has ever seen!—Who has ever heard tell, in times past, that powerful princes of the world, that men brought up in honour and in wealth, that nobles, men and women, have bent their proud and haughty necks to the harness of carts, and that, like beasts of burden, they have dragged to the abode of Christ these wagons, loaded with wines, grains, oil, stone, wood, and all that is necessary for the wants of life, or for the construction of the church? But while they draw these burdens, there is one thing admirable to observe; it is that often when a thousand persons and more are attached to the chariots,—so great is the difficulty,—yet they march in such silence that not a murmur is heard, and truly if one did not see the thing with one's eyes, one might believe that among such a multitude there was hardly a person present. When they halt on the road, nothing is heard but the confession of sins, and pure and suppliant prayer to God to obtain pardon. At the voice of the priests who exhort their hearts to peace, they forget all hatred, discord is thrown far aside, debts are remitted, the unity of hearts is established. But if any one is so far advanced in evil as to be unwilling to pardon an offender, or if he rejects the counsel of the priest who has piously advised him, his offering is instantly thrown from the wagon as impure, and he himself ignominiously and shamefully excluded from the society of the holy. There one sees the priests who preside over each chariot exhort every one to penitence, to confession of faults, to the resolution of better life! There one sees old people, young people, little children, calling on the Lord with a suppliant voice, and uttering to Him, from the depth of the heart, sobs and sighs with words of glory and praise! After the people, warned by the sound of trumpets and the sight of banners, have resumed their road, the march is made with such ease that no obstacle can retard it. . . . When they have reached the church they arrange the wagons about it like a spiritual camp, and during the whole night they celebrate the watch by hymns and canticles. On each wagon they light tapers and lamps; they place there the infirm and sick, and bring them the precious relics of the Saints for their relief. Afterwards the priests and clerics close the ceremony by processions which the people follow with devout heart, imploring the clemency of the Lord and of his Blessed Mother for the recovery of the sick.

ABBOT HAIMON

WISDOM AND THE CHURCH OF GOD

Alfred, the king, greets bishop Werferth, with his words lovingly and in friendly wise; and I let it be known to thee that it has very often come to my mind what wise men there were formerly among the English, both of godly and of worldly office, and what happy times were those throughout England; and how the kings who had rule of the folk in those days obeyed God and His ministers; and how within their borders they maintained their peace, their customs, and their might, and at the same time extended their territory beyond; how they prospered both in war and in wisdom; and also how zealous were those of the religious life in teaching and in learning and in all those services which they owed to God; and how foreigners came hither to this land seeking wisdom and learning, and how we must now get them from abroad if we are to have them. So clean was learning fallen away among the English, that there were very few on this side of the Humber who could understand their service-book in English, or translate a letter from Latin into English; and I ween there were not many beyond the Humber. So few of them were there that I cannot think of one south of the Thames when I came to the throne. To God Almighty be the thanks that we have any supply of teachers now. And therefore I bid thee, as I believe thou art willing, as often as thou art able, to free thyself from worldly affairs, that thou mayest apply the wisdom that God gavest thee wherever thou canst. Think what punishments came upon us on account of this world, when we neither loved wisdom ourselves nor allowed it to other men: the name alone of being Christians we loved, and very few of the practises.

When I remembered all this, I also recalled that I saw, before it was all laid waste and burnt, how the churches throughout England stood filled with treasures and books, and also a great number of God's servants; but they knew very little use of those books, since they were able to understand no whit of them, for they were not written in their own tongue. As if they had said, "Our elders, who held these places of old, loved wisdom, and through it they got wealth and left it to us.

Here we can yet see their tracks, but we know not how to follow them, and therefore we have lost both the wealth and the wisdom, because we would not bend our minds to follow their path."

When I remembered all this, I wondered very greatly, concerning the good wise men who were formerly among the English and had fully learned all those books, that they had turned no part of them into their own language. But I soon answered myself and said, "They did not think that men would ever become so careless and that learning would so fall away; hence they neglected it, through the desire that there might be the more wisdom here in the land the more we knew of languages."

Then I called to mind how the law was first found in Hebrew; and again, when the Greeks learned it, they translated all of it into their own tongue, and also all other books. And again, the Romans likewise, after they learned them, translated the whole of them, through wise interpreters, into their own language. And also all other Christian peoples turned some part of them into their own tongues. Therefore it seems better to me, if it seems so to you, that we also translate some books that are most needful for all men to know, into that language which we are all able to understand; and that, as we very easily can with God's help if we have peace, we cause all the youth now in England of the class of freemen, who are rich enough to be able to apply themselves to it, to be set to learn, the while they can be put to no other employment, until they are well able to read English writing; and afterward let those be taught in the Latin tongue who are to be taught further and to be put in a higher office. When I remembered how, before now, the knowledge of Latin had fallen away among the English and yet many knew how to read English writing, I began, among other various and manifold concerns of this kingdom, to translate into English the book that in Latin is called "Pastoralis," and in English, "Shepherd's Book,"—at times word by word, and again according to the sense, as I had learned it from Plegmund my archbishop, and from Asser my bishop, and from Grimbold my mass-priest, and from John my mass-priest. After I had learned it, I turned it into English as I understood it and could most clearly expound it;

and to every bishopric in my kingdom I wish to send one; and in each there is a book-mark worthy fifty mancuses. And I command in God's name that no man take the book-mark from the book, nor the book from the minister. We know not how long there may be such learned bishops as, God be thanked, there now are nearly everywhere. Therefore, I would that they may always be in their place, unless the bishop wishes to have them with him, or they be lent anywhere, or anyone copy them.

KING ALFRED

THE LIFE OF MAN

King Edwin, therefore, delaying to receive the word of God at the preaching of Paulinus, and using for sometime, as has been said, to sit several hours alone, and seriously to ponder within himself what he was to do, and what religion he was to follow, the man of God came to him, laid his right hand on his head, and asked, "Whether he knew that sign?" The king in a trembling condition, was ready to fall down at his feet, but he raised him up, and in a familiar manner said to him, "Behold by the help of God you have escaped the hands of the enemies whom you feared. Behold you have of His gift obtained the kingdom which you desired. Take heed not to delay that which you promised to perform; embrace the faith, and keep the precepts of Him who, delivering you from temporal adversity, has raised you to the honour of a temporal kingdom; and if, from this time forward, you shall be obedient to His will, which through me He signifies to you, He will not only deliver you from the everlasting torments of the wicked, but also make you a partaker with Him of His eternal kingdom in heaven."

The king, hearing these words, answered that he was both willing and bound to receive the faith which he taught; but that he would confer about it with his principal friends and counsellors, to the end that if they also were of his opinion, they might all together be cleansed in Christ, the Fountain of Life. Paulinus consenting, the king did as he said; for, holding a counsel with the wise men, he asked of everyone in particular what he thought of the new doctrine, and the new worship that was preached? To which the chief of his own priests, Coifi, immediately answered, "O king, consider what this is which is now preached to us; for I verily declare to you, that the religion which we have hitherto professed has, as far as I can learn, no virtue in it. For none of your people has applied himself more diligently to the worship of our gods than I; and yet there are many who receive greater favours from you, and are more preferred than I, and are more prosperous in all their undertakings. Now if the gods were good for anything, they would rather forward me, who have been more careful to serve them. It remains, therefore, that if upon examination you find those new doctrines, which are now preached to us, better and more efficacious, we immediately receive them without any delay."

Another of the king's chief men, approving of his words and exhortations, presently added: "The present life of man, O king, seems to me, in comparison of that time which is unknown to us, like to the swift-flight of a sparrow through the room wherein you sit at supper in winter, with your commanders and ministers, and a good fire in the midst, whilst the storms of rain and snow prevail abroad; the sparrow, I say, flying in at one door, and immediately out at another, whilst he is within, is safe from the wintry storm; but after a short space of fair weather, he immediately vanished out of your sight, into the dark winter from which he had emerged. So this life of man appears for a short space, but of what went before, or what is to follow, we are utterly ignorant. If, therefore, this new doctrine contains something more certain, it seems justly to deserve to be followed." The other elders and king's counsellors, by divine inspiration, spoke to the same effect.

VENERABLE BEDE

THE DEATH OF CAEDMON

For when the time of his departure drew near, he laboured for the space of fourteen days under a bodily infirmity which seemed to prepare the way, yet so moderate that he could talk and walk the whole time. In his neighbourhood was the house to which those that were sick, and like shortly to die, were carried. He desired the person that attended him, in the evening, as the night came on in which he was to depart this life, to make ready a place there for him to take his rest. This person, wondering why he should desire it, because there was as yet no sign of his dying soon, did what he had ordered. He accordingly went there, and conversing pleasantly in a joyful manner with the rest that were in the house before, when it was past midnight, he asked them whether they had the Eucharist there? They answered, "What need of the Eucharist? for you are not likely to die, since you talk so merrily with us, as if you were in perfect health."—"However," said he, "bring me the Eucharist." Having received the same into his hand, he asked whether they were all in charity with him and without any enmity or rancour? They answered, that they were all in perfect charity, and free from anger; and in their turn asked him, whether he was in the same mind towards them? He answered, "I am in charity, my children, with all the servants of God." Then strengthening himself with the heavenly Viaticum, he prepared for the entrance into another life, and asked, how near the time was when the brothers were to be awakened to sing the nocturnal praises of our Lord? They answered, "It is not far off." Then he said, "Well, let us wait that hour," and signing himself with the sign of the cross, he laid his head on the pillow, and falling into a slumber ended his life so in silence.

Thus it came to pass, that as he had served God with a simple and pure mind, and undisturbed devotion, so he now departed to His presence, leaving the world by a quiet death, and that tongue, which had composed so many holy words in praise of the Creator, uttered its last words whilst he was in the act of signing himself with the cross, and recommending himself into His hands, and by what has been here said, he seems to have had foreknowledge of his death.

VENERABLE BEDE

KING CANUTE PASSES

On a certain occasion, king Canute, accompanied by his queen Emma, and by magnates of the realm, was proceeding to Ely by boat, intending there to celebrate, according to custom, the purification of Saint Mary; for since the beginning of their order, the abbots of Ely have held the ceremony in the presence of the king's court. As they were approaching the bank, the king, rising in the midst of his men, signalled to the boatmen to pull more swiftly to the little gate, and commanded them to pass through it slowly. Thereupon, lifting his eyes toward the church, which stood out distinctly on the summit of a rock, he heard upon all sides a sound of great sweetness; and listening intently, the better to hear the melody in all its fulness, he began to sigh. He perceived that it was the monks singing in the dining-hall, and chanting the hours. Thereupon, he requested certain ones in the boats to come round to him and to sing with him. Then the king himself, expressing with his own mouth the gladness of his heart, composed a song in English in these words:

Sweetly sang the monks in Ely
When Canute the king rowed by!
"Row, Knights, near the land
And hear the monks' sweet song,"

which, even to-day, are sung publicly in chorus and are remembered in proverbs. The king beginning thus, did not cease to sing piously and sweetly in chorus with the venerable college, until he came to land, and, being worthily received by the brothers in procession as their custom is with the most distinguished person, was led into the church. Presently, by his privilege and authority he confirmed in perpetuity the rights and benefits granted to the church by his predecessors, the kings of the English; and before the high altar, where rests the sacred body of the virgin and spouse of Christ, Aetheldreda, he declared, in the presence of the church and of the world, that the rights and privileges of the place should be free in perpetuity.

THOMAS OF ELY

LOVE WITHOUT ENDING

Afore this time I had great longing and desire of Gods gifts to be delivered of this world, and of this life; for oft-times I beheld the woe that is here, and the weal and the blessed being that is there. And if there had no pain been in this life, but the absence of our Lord, methought sometime that it was more than I might bear. And this made me to mourn and busily to long. And also of my own wretchedness, sloth and weariness, that me liked not to live and to travel as me fell to do. And to all this our courteous Lord answered for comfort and patience, and said these words: "Suddenly thou shalt be taken from all thy pain, from all thy sickness, from all thy disease, and from all thy woe. And thou shalt come up above, and thou shalt have Me to thy meed, and thou shalt be fulfilled of joy and bliss; and thou shalt never more have no manner of pain, no manner of sickness, no manner misliking, no wanting of will, but ever joy and bliss without end. What should it then grieve thee to suffer a while, sithen it is my will and my worship?" And in this word (suddenly thou shalt be taken) I saw that God rewarded man of the patience that he hath in abiding of Gods will, and of his time; and that man lengeth his patience over the time of his living; for unknowing the time of his passing. This is a great profit; for if a man knew his time, he should not have patience over that time. And also God will that while the soul is in the body, it seem to it self that it is ever at the point to be taken, for all this life and this longing that we have here is but a point. And when we be taken suddenly out of pain into bliss, then pain shall be nought. And in this time I saw a body lying on the earth: which body shewed heavy and fearful, and without shape and form, as it were a swilge stinking myre. And suddenly out of this body sprung a full fair creature, a little child full shapen and formed, swift and lively, and whiter than the lilly, which sharply glided up into heaven. The swilge of the body betokeneth great wretchedness of our deadly flesh: and the littleness of the child betokeneth the cleanness and the pureness of our soul.

And I thought with this body bliveth no fairness of this child, ne of this child dwelleth no foulness of this body. It is full bliss-ful (for) man to be taken from pain, more than pain to be taken from man; for if pain be taken from us, it may come again. Therefore this is a sovereign comfort, and a bless-ful beholding in a longing soul, that we shall be taken from pain; for in this behest I saw a merciful compassion that our Lord hath in us for our woe, and a courteous behighting of clear deliverance: for He will that we be comforted in the over-passing joy. And that He shewed in these words; "And thou shalt come up above; and thou shalt have me to thy meed, and thou shalt be fulfilled of joy and bliss." It is Gods will that we set the point of our thought in this blissful beholding as oft-time as we may, and as long time keep us therein with his grace; for this is a blissful contemplation to the soul that is led of God, and full much to His worship for the time that it lasteth. And when we fall again to our self by heaviness and ghostly blindness, and feeling of pains ghostly and bodily by our fragility, it is Gods will that we know, that He hath not forget us. And so meaneth He in these words, and saith for comfort; "And thou shalt never more have pain in no manner; nor no manner of sickness, no manner of mis-liking, no want of will, but ever joy and bliss without end: what should it then agrieved thee to suffer a while, sithen it is my will and my worship?" It is Gods will that we take His behests and His comfortings as largely and as mightily as we may take them. And also He will that we take our abidings and our dis-eases as lightly as we may take them, and set them at naught: for the lightlier that we take them, and the less price that we set at them for love, less pain shall we have in the feeling of them, and the more thank and meed shall we have for them.

And thus I understood that what man or woman wilfully choseth God in this life for love, he may be sure that he is loved without end, with endless love that worketh in him that grace; for he will we keep this trustily, that we be as sicker in hope of the bliss of heaven whiles we are here, as we shall be in surety when we are there. And ever the more liking and joy that we take in this sickerness, with reverence and meekness, the better liketh him. For as it was shewed, this reverence that I mean, is a holy, courteous dread of our Lord, to which meekness is knit; and that is, that a creature see the Lord marvellous great, and her self marvellous litle: for these vertues are had endlessly to the loved of God. And it may now be seen and felt in measure by the gracious presence of our Lord, when it is: which presence in all thing is most desired; for it worketh that marvellous sickerness in true faith, and siker hope by greatness of charity in dread that is sweet and delectable. It is Gods will that I see myself as much bound to Him in love, as if He had done for me all that he hath done. And thus should every soul think in regard of His love; that is to say, the charity of God maketh in us such a unity, that when it is truly seen no man can part himself from other. And thus ought each soul to think that God hath done for him all that He hath done. And this sheweth He to make us to love Him, and liken Him, and nothing dread but Him; for it is His will we know that all the might of our enemies is locked in our friends hands. And therefore the soul that knoweth this sickerly, he shall not dread but Him that she loveth. All other dreads she set them among passions, and bodily sickness, and imaginations. And therefore though we been in so much pain, woe and disease that us thinketh, we can think right naught but that we are in, or that we feel; as soon as we may we pass it lightly over, and set we it at naught. And why? for God will be known; for if we know Him, and love Him, and reverently dread Him, we shall have patience, and be in great rest. And it should been great liking to us all that he doth. And this shewed our Lord in these words: "What should it then agrieve thee to suffer a while, seeing it is My will and My worship?"

BLESSED JULIANA OF NORWICH

THE CROSS

Now they lead Thee forth, naked as a worm, the tormentors and armed knights about Thee. The press of the people was amazingly strong. They hustled Thee and harried Thee so shamefully, they spurned Thee with their feet as if Thou hadst been a dog. I see in my soul how ruefully Thou goest, Thy body is so bloody, so torn and blistered, Thy crown is so sharp that sits upon Thy head; Thy hair moveth with the wind, plastered with Thy blood; Thy lovely face is so wan and so swollen with buffeting and with beating, with spitting and spouting, running with blood, that I shudder at the sight. So loathly and so abominable have the Jews made Thee that Thou art more like to myself than to a clean man. The Cross is so heavy, so high and so stark, that they hung on Thy bare back, trussed so hard!

Ah, Lord, how Thou didst groan, so sore and so hard did it press to the bone! Thy body is so sick, so feeble and so weary, what with great fasting and watching all night without any rest before Thou wert taken, and being so dreadfully used with beating and buffeting, that Thou goest all stooping and Thy face is grim. The flesh where the Cross sitteth is all made raw, the bruises and the blisters are wan and blue; the pain of that burden sitteth on Thee so sorely that each foot Thou goest, it stingeth to Thine heart. Thus, in this groaning and great pain, Thou goest out of Jerusalem to Thy death. The city is so noble! The people are so many! The folk come running out of each street. Then the folk stand up in a great crowd, that men may wonder that think thereon. No thief was ever led to death with such a procession of worldly wondering. There were some of the common people who sighed sorely and greatly for Thy woe, knowing Thee so tormented, and that it was for envy, because the princes and bishops that dispensed the law did Thee to death for Thy wise sayings, when Thou wouldst reprove them for their errors. The people knew it was outrage and wrong that Thou didst suffer, and followed Thee weeping and sighing sorely. Then Thou didst tell them what afterwards happened, Thou didst bid them weep for themselves and for the great vengeance that should fall, because of Thy death, upon them and their children, and upon all the city, that afterwards was destroyed, when for the avenging of their own guilt they were chased out of their place.

Ah, Lord, the sorrow that fell upon Thy heart when Thou didst cast Thine eyes upon Thy Mother! Thou sawest her follow after among the great throng as a woman out of herself; she wrung her hands; weeping and sighing, she cast her arms about; her tears dropped at her feet; more than once she fell in a dead swoon for sorrow, because of the pains that smote her to the heart. The sorrowing and the great dole that she made increased all Thine other pains manifold! So when she knew that it was so, she was much worse, and Thou didst weep also for her. So was your sorrow for one another growing manifold with heaping sorrows! The love of your hearts that over all other loves was without equal, burning keenly, made you to burn for each other with sorrow unlike to any other woe. As the love was without equal, so the sorrow was without equal. It pierced your hearts as if it were death.

Ah, Lady, mercy! why were thou so bold as to follow so nigh among so many keen foes? How was it that awareness of womankind or the shame of maidenhood had not withdrawn thee? For it was not seemly to follow such a rout, so vile and so shameful, so horrible to see! But thou hadst no regard for the fear of any man, nor for aught else that should hinder thee, but, as if thou wert out of thyself, all thine heart was set in dole and sorrow for thy Son's passion. Thy love was so keen, the one for the other, and so burning hot, thy sighs were so deep, the sadness of thy face was woeful as death. The love and the sorrow that pierced thy breast bereft thee of all recking of bodily fear, and of worldly shame, and all manner of hindrances, so that thy sorrow had taken thee out of thyself.

RICHARD ROLLE

MEDITATION

And therefore, when thou purposest thee to this work, and feelest by grace that thou art called by God, lift up thine heart unto God with a meek stirring of love. And mean God that made thee, and bought thee, and that graciously hath called thee to thy degree: and receive none other thought of God. And yet not all these, except thou desirest; for a naked intent directed unto God, without any other cause than himself, sufficeth wholly.

And if thou desirest to have this intent lapped and folden in one word, so that thou mayest have better hold thereupon, take thee but a little word of one syllable, for so it is better than of two; for the shorter the word, the better it accordeth with the work of the spirit. And such a word is this word GOD or this word LOVE. Choose whichever thou wilt, or another: whatever word thou likest best of one syllable. And fasten this word to thine heart, so that it may never go thence for anything that befalleth.

This word shall be thy shield and thy spear, whether thou ridest on peace or on war. With this word, thou shalt beat on this cloud and this darkness above thee. With this word, thou shalt smite down all manner of thought under the cloud of forgetting. Insomuch, that if any thought press upon thee to ask thee what thou wouldst have, answer with no more words but with this one word. And if he offer of his great learning to expound to thee that word and to tell thee the conditions of that word, say to him that thou wilt have it all whole, and not broken nor undone. And if thou wilt hold fast to this purpose, be thou sure that that thought will no while bide. And why? Surely because thou wilt not let him feed himself on such sweet meditations of God touched before.

THE CLOUD OF UNKNOWING

TESTIMONY OF ST. JEANNE D'ARC

Whereupon master Jean de La Fontaine, specially charged and deputed by us to this end, interrogated the said Jeanne. And he asked her, by the oath she had taken, whence she had come when she last went to Compiègne. She answered that she had come from the town of Crespy-en-Valois.

Asked whether she spent several days at Compiègne before she made any sally or attack therefrom, she answered that she came there secretly in the morning; and entered the town unknown, she thought, to the enemy; and the same day, towards evening, she made the sally (in French la saillie) in which she was taken.

Asked whether, when she was attacked, the bells were rung, she replied that if they were, it was not at her order or with her knowledge; she did not think so, or remember saying they were rung.

Asked whether she made the sally at the instruction of her voice, she answered that in Easter week last, when she was in the trenches at Melun, she was told by her voices, namely by St. Catherine and St. Margaret, that she would be captured before St. John's Day; it had to be so; and she should not be distressed, but take it in good part, and God would aid her.

Asked if since Melun she had been told by her voices that she would be taken, she answered yes, several times, nearly every day. And she asked of her voices, that when she was taken, she might die quickly without long suffering in prisons; and the voices told her to be resigned to everything, that it must so happen; but they did not tell her when. If she had known the hour, she would not have gone. She had often asked them at what hour she would be taken, but they did not tell her.

Asked whether, if her voices had ordered her to make this attack from Compiègne, and had signified that she would be captured, she would have gone, she answered that if she had known when she was to be taken she would not have willingly gone; nevertheless she would have done their bidding in the end, whatever it cost her.

THE TRIAL OF JEANNE D'ARC

ST. FRANCIS AND THE STIGMATA

Coming to the third consideration, to wit the seraphic vision and the imprinting of the most holy stigmata, it is to be considered that when the festival of the most Holy Cross of the month of September was drawing nigh, Friar Leo went one night, at the accustomed hour, to say matins with St. Francis, and calling, as he was wont, from the head of the bridge: *Domine, labia mea aperies,* and St. Francis making no answer, Friar Leo turned not back again as St. Francis had commanded him; but, with good and holy purpose, he crossed over the bridge and softly entered the cell; and, finding him not, he thought that he was somewhere in the wood in prayer; wherefore he came forth and, by the light of the moon, went searching softly through the wood; and finally he heard the voice of St. Francis; and, drawing nigh, he saw him on his knees in prayer, with face and hands raised to heaven; and in fervour of spirit he was speaking thus: "Who art Thou, my most sweet God? What am I, most vile worm and Thine unprofitable servant? What am I, most vile worm and Thine unprofitable servant?" And these same words alone did he repeat, and said no other thing.

For the which cause, Friar Leo, marvelling thereat, raised his eyes and gazed toward heaven; and as he looked, he beheld, coming down from heaven, a torch of fire, most beautiful and bright, which descended and lighted upon the head of St. Francis; and from out the said flame he heard a voice come which spake with St. Francis; but Friar Leo understood not the words. Hearing this, and deeming himself unworthy to abide so near to that holy place, where was that marvellous apparition, and fearing also to offend St. Francis, or to disturb him in his contemplation, if he should be perceived by him, he softly drew back, and, standing afar off, waited to see the end; and, gazing fixedly, he saw St. Francis stretch out his hands three times to the flame; and finally, after a long time, he saw the flame return to heaven. Wherefore he gat him thence, deeming himself unseen and glad of the vision, and was returning to his cell. And, as he went confidently, St. Francis perceived him by the rustling which his feet made upon the leaves, and commanded him to wait for him and not to move. Then Friar Leo, obedient, stood still and waited for him, with such fear that, as he afterwards told his companions, he would rather, at that moment, that the earth had swallowed him up than wait for St. Francis, who he thought was angered with him; because with very great diligence he took heed not to offend his fatherhood, lest, through fault of his, St. Francis should deprive him of his company. Then, when he had come up to him, St. Francis asked him: "Who art thou?" and Friar Leo, all trembling, replied: "My father, I am Friar Leo;" and St. Francis said unto him: "Wherefore didst thou come hither, friar little sheep? Did I not tell thee not to come and watch me? For holy obedience, tell me whether thou sawest or heardest aught." Friar Leo replied: "Father, I heard thee speak and say many times: 'Who art Thou, my most sweet God? What am I, most vile worm and Thine unprofitable servant?'" And then Friar Leo, kneeling down before St. Francis, confessed himself guilty of disobedience, in that he had done contrary to his commandment, and besought his pardon with many tears. And thereafter he prayed him devoutly that he would explain those words which he had heard, and would tell him those which he had not understood.

Then, seeing that to the humble Friar Leo God had revealed or granted to hear and to see certain things, by reason of his simplicity and purity, St. Francis condescended to reveal and to explain unto him that which he asked; and he spake as follows: "Know, friar little sheep of Jesus Christ, that when I was saying those words which thou heardest, then were shown unto me two lights for my soul; the one of knowledge and understanding of my own self, the other of knowledge and understanding of the Creator. When I said: 'Who art thou, O my most sweet God?' then I was in a light of contemplation wherein I saw the abyss of the infinite goodness and wisdom and power of God; and when I said: 'What am I?' I was in a light of contemplation in the which I beheld the depth of my baseness and misery; and therefore I said: 'Who art Thou, Lord of infinite goodness and wisdom, that deignest to visit me, that am a vile worm and abominable?' And in that flame which thou sawest was God; who in that form spake with me, even as of old He spake unto Moses. And, among other things which He said unto me, He asked me to give Him three gifts; and I made answer: 'Lord, I am all Thine; Thou knowest well that I have nothing beside the habit and the cord and the breeches, and even these three things are Thine; what then can I offer or give unto Thy majesty?' Then God said unto me: 'Search in thy bosom, and give Me that which thou findest therein.' I searched and found a ball of gold; and I offered it to God; and thus did I three times, even as God three times commanded me; and thereafter I kneeled me down three times and blessed and thanked God who had given me wherewith to offer Him. And straightway, it was given me to understand that these three offerings signified holy obedience, highest poverty and most resplendent chastity; the which God, through His grace, hath permitted me to observe so perfectly that my conscience accuseth me of nothing. And as thou sawest me put my hands in my bosom and offer to God those three virtues symbolised by those three balls of gold, which God had placed in my bosom; so hath God given me such virtue in my soul that, for all the benefits and all the graces which He hath granted me of His most holy goodness, I ever praise and magnify Him with heart and mouth. These are the words which thou heardest when I thrice lifted up my hands, as thou sawest. But look to it, friar little sheep, that thou watch me no more; but return to thy cell with the blessing of God, and do thou have diligent care of me; because, a few days from now, God will do such great and marvellous things upon this mountain that all the world shall wonder thereat; for He will do certain new things, the which He hath never done unto any creature in this world."

And, when he had spoken these words, he caused the book of the Gospels to be brought unto him; for God had put it in his mind that, by the opening of the book of the Gospels three times, that which it was the will of God to do unto him should be revealed. And, when the book was brought unto him, St. Francis betook himself to prayer; and, when he had finished his prayer, he caused the book to be opened three times by the hand of Friar Leo, in the name of the Most Holy Trinity; and, as it pleased the Divine Providence, in those three times ever there appeared before him the Passion of Christ. By the which thing it was given him to understand that, even as he had followed Christ in the actions of his life, so he must follow Him, and be conformed to Him in afflictions and sorrows and in his passion, before he departed from this life. And from that moment St. Francis began to taste and to feel more abundantly the sweetness of Divine contemplation and of the Divine visitations. Among the which he had one which was an immediate preparative for the imprinting of the most holy stigmata; and it was upon this wise: On the day before the festival of the most Holy Cross of the month of September, while St. Francis was secretly praying in his cell, the angel of God appeared unto him, and said unto him in God's name: "I exhort thee and admonish thee that thou prepare and dispose thyself, humbly and with all patience, to receive that which God willeth to give thee, and to work in thee." St. Francis made answer: "I am ready to bear patiently everything that my Lord willeth to do unto me;" and, when he had said this, the angel departed. The next day came, to wit the day of the most Holy Cross, and St. Francis, betimes in the morning, or ever it was day, betook himself to prayer before the entrance of his cell, and turning his face towards the East, prayed after this manner: "O my Lord Jesus Christ, two graces do I beseech Thee to grant me before I die: the first, that, during my lifetime, I may feel in my soul and in my body, so far as may be possible, that pain which Thou, sweet Lord, didst suffer in the hour of Thy most bitter passion; the second is that I may feel in my heart, so far as may be possible, that exceeding love, whereby Thou, Son of God, wast enkindled willingly to bear such passion for us sinners." And, when he had continued long time in this prayer, he knew that God would hear him, and that, as far as was possible for a mere creature, so far would it be granted to him to feel the aforesaid things.

Having this promise, St. Francis began to contemplate with very great devotion the Passion of Christ and His infinite charity; and so much did the fervour of devotion increase in him that he altogether transformed himself into Jesus through love and pity. And, being thus self-inflamed in this contemplation, on that same morning, he saw, coming from heaven, a Seraph, with six wings resplendent and ablaze; the which Seraph, flying swiftly, drew near unto St. Francis, so that he was able to discern Him clearly, and he perceived that He bore the likeness to a crucified Man; and His wings were so disposed that two wings extended above His head, two were spread out to fly, and the other two covered all His body. Seeing this, St. Francis was sore afraid, and, at the same time, was filled with joy and grief and wonder. He had passing great joy of the gracious aspect of Christ, who appeared to him so familiarly and regarded him so kindly; but, on the other hand, seeing Him crucified upon the cross, he felt immeasurable grief for pity's sake.

Next, he marvelled much at so strange and stupendous a vision, knowing well that the infirmity of suffering agreeth not with the immortality of the seraphic spirit. And, while he thus marvelled, it was revealed unto him by Him who appeared to him: that that vision had been shown unto him in that form, by the Divine providence, to the end that he might understand that, not by corporal suffering but by enkindling of the mind, he must be altogether transformed ino the express image of Christ crucified, in that marvellous vision. Then all the mountain of Alvernia seemed to burn with the brightest flame, which shone forth and lighted up all the mountains and the valleys round about, even as if the sun had risen upon the earth; wherefore the shepherds, who kept watch in those regions, beholding the mountain all on fire and so great a light round about it, were very much afraid, according as they afterward related to the friars, declaring that the flame continued upon the mountain of Alvernia for the space of an hour or more. In like manner, by reason of the brightness of this light, which shone through the windows into the hostelries of the countryside, certain muleteers, who were journeying into Romagna, rose up, believing that the sun had risen, and saddled and loaded their beasts; and, as they went upon their way, they beheld the said light die out, and the material sun arise.

In the said seraphic vision, Christ, who appeared to St. Francis, spake unto him certain high and secret things, the which St. Francis was never willing to reveal to any one during his life; but, after his death, he revealed it, even as is set forth below; and the words were these: "Knowest thou," said Christ, "that which I have done unto thee? I have given thee the stigmata, which are the tokens of My Passion, so that thou mayest be My standard-bearer. And even as I, on the day of My death, descended into Limbo, and, in virtue of these My stigmata, drew out thence all the souls which I found there; so to thee do I grant that, every year on the day of thy death, thou shalt go to purgatory, and in virtue of thy stigmata, shalt draw out thence all the souls of thy three Orders, to wit minors, sisters and continents, and also those others who have borne great devotion unto thee, and shall lead them unto the glory of paradise, to the end that thou mayest be conformed to Me in death as thou art in life." Now when, after long and secret converse, this marvellous vision vanished away, it left an exceeding ardour and flame of Divine love in the heart of St. Francis, and in his flesh a marvellous image and imprint of the Passion of Christ. For anon, in the hands and in the feet of St. Francis the marks of nails began to appear after the same fashion as he had just seen in the body of Jesus Christ crucified, the which had appeared unto him in the form of a seraph; and even so were his hands and his feet pierced through the midst with nails, the heads whereof were in the palms of the hands and in the soles of the feet, outside the flesh; and the points came out through the back of the hands and of the feet, where they showed bent back and clinched on such wise that, under the clinching and the bend, which all stood out above the flesh, it would have been easy to put a finger of the hand, as in a ring; and the heads of the nails were round and black. In like manner, in his right side appeared the likeness of a lance wound, open, red and bloody; the which oftentimes thereafter spouted blood from the holy breast of St. Francis, and covered his habit and breeches with blood.

Wherefore his companions, before they knew thereof from him, perceiving nevertheless that he uncovered neither his hands nor his feet, and that he could not put the soles of his feet to the ground; and therewithal finding his habit and breeches all bloody, when they washed them, knew certainly that he bore, imprinted on his hands and feet and likewise on his side, the express image and likeness of our Lord Jesus Christ crucified. And although he very earnestly endeavoured to conceal and to hide those most holy and glorious stigmata which were so clearly imprinted on his flesh, he perceived that he could but ill conceal them from his familiar companions; and therefore he stood in very great doubt, fearing to make public the secrets of God, and knowing not whether he ought to reveal the seraphic vision and the imprinting of the most holy stigmata. At the last, being goaded thereunto by this conscience, he called to him certain of his most intimate friends among the friars, and, setting before them his doubt in general terms, yet without explaining the actual fact, he asked their advice; and among the said friars was one of great sanctity, who was called Friar Illuminatus. Now this man, being of a truth illuminated by God, and understanding that St. Francis must have seen marvellous things, answered him after this manner: "Friar Francis, know thou that, not for thy sake only but also for the sake of others, God manifesteth unto thee at divers times His mysteries; and therefore thou hast good reason to fear that, if thou keepest secret that which God hath shown thee for the benefit of others, thou wilt be worthy of blame."

Then St. Francis, being moved by these words, with great dread related unto them all the manner and form of the aforesaid vision; adding that Christ, who had appeared unto him, had spoken certain things unto him which he would never repeat as long as he lived. And, albeit those most holy wounds, inasmuch as they were imprinted by Christ, gave very great joy to his heart; nevertheless to his flesh and to his corporal senses they gave intolerable pain. Wherefore, being compelled thereunto by necessity, he chose Friar Leo, as more simple and pure than the others, and to him he revealed everything; permitting him to see and to touch those sacred wounds and to bind them with certain handkerchiefs, for the allaying of the pain, and to catch the blood which issued and flowed from the said wounds; the which bandages, in time of sickness, he permitted him to change frequently, and even daily, except from Thursday evening to Saturday morning, during which time our Saviour Jesus Christ was taken for our sakes and crucified, slain and buried; and therefore, during that time, St. Francis would not suffer that the pain of the Passion of Christ, which he bore in his body, should be assuaged in anywise by any human remedy or medicine whatsoever. It befel, sometimes, that, as Friar Leo was changing the bandage of the wound in his side, St. Francis, for the pain which he felt when that blood-soaked bandage was plucked away, laid his hand upon the breast of Friar Leo; whereby, from the touch of those sacred hands, Friar Leo felt such sweetness of devotion in his heart, that he well-nigh fell swooning to the ground.

And finally, as touching this third consideration, St. Francis having finished the fast of St. Michael the Archangel, prepared himself, by Divine revelation, to return to Santa Maria degli Angeli. Wherefore he called unto him Friar Masseo and Friar Agnolo, and, after many words and holy admonishments, he commended unto them that holy mountain with all possible earnestness, telling them that it behoved him, together with Friar Leo, to return to Santa Maria degli Angeli. And when he had said this, he took leave of them and blessed them in the name of Jesus crucified; and, yielding to their entreaties, he gave them his most holy lands, adorned with those glorious and sacred stigmata, to see, to touch and to kiss; and so leaving them consoled, he departed from them and descended the holy mountain.

THE "LITTLE FLOWERS OF ST. FRANCIS"

A PARABLE

In the Divine Office Brother Albert always stood most devoutly, and, with shut eyes, avoided wandering of mind. In the company of the Brethren he was ever gay and cheerful, and won to himself the affection of all.

Thus, when he had once been let blood, together with the others in the convent, he set forth a parable of this sort among his companions, chiefly on account of a certain novice who was present, who was too wise in his own eyes and presumed to interfere in matters that did not concern him. He spake as follows. A certain countryman, hearing of the great peace in Paradise and of its many delights, set forth to find where it was, to see if by chance by some means or other he could enter it. And when he had at last come to the gate, he found Saint Peter and begged for admission. When Peter asked him if he could keep the laws of Paradise and intended to do so, he said yes, if only he would deign to tell him. Wherefore Peter told him that the only thing needful was to keep silence. This he willingly agreed to, and was admitted. Then as he went through Paradise he saw a man ploughing with two oxen, one lean and one fat, and the fat one he allowed to go as it would and the lean one he kept on prodding. And the countryman, running up, showed him his mistake. And at once Saint Peter came up, and wanted to turn him out, yet he spared him that time, and bade him be careful. And straightway he went on farther, and saw a man carrying a long beam, and desirous of entering a house, yet he kept on turning the beam lengthwise to the door. The countryman ran up and showed him how he should put forward one end of the beam. And at once Saint Peter came up and wanted by all means to turn him out, yet he spared him that time also. A third time the countryman went forward, and saw a man cutting down trees in a wood, and always he spared the old trunks and crooked oaks, and felled and sawed those that were straight and green and finest. And, running up, he blamed him. Then at once Saint Peter came up and turned him out.

THOMAS OF ECCLESTON

OF THE NATIVITY OF OUR LORD JESUS CHRIST

When nine months from the conception of blessed Jesus were drawing to an end, Caesar Augustus, the Emperor of Rome, sent out a command, or a behest, that all the world subject to him should be enrolled; so that he might know the number of regions, of cities, and of heads belonging to them that were subject to the Emperor of Rome; and herefore he ordained and bade that all men wheresoever they dwelled should go to the city of their origin and proper lineage. Wherefore Joseph, who was of the lineage of David, whose city was Bethlehem, took with him his spouse, blessed Mary, who was at that time great with child, and went from Nazareth to the city of Bethlehem, there to be numbered among the others as subject to the Emperor. And so, leading with them an ox and an ass, they went all that long way together, as poor folk, having no other worldly goods but those two beasts. And when they came to Bethlehem, by reason of the great multitude that was there at the same time for the same cause, they could get no shelter in any house, but needed to rest and abide all that time in a public place between two houses, that was covered over for men to stand there out of the rain, and was called a diversory. And in that place Joseph, who was a carpenter, made them a closure and a crib for their beasts.

Now take here good heed and have inward compassion of that blessed lady and maiden, Mary; how she, so young and of so tender age, that is to say of fifteen years, and great with child, being near the birth, traveleth that long way of sixty miles and ten or more, in so great poverty. And yet when she came to the City aforesaid, where she should rest, and with her spouse asked harbourage in divers places, shamefacedly, being among strange folk, all refused them and made them go away; and so, for need, at last they took as their shelter that common place aforesaid.

But now to speak further of the blessed birth of Jesus, and of that pure and holy deliverance of His dear mother Mary, as it is written in part from a revelation made by our Lady to a devout man. When the time of that blessed birth was come, that is to say the Sunday at midnight, God's Son of Heaven, as He was conceived in His mother's womb by the Holy Ghost without seed of man, so, going out of that womb without travail or sorrow, suddenly was upon the hay at His mother's feet. And anon she, devoutly bending over, with sovereign joy took Him in her arms, and sweetly clasping and kissing Him, laid him in her bosom; and with a full pap, as she was taught by the Holy Ghost, washed Him all about with her sweet milk, and so wrapped Him in the kerchiefs of her head, and laid Him in the crib. And anon the Ox and the Ass kneeling down, laid their mouths on the crib, breathing through their noses upon the child, as they knew by reason that in that cold weather, the child so simply clad had need to be warmed in that manner. And then His mother, kneeling down, worshipped and praised God, inwardly giving thanks and saying in this manner: Lord God, holy Father of Heaven, I thank Thee with all my might, Who hast given me Thy dear Son; and I honour the almighty God, God's Son and mine. Joseph, also honouring and worshipping the child God and man, took the saddle from the Ass and made thereof a cushion for our Lady to sit on, and a support to lean upon.

And so sat the Lady of all the world in that simple array beside the crib, having her mild mien and her lovely eyes, together with her inward affection, upon her sweet beloved child. But in this poor and simple worldly array, what ghostly riches and inward comfort she had no tongue may tell. Wherefore if we will to feel the true joy and comfort of Jesus, we must, with Him and with His mother, love poverty, meekness, and bodily penance, as He gave us example of all these here in His birth and first coming into this world. For of the first, that is poverty, Saint Bernard in a sermon on the Nativity of our Lord, telling how He was born unto the comfort of mankind, saith in this manner: "God's Son comforteth His people. Wilt thou know His people? That is, the people of whom David speaketh in the psalter and saith: Lord, to Thee is left the poor people, And He Himself saith in the gospel: Woe to you rich men that have your comfort here. For how should He comfort them that have their own comfort here? Wherefore Christ's innocence and childhood comfort not wranglers and great speakers; Christ's weepings and tears comfort not dissolute lawyers; His simple clothing comforteth not them that go in proud clothing; and His stable and crib comfort not them that love first seats and worldly honours. And also the angels, appearing at Christ's nativity to the waking shepherds, comfort none others than the poor labourers; and to them they tell the joy of new light, and not to the rich men that have their comfort here.

Also as to the second: at this birth, both in Christ and in His mother, we may see perfect meekness; for they were not squeamish of the stable, nor of the beasts, nor of hay and such other abject simpleness. But both our Lord and our Lady kept this virtue of meekness perfectly in all their deeds, and commend it sovereignly to us; wherefore let us busy ourselves with all our might to obtain this virtue, knowing that without it there is no salvation. For there is no work or deed of ours that may please God with pride.

Also as to the third: we may see in them both, and specially in the child Jesus, not a little bodily penance; of the which Saint Bernard saith thus: God's Son, when He willed to be born, having in His own free will to choose what time He would take thereto, chose the time that was most troublesome and hard, namely the cold winter, specially to a young child and a poor woman's son, who scarcely had clothes to wrap him in, and a crib for a cradle to lay him in; and yet, though there was so much need, I find no mention of furs and robes of skin. And since Christ, who is not deceived, chose that which is most hard to the flesh, soothly that is best, most profitable, and rather to be chosen; and whoso teacheth or biddeth otherwise is as a false deceiver, to be fled from and forsaken. All this saith Saint Bernard. And thus much of these virtues at this time.

ST. BONAVENTURE

THE HAIL MARY

Now take good heed and understand how worthy this feast and this solemnity is; and have therefore a spiritual gladness and make a special feast, in thy soul thanking God inwardly; for such was never heard before. For this is the solemnity of all the Holy Trinity, Father, and Son, and Holy Ghost, by whom this sovereign deed of the Incarnation was wrought and fulfilled, as it is said before. This also is a special feast of our lady Saint Mary, who on this day was chosen by the Father of Heaven to be His dear daughter; and of the Son to be his mild mother; and of the Holy Ghost to be His special spouse. This day also is a special solemnity of all the blessed spirits of Heaven; for this day was begun the restoring of their company and fellowship, that fell down by sin of Lucifer. But above all this day is an high feast and a special solemnity of all mankind; for this day was mankind sovereignly honoured, in that it was united and joined to the godhead in Christ without division. And this day began the healing and the redemption of mankind, and the reconciling to the Father of Heaven. For until this time God was wroth toward mankind for the sin and the trespass of our first fathers; but from this time forth He may no longer be wroth, seeing His dear Son become man; and therefore is this day rightfully called the fulness of time to man. And so this day ought ever to be remembered by man and woman; for this day was man made to the likeness and the image of God, and set in that joyful place of paradise, that he might live ever without death. And this day the first man, Adam, by the fruit of the forbidden tree, deformed the image of God in himself, and lost that joyful place of paradise, and was condemned to death without ending. But this day the second Adam, Christ God and man, reformed this image in His incarnation, and afterward, by virtue of the blessed fruit of His body hanging on the tree of the cross, restored man to bliss and life everlasting. Also this day the first woman, Eve, through pride assenting to the serpent, the devil of Hell, was cause of man's damnation. And this day the blessed maiden Mary, through meekness believing the angel Gabriel, was cause of man's salvation. And so this day hath man matter of great joy and of great sorrow: first of great joy for the sovereign goodness, honour, and grace of God done to him; and also of great sorrow for his great sin and unkindness done against God. And thus must thou have thy contemplation of this day and of this blessed feast of Christ's Incarnation, and our Lady's annunciation.

And forasmuch as that blessed greeting of the angel Gabriel, wherewith we honour and greet our Lady every day, is grounded in this Gospel, as thou hast heard before, therefore I shall tell thee somewhat more hereof, as me thinketh, to guide thy devotion more in reciting that greeting, *Ave Maria.* As I understand this greeting in manner as holy Church hath ordained it to be said, it hath five parts; in the which may be understood specially the five joys of our Lady, and in those five joys, five virtues that she had in them sovereignly, above all earthly creatures: the which are meekness, chastity, faith, hope, and charity. In the first part of this greeting, that consisteth in these two words *Hail Mary,* thou mayest understand the first joy that she had in Jesus' gracious conception, of the which meekness was the ground, as thou hast heard before. And as these words *Hail Mary* are the first and beginning of this greeting, so this feast was the beginning of and ground of all others; and as meekness was the beginning of Mary's joy and all mankind's, so is it the beginning and ground of all virtues. And therefore in these first words, *Hail Mary,* thou mayest with reason understand the first joy that she had in her annunciation of the conceiving of her blessed son Jesus, and that specially through the virtue of meekness. In the second part, that consists in these words *Full of grace,* may be understood the second joy that Mary had in Jesus' birth and her joyful child-bearing, in the which she had sovereignly the virtue of chastity and purity; and therefore then was she specially full of grace, in that she, clean maiden and mother, bore child without sorrow, which no woman ever did but she all only. In the third part, that is in these words *Our Lord is with thee,* may be understood the third joy that she had in the glorious resurrection of her son Jesus, specially by the virtue of steadfast faith and true belief. For from His death until that time, He dwelled only with her, by the steadfast belief that she had in Him as God, when all His apostles and disciples were separated from Him by misbelief, and by despair that He was God. And therefore the faith of holy church stayed in her alone for those three days; so that in that time it might specially be said to her, Our Lord is with thee, that is to say by true faith and belief. And afterwards, at His resurrection, *Our Lord is with thee* was fulfilled more specially by His bodily presence, which first appeared to her. In the fourth part, that is in these words, *Blessed art thou among women,* or else, *above all women,* may be understood the fourth joy that she had, in the sight of her Son Jesus mightily ascending to Heaven: in the which sight the hope that she had in His godhead was fully strengthened and confirmed, seeing that which no other woman ever did, when that part which He took of her in flesh and blood was bodily borne up to Heaven through power of the godhead; and so hoping without doubt that she should follow after. Well then might it be said to her, then and now, Blessed art thou sovereignly among women, seeing thy Son Jesus mightily to Heaven ascending. In the fifth part, that is, *Blessed is the fruit of thy womb, Jesus,* may be understood the last joy that she had in her blessed son Jesus, when He took her up with Him to bliss, and there honourably crowned her queen of Heaven everlasting. Then was her desire of love fulfilled, when, through fulness of charity, she was forever joined to her blessed son Jesus, and He to her, and was so fed with that blessed fruit that she hungered no more; for thereby she was filled with all goodness, bliss, and joy without end. And thus briefly in the fifth part of this salutation *Ave Maria,* may be understood the five joys of blessed Mary, with five virtues that she had sovereignly in them, as I have now said. The which greeting, according to the common understanding, may thus be said in English tongue: Hail, Mary, full of grace, Our Lord is with thee. Blessed art thou sovereignly among women, and ever blessed is the fruit of thy womb, Jesus! And as the list in this greeting specifies the five joys with the five virtues aforesaid, thou mayest say thus in short words: Hail Mary, maiden meekest, greeted by the angel Gabriel in Jesus' gracious conception; full of grace, as mother chaste, bearing thy son Jesus without sorrow or pain! Our Lord is with thee by true faith and belief at Jesus' joyful resurrection. Blessed art thou sovereignly among women by firm hope, seeing thy son Jesus with power to Heaven ascending. And blessed is the fruit of thy womb, Jesus, in everlasting bliss, through perfect charity gloriously crowning thee queen of Heaven. Obtain for us these virtues, that for our gain we may be pleasing to thy son Jesus and to thee. Be thou our help in all our need, and our succour at our last ending. Amen.

ST. BONAVENTURE

POPE BENEDICT XII

In the year of our Lord 1342 died Pope Benedict XII, on the day of St. Gregory the Pope and in the seventh year of his pontificate; of whom it is said that there was none more righteous than he since St. Gregory. On his deathbed, the cardinals prayed him to commit his powers to one of them, who might thus give him plenary absolution for all that he had committed; but he refused, saying: "I will not give my glory to another; but I submit myself to God's mercy."

Again when they prayed him to think of his kinsfolk and friends, and to distribute of his goods among them, he made answer: "I am a monk, and possess nought of mine own; whereof then could I make a testament or a distribution? Think not that I shall take away the goods of the church to give them to my kinsfolk." They prayed him therefore to fix the place where he should be buried; but he answered: "I may not choose mine own sepulchre, seeing that I am a monk." For he had so loved his monastic state that, even as a Pope, he ever wore a cowl for his outer garment in his lower closet; and daily he sang Mass in his monk's cowl within his private chapel. When therefore he must needs leave his closet and go in the sight of the people and put on his pontificals according to custom, then he would kiss his cowl as he laid it down, saying, "Farewell, monk!" and taking his pontificals he would say, "Welcome, lord Pope!" On his return, as he laid aside his pontificals and resumed his cowl, then would he say, "Farewell, Pope! and thou, monk, come hither!" For he was most humble and affable and ready to jest with all men; wherefore it is said that, while he drew almost his last breath, he was asked by those that stood by whether he could eat aught; to which he made answer: "No indeed, nor yet drink, whereof we have a more evil report." So he held the papal see for six years and four months and twelve days, and died, and was buried in the cathedral church of Avignon.

THOMAS DE BURTON

HUSBAND AND WIFE

Thirdly, marriage is love. What saith Paul in the fifth chapter of his epistle to the Ephesians?—"Husbands, love your wives as Christ also loved the Church." . . . Wouldst thou have a faithful wife? Then keep faith with her. Many men would fain take a wife and can find none; knowst thou why? The man saith: I must have a wife full of wisdom—and thou thyself art a fool. This sorteth not: he-fool sorteth well with she-fool.—How wouldst thou have thy wife?—I would have her tall—and thou art a mere willow-wren; this sorteth not. There is a country where women are married by the ell-yard. It came to pass that one of these people wanted a wife, and would fain see her first: so the girl's brothers brought him to see her, and she was shown to him without shoes or head-gear; and, measuring her stature, he found her tallest of all the maidens, and he himself was one of those puny weaklings! In short, they asked of him, "Well, is she to thy mind?" "Yes, truly, she pleaseth me well." But she, seeing how miserable was his presence, said, "Yet art thou not to my mind." Lo, was that not right?—But to my point again. How wouldst thou have this thy wife?—I will have her an honest woman—and thou art dishonest: that again is not well. Once more how wouldst thou have her?—I would have her temperate—and thou art never out of the tavern: thou shalt not have her! O, how wouldst thou have this wife of thine?—I would not have her gluttonous—and thou art ever at thy fegetelli: that is not well. I would have her active—and thou art a very sluggard. Peaceful—and thou wouldst storm at a straw if it crossed thy feet. Obedient—and thou obeyest neither father nor mother nor any man; thou deservest her not. I would not have a cock—well, thou art no hen. I would have her good and fair and wise and bred in all virtue.—I answer, if thou wouldst have her thus, it is fitting that thou shouldst be the same; even as thou seekest a virtuous, fair and good spouse, so think likewise how she would fain have a husband prudent, discreet, good, and fulfilled of all virtue. . . .

ST. BERNARDINE OF SIENA

SAINT MARTIN

It chanced one winter day that Martin was passing through the gate of Amiens, and came upon a poor and almost naked beggar. The poor man had received no alms that day, and Martin considered that he was reserved to himself; wherefore he drew his sword, divided his cloak in two parts, gave one part to the beggar, and wrapped himself in the other. On the following night, in a vision, he saw Christ wearing the part of his cloak with which he had covered the beggar, and heard Him saying to the angels who surrounded Him: "Martin, while yet a catechumen, has clothed me with this garment!" Hence the holy man, not puffed up with pride, but acknowledging the goodness of God, had himself baptized. He nevertheless continued in the profession of arms for two years, at the insistence of his tribune, who in turn promised that when his term as tribune was completed, he would renounce the world.

Meanwhile the barbarians were breaking into the Empire, and the Emperor Julian, before setting out to war against them, distributed a gift of money to his soldiery. But Martin, being unwilling to bear arms any longer, refused the donative, and said to Caesar: "I am the soldier of Christ, and it is not lawful for me to do battle!" Being angered at this, Julian said that it was not for the sake of religion that he renounced the soldierly profession, but for fear of the impending war. Unshaken, Martin responded: "If thou chargest this to cowardice and not to faith, tomorrow I shall face the enemy unarmed, and in the name of Christ, protected not with shield and helmet but with the sign of the cross, I shall pierce their ranks in safety!" Hence he was put under guard, in order that he might not stand before the enemy unarmed, as he had said. But on the morrow, the enemy sent legates, and surrendered themselves and their goods. Hence there is no doubt that the bloodless victory was gained by the merits of the saint.

After this Martin abandoned the military life, and betook himself to Saint Hilary, the bishop of Poitiers, who ordained him an acolyte.

JACOBUS DE VORAGINE

SAINT ELIZABETH

Established as she was in the highest station, she yearned for the state of poverty, that she might repay the poverty of Christ, and that the world might have naught of its own in her. Wherefore, when she was alone with her maids, she sometimes put on mean garments, and covered her head with a shabby veil, saying: "So shall I go about, when I shall have reached the state of poverty." And while she imposed the curb of abstinence upon herself, she lavished such liberality upon the poor that she would suffer none to go hungry, but succoured all most generously; whence all acclaimed her as the mother of the poor. Thus she laboured with all diligence in performing the seven works of mercy, in order to reign forever in the everlasting Kingdom, and to receive the blessing of the Father with those who would be set on His right hand. She clothed the naked, and bestowed garments for the burial of pilgrims and poor men, and for the baptism of children; and these she often lifted from the sacred font with her own hands, in order that, having become their godmother, she might provide for them the more freely. And once she chanced to give a choice garment to a poor little woman, who was so overwhelmed with joy at the sight of so splendid a gift that she might have been the cause of the poor woman's death; but she prayed for her, and the woman straightway arose, completely restored. She often spun wool thread with her own hands, and then ordered clothing to be made thereof; for she wished to gain the glorious fruit of these good works, and to give an alms to God of the toil of her own body.

She likewise provided food for the hungry. Once when her husband the landgrave had gone to the court of the Emperor Frederick, which was then at Cremona, she collected all the stores of wheat from his granges, and thus supplied the needs of the poor people gathered from all sides, for at that time they were threatened with want and dire famine. And whenever money was lacking for her alms deeds, she sold her adornments or those of her women, in order to assist the poor.

She gave drink to the thirsty. One day she meted out beer to a number of poor men, and when each had had as much as he desired, it was found that the jug still contained the same measure as before.

In order to give shelter to pilgrims and to the homeless, she had a large house built at the foot of her lofty castle. In this house she cared for a great multitude of the sick, visiting them each day maugre the steepness of the way, ministering to their needs and exhorting them to patience. And although she was sorely distressed by the least taint of the air, she shrank not from the sores of the sick, even in summer weather, for the love of God. She applied their remedies, cleansed their wounds with the veil of her head, and handled them with her own hands, paying no heed to the protests of her handmaidens. In this same house she caused the children of poor women to be fed with utmost care, and showed herself so kindly and so humble in their regard that all called her their mother, and crowded about her when she entered the house as children follow their mother. And once she bought a number of dishes and rings and other things made of glass for the children's games; and as she rode toward the castle, carrying these things in her mantle, they fell from a high cliff upon the rocks below, but not one of them was broken.

She provided for the burial of the poor, dressing their bodies with her own hands in garments which she had sewn. Once she cut her large linen veil in several pieces, and wrapt the body of a dead pauper therein. She also assisted at their burial with all devotion.

In all these things the piety of her husband is worthy of praise, for although he was concerned with a great number of affairs, he was yet devout in the service of God; and since he could not personally see to these matters, he provided his wife with the means of attending to all that regarded God's honour and the salvation of his soul.

JACOBUS DE VORAGINE

SAINT MARCELLINUS

Pope Saint Marcellinus governed the church of Rome for nine years and four months. At the order of Diocletian and Maximian, he was arrested and enjoined to offer sacrifice to the idols. At first he refused; but when he was threatened with divers tortures, the fear of suffering made him consent to sacrifice two grains of incense on the altar. Great was the joy of the infidels, and greater still the sorrow of the faithful. These came in large numbers to Marcellinus, and reproached him with his lack of courage; and Marcellinus, overwhelmed with confusion, asked to be judged by an assembly of bishops. But the bishops made answer: "As sovereign pontiff, no man on earth can be thy judge; but enter into thyself, and pronounce thine own judgement!" Then Marcellinus, stricken with remorse and weeping bitterly, abdicated the papal office; but the multitude at once reëlected him. When the emperors learned of this, they commanded that he be taken into custody once more. And when he firmly refused to offer sacrifice to the gods, they ordered him to be beheaded: and after this was done, their rage waxed to such a point that in one month they put to death seventeen thousand Christians.

Marcellinus had deemed himself unworthy of Christian burial, and had decreed, before his death, that any who should attempt to bury him would be excommunicated. Thus his body remained unburied for thirty-five days. But at the end of this time, Saint Peter appeared to his successor, Pope Marcellus, and said to him: "Brother Marcellus, wherefore dost thou keep me so long without burial?" And Marcellus answered: "But, Master, art thou not buried long since?" To this the apostle replied: "As long as I shall see Marcellinus deprived of sepulture, I shall hold myself to be unburied." But the Pope protested: "But, Master, knowest thou not that he laid an excommunication on all those who should take it in mind to bury him?" And Saint Peter responded: "Knowest thou not that it is written that he who humbles himself shall be exalted? Go straight, and lay Marcellinus to rest at the foot of my tomb!" And this the pope did, in obedience to the apostle's command.

JACOBUS DE VORAGINE

THE JUST WAR

I reply that it must be said that, in order that a war may be just, three things are necessary.

In the first place, the authority of the prince, by whose order the war is undertaken; for it does not belong to a private individual to make war, because, in order to obtain justice, he can have recourse to the judgment of his superior. Neither does it belong to a private individual to summon a multitude of people together as must be done to engage in war. But, since the care of the State is confided to princes, it is to them that it belongs to defend the city, the kingdom or province which is subject to their authority. Just as it is permissible for them to defend these, by the material sword, against those who trouble them from within, by punishing the evil-doers according to the word of the Apostle: "The prince beareth not the sword in vain for he is the minister of God to execute His vengeance against him who doeth evil" (Romans xiii: 4), so, in like manner, it is to them that it belongs to bear the sword in combats for the defence of the State against external enemies. Also, the Psalmist says to princes: "Snatch the poor and deliver the needy out of the hands of the sinner" (Psalm lxxxi: 4). This is what makes St. Augustine say (*Contra Faustum,* XXII, 75): "The natural order, which would have peace amongst men, requires that the decision and power to declare war should belong to princes."

In the second place, there must be a just cause; that is to say, those attacked must have, by a fault, deserved to be attacked. This is what makes St. Augustine say in Book VI, Question 16, of Questions on Joshua: "Just wars are usually defined as those which avenge injuries, when the nation or city against which warlike action is to be directed has neglected either to punish wrongs committed by its own citizens or to restore what has been unjustly taken by it. Further, that kind of war is undoubtedly just which God Himself ordains."

In the third place, it is necessary that the intention of those who fight should be right; that is to say, that they propose to themselves a good to be effected or an evil to be avoided. This is what made St. Augustine say in the book De Verbis Domini: "With the true servants of God wars themselves are pacific, not being undertaken through cupidity or cruelty, but through the love of peace, with the object of repressing the wicked and encouraging the good." Consequently, it may happen that, although the war has been declared by the legitimate authority and for a just cause, it may nevertheless be rendered illicit by the perversity of the intention of him who makes it. "For," says St. Augustine (*Contra Faustum,* I, XXII, Chap. 74), "what is blamed in war? Is it the death of those who must die sooner or later, but who give up their lives to bring peace by overcoming guilty men? To blame this is the cry of cowards, not of religious people. The desire for harming, the cruelty of avenging, an unruly and implacable animosity, the rage of rebellion, the lust of domination and the like—these are the things which are to be blamed in war."

To the second argument (viz. that war is a sin, as being "contrary to a divine precept") it must be replied that these precepts, as St. Augustine says (*De Serm. Domini in monte,* I, 34), ought always to be observed in relation to the disposition of the soul; that is to say, that man ought always to be ready, if necessary, not to resist or not to defend himself. But sometimes we must act otherwise for the common good, and even for the good of those against whom we fight. This it is that causes St. Augustine to say, in the Fifth Epistle Ad Marcellinum: "There are many things that must be done against the will of those whom one ought to correct with a beneficent severity."

To the third argument the reply is, that those who wage wars justly have peace as the object of their intention, and so they are not opposed to peace, but only to that evil peace which the Lord did not come on earth to bring (St. Matthew x: 34). Hence Augustine says (*Ep. ad Bonifacium,* CLXXXIX): "For peace is not sought in order to the kindling of war, but war is waged in order that peace may be obtained. Therefore, even in waging war, cherish the spirit of the peacemaker, that, by conquering those whom you attack, you may lead them back to the advantages of peace. . . ."

To the fourth argument the reply is that manly exercises in warlike feats of arms are not all forbidden but those which are inordinate and perilous, and end in slaying or plundering. In olden times warlike exercises presented no such danger and hence they were called exercises of arms or bloodless wars.

ST. THOMAS AQUINAS

THE EVIL MEN DO

More sins abound in our times than in any past age, and sin is not to be reconciled with wisdom. Let us examine into all conditions that prevail in the world, studying them diligently:—everywhere we find boundless corruption, first of all in the Head. The Court of Rome, once ruled by God's wisdom (as it should always be), is now debased by constitutions enacted by lay Emperors, though these are properly made for the governing of lay people and are contained in the code of civil law. The Holy See is therefore torn by the deceit and fraud of unjust men. Justice is dying, all peace is disrupted, infinite scandals are created. The fruit of all this is utterly perverse conduct:—pride reigneth, covetousness burneth, envy gnaweth everyone. The whole Court has the ill-fame of lechery; gluttony is the lord all serve. . . . If this be so in the Head, what shall we say of what prevails among the members?

Look at the prelates. How they run after money, neglect the care of souls, promote the interests of their nephews and other carnal friends, and foster wily lawyers whose counsel ruins everybody. For they despise students of philosophy and theology, and prevent the two Orders which arose to serve God without wages from living in freedom and working for the salvation of souls. Let us consider the religious Orders—I exclude none from my remarks. See how one and all have fallen from their proper state. The new Orders are already horribly decadent, and have lost their original dignity. The whole clergy is intent upon pride, lechery and avarice. Wheresoever clerks are assembled, be it at Paris or Oxford, they scandalize the laity by reason of their fights and quarrels and other vicious practices. Princes, barons and knights oppress and rob one another; they pester their subjects with endless wars and exactions, wherein each one seeks to despoil the other even of duchies and kingdoms, as we see in these times. It is notorious that the King of France has most unjustly robbed the King of England of that great territory; and Charles has even now crushed the heirs of Frederick in mighty battles. Men do not care what happens or how it happens; if only they may have their will, they heed not right and wrong. Meanwhile they are slaves to gluttony, lechery and the wickedness of other sins. The people hate their princes, who harass them, and keep no fealty save that which can be enforced. In addition, being corrupted by the evil example of their betters, they oppress, deceive and defraud one another, as we see everywhere with our own eyes. They are wholly given over to lechery and gluttony, and are more debased than tongue can tell. Nothing different can be said about merchants and craftsmen, because fraud and deceit and guile dominate beyond measure in everything they say and do.

There is another way to measure the effect of this corruption. For the faith of Christ has been made manifest to the world, and is already attested to by saints beyond number. . . . And we have Our Lord, Jesus Christ, in the Blessed Sacrament of the altar. Everywhere, every day, we renew that Sacrament at our will, in accordance with His precept, "Do this in commemoration of Me." We eat and drink Him, and are turned into Him, to become Gods and Christs. Surely if men had faith, reverence and devotion, as they ought to have when they approach this Sacrament, they would not make themselves vile with so many errors, sins and wickednesses, but would know all wisdom and wholesome truth in this life. Wherefore, seeing that they play the fool here below, and as a rule are infirm and weak and asleep (to use the Apostle's words), they must, then, needs become unsteady and weak in all that region of wisdom and sleep the sleep of death and play the ass in an unparalleled way. For the Sacrament is at the end of the glory and goodness and comeliness of wisdom, and hath more certain proofs than any other kind.

ROGER BACON

SCIENCE

But besides these sciences is one more perfect than all others, to which all are subject and which in a wonderful way proves them all; and this is called experimental science, which disregards arguments, because they cannot prove, be they never so strong, unless the conclusion is also found true to experience, as I am setting forth in a dissertation on this science. And this science teaches that the noble conclusions of all the sciences should be tested by experiment; which in other sciences are either proved by arguments or investigated only by poor and imperfect trials; and this is its one special privilege, as I am now showing in the Sixth Part of the Opus Majus, in the conclusions of natural philosophy and optics and their truths about the rainbow, about coloured circles round the moon, and about the sun and the stars.

And I am setting forth there the immense importance of this science in proving the other sciences. Fools busy themselves about proving statements in the De Meteoris of Aristotle and in Optics, but quite uselessly. Because here things cannot be proved by argument, but only by experiment. And therefore I place the roots of experiments around these matters; which none of the Latins can understand, except one, viz., Master Peter.

ROGER BACON

III

THE EARLY RENAISSANCE

SERMON PREACHED AGAINST TYRANTS

Even as the rule of a single person, when he is good, is the best kind of government, so also is absolute power in the hands of an unjust and wicked individual of necessity the worst of all possible kinds of bad government. Nevertheless there is a great difference between the sovereignty of a natural, legitimate monarch who has developed into a tyrant, and the rule of an ordinary citizen who has transformed himself into a tyrant. The second fosters many more unbearable situations than does the first. For if a simple citizen wishes to establish himself in the power to which he had no right to aspire he must render his fellow citizens harmless by resorting to murder, banishment and other crimes not merely against his enemies but against all those who are his equals in rank, wealth or repute. In short, he must dispose of everyone who could conceivably become dangerous to him and must, therefore, be the author of innumerable evils. On the other hand, when the rightful ruler becomes an autocrat he can abstain from such actions since there can be no one who is his equal. Citizens are accustomed to obeying him and will not seek to rebel against his rule. Accordingly he need not live in the condition of permanent unrest which is the lot of the citizen become a tyrant.

Now because peoples who live under a democratic or oligarchical constitution are exposed, by reason both of the disagreements which arise in daily life and of the intrigues of the innumerable criminals, flatterers and calumniators who are always active, to the peril of divisions out of which tyranny can easily derive, they must proceed with all possible diligence and care to prevent, with laws of the utmost rigor, the assumption by anyone of tyrannical rule. They must impose the heaviest penalties on anyone who even tends in the slightest degree to play with the idea of becoming a dictator. Whosoever is lenient in this matter or fails to impose the required punishment, sins most grievously against God, because he prepares the way for the tyrant whose government is productive of numberless evils.

The word 'tyrant' is applied to a vicious, thoroughly wicked person who wishes to dominate over all others by force, and is especially apt when the person happens to be an ordinary citizen who has turned himself into a dictator. In the first place, he must be called arrogant, for he has sought to raise himself above his equals and, indeed, over his betters, to whom he ought to be subject. In addition he is envious and is always distressed about the fame of other people, particularly his fellow citizens. He cannot endure hearing others praised, although he may be ready to conceal his real feelings and listen with anguish of heart. On the other hand he rejoices over the shame of others in such a fashion that it is evident he would like to degrade everyone else in order to bask alone in the sunlight of glory. Because he is constantly tormented by the great anxieties, troubles and fears which always beset him, he seeks relief from his sullen mood in distractions. In order to acquire these and to maintain himself in his position he needs a great deal of money and therefore does not shrink from getting it in unlawful ways. Thus every tyrant is covetous and given to robbery. He not only steals from the whole people its freedom, but he also lays his hands on community funds in addition to taking from private citizens what they possess, either cautiously or stealthily or, it may be, quite openly.

He likewise does harm to religion. He expropriates ecclesiastical property, lending it to or distributing it among his camp-followers and his helpers' helpers. He is given to nepotism in behalf of his and their sons, too, and accordingly acquires the goods of clerical and lay persons. He does not want any other citizen to do anything important—such as building larger palaces, monasteries and churches, or showing prowess in war or peace,—because he would shine alone. Frequently he conspires to humble great men, so that after they have been brought low he may raise them up again to stations higher than those they had occupied previously, in this way making them conscious of their dependence upon him even while deluding the common people into thinking him generous and magnanimous, which thinking helps to make him more popular. He takes a hand in the juridical labors of the established judges in order that he may, as his whim dictates, favor this person and either degrade or get rid of that person. He expropriates the public funds and is quick to invent new burdens and pressures that will raise more money. This wealth he uses to support his hirelings and to employ princes and other military leaders, often not because the state has need of them but only because he wishes to bribe them into being his friends or because he seeks to mislead the people into thinking that he has a decent excuse for new tax levies—namely the excuse that the army and its captains must be paid.

For similar reasons the tyrant also wages war. He may not expect any benefit to accrue from such action; he may not expect a victory or a conquest of other territory. He merely seeks to keep the people down, and himself in the saddle. Very frequently he also uses public funds in order to erect huge palaces and temples on which his coat of arms can be displayed. In addition he supports a number of male and female singers, so that their reputation may reflect on him alone. His protegées, persons of base origin, he marries to the daughters of prominent citizens, in the hope that thus the second may be humbled and deprived of their social status even while the first are elevated in rank. The profiteers in such cases lack all noble sentiment and therefore remain faithful only because they are dependent on their master.

While the rule of the tyrant is in every sense evil, it is particularly harmful to the Christian mission. For the object of all Christian governments must be the attainment of the bliss promised to us by Christ. This is, however, possible only when conduct is righteous and Christian. Accordingly Christians must take care so to construct their constitutions, in principle and in detail, that they serve above all to lead to virtuous living. Such living depends in turn upon the fostering and flowering of genuine religion; and therefore that religion must be nourished, maintained and advanced to greater fervor not merely with ceremonies but with truth and with the help of pious, holy and learned servants of the Church and religious. On the other hand, bad priests and monks must be removed from their posts whenever possible; for according to the testimony of the saints there are no men more injurious to true religion, Christian conduct and good government than such priests and monks. It is far better to have fewer and good priests than to have many and bad priests, for these last call down the anger of God upon the cities and the peoples. It is the fault of such that God, the author of all good government, withdraws his protecting hand from cities and peoples, withholding the blessing of a worthy ruler by reason of the gravity and number of their sins, which visit punishment on the people as well as upon the guilty ones.

Nothing is more abhorrent to the tyrant than the service of Christ and a virtuous Christian life. For these are diametrically opposed to his own habits. Since one extreme excludes the other, the tyrant seeks in every way possible to undermine the true service of Christ, though often he may act only secretly. Should he encounter a good bishop, priest or religious, who still courageously speaks the truth, he will try either to get him out of the city or to bribe him with flattery and gifts. He will transfer the benefices to bad priests, his retainers and boon companions, even as he will favor unworthy religious and those among the brethren who flatter him.

GIROLAMO SAVONAROLA

THE MEETING WITH BEATRICE

Nine times already since my birth had the heaven of light returned to the selfsame point almost, as concerns its own revolution, when first the glorious Lady of my mind was made manifest to mine eyes; even she who was called Beatrice by many who knew not wherefore. She had already been in this life for so long as that, within her time, the starry heaven had moved towards the Eastern quarter one of the twelve parts of a degree; so that she appeared to me at the beginning of her ninth year almost, and I saw her almost at the end of my ninth year. Her dress, on that day, was of a most noble colour, a subdued and goodly crimson, girdled and adorned in such sort as best suited with her very tender age. At that moment, I say most truly that the spirit of life, which hath its dwelling in the secretest chamber of the heart, began to tremble so violently that the least pulses of my body shook therewith; and in trembling it said these words: Ecce deus fortior me, qui veniens dominabitur mihi. At that moment the animate spirit, which dwelleth in the lofty chamber whither all the senses carry their perceptions, was filled with wonder, and speaking more especially unto the spirits of the eyes, said these words: Apparuit jam beatitudo vestra. At this moment the natural spirit, which dwelleth there where our nourishment is administered, began to weep, and in weeping said these words: Heu miser! quia frequenter impeditus ero deinceps.

I say that, from that time forward, Love quite governed my soul; which was immediately espoused to him, and with so safe and undisputed a lordship (by virtue of strong imagination) that I had nothing left for it but to do all his bidding continually. He oftentimes commanded me to seek if I might see this youngest of the Angels: wherefore I in my boyhood often went in search of her, and found her so noble and praiseworthy that certainly of her might have been said those words of the poet Homer, "She seemed not to be the daughter of a mortal man, but of God." And albeit her image, that was with me always, was an exultation of Love to subdue me, it was yet of so perfect a quality that it never allowed me to be overruled by Love without the faithful counsel of reason, whensoever such counsel was useful to be heard. But seeing that were I to dwell overmuch on the passions and doings of such early youth, my words might be counted something fabulous, I will therefore put them aside; and passing many things that may be conceived by the pattern of these, I will come to such as are writ in my memory with a better distinctness.

After the lapse of so many days that nine years exactly were completed since the above-written appearance of this most gracious being, on the last of those days it happened that the same wonderful lady appeared to me dressed all in pure white, between two gentle ladies elder than she. And passing through a street, she turned her eyes thither where I stood sorely abashed: and by her unspeakable courtesy, which is now guerdoned in the Great Cycle, she saluted me with so virtuous a bearing that I seemed then and there to behold the very limits of blessedness. The hour of her most sweet salutation was exactly the ninth of that day; and because it was the first time that any words from her reached mine ears, I came into such sweetness that I parted thence as one intoxicated. And betaking me to the loneliness of mine own room, I fell to thinking of this most courteous lady, thinking of whom I was overtaken by a pleasant slumber, wherein a marvellous vision was presented to me: for there appeared to be in my room a mist of the colour of fire, within the which I discerned the figure of a lord of terrible aspect to such as should gaze upon him, but who seemed therewithal to rejoice inwardly that it was a marvel to see. Speaking he said many things, among the which I could understand but few; and of these, this: Ego dominus tuus. In his arms it seemed to me that a person was sleeping, covered only with a blood-coloured cloth; upon whom looking very attentively, I knew that it was the lady of the salutation who had deigned the day before to salute me. And he who held her held also in his hand a thing that was burning in flames; and he said to me, Vide cor tuum. But when he had remained with me a little while, I thought that he set himself to awaken her that slept; after the which he made her to eat that thing which flamed in his hand; and she ate as one fearing. Then, having waited again a space, all his joy was turned into most bitter weeping; and as he wept he gathered the lady into his arms, and it seemed to me that he went with her up towards heaven: whereby such a great anguish came upon me that my light slumber could not endure through it, but was suddenly broken.

DANTE ALIGHIERI

DANTE

Our poet was of moderate height, and, after reaching maturity, was accustomed to walk somewhat bowed, with a slow and gentle pace, clad always in such sober dress as befitted his ripe years. His face was long, his nose aquiline, and his eyes rather large than small. His jaws were large, and the lower lip protruded beyond the upper. His complexion was dark, his hair and beard thick, black, and curled, and his expression ever melancholy and thoughtful. And thus it chanced one day in Verona, when the fame of his works had spread everywhere, particularly that part of his Commedia entitled the Inferno, and when he was known by sight to many, both men and women, that, as he was passing before a doorway where sat a group of women, one of them softly said to the others,—but not so softly but that she was distinctly heard by Dante and such as accompanied him —"Do you see the man who goes down into hell and returns when he pleases, and brings back tidings of them that are below?" To which one of the others naïvely answered, "You must indeed say true. Do you not see how his beard is crisped, and his colour darkened, by the heat and smoke down there?" Hearing these words spoken behind him, and knowing that they came from the innocent belief of the women, he was pleased, and smiling a little as if content that they should hold such an opinion, he passed on.

In both his domestic and his public demeanour he was admirably composed and orderly, and in all things courteous and civil beyond any other. In food and drink he was most temperate, both in partaking of them at the appointed hours and in not passing the limits of necessity. Nor did he show more epicurism in respect of one thing than another. He praised delicate viands, but ate chiefly of plain dishes, and censured beyond measure those who bestowed a great part of their attention upon possessing choice things, and upon the extremely careful preparation of the same, affirming that such persons do not eat to live, but rather live to eat.

None was more vigilant than he in study and in whatever else he undertook, insomuch that his wife and family were annoyed thereby, until they grew accustomed to his ways, and after that they paid no heed thereto. He rarely spoke unless questioned, and then thoughtfully, and in a voice suited to the matter whereof he treated. When, however, there was cause he was eloquent and fluent in speech, and possessed of an excellent and ready delivery. In his youth he took the greatest delight in music and song, and enjoyed the friendship and intimacy of all the best singers and musicians of his time. Led on by this delight he composed many poems, which he made them clothe in pleasing and masterly melody.

How devoted a vassal to love Dante was, has already been shown.

It is the firm belief of all that this love inspired his genius to compose poetry in the vulgar tongue, first through imitation, afterwards through a desire for glory and for a more perfect manifestation of his feelings. By a careful training of himself in the vernacular, he not only surpassed all his contemporaries, but so elucidated and beautified the language that he made then, and has made since, and will make in the future, many persons eager to be expert therein. He delighted also in being alone and removed from people, to the end that his meditations might not be disturbed. If, moreover, any particularly pleasing contemplation came upon him when he was in company, it mattered not what it was that was asked of him, he would never answer the question until he had ended or abandoned his train of thought. This peculiarity often showed itself when he was at table, or in travel with companions, and elsewhere.

In his studies he was most assiduous, insomuch that while he was occupied therewith no news that he heard could divert him from them. Some trustworthy persons relate, anent this complete devotion of his to the thing that pleased him, that once, when he chanced to be at an apothecary's shop in Siena, there was brought him a little book, very famous among men of understanding, but which he had not yet seen, although it had been promised him. He did not have, as it happened, room to place it elsewhere, so, lying breast-downwards upon a bench in front of the apothecary's, he laid the book before him and began to read with great eagerness. Now a little later in this same neighborhood, by reason of some general festival of the Sienese, there took place a grand tournament of young noblemen which created among the bystanders a great uproar—such noise as many instruments and applauding voices are wont to produce. And though many other things were done to attract attention, such as dancing by fair ladies and numerous games of youths, none saw Dante move from his position, or once lift his eyes from his book. Indeed, although he had taken his station there about the hour of three, it was after six before, having examined and summarized all the points of the book, he rose from his position. Yet he afterwards declared to some who asked him how he could keep from watching so fine a festival as had taken place before him, that he had heard nothing. Whereupon to the first wonder of the questioners was not unduly added a second.

GIOVANNI BOCCACCIO

O STELLIFERI CONDITOR ORBIS

O Thou Maker of the whele that bereth the sterres, which that art y-fastned to thy perdurable chayer, and tornest the hevene with a ravisshing sweigh, and constreinest the sterres to suffren thy lawe; so that the mone somtyme shyning with hir ful hornes, meting with alle the bemes of the sonne hir brother, hydeth the sterres that ben lesse; and somtyme, whan the mone, pale with hir derke hornes, approcheth the sonne, leseth hir lightes; and that the eve-sterre Hesperus, whiche that in the firste tyme of the night bringeth forth hir colde arysinges, cometh eft ayein hir used cours, and is pale by the morwe at the rysing of the sonne, and is thanne cleped Lucifer. Thou restreinest the day by shorter dwelling, in the tyme of colde winter that maketh the leves to falle. Thou dividest the swifte tydes of the night, whan the hote somer is comen. Thy might atempreth the variaunts sesons of the yere; so that Zephirus the deboneir wind bringeth ayein, in the first somer sesoun, the leves that the wind that highte Boreas hath reft awey in autumpne, that is to seyn, in the laste ende of somer; and the sedes that the sterre that highte Arcturus saw, ben waxen heye cornes whan the sterre Sirius eschaufeth hem. Ther nis nothing unbounde from his olde lawe, ne forleteth the werke of his propre estat.

O thou governour, governinge alle thinges by certein ende, why refusestow only to governe the werkes of men by dewe manere? Why suffrest thou that slydinge Fortune torneth so grete entrechaunginges of thinges, so that anoyous peyne, that sholde dewely punisshe felouns, punissheth innocents? And folk of wikkede maneres sitten in heye chayres, and anoyinge folk treden, and that unrightfully, on the nekkes of holy men? And vertu, cler-shyninge naturelly, is hid in derke derkenesses, and the rightful man bereth the blame and the peyne of the feloun. Ne forsweringe ne the fraude, covered and kembd with a fals colour, ne anoyeth nat to shrewes; the whiche shrewes, whan hem list to usen hir strengthe, they rejoysen hem to putten under hem the sovereyne kinges whiche that people with-outen noumbre dreden.

O thou, what so ever thou be that knittest alle bondes of thinges, loke on thise wrecchede erthes; we men that ben nat a foule party but a fayr party of so grete a werk, we ben tormented in this see of fortune. Thou Governour, withdraw and restreyne the ravisshinge flodes, and fastne and ferme thise erthes stable with thilke bonde with whiche thou governest the hevene that is so large.

GEOFFREY CHAUCER

IV

RELIGIOUS HUMANISM

OF BOOKS

O Celestial gift of divine liberality, descending from the Father of light to raise up the rational soul even to heaven. . . . Undoubtedly, indeed, thou hast placed thy desirable tabernacle in books, where the Most High, the Light of Light, the Book of Life, hath established thee. Here then all who ask receive, all who seek find thee, to those who knock thou openest quickly. In books cherubim expand their wings, that the soul of the student may ascend and look around from pole to pole, from the rising and the setting sun, from the north and from the sea. In them the most high and incomprehensible God Himself is contained and worshipped.

RICHARD DE BURY

OF PARADISE

Of paradys ne can I not speken propurly for I was not there; it is fer beyonde and that forthinketh me. And also I was not worthi. But as I have herd seye of wyse men beyonde, I schall telle you with gode will. PARADYS TERRESTRE, as wise men seyn, is the highest place of erthe that is in all the world and it is so high that it toucheth nygh to the cercle of the mone, there as the mone maketh hire torn. For sche is so high that the flode of Noe ne myght not come to hire, that solde have covered all the erthe of the world all abowte and aboven and benethen, saf PARADYS only allone. And this PARADYS is enclosed all aboute with a wall and men wyte not whereof it is. For the walles ben covered all over with mosse, as it semeth. And it semeth not that the wall is ston of nature ne of non other things that the wall is. And that wall streccheth fro the south to the north. And it hath not but one entree that is closed with fyre brennynge, so that noman that is mortall ne dar not entren. And in the most high place of PARADYS, evene in the myddel place, is a welle that casteth out the .iiij. flodes that rennen be dyverse londes. Of the whiche the first is clept PHISON or GANGES, that is all one, and it renneth throughout YNDE or EMLAK. In the which Ryvere ben manye preciouse stones, and mochel of Lignum Aloes, and moche gravell of gold. And that other Ryvere is clept NILUS or GYSON, that goth be ETHIOPE and after be EGYPT. And that other is clept TIGRIS, that renneth be ASSIRYE and be ARMENYE the grete. And that other is clept EUFRATE that renneth also be MEDEE and be ARMONYE and be PERSYE. And men there beyonde seyn that alle the swete watres of the world aboven and benethen taken hire begynnynge of that welle of PARADYS, and out of that welle all watres comen and gon. . . . And yee schull understonde that noman that is mortell ne may not approchen to that Paradys. For be londe noman may go for wylde bestes that ben in the desertes and for the high mountaynes and grete hugh roches, that noman may passe by, for the derke places that ben there and that manye. And be the ryveres may noman go, for the water renneth so rudely and so scharply, because that it cometh doun so outrageously from the high places aboven, that it renneth in so grete wawes that no schipp may not rowe ne seyle agenes it. And the water roreth so and maketh so hugh noyse and so gret tempest that noman may here other in the schipp, though he cryede with all the craft that he cowde in the hieste voys that he myghte. Many grete lordes han assayed with gret wille many tymes for to passen be tho ryveres toward PARADYS with full grete companyes, but thei myghte not speden in hire viage. And manye dyeden for weryness of rowynge agenst tho stronge wawes. And many of hem becamen blynde and many deve for the noyse of the water. And summe weren perisscht and loste withinne the wawes. So that no mortell man may approche to that place withouten specyall grace of God, so that of that place I can sey you nomore.

SIR JOHN MANDEVILLE

A MORALITY

The world resembles a chessboard which is chequered white and black, the colors showing the two conditions of life and death, or praise and blame. The chessmen are men of this world who have a common birth, occupy different stations and hold different titles in this life, who contend together, and finally have a common fate which levels all ranks. The King often lies under the other pieces in the bag.

The King's move and powers of capture are in all directions, because the King's will is law.

The Queen's move is aslant only, because women are so greedy that they will take nothing except by rapine and injustice.

The Rook stands for the itinerant justices who travel over the whole realm, and their move is always straight, because the judge must deal justly . . .

The Pawns are poor men. Their move is straight except when they take anything: so also the poor man does well so long as he keeps from ambition . . .

In this game the Devil says 'Check!' when a man falls into sin; and unless he quickly cover the check by turning to repentance, the Devil says, 'Mate!' and carries him off to hell, whence is no escape. For the Devil has as many kinds of temptations to catch different types of man, as the hunter has dogs to catch different types of animals.

INNOCENT MORALITY

FROM THE MORTE D'ARTHUR

How Sir Launcelot departed to seek the queen Guenever, and how he found her at Almesbury.

Then came Sir Bors de Ganis, and said, My lord Sir Launcelot, what think ye for to do, now to ride in this realm? wit thou well ye shall find few friends. Be as be may, said Sir Launcelot, keep you still here, for I will forth on my journey, and no man nor child shall go with me. So it was no boot to strive, but he departed and rode westerly, and there he sought a seven or eight days, and at the last he came to a nunnery, and then was Queen Guenever ware of Sir Launcelot as he walked in the cloister, and when she saw him there she swooned thrice, that all the ladies and gentlewomen had work enough to hold the queen up. So when she might speak, she called ladies and gentlewomen to her, and said, Ye marvel, fair ladies, why I make this fare. Truly, she said, it is for sight of yonder knight that yonder standeth: wherefore, I pray you all, call him to me. When Sir Launcelot was brought to her, then she said to all the ladies, Through this man and me hath all this war been wrought, and the death of the most noblest knights of the world; for through our love that we have loved together is my most noble lord slain. Therefore, Sir Launcelot, wit thou well I am set in such a plight to get my soul's health; and yet I trust, through God's grace, that after my death to have a sight of the blessed face of Christ, and at doomsday to sit on his right side, for as sinful as ever I was are saints in heaven. Therefore, Sir Launcelot, I require thee and beseech thee heartily, for all the love that ever was betwixt us, that thou never see me more in the visage; and I command thee on God's behalf, that thou forsake my company, and to thy kingdom thou turn again and keep well thy realm from war and wrack. For as well as I have loved thee, mine heart will not serve me to see thee; for through thee and me is the flower of kings and knights destroyed. Therefore, Sir Launcelot, go to thy realm, and there take thee a wife, and live with her with joy and bliss, and I pray thee heartily pray for me to our Lord, that I may mend my mis-living. Now, sweet madam, said Sir Launcelot, would ye that I should return again unto my country, and there to wed a lady? Nay, madam, wit you well that shall I never do: for I shall never be so false to you of that I have promised, but the same destiny that ye have taken you to, I will take me unto, for to please Jesu, and ever for you I cast me specially to pray. If thou wilt do so, said the queen, hold thy promise; but I may never believe but that thou wilt turn to the world again. Well, madam, said he, ye say as pleaseth you, yet wist you me never false of my promise, and God defend but I should forsake the world as ye have done. For in the quest of the Sancgreal I had forsaken the vanities of the world, had not your lord been. And if I had done so at that time with my heart, will and thought, I had passed all the knights that were in the Sancgreal, except Sir Galahad my son. And therefore, lady, sithen ye have taken you to perfection, I must needs take me to perfection of right. For I take record of God, in you I have had mine earthly joy. And if I had found you now so disposed, I had cast me to have had you into mine own realm.

How Sir Launcelot came to the hermitage where the archbishop of Canterbury was, and how he took the habit on him.

But sithen I find you thus disposed, I insure you faithfully I will ever take me to penance, and pray while my life lasteth, if that I may find any hermit either grey or white that will receive me. Wherefore, madam, I pray you kiss me, and never no more. Nay, said the queen, that shall I never do, but abstain you from such works. And they departed. But there was never so hard and hearted man, but he would have wept to see the dolour that they made. For there was lamentation as they had been stung with spears, and many times they swooned. And the ladies bare the queen to her chamber, and Sir Launcelot awoke, and went and took his horse, and rode all that day and all that night in a forest, weeping. And at the last he was ware of an hermitage and a chapel stood betwixt two cliffs, and then he heard a little bell ring to mass, and thither he rode and alight, and tied his horse to the gate, and heard mass. And he that sang mass was the bishop of Canterbury. Both the bishop and Sir Bedivere knew Sir Launcelot, and they spake together after mass. But when Sir Bedivere had told his tale all whole, Sir Launcelot's heart almost brast for sorrow, and Sir Launcelot threw his arms abroad, and said, Alas, who may trust this world! And then he kneeled down on his knees, and prayed the bishop to shrive him and assoil him. And then he besought the bishop that he might be his brother. Then the bishop said, I will gladly: and there he put an habit upon Sir Launcelot, and there he served God day and night with prayers and fastings.

Thus the great host abode at Dover. And then Sir Lionel took fifteen lords with him, and rode to London to seek Sir Launcelot. And there Sir Lionel was slain and many of his lords. Then Sir Bors de Ganis made the great host for to go home again. And Sir Bors, Sir Ector de Maris, Sir Blamor, Sir Bleoberis, with more other of Sir Launcelot's kin, took on them to ride all England overthwart and endlong, to see Sir Launcelot. So Sir Bors by fortune rode so long till he came to the same chapel where Sir Launcelot was. And so Sir Bors heard a little bell knell that rang to mass, and there he alight, and heard mass. And when mass was done, the bishop, Sir Launcelot, and Sir Bedivere came to Sir Bors. And when Sir Bors saw Sir Launcelot in that manner clothing, then he prayed the bishop that he might be in the same suit. And so there was an habit put upon him, and there he lived in prayers and fasting. And within half a year there was come Sir Galihud, Sir Galihodin, Sir Blamor, Sir Bleoberis, Sir Williars, Sir Clarrus and Sir Gahalantine. So all these seven noble knights there abode still. And when they saw Sir Launcelot had taken him unto such perfection, they had no list to depart, but took such an habit as he had. Thus they endured in great penance six year, and then Sir Launcelot took the habit of priesthood, and a twelvemonth he sang mass. And there was none of these other knights but they read in books, and holp to sing mass, and rang bells, and did bodily all manner of service. And so their horses went where they would, for they took no regard of no worldly riches. For when they saw Sir Launcelot endure such penance, in prayers and fasting, they took no force what pain they endured, for to see the noblest knight of the world take such abstinence, that he waxed full lean. And thus upon a night there came a vision to Sir Launcelot, and charged him in remission of his sins, to haste him unto Almesbury,— And by then thou come there, thou shalt find queen Guenever dead: and therefore take thy fellows with thee, and purvey them of an horse bier, and fetch thou the corpse of her, and bury her by her husband the noble king Arthur. So this vision came to Launcelot thrice in one night.

How Sir Launcelot went with his seven fellows to Almesbury, and found there queen Guenever dead, whom they brought to Glastonbury.

Then Sir Launcelot rose up or day, and told the hermit. It were well done, said the hermit, that ye made you ready, and that ye disobey not the vision. Then Sir Launcelot took his seven fellows with him, and on foot they went from Glastonbury to Almesbury, the which is little more than thirty miles. And thither they came within two days, for they were weak and feeble to go. And when Sir Launcelot was come to Almesbury, within the nunnery, queen Guenever died but half an hour before. And the ladies told Sir Launcelot that queen Guenever told them all, or she passed, that Sir Launcelot had been priest near a twelvemonth,— And hither he cometh as fast as he may to fetch my corpse: and beside my lord king Arthur he shall bury me. Wherefore the queen said in hearing of them all, I beseech Almighty God that I may never have power to see Sir Launcelot with my worldly eyes. And thus, said all the ladies, was ever her prayer these two days, till she was dead. Then Sir Launcelot saw her visage, but he wept not greatly, but sighed. And so he did all the observance of the service himself, both the Dirige, and on the morn he sang mass. And there was ordained an horse bier; and so with an hundred torches ever burning about the corpse of the queen, and ever Sir Launcelot with his eight fellows went about the horse-bier singing and reading many an holy orison, and frankincense upon the corpse incensed. Thus Sir Launcelot and his eight fellows went on foot from Almesbury unto Glastonbury; and when they were come to the chapel and the hermitage, there she had a Dirige with great devotion. And on the morn the hermit, that sometime was bishop of Canterbury, sang the mass of Requiem with great devotion: and Sir Launcelot was the first that offered, and then all his eight fellows. And then she was wrapped in cered cloth of Raines, from the top to the toe in thirty fold, and after she was put in a web of lead, and then in a coffin of marble. And when she was put in the earth, Sir Launcelot swooned, and lay long still, while the hermit came out and awaked him, and said, Ye be to blame, for ye displease God with such manner of sorrow making. Truly, said Sir Launcelot, I trust I do not displease God, for He knoweth mine intent, for my sorrow was not, nor it not, for any rejoicing of sin, but my sorrow may never have end. For when I remember of her beauty, and of her noblesse, that was both with her king and with her; so when I saw his corpse and her corpse so lie together, truly mine heart would not serve to sustain my careful body. Also when I remember me, how by my default, mine orgule, and my pride, that they were both laid full low, that were peerless that ever was living of christian people, wit you well, said Sir Launcelot, this remembered, of their kindness and mine unkindness, sank so to my heart, that I might not sustain myself.

SIR THOMAS MALORY

HOLY POVERTY

Those brothers to whom God has given the ability to labour, shall labour faithfully and devoutly; in such way that idleness, the enemy of the soul, being excluded, they may not extinguish the spirit of holy prayer and devotion; to which other temporal things should be subservient. As a reward, moreover, for their labour, they may receive for themselves and their brothers the necessaries of life, but not coin or money; and thus humbly as becomes servants of God and the followers of most holy poverty. The brothers shall appropriate nothing to themselves, neither a house nor a place nor anything; but as pilgrims and strangers in this world, in poverty and humility serving God, they shall go confidently seeking for alms. Nor need they be ashamed, for the Lord made Himself poor for us in this world.

RULE OF ST. FRANCIS

THE CUSTOMS OF CHIVALRY

You have heard how the town of Entenca surrendered to the Duke of Lancaster, for the king of Castille sent thither no assistance; and how the duchess of Lancaster and her daughter visited the king and queen of Portugal at Oporto, when the king and his court, as was right, received them most honorably. During the stay of the duke of Lancaster in Entenca, a herald arrived from Valladolid, who demanded where Sir John Holland was lodged. On being shown thither, he found Sir John within; and, bending his knee, presented him a letter, saying, "Sir, I am a herald at arms, whom Sir Reginald de Roye sends hither; he salutes you by me, and you will be pleased to read this letter." Sir John answered, he would willingly do so. Having opened it, he read that Sir Reginald de Roye entreated him, for the love of his mistress, that he would deliver him from his vow, by tilting with him three courses with the lance, three attacks with the sword, three with the battle-axe, and three with the dagger; and that, if he chose to come to Valladolid, he had provided him an escort of sixty spears; but, if it were more agreeable to him to remain in Entenca, he desired he would obtain from the duke of Lancaster a passport for himself and thirty companions.

When Sir John Holland had perused the letter, he smiled, and looking at the herald said, "Friend, thou art welcome; for thou hast brought me what pleases me much, and I accept the challenge. Thou wilt remain in my lodging with my people, and in the course of tomorrow thou shalt have my answer, whether the tilts are to be in Galicia or Castille." The herald replied, "God grant it." He remained in Sir John's lodgings, where he was made comfortable; and Sir John went to the duke of Lancaster, whom he found in conversation with the marshal, and showed the letter the herald had brought. "Well," said the duke, "and have you accepted it?" "Yes, by my faith, have I; and why not? I love nothing better than fighting, and the knight entreats me to indulge him: consider, therefore, where you would choose it should take place." The duke mused awhile, and then said, "It shall be performed in this town: have a passport made out in what terms you please, and I will seal it." "It is well said," replied Sir John; "and I will, in God's name, soon make out the passport." The passport was fairly written and sealed, for thirty knights and squires to come and return; and Sir John Holland, when he delivered it to the herald, presented him with a handsome mantle lined with minever, and twelve nobles. The herald took leave and returned to Valladolid, where he related what had passed, and shewed his presents.

News of this tournament was carried to Oporto, where the king of Portugal kept his court. "In the name of God," said the king, "I will be present at it, and so shall my queen and the ladies." "Many thanks," replied the duchess; "for I shall be accompanied by the king and queen when I return." It was not long after this conversation that the king of Portugal, the queen, the duchess, with her daughter, and the ladies of the court, set out for Entenca, in grand array. The duke of Lancaster, when they were near at hand, mounted his horse; and, attended by a numerous company, went to meet them. When the king and queen met, they embraced each other most kindly, and entered the town together, where their lodgings were as well prepared as they could be in such a place, though they were not so magnificent as if they had been at Paris. Three days after the arrival of the king of Portugal, came Sir Reginald de Roye, handsomely accompanied by knights and squires, to the amount of six score horse. They were all properly lodged; for the duke had given his officers strict orders that they should be well taken care of. On the morrow, Sir John Holland and Sir Reginald de Roye armed themselves, and rode into a spacious close in Entenca, well sanded, where the tilts were to be performed. Scaffolds were erected for the ladies, the king, the duke and many English lords who had come to witness the combat; for none had stayed at home.

The two knights who were to perform this deed of arms, entered the lists so well armed and equipped that nothing was wanting. Their spears, battle-axes and swords, were brought them; and each, being mounted on the best of horses, placed himself about a bow-shot distant from the other, but, at times, they all pranced about on their horses most gallantly, for they knew every eye to be upon them. All being now arranged for their combat, which was to include everything, except pushing it to extremity, though no one could foresee what mischief might happen, not how it would end; for they were to tilt with pointed lances, then with swords, which were so sharp that scarcely a helmet could resist their strokes; and these were to be succeeded by battle-axes and daggers, each so well tempered that nothing could resist them. Now, consider the perils those run who engage in such combats to exalt their honor; for one unlucky stroke puts an end to the business.

Having braced their targets and examined each other through the visors of their helmets, they spurred on their horses, spear in hand. Though they allowed their horses to gallop as they pleased, they advanced on as straight a line as if it had been drawn with a cord, and hit each other on the visors, with such force that Sir Reginald's lance was shivered into four pieces, which flew to a greater height than they could have been thrown. All present allowed this to be gallantly done. Sir John Holland struck Sir Reginald likewise on the visor, but not with the same success, and I will tell you why. Sir Reginald had but slightly laced on his helmet, so that it was held by one thong only, which broke at the blow, and the helmet flew over his head, leaving Sir Reginald bare-headed. Each passed the other, and Sir John bore his lance without halting. The spectators cried out that it was a handsome course. The knights returned to their stations, when Sir Reginald's helmet was fitted on again, and another lance was given to him: Sir John grasped his own, which was not worsted. When ready, they set off full gallop, for they had excellent horses under them, which they well knew how to manage, and again struck each other on the helmets, so that sparks of fire came from them, but chiefly from Sir John Holland's. He received a very severe blow, for this time the lance did not break; neither did Sir John's, which hit the visor of his adversary without much effect, passing through and leaving it on the crupper of the horse, and Sir Reginald was once more bare-headed. "Ha," cried the English to the French, "he does not fight fair; why is not his helmet buckled on as well as Sir John Holland's? We say he is playing tricks: tell him to put himself on an equal footing with his adversary." "Hold your tongues," said the duke, "and let them alone. In arms every one takes what advantage he can: if Sir John think there is any advantage in thus fastening on the helmet, he may do the same. But, for my part, were I in their situations, I would lace my helmet as tight as possible; and if one hundred were asked their opinions, there would be forescore of my way of thinking." The English, on this, were silent, and never again interfered. The ladies declared they had nobly jousted; and they were much praised by the king of Portugal, who said to Sir John Fernando, "In our country they do not tilt so well, nor so gallantly: what say you, Sir John?"

After the courses of the lance, they fought three rounds with swords, battle-axes, and daggers, without either of them being wounded. The French carried off Sir Reginald to his lodgings, and the English did the same to Sir John Holland. The duke of Lancaster entertained this day at dinner all the French knights and squires; the duchess was seated beside him, and Sir Reginald de Roye next to her. After dinner they entered the presence-chamber; and the duchess, taking Sir Reginald by the hand, led him thither. They were followed by the other knights, who conversed on arms and other subjects a long time, almost until wine was brought. The duchess then drew nearer to the French knights, and thus spoke, "I wonder greatly how you knights of France can think of supporting the claims of a bastard; for it is well known to the whole world that Henry, who called himself king of Castille, was a bastard, and how can you thus, with your arms and counsel, disinherit the right heir of Castille and deprive him of the crown? For this I know, that myself and sister are the legal daughters of the late king, Don Pedro; and God, who is Truth itself, knows that our claim on Castille is just." The lady, when speaking of her father, Don Pedro, could not refrain from tears, as she doated on him. Sir Reginald de Roye bowed to her, and thus replied, "Madam, we know that what you have said is true; but our lord, the king of France, holds a different opinion from yours; and, as we are his subjects, we must make war for him, and go whithersoever he may send us, for we cannot disobey him."

SIR JOHN FROISSART

ALL WORK AND NO PLAY

Let us now come to the sports and pastimes, seeing it is fit that a city should not only be commodious and serious, but also merry and sportful; whereupon in the seals of the popes, until the time of Pope Leo, on the one side was St. Peter fishing, with a key over him, reached as it were by the hand of God out of heaven, and about it this verse:

Tu pro me navem liquisti, suscipe clavem.

And on the other side was a city, and this inscription on it: "Aurea Roma." Likewise to the praise of Augustus Caesar and the city in respect of the shows and sports was written:

Nocte pluit tota, redeunt spectacula mane, etc.

"All night it raines, and shows at morrow tide returne again,
And Caesar with almighty Jove hath matcht an equal raign."

But London, for the shows upon the theatres, and comical pastimes, hath holy plays, representations of miracles, which holy confessors have wrought, or representations of torments wherein the constance of martyrs appeared. Every year also at Shrove Tuesday, that we may begin with children's sports, seeing we all have been children, the schoolboys do bring cocks of the game to their master, and all the forenoon they delight themselves in cock-fighting: after dinner, all the youths go into the fields to play at the ball.

The scholars of every school have their ball, or baton, in their hands; the ancient and wealthy men of the city come forth on horseback to see the sport of the young men, and to take part of the pleasure in beholding their agility. Every Friday in Lent a fresh company of young men comes into the field on horseback and the best horseman conducteth the rest. Then march forth the citizens' sons, and other young men, with disarmed lances and shields, and there they practise feats of war. Many courtiers likewise, when the king lieth near, and attendants of noblemen, do repair to these exercises; and while the hope of victory doth inflame their minds, do show good proof how serviceable they would be in martial affairs.

In Easter holidays they fight battles on the water; a shield is hung upon a pole, fixed in the midst of the stream, a boat is prepared without oars, to be carried by violence of the water, and in the fore part thereof standeth a young man, ready to give charge upon the shield with his lance; if so be he breaketh his lance against the shield, and doth not fall, he is thought to have performed a worthy deed; if so be, without breaking his lance, he runneth strongly against the shield, down he falleth into the water, for the boat is violently forced with the tide; but on each side of the shield ride two boats, furnished with young men, which recover him that falleth as soon as they may. Upon the bridge, wharfs, and houses, by the river's side, stand great numbers to see and laugh thereat.

In the holidays all the summer the youths are exercised in leaping, dancing, shooting, wrestling, casting the stone, and practising their shields; the maidens trip in their timbrels, and dance as long as they can well see. In winter, every holiday before dinner, the boars prepared for brawn are set to fight, or else bulls and bears are baited.

When the great fen, or moor, which watereth the walls of the city on the north side, is frozen, many young men play upon the ice; some, striding as wide as they may, do slide swiftly; others make themselves seats of ice, as great as millstones; one sits down, many hand in hand to draw him, and one slipping on a sudden, all fall together; some tie bones to their feet and under their heels; and shoving themselves by a little picked staff, do slide as swiftly as a bird flieth in the air, or an arrow out of a cross-bow. Sometime two run together with poles, and hitting one the other, either one or both do fall, not without hurt; some break their arms, some their legs, but youth desirous of glory in this sort exerciseth itself against the time of war. Many of the citizens do delight themselves in hawks and hounds; for they have liberty of hunting in Middlesex, Hertfordshire, all Chiltern, and in Kent to the water of Cray.

FITZSTEPHEN

AT THE TABLE

Servant. My mistress bids me tell you, Sir, that Dinner will be spoil'd. *Eusebius.* A little Patience, tell her, and we come. Let's wash first, my Masters, that we may bring clean Hands to the Table, as well as clean Hearts: the very Pagans us'd a kind of Reverence in this case; how much more then should Christians do it; if it were but in Imitation of that Sacred Solemnity of our Saviour with his Disciples at his last Supper! The washing of the hands is but an Emblem of purging the Mind. And so long as there is any uncleanness in the one, or any Envy or Rancour in the other, we ought not to usurp upon the Blessings of the Table: The very Body is the founder, and Meat the wholesomer for a purifi'd Mind. *Timotheus.* Most undoubtedly. *Eusebius.* It is evident from several Instances in the Scriptures, that it was the Practice of our Saviour, to bless the Table, both before and after Meat. Wherefore, if you please, I'le say you a Grace that St. Chrysostome, in one of his Homilies commends to the Skies, and he himself was the Interpreter of it. *Timotheus.* Pray'e do.

Blessed be thou, O God, who has susteined us from our youth, and providest Food for all Flesh: Fill our Hearts with joy and comfort, that partaking abundantly of thy Bounties, we may likewise abound in all good works, through Jesus Christ our Lord, to whom with thee and the Holy Ghost, be Glory, Honour, and Power, world without end. *Timotheus.* Amen.

Eusebius. Sit down now, and let every man take his Friend next to him. The first place is yours, Timothy, in the right of your grey hairs. *Timotheus.* The only thing in the world that gives me a Title to't. *Eusebius.* We can only judge of what we see, and must leave the rest to God. Sophronius, keep you close to your Principal. There's the right side of the Table for Theophilus and Eulalius: and the left for Chrysoglottus, and Theodidactus. Euramius, and Nephalius must make a shift with what's left, and I'le stick here to my old Corner. *Timotheus.* This must not be; the Master of the House sure shall take the first place. *Eusebius.* The House is as much yours as mine Gentlemen, or however if I may govern within my own Jurisdiction, I'le sit where I please, and I have made my choice. Now Christ be with us and among us; without whom there can be no true joy and comfort. *Timotheus.* Amen. But where shall he sit? for the places are all taken up. *Eusebius.* I would have him in every Drop, and Morsel that we eat, or Drink; but principally in our Minds. And the better to fit us for the reception of so Divine a Guest, if you please, wee'l have some piece of Scripture read in the Interim, which will not at all hinder us in the business of our Dinner. *Timotheus.* With all my Soul. *Eusebius.* This Entertainment pleases me so much the better because it puts off Vain and frivolus discourse, and brings profit beside. I am none of those that think no Society diverting, unless it be season'd with the foppery of wanton Stories and Bawdy Songs. There's no true joy but in a clear and open Conscience, and those are the happy Conversations, where only such things are spoken and heard as we can reflect upon afterward with Satisfaction; and without any Mixture either of Shame, or Repentance. *Timotheus.* It were well if we were as Careful in this Point, as we are sure of the Truth on't. *Eusebius.* And 'tis not all neither, that the Benefit is valuable and Certain; but one Months using of it would make it pleasant too. *Timotheus.* And therefore 'tis the best Course we can take to wont our selves to that which is good.

ERASMUS

FAITH AND COMFORT

Syth all our principall coumforte must come of God, we must first presuppose in hym to whome we shall with anye ghostely counsell geue any effectuall counfort, one ground to begyn withall: whereuppon, all that we shall build must be supported and stand, that is to witte, the grounde and foundacion of fayth, without which had ready before, all the spiritual counfort that any man maye speake of, can neuer auaile a flye. For likewise as it wer vtterlye vayne to lay natural resons of counfort, to him that hath no witte, so were it vudoutedlye frustrate to laye spirituall causes of coumforte, to hym that hath no faythe. For except a man first belieue, that holye scripture is the woorde of God, and that the woorde of God is true, how can a man take any coumforte of that, that the scripture telleth him therein? Nedes must the man take little fruit of the scripture, if he either belieue not that it were the woorde of God, or els wene yt though it wer, it might yet be for al that vntrue. This fayth as it is more faynte or more strong, so shall the coumfortable woordes of holye scripture stande the man in more stede or lesse. This vertue of fayth, can neither any man geue himselfe, nor yet any one manne another: but though men maye with preaching be ministers unto God therein, and the man with hys own free will obeying freely the inward inspiracion of God, be a weake woorker with almighty god therin: yet is ye faith in dede the gracious gift of god himself. For as Saynt James saith, Omne datum optimum et omne donum perfectum de sursum est descendens a patre luminum. Euery good gyft and euery perfit gyft, is geuen from aboue, descending from the father of lightes. Therefore feelyng our fayth by manye tokens very faynt, lette vs praye to him that geueth it, that it may please him to helpe and encrease it. And lette vs first saye with him in the ghospel: Credo domine, adiuua incredulitatem meam; I belieue good Lorde, but helpe thou the lacke of my beliefe. And after lette vs pray with the Apostles: Domine, adauge nobis fidem; Lord encrease our fayth. And finallye, lette vs consider by Chrystes saying vnto them, that if we would not suffer the strength and feruour of our fayth to waxe luke warme, or rather key cold, and in maner lese his vigor by scatteryng our mindes abroade about so many tryfling thinges, that of the matters of our faith, we very seldom thinke but yt we woulde withdrawe our thought fro the respect and regard of all worldly fantasies, and so father our fayth together into a little narrowe rowme. And lyke the lyttle grayne of musterde seede, whiche is of nature hote: sette it in the garden of our soule, all weedes pulled out for the better feding of our faith, then shall it growe, and so spreade vppe in heyght, that the byrdes, that is to wit the holy Aungelles of heauen shal brede in our soule, and bring furth vertues in the branches of our fayth, and then with the faithfull trust, that through the true beliefe of Goodes woorde, we shall putte in his promyse, we shall be well hable to commaund a great mountayn of tribulacion, to voyde from the place where he stode in our hert, whereas with a verye fieble fayth and a faynte, we shall be scant hable to remoue a lyttle hillocke. And therefore, as for the fyrst conclusion, as we must of necessitie before any spirituall coumfort presuppose the foundacion of fayth: So syth no man can geue vs faith but only God, lette vs neuer cease to cal vpon God therefore.

Vyncent. Forsooth, good vncle, me thynketh that this foundacion of fayth, which as you saye must be layde first, is so necessarily requisite, that without it, all spirituall coumforte wer vtterly geuen in vayn. And therefore now shal we pray God for a full and a fast fayth.

ST. THOMAS MORE

LAST LETTER TO HIS DAUGHTER

OURE Lorde blesse you, good doughter, and youre good husbande, and youre lyttle boye, and all yours, and all my chyldren, and all my Goddechyldren and all oure frendes. Recommende me whan ye maye, to my good doughter Cicily, whom I beseche oure Lorde to coumforte. And I sende her my blessyng, and to all her children, and praye her to praye for me. I sende her an handkercher: and God coumfort my good soon her husbande. My good doughter Daunce hathe the picture in parchemente, that you delyuered me from my ladye Coniers, her name is on the backeside. Shewe her that I hartelye praye her, that you may sende it in my name to her agayne, for a token from me to praye for me. I lyke speciall wel Dorothe Coly, I pray you be good unto her. I woulde wytte whether thys be she that you wrote me of. If not yet I praye you bee good to the tother, as you maye in her affliccion, and to my good doughter Joone Aleyn too. Geve her I praye you some kynde aunswere, for she sued hither to me this day to pray you be good to her. I comber you good Margaret much, but I would be sory, if it should be any longer than tomorrow. For it is saint Thomas euen, and the utas of saint Peter: & therefore tomorow long I to go to God: it were a day verye mete and conuenient for me. I never liked your maner toward me better, than when you kissed me laste: for I love when doughterly loue and deere charitye hath no laysure to loke to worldlye curtesy. Fare well my dere chylde, and pray for me, and I shall for you and all youre frendes, that we may merelye mete in heauen. I thanke you for youre gret cost. I sende now to my good doughter Clement her algorisme stone, and I send her and my godsonne and all hers, Gods blessing and myne. I praye you at time conuenient recommende me to my good sonne John More. I liked wel his naturall fashion. Our Lord blesse hym & his good wyfe my louyng doughter, to whom I praye him be good as he hathe greate cause: and that yf the lande of myne come to his hande, he breake not my wyll concernynge hys sister Daunce. And oure Lord Blisse Thomas and Austen and all that they shal haue.

ST. THOMAS MORE

THE FAREWELL OF SAINT THOMAS MORE

And so vppon the next morowe, beinge Tuesdays, St. Thomas even, and the vtas of Saincte Peeter, in the yeare of our lord, one thowsand five hundreth thirtye and five (according as he in his letter the daye before had wished) earlye in the morninge came to him Sir Thomas Pope, his singuler freind, on message from the kinge and his Councell, That he should before nyne of the clock the same morning suffer death; and that therefore furthwith he should prepare him self therunto:

"Master Pope," quoth he, "for your good tydings I most hartelye thancke you. I haue bine alwaies much bounden to the Kings highnes for the benefites and honoures that he hath still from tyme to tyme most bountyfully heaped vppon me; and yeat more bound am I to his grace for putting me into this place, where I haue had convenient time and space to haue remembraunce of my end. And so helpe me, god, most of all, master Pope, am I bound to his highnes that it pleaseath him so shortly to ridde me out of the miseries of this wretched woorld. And therefore will I not faile ernestly to pray for his grace, bothe heare and also in another world."

"The kings pleasure is further," quoth master Pope, "that at your execution you shall not vse many words."

"Master Pope," quothe he, "you do well to geeue me warninge of his graces pleasure, for other wise I had purposed at that tyme somewhat to have spoken, but of no matter wherewith his grace, or any other, should haue had cause to be offended. Neuertheles, whatsoeuer I intended, I am ready obediently to conforme my self to his graces commandementes. And I beseeke you, good master Pope, to be a meene vnto his highnes that my daughter Margaret may be at my buriall."

"The kinge is content already," quoth master Pope, "that your wife, children and other (your) freinds shall haue libertie to be present thereat."

"O howe much beholden then," said Sir Thomas Moore, "am I to his grace, that vnto my poore buriall vouchsafeth to haue so graciouse consideracion."

Wherewithall master Pope, takinge his leaue of hym, could not refrayne from wepinge. Which Sir Thomas Moore perceiuinge, comforted him in this wise: "Quiet your self, good master Pope, and be not discomforted; For I trust that we shall, once in heaven, see eche other full merily, where we shalbe sure to live and loue together, in ioyful blisse eternally."

Vppon whose departure, Sir Thomas Moore, as one that had bine invited to some solempne feaste, chaunged himself into his best apparell; which master Leiuentenaunt espienge, advised him to put it of, sayenge that he that should haue it was but a Javill.

"What, master Leiuentenaunt," quoth he, "shall I accompte him a Javill that shall doe me this day so singuler a benefitt? Nay, I assure you, were it clothe of gold, I wolde accompt it well bestowed on him, as St. Ciprian did, who gaue his executioner thirtie peeces of gould." And albeit at length, throughe master Leiuetenauntes importunate persuasion, he altered his apparell, yeat after thexample of that holy martir St. Ciprian, did he, of that litle money that was lefte him, send one Angell of gold to his executioner.

And so was he by master Leiuentenaunte brought out of the Tower, and from thence led to (wardes) the place of execution. Where, goinge vppe the scaffold, which was so weake that it was ready to fall, he saide merilye to master Leiuetenaunte: "I pray you, master Leiuetenaunte, see me salf vppe, and for my cominge downe let me shifte for my self."

Then desired he all the people thereaboute to pray for him, and to beare witnes with him that he should (nowe there) suffer death in and for the faith of the holy chatholik churche. Whiche done, he kneled downe, and after his prayers said, turned to the executioner, and with a cheerefull countenaunce spake thus to him:

"Plucke vpp thy spirites, man, and be not afrayde to do thine office; my necke is very shorte; take heede therefore thow strike not awrye, for savinge of thine honestye."

So passed Sir Thomas Moore out of this world to god, vppon the very same daye in which himself had most desired.

Soone after whose deathe came intelligence thereof to the Emperour Charles. Whervppon he sent for Sir Thomas Elliott, our english Embassadour, and said unto him: "My Lord Embassador, we vnderstand that the Kinge, your master, hath put his faithfull seruaunt and grave, wise Councelour, Sir Thomas Moore, to deathe." Wherunto Sir Thomas Elliott awneswered that he vnderstood nothing thereof. "Well," said the Emperour, "it is too true. And this will we say, that if we had bine maister of such a servante, of whose doings our selfe haue had these many yeares no small experience, we wold rather haue lost the best city of our dominions than haue lost such a worthy councellour." Which matter was by the same Sir Thomas Elliott to my self, to my wife, to maister Clement and his wife, to master John Haywood and his wife, and diuers other his Freinds accordingly reported.

WILLIAM ROPER

THE DEATH OF THE LADY MARGARET

But specyally whan they sawe the dethe so hast vpon her and that she must nedes departe from them, and they sholde forgo so gentyll a maystris, so tender a lady, then wept they meruayllously, wepte her ladyes and kynneswomen to whom she was full kynde, wepte her poore gentylwomen whom she had loued so tenderly before, wept her chamberers to whome she was full deare, wepte her chapelaynes and preestes, wepte her other true and faythfull seruauntes. And who wolde not haue wept that there had ben presente All Englonde for her dethe had cause of wepynge. The poore creatures that were wonte to receyue her almes, to whome she was alwaye pyteous and mercyfull. The studyentes of bothe the vnyuersytees to whome she was as a moder. All the lerned men of Englonde to whome she was a veray patronesse. All the vertuous and deuoute persones to whom she was as a louynge syster, all the good relygyous men and women whom she so often was wont to vysyte and comforte. All good preestes and clerkes to whome she was a true defenderesse. All the noble men and women to whome she was a myrroure and exampler of honoure. All the comyn people of this realme for whom she was in theyr causes a comyn mediatryce, and toke ryght grete dyspleasure for them, and generally the hole realme hathe cause to complayne & to morne her dethe . . .

Now therefore wolde I aske you this one questyon. Were it, suppose ye, al this considered, a meetly thyng for vs to desyre to haue this noble princes here amongest vs agayn to forgo the ioyous lyfe aboue, to wante the presence of the gloryous Trynyte' whom she so longe hathe sought & honoured, to leue that moost noble kyngdome, to be absent frome the moost blessyd company of sayntes & sayntesses, & hether to come agayn to be wrapped & endaungered with the myseries of this wretched worlde, with the paynfull dyseases of her age, with the other encomberaunces that dayly happethe in this myserable lyfe? Were this a reasonable request of oure partye, were this a kynde desyre, were this a gentyl wysshe, that where she hathe ben so kinde & louyng a maystresse vnto us, all we sholde more regarde our owne prouffytes then her more synguler wele & comfort? The moder that hathe so grete affeccyon vnto her sone that she wyll not suffre hym to departe from her to his promocyon & furtheraunce but alway kepe hym at home, more regardynge her owne pleasure than hys wele, were not she an vnkinde & vngentyl moder? Yes verayly, let vs therefore thynke out moost louyng maystres is gone hens for her promocyon, for her grete furtheraunce, for her moost wele & prouffyte. And herin comforte vs, herin reioyse ourselfe & thanke almyghty God whiche of his infynyte mercy so gracyously hathe dysposed for her.

JOHN FISHER

THE LADY MARGARET

She was by birth second to none, but unto the first in the realm; yet she measured only greatness by goodness, making nobility but the mirror or virtue, as able to shew things worthy to be seen, as apt to draw many eyes to behold it; she suited her behaviour to her birth, and ennobled her birth with her piety, leaving her house more beholden to her for having honoured it with the glory of her virtues, than she was to it, for the titles of her degree; she was high-minded in nothing but in aspiring to perfection and in the disdain of vice; in other things covering her greatness with humility among her inferiors, and shewing it with courtesy amongst her peers.

Of the carriage of herself, and her sober government it may be sufficient testimony, that envy herself was dumb in her dispraise, finding in her much to repine at, but nought to reprove: the clearness of her honour I need not to mention, she having always armed it with such modesty as taught the most untemperate tongues to be silent in her presence, and answered their eyes with scorn and contempt that did but seem to make her an aim to passion; yea, and in this behalf, as almost in all others, she hath the most honourable and known ladies of the land, so common and known witnesses, that those that least loved her religion, were in love with her demeanour, delivering their opinions in open praises. How mildly she accepted the check of fortune, fallen upon her without desert, experience has been a most manifest proof; the temper of her mind being so easy that she found little difficulty in taking down her thoughts to a mean degree, which true honour, not pride, has raised to a former height. Her faithfulness and love, where she found true friendship, is written with tears in many eyes, and will be longer registered in grateful memories of divers that have tried her in that kind, avowing her for secrecy, wisdom, and constancy, to be a miracle in that sex: yes, when she found least kindness in others, she never lost it in herself, more willingly suffering, than offering wrong, and often weeping for their mishaps, whom though less loving her, she could not but affect.

Of the innocency of her life, in general, all can aver, that as she was grateful many ways, and memorable for virtues, so was she free from all blemish of any vice, using, to her power, the best means to keep continually an undefiled conscience. Her attire was ever such as might both satisfy a curious eye, and yet bear witness of a sober mind; neither singular nor vain, but such as her peers of least report used.

If our souls be possessed in our patience, surely her soul was truly her own, whose rock, though often stricken with the rod of adversity, never yielded any more than to give issue of eye-streams; and though these, through the tenderness of her nature and aptness of her sex, were the customary tributes that her love paid more to her friends than her own misfortunes, yet were they not accompanied with distempered words or ill seeming actions; reason never forgetting decency, though remembering pity.

Her devotions she daily observed, offering the daily sacrifice of an innocent heart, and stinting herself to her times of prayer, which she performed with so religious a care as well shewed that she knew how high a Majesty she served. I need not write how dutifully she discharged all the behoofs of a most loving wife, since that was the commonest theme of her praise; yet this may be said without improof to any, that whosoever in this behalf may be counted her equal, none can justly be thought her superior: where she owned, she payed duty; where she found, she turned courtesy: wheresoever she was known, she deserved amity; desirous of the best, yet disdaining none but evil company, she was readier to require benefits than revenge wrongs; more grieved than angry with unkindness of friends, when either mistaking or misreport occasioned any breaches; for if their words carry credit, who entered deepest into her thoughts, they have acquitted her from all spice of malice, not only against her friends, whose dislikes were but a retire to slip further into friendship, but even her greatest enemies, to whom if she had been a judge as she was a suppliant, I assuredly think she would have redressed, but not revenged her wrongs. In sum, she was an honour to her predecessors, a light to her age, and a pattern to her posterity; neither was her conclusion different from her premises, or her death from her life; she shewed no dismay, being warned of her danger, carrying in her conscience the safe conduct of innocency. But having sent her desires to heaven before, with a mild countenance and a most calm mind, in more hope than fear, she expected her own passage; she commended both her duty and goodwill to all her friends, and cleared her heart from all grudge towards her enemies, wishing true happiness to them both, as best became so soft and gentle a mind, in which anger never stayed but as an unwelcome stranger.

ROBERT SOUTHWELL

MARY, QUEEN OF SCOTS

Night having fallen, she retired to her chapel, where she prayed to God two full hours, kneeling on her bare knees on the floor, as the women who saw her attest. Returning to her chamber she said to them, "I think it were well, my dears, that I should eat something and then retire, that on the morrow I may do nothing undignified, or lack courage."

What generosity! What fortitude!

She then ate food and retired to bed, but slept very little, spending the greater part of the night saying prayers.

She rose two hours before dawn, and dressed herself as neatly as possible, more so than usual, in a dress of black velvet, a jacket of crimson satin, and a black veil. These were all her clothes she had kept for herself; so she said to her women, "I would have given you this costume yesterday, my dears, but that I must go to my death with a certain dignity, since I owe this to my exalted position. Here is a handkerchief I have also kept. With this my eyes will be covered as I approach the place. I give this to you (indicating one of the women), since I shall request of you this last favour of blindfolding my eyes."

She then retired once more to her chapel, and after bidding farewell to her women and kissing them all, she gave them detailed messages that she wished them to take to the King, the Queen and her relatives, uttering no word of vengeance, but much against it. She then performed the ceremony of the Sacrament by means of a wafer consecrated by the good Pope Pius V, which he had sent to her for such use. This she had always kept as an object of great sanctity.

Her prayers were long, for she said them all, and the sun was already risen when she had ended, and gone into her chamber. There she sat herself before the fire, conversing with her women and consoling them—instead of their consoling her—as before—telling them that the joys of this world were as naught, and that she should serve as an example to all the great ones of the earth and all the small; that she, who had once been Queen over the kingdoms of France and Scotland—over the one by right of birth and over the other by the changes of fortune—after enjoying triumphs and honours, thus found herself at last in the hands of the hangman, though wholly innocent. This was at least some consolation. The best pretext used by her enemies was that she was being killed because of her adherence to the Catholic religion, so good and so holy, which she would not abandon so long as she breathed, since she had been baptized in it. She desired in dying no other glory save that her determination should be known far and wide in France, and that her women should tell this when they returned thither. Though she knew it would grieve them to see her on the scaffold and be witnesses of so dark a tragedy, yet she wished them to be present at her death, knowing well she could have no more faithful friends with her to report afterward what had occurred.

Just as she was finished speaking there came a loud knocking at the door. The women, fearing that the time had come to fetch the Queen, wished to prevent the gaolers from entering, but the Queen said to them, "That would be useless, my dears. Open the door."

PIERRE DE BOURDEILLE

LETTER TO POPE GREGORY XI

Most holy and dear and sweet father in Christ sweet Jesus: I your unworthy daughter Catherine, servant and slave of the servants of Jesus Christ, write to you in His precious Blood. With desire have I desired to see in you the fulness of divine grace, in such wise that you may be the means, through divine grace, of pacifying all the universal world. Therefore, I beg you, sweet my father, to use the instrument of your power and virtue, with zeal, and hungry desire for the peace and honour of God and the salvation of souls. And should you say to me, father—"The world is so ravaged! How shall I attain peace?" I tell you, on behalf of Christ crucified, it befits you to achieve three chief things through your power. Do you uproot in the garden of Holy Church the malodorous flowers, full of impurity and avarice, swollen with pride: that is, the bad priests and rulers who poison and rot that garden. Ah me, you our Governor, do you use your power to pluck out those flowers! Throw them away, that they may have no rule! Insist that they study to rule themselves in holy and good life. Plant in this garden fragrant flowers, priests and rulers who are true servants of Jesus Christ, and care for nothing but the honour of God and the salvation of souls, and are fathers of the poor. Alas, what confusion is this, to see those who ought to be a mirror of voluntary poverty, meek as lambs, distributing the possessions of Holy Church to the poor: and they appear in such luxury and state and pomp and worldly vanity, more than if they had turned them to the world a thousand times! Nay, many seculars put them to shame who live a good and holy life. But it seems that Highest and Eternal Goodness is having that done by force which is not done by like; it seems that He is permitting dignities and luxuries to be taken away from His Bride, as if He would show that Holy Church should return to her first condition, poor, humble, and meek as she was in that holy time when men took note of nothing but the honour of God and the salvation of souls, caring for spiritual things and not for temporal. For ever since she has aimed more at temporal than at spiritual, things have gone from bad to worse. See therefore that God, in judgment, has allowed much persecution and tribulation to befall her. But comfort you, father, and fear not for anything that could happen, which God does to make her state perfect once more, in order that lambs may feed in that garden, and not wolves who devour the honour that should belong to God, which they steal and give to themselves. Comfort you in Christ sweet Jesus; for I hope that His aid will be near you, plentitude of divine grace, aid and support divine in the way that I said before. Out of war you will attain greatest peace; out of persecution, greatest unity; not by human power, but by holy virtue, you will discomfit those visible demons, wicked men, and those invisible demons who never sleep around us.

But reflect, sweet father, that you could not do this easily unless you accomplished the other two things which precede the completion of the other: that is, your return to Rome and uplifting of the standard of the most holy Cross. Let not your holy desire fail on account of any scandal or rebellion of cities which you might see or hear; nay, let the flame of holy desire be more kindled to wish to do swiftly. Do not delay, then, your coming. Do not believe the devil, who perceives his own loss, and so exerts himself to rob you of your possessions in order that you may lose your love and charity and your coming be hindered. I tell you, father in Christ Jesus, come swiftly like a gentle lamb. Respond to the Holy Spirit who calls you. I tell you, Come, come, come, and do not wait for time, since time does not wait for you. Then you will do like the Lamb Slain whose place you hold, who without weapons in His hand slew our foes, coming in gentleness, using only the weapons of the strength of love, aiming only at care of spiritual things, and restoring grace to man who had lost it through sin.

Alas, sweet my father, with this sweet hand I pray you, and tell you to come to discomfit our enemies. On behalf of Christ crucified I tell it you: refuse to believe the counsels of the devil, who would hinder your holy and good resolution. Be manly in my sight, and not timorous. Answer God, who calls you to hold and possess the seat of the glorious Shepherd St. Peter, whose vicar you have been. And raise the standard of the holy Cross; for as we were freed by the Cross—so Paul says—thus raising this standard, which seems to me the refreshment of Christians, we shall be freed—we from our wars and divisions and many sins, the infidel people from their infidelity. In this way you will come and attain the reformation, giving good priests to Holy Church. Fill her heart with the ardent love that she has lost; for she has been so drained of blood by the iniquitous men who have devoured her that she is wholly wan. But comfort you, and come, father, and no longer make to wait the servants of God, who afflict themselves in desire. And I, poor, miserable woman, can wait no more; living, I seem to die in my pain, seeing God thus reviled.

ST. CATHERINE OF SIENA

LETTER TO SISTER DANIELLA OF ORVIETO

Dearest daughter in Christ sweet Jesus: I Catherine, servant and slave of the servants of Jesus Christ, write to you in His precious Blood: with desire to see thee in true and very perfect light, that thou mayest know the truth in perfection. Oh, how necessary this light is to us, dearest daughter! For without it we cannot walk in the Way of Christ crucified, a shining Way that brings us to life; without it we shall walk among shadows and abide in great storm and bitterness. But, if I consider aright, it behooves us to possess two orders of this light. There is a general light, that every rational creature ought to have, for recognizing whom he ought to love and obey—perceiving in the light of his mind by the pupil of most holy faith, that he is bound to love and serve his Creator, loving Him directly, with all his heart and mind, in obeying the commandments of the law to love God above everything, and our neighbour as ourselves. These are the principles by which all men beside ourselves are held. This is a general light, which we are all bound by; and without it we shall die, and shall follow, deprived of the life of grace, the darkened way of the devil. But there is another light, which is not apart from this, but one with it—nay, by this first, one attains to the second. There are those who, observing the commandments of God, grow into another most perfect light; these rise from imperfection with great and holy desire, and attain unto perfection, observing both commandments and counsels in thought and deed. One should use this light with hungry desire for the honour of God and the salvation of souls, gazing therewith into the light of the sweet and loving Word, where the soul tastes the ineffable love which God has to His creatures, shown to us through that Word, who ran enamoured to the shameful death of the Cross, for the honour of the Father and for our salvation.

When the soul has known this truth in the perfect light, it rises above itself, above its natural instincts; with intense, sweet and loving desires, it runs, following the footsteps of Christ crucified, bearing pains, bearing shame, ridicule and insult with much persecution, from the world, and often from the servants of God under pretext of virtue. Hungrily it seeks the honour of God and the salvation of souls; and so much does it delight in this glorious food, that it despises itself and everything else: this alone it seeks, and abandons itself. In this perfect light lived the glorious virgins and the other saints, who delighted only in receiving this food with their Bridegroom, on the table of the Cross. Now to us, dearest daughter and sweet my sister in Christ sweet Jesus, He has shown such grace and mercy that He has placed us in the number of those who have advanced from the general light to the particular—that is, He has made us choose the perfect state of the Counsels: therefore we ought to follow that sweet and straight way perfectly, in true light, not looking back for any reason whatever; not walking in our own fashion but in the fashion of God, enduring sufferings without fault even unto death, rescuing the soul from the hands of devils. For this is the Way and the Rule that the Eternal Truth has given thee; and He wrote it on His body, not with ink, but with His Blood, in letters so big that no one is of such low intelligence as to be excused from reading. Well thou seest the initials of that Book, how great they are; and all show the truth of the Eternal Father, the ineffable love with which we were created—this is the truth—only that we might share His highest and eternal good. Thus our Master is lifted up on high upon the pulpit of the Cross, in order that we may better study it, and should not deceive ourselves, saying: "He teaches this to me on earth, and not on high." Not so: for ascended upon the Cross, and uplifted there in pain, He seeks to exalt the honour of the Father, and to restore the beauty of souls. Then let us read heartfelt love, founded in truth, in this Book of Life. Lose thyself wholly; and the more thou shalt lose the more thou shalt find; and God will not despise thy desire. Nay, He will direct thee, and show thee what thou shouldst do; and will enlighten him to whom thou mightest be subject, if thou dost according to His counsel. For the soul that prays ought to have a holy jealousy, and let it always rejoice to do whatever it does with the help of prayer and counsel.

ST. CATHERINE OF SIENA

DIALOGUE OF THE HEART

Worldly Heart. Prithee tell me, Solitary Heart, why dost thou keep in this desert place? How canst thou live thus hidden away from the world, with none other to comfort thee and be thy companion?

Solitary Heart. Let me assure thee, Worldly Heart, that I am not in the least sad, but rather that I keep cheerful and free.

Worldly Heart. Whence, then, cometh the happiness thou canst have in this place? Thou art solitary; and love is something that can only exist when there is more than one.

Solitary Heart. Thou canst not, I tell thee, Worldly Heart, perceive that which causes my ecstasy within.

Worldly Heart. And why not, prithee? Dost thou think me blind, or without eyes to behold, or minus understanding? Thou thinkest me foolish, seemingly, though the world judges me wise.

Solitary Heart. Permit God to make answer for me with the

words of His Prophet, *homo cum in honore esset non intellexit.* He who striveth not to raise himself up unto God, and so to know, love, praise and honor Him, is like unto a wild beast, which is without understanding, liveth only for his body's pleasure, and acteth as if he had not been fashioned according to the very image and likeness of God.

JOHN GERSON

O SWEET AND SAVOURY WORD

Behold my God and my all.

What can I wish more; and what happier thing can I long for?

O sweet and savoury word; to him that is who loveth the Word: not the world nor the things that are in the world.

My God and my all.

To him that understands enough is said: and to repeat it often is delightful to him that loveth. For when Thou art present all things are delightful: but when Thou art absent, all is wearisome. Thou makest quietness of heart and great peace: and festive joy. Thou makest us to think well of all things and in all to praise Thee: neither can any thing please long without Thee; but if it is to be pleasant and palatable: Thy grace must be present, and it must be seasoned with the seasoning of Thy Wisdom. If Thou art sweet, all is sweet: if Thou art not sweet; what can please?

But the wise men of the world and they to whom the flesh is sweet are poor in Thy sweet wisdom: for in the world is utter vanity, and in the flesh is death. But they that follow Thee through contempt of worldly things and mortification of the flesh; are known to be truly wise: for they are translated from vanity to truth from flesh to spirit. To these God is sweet; and what good soever is found in creatures: they make the theme for praise of their Creator.

But great yea very great is the difference between the sweetness of the Creator and of the creature: of Eternity and of time: of Light uncreated and of light enlightened.

O Everlasting Light, surpassing all created luminaries: dart the beams of Thy brightness from above and penetrate all the corners of my heart. Purify, beatify, beautify and vivify my spirit with all its powers: that I may cleave unto Thee with transports of jubilation.

O for the coming of that blessed and desirable hour; when Thou wilt satisfy me with Thy presence: and be unto me all in all. So long as this is not granted: neither will my joy be full. Still alas the old man lives in me: not wholly is he crucified, not perfectly is he dead. Still lusts he mightily against the Spirit, stirs up inward wars: nor suffers the kingdom of the soul to be in peace.

But Thou that rulest the Power of the sea and stillest the tossing of its waves: arise and help me. Scatter the nations that delight in war: quell Thou them in Thy might; shew forth Thy wonderful works I beseech Thee: and let Thy right hand be glorified; for there is no other hope or refuge for me: save in Thee, O Lord my God.

THOMAS À KEMPIS

THINGS THAT BRING MUCH PEACE

Son, now will I teach thee the way of peace and true freedom. Lord do as Thou sayest: for this is delightful to me to hear. Study son to do the will of another rather than thine own. Choose always to have less rather than more.

Seek always the lowest place: and to be the inferior to every one.

Wish always and pray: that the will of God may be wholly fulfilled in thee.

Behold such a man enters the land of peace and rest.

Lord this brief discourse of Thine: contains within itself much perfection. It is small in speech: but full of meaning and rich in fruit. For if I could faithfully keep it: I should not be so easily disturbed. For as often as I feel myself restless and heavy: I find that I have gone back from this doctrine. But Thou who canst do all things and ever lovest the profit of my soul; increase in me Thy grace: that I may be able to fulfil Thy words, and to work out my salvation.

THOMAS À KEMPIS

A PRAYER AGAINST EVIL THOUGHTS

Lord my God be not Thou far from me: my God have regard to help me; for there have risen up against me various thoughts and great fears: afflicting my soul. How shall I pass through unhurt? how shall I break them to pieces?

I will go before thee saith He: and will humble the great ones of the earth. I will open the doors of the prison: and reveal unto thee hidden secrets.

Do Lord as Thou sayest: and let all evil thoughts fly from Thy face. This is my hope my one only consolation, to flee unto Thee in every tribulation; to trust in Thee, to call upon Thee from my inmost heart: and to wait patiently for Thy consolation.

THOMAS À KEMPIS

A PRAYER FOR MENTAL ILLUMINATION

O good Jesu enlighten me with the shining of inner light: and remove away all darkness from the habitation of my heart; Repress Thou my many wandering thoughts: and break in pieces those temptations which violently assault me. Fight Thou strongly for me and vanquish the evil beasts, I mean the alluring desires of the flesh; that peace may be obtained by Thy power: and that Thine abundant praise may resound in Thy holy court that is in a pure conscience. Command the winds and tempests: say unto the sea Be still and to the north wind Blow not: and there shall be a great calm. Send out Thy Light and Thy Truth that they may shine upon the earth; for I am earth without form and void: until Thou enlighten me. Pour forth Thy grace from above, sprinkle my heart with heavenly dew; supply streams of devotion, to water the face of the earth: that it may bring forth fruit good and excellent.

Lift Thou up my mind which is pressed down by a load of sins: and draw up my whole desire to things heavenly; that when I have tasted the sweetness of celestial happiness: it may be irksome to me to think about earthly things. Do Thou snatch me and deliver me from all fleeting comfort of created things: for no created thing can fully satisfy my desires or console.

Join Thou me to Thyself with an inseparable band of love; for Thou alone canst satisfy him that loves: and without Thee all things are futile.

THOMAS À KEMPIS

TRUE COMFORT

Whatsoever I can desire or imagine for my comfort: I look for it not here, but hereafter. For if I might alone have all the comforts of the world and enjoy all its delights: it is certain that they could not long endure.

Wherefore O my soul thou canst not be fully comforted nor perfectly refreshed: except in God the Comforter of the poor and Sponsor of the humble. Wait a little while O my soul; wait for the divine promise: and thou shalt have abundance of all good things in heaven. If thou desire inordinately the things that are present: thou shalt lose those which are eternal and heavenly. Use temporal things: desire eternal. Thou canst not be satisfied with any temporal good: because thou are not created to enjoy them. Although thou shouldest possess all created goods, yet couldest thou not be happy nor blessed; but in God who created all things, stands thy whole blessedness and felicity: not such as is seen and praised by the foolish lovers of the world; but such as good and faithful servants of Christ wait for, and of which the spiritual and pure in heart: whose conversation is in heaven sometimes have a foretaste.

Vain and brief is all human solace. Blessed and true is the solace: which is received inwardly from the Truth. A devout man bears every where about with him his own Comforter Jesus: and saith unto Him. Be Thou with me Lord Jesu in every place and time. Let this be my consolation: gladly to forego all human comfort. And if Thy consolation be wanting: gladly to forego all human comfort.

And if Thy consolation be wanting: let Thy will and just trial of me be unto me the greatest comfort. For Thou wilt not always be angry: neither wilt Thou threaten for ever.

THOMAS À KEMPIS

HOW GREAT IS THE ABUNDANCE

Now I will speak again Lord and not be silent; I will say in the ears of my God, my Lord and my King: who is on high. O how great is the abundance of Thy sweetness Lord: which Thou hast laid up in secret for them that fear Thee. But what art Thou to those who love Thee; what to those who serve Thee with their whole heart? Truly unspeakable is the sweetness of Thy contemplation: which Thou bestowest on them that love Thee. In this especially Thou hast shewed me the sweetness of Thy charity, that when I was not Thou madest me: when I went far astray from Thee, Thou broughtest me back again that I might serve Thee: and hast commanded me to love Thee.

O Fount of Love unceasing. What shall I say concerning Thee? How can I forget Thee; who hast deigned to remember me, even after I had wasted away and perished? Thou hast shewed mercy to Thy servant beyond all hope: and hast granted favour and friendship beyond all desert. What return shall I make to Thee for this grace? For it is not granted to all, to forsake all renounce the world: and assume the monastic life. Is it a great thing that I should serve Thee; whom all creation is bound to serve? It ought not to seem a great thing to me to serve Thee; but rather this appears great to me and wonderful: that Thou dost condescend to receive into Thy service one so poor and unworthy and to make him one with Thy beloved servants.

Behold all that I have and whereby I serve Thee: is Thine. And yet Thou servest me rather than I Thee.

Behold heaven and earth which Thou hast created for the service of man wait upon Thee: and daily perform whatever Thou hast commanded. And this is little: Thou hast also appointed Angels in their orders to minister to man. Yet is it more adorable than all, that Thou Thyself hast deigned to serve man: and hast promised to give Thyself unto him.

What shall I give Thee for all these thousands of benefits? Would I could serve Thee all the days of my life. Would I were able for one single day to do Thee worthy service. Truly Thou art worthy of all service: all honour and eternal praise. Truly Thou art my Lord, and I Thy poor servant; who am bound to serve Thee with all my might: neither ought I ever to be weary of praising Thee. This is my wish this my desire: and whatsoever is wanting unto me, do Thou vouchsafe to supply.

THOMAS À KEMPIS

JUDGMENT DAY

But at the last day, at the Judgment of God, when we rise again with glorious bodies, in the power of the Lord, these bodies will be white and resplendent as the snow, more brilliant than the sun, more transparent than crystal, and each one will have a special mark of honour and glory, according to the support and endurance of torments and sufferings, willingly and freely borne to the honour of God. For all things shall be regulated and recompensed according to the Wisdom of God and the nobility of our works; and the Christ, our Preceptor and Choir-Master, shall sing with His sweet triumphant voice an eternal canticle to the Praise and Glory of the Heavenly Father. We also shall sing the same hymn, with joyous spirit and clear voice, eternally without end. The happiness and glory of the Soul shall be reflected in our senses and members, as we contemplate one the other with glorified vision, hearing, speaking, and chanting the Praise of our Lord with unfailing voice. The Christ will serve us and show us His illuminated Visage and glorious Body bearing the marks of love and fidelity printed on them.

We shall, too, contemplate the glorified bodies of the Just, clothed in numberless marks of love, spent in the service of God since the beginning of the world; and our sensitive life shall be filled, exteriorly and interiorly, with the Glory of God; the heart full of life burning with ardent love of God, the powers of the Soul resplendent with Glory, ornamented with the gifts of God and the practice of all virtue on earth.

Finally, and beyond all else, ravished out of self into the Glory of God, without limit, incomprehensible, immense, we are to enjoy Him for ever and ever.

The Christ in His human nature shall lead the Choir on the right, for He is the highest and most sublime creation of God, and to this Choir belong all who live in Him and He in them. The other Choir is the angelic, for although they are by Nature the more noble, we have been dowered in a more sublime fashion in Jesus Christ, with Whom we are one. He shall be the supreme Pontiff in the midst of the Choir of Angels and men before the throne of the sovereign Majesty of God, and will offer and renew before His heavenly Father, God Almighty, all offerings that were ever presented by Angels and men, fixed in the Glory of God for ever and ever.

Thus, then, shall our bodies and senses by which we serve God now be glorified and beatified, like unto the glorious Body of the Christ; that Body in which He served God and man. Our Souls, by which we now and always love, thank, and praise God, will then be blessed and glorious spirits, like to the blessed and glorious Soul of the Christ, the Angels and all spirits who love, praise, and bless God; and through the Christ we shall be ravished in God to be with Him in fruition and eternal Beatitude.

BLESSED JOHN RUYSBROECK

ADDRESS TO THE BELOVED

Thou hast placed me, O my Beloved, between my evil and Thy good. On Thy part may there be mercy and pity, patience, humility, pardon, restoration and help; on mine let there be contrition, perseverance and remembrance of Thy sacred passion, with sighs and tears.

O Beloved, thou makest me to love, if Thou aidest me not, why didst Thou will to create me, and why didst Thou endure grief for my sake and bear Thy so grievous passion? Since Thou didst help me thus to rise, my Beloved, help me also to descend to the remembrance and hatred of my faults and failings, that my thoughts may the better rise again to desire, honor and praise Thee.

My will, O Beloved, hast Thou made free to love Thy honor or despise Thy worth, that in my will my love to Thee may be increased; and in granting me this liberty, O Beloved, hast Thou put my will into danger. Remember, then, Thy lover in this danger, that I may place in servitude my free will, praise Thy honor, and multiply tears and grief in my heart.

O Beloved, never from Thee came fault nor failing to Thy Lover, nor can Thy Lover attain to perfection but through Thy grace and mercy. Then, since the Lover has Thee in such possessions, do Thou remember him in his perils and tribulations.

O Beloved, who in one name, Jesus Christ, art called both God and Man, by that name my will seeks to adore Thee as God and Man. And if Thou, Beloved, hast so greatly honored Thy Lover, through none of his merits, why honorest Thou not so many ignorant men, who knowingly have been less guilty of dishonoring Thy name, Jesus Christ, than has this Thy Lover?

RÁMON LULL

QUESTIONS

The Lover passed through divers places and found many men who were rejoicing, laughing and singing and living in great joy and comfort. And he wondered if this world were meant for laughing or for weeping.

So the Virtues came, to pronounce upon that question. And Faith said: "It is for weeping, because the faithless are more in number than the believers." Hope said: "It is for weeping, because few are those who hope in God, whereas many put their trust in the riches of earth." Charity said: "It is for weeping, because so few are those who love God and their neighbor." And there followed the other Virtues, and so they declared all.

The lovers sought to prove Love's messenger, and they said that they should go through the world, crying that worshippers must honor servants as servants and the Lord as a Lord, so that their requests might better be heard, and because there needs not to love, save the Beloved.

They asked Love's messenger whence came to the Beloved so many useless servants, vile, more abject, and more contemptible than secular men. Love's messenger answered and said: "They come through the fault of those whose task it is to furnish their Sovereign, —the King of Kings,—the Beloved,—with servants. They make no question, as they ought, concerning the wisdom nor the lives of those whom they choose. And those whom they will not take for His train they allow to serve the Eternal King in his palace, and in the most holy ministry of His table. Wherefore ought they to fear the severest retributions when they are called by the Beloved to their account."

They asked the Lover: "In which is love greater, in the Lover who lives or in the Lover who dies." He answered: "In the Lover who dies." "And why?" "Because in one who lives for love it may yet be greater, but in one who dies for love it can be no greater."

RÁMON LULL

HOPE IN THE MERCY OF GOD

When I was in the midst of the pleasures of the world, the remembrance of what I owed to God made me sad, and when I was praying to God my worldly affections disturbed me. This is so painful a struggle that I know not how I could have borne it for a month, let alone for so many years. Nevertheless, I can trace distinctly the great mercy of our Lord to me, while thus immersed in the world, in that I had still the courage to pray. I say courage, because I know of nothing in the whole world which requires greater courage than plotting treason against the King, knowing that He knows it, and yet never withdrawing from His presence; for, granting that we are always in the presence of God, yet it seems to me that those who pray are in His presence in a very different sense; for they, as it were, see that He is looking upon them, while others may be for days together without even once recollecting that God sees them.

It is true, indeed, that during these years there were many months, and, I believe, occasionally a whole year, in which I so kept guard over myself that I did not offend our Lord, gave myself much to prayer, and took some pains, and that successfully, not to offend Him. I speak of this now because all I am saying is strictly true; but I remember very little of those good days, and so they must have been few, while my evil days were many. Still, the days that passed over without my spending a great part of them in prayer were few, unless I was very ill, or very much occupied.

When I was ill, I was well with God. I contrived that those about me should be so, too, and I made supplications to our Lord for this grace, and spoke frequently of Him. Thus, with the exception of that year of which I have been speaking, during eight and twenty years of prayer, I spent more than eighteen in that strife and contention which arose out of my attempts to reconcile God and the world. As to the other years, of which I have now to speak, in them the grounds of the warfare, though it was not slight, were changed; but inasmuch as I was—at least, I think so—serving God, and aware of the vanity of the world, all has been pleasant, as I shall show hereafter.

The reason, then, of my telling this at so great length is that, as I have just said, the mercy of God and my ingratitude, on the one hand, may become known; and, on the other, that men may understand how great is the good which God works in a soul when He gives it a disposition to pray in earnest, though it may not be so well prepared as it ought to be. If that soul perseveres in spite of sins, temptations, and relapses, brought about in a thousand ways by Satan, our Lord will bring it at last—I am certain of it—to the harbour of salvation, as He has brought me myself; for so it seems to me now. May His Majesty grant I may never go back and be lost! He who gives himself to prayer is in possession of a great blessing, of which many saintly and good men have written—I am speaking of mental prayer—glory be to God for it! and, if they had not done so, I am not proud enough, though I have but little humility, to presume to discuss it.

I may speak of that which I know by experience; and so, I say, let him never cease from prayer who has once begun it, be his life ever so wicked; for prayer is the way to amend it, and without prayer such amendment will be much more difficult. Let him not be tempted by Satan, as I was, to give it up, on the pretence of humility; let him rather believe that His words are true Who says that, if we truly repent, and resolve never to offend Him, He will take us into His favour again, give us the graces He gave us before, and occasionally even greater, if our repentance deserves it. And as to him who has not begun to pray, I implore him by the love of our Lord not to deprive himself of so great a good.

Herein there is nothing to be afraid of, but everything to hope for. Granting that such a one does not advance, nor make an effort to become perfect, so as to merit the joys and consolations which the perfect receive from God, yet he will by little and little attain to a knowledge of the road which leads to heaven. And, if he perseveres, I hope in the mercy of God for him, seeing that no one ever took Him for his friend that was not amply rewarded; for mental prayer is nothing else, in my opinion, but being on terms of friendship with God, frequently conversing in secret with Him Who, we know, loves us. Now, true love and lasting friendship require certain dispositions; those of our Lord, we know, are absolutely perfect; ours, vicious, sensual, and thankless; and you cannot, therefore, bring yourselves to love Him, as He loves you, because you have not the disposition to do so; and if you do not love Him, yet, seeing how much it concerns you to have His friendship, and how great is His love for you, rise above that pain you feel at being much with Him Who is so different from you.

O infinite Goodness of my God! I seem to see Thee and myself in this relation to one another. O Joy of the angels! when I consider it, I wish I could wholly die of love! How true it is that Thou endurest those who will not endure Thee! Oh, how good a friend art Thou, O my Lord! how Thou comfortest and endurest, and also waitest for them to make themselves like unto Thee, and yet, in the meanwhile, art Thyself so patient of the state they are in! Thou takest into account the occasions during which they seek Thee, and for a moment of penitence forgettest their offences against Thyself.

ST. TERESA OF AVILA

ON THE DISTRIBUTION OF ALMS

Do you feel inclined to give a part of your goods to your relations and friends from the lively affection you bear them? Submit this disposition to the four rules already given for election, which when developed somewhat farther are as follows:

1. All the love I bear my neighbor should, in order to be perfect, be derived from the love of God. Such charity towards Him is, I ought to feel, the beginning and the end of all my affections and attachments. It should be the principal motive governing my conduct, here as in other things.

2. If an unknown person, one I desired to see performing the duties proper to his state in life, one moreover who does perform them with all the perfection of which he is capable, came to seek my advice, what would I counsel him to undertake in order that the Divine glory be served and his own progress towards perfection increased? It should be a course I would adopt myself.

3. Were I at the point of death, what should I wish I had done here and now? Precisely that is what I should be doing.

4. When I am called before the Divine tribunal, what will I wish I had done with my worldly goods? This certainly is what I ought to do at the present moment.

5. If I feel that my heart is too deeply attached to those persons who are united with me by the bonds of nature, I must first submit this attachment itself to the four rules thus far given, without concerning myself as yet with the question of how I shall distribute my possessions or alms. This too complete attachment must be corrected before I make the final arrangement.

6. What portion of the revenues collected in his church should a

perfect ecclesiastic expend upon himself? This question occasions numerous scruples, and many are in constant fear of going too far. The rules mentioned above should be employed in seeking to answer the question and to determine the proper amount.

7. In so far as our expenditures on our person, our house, our furniture, or our servants are concerned, the most perfect and dependable way is to retrench as far as possible whatever is to our convenience or comfort, so that we may conform perfectly with the example given by Jesus Christ, our great High Priest. It is after this general rule, which is applicable to all states in life (although we must make due allowance for different persons and even different conditions) that the Third Council of Carthage, at which Saint Augustine assisted, decided that all the furniture belonging to a bishop should be of low price and should reflect poverty. In the married state, the best example we can cite is that of Saint Joachim and Saint Anne, who every year divided their income into three parts. One was for the poor, the second for the temple and the divine service, and the third for themselves.

ST. IGNATIUS LOYOLA

MICHAELANGELO AND RELIGIOUS ART

Here Messer Lattanzio, who had for some time been silent, said:

One thing I cannot forgive bad painters, and that is their lack of taste in painting images without devotion or judgment in the churches. And I should like our discussion to end with this subject. And certainly no one can approve the want of care with which a very unskilful painter (to call him a painter) sets himself to paint holy images so rashly and ignorantly that, instead of moving men to tears and devotion, they sometimes rather provoke to laughter.

Indeed this is so high an undertaking, went on Michael Angelo, that in order to imitate in some degree the venerable image of Our Lord, it is not enough to be a painter, a great and skilful master; I believe that he must further be of blameless life, even if possible a saint, that the Holy Spirit may inspire his understanding. We read that Alexander the Great forbade on pain of a heavy penalty any other painter to paint him except Apelles, considering him alone capable of painting him with that severity of aspect and liberal look which could not be seen by the Greeks without being praised nor by the barbarians without being feared and worshipped. And if a poor man of this earth made this edict about his portraits, how much more should princes of the Church or State most carefully enact that no one should paint the loving-kindness and mercy of Our Redeemer nor the purity of Our Lady and of the saints except the most eminent painters they can find in their kingdoms and domains. Such a decree would bring fame and praise to any ruler. And in the Old Testament it was the will of God the Father that those who had merely to adorn and paint the ark of the covenant should not only be great and eminent masters but should be inspired with His grace and wisdom; for God said unto Moses that He would fill them with the wisdom and understanding of His spirit in order that they might be able to devise and do all that it could devise and do. And if it was the will of God the Father that the ark of His law should be skilfully adorned and painted, how much more must it be His will that care and judgement should be bestowed on copying His serene countenance and that of His Son our Lord, and the tranquillity, chastity, and beauty of the glorious Virgin Mary, copied by St. Luke the Evangelist; and likewise in the Holy of Holies the countenance of the Saviour which is in San Giovanni Laterano, as we all know, and Messer Francisco better than any. For often badly wrought images distract the attention and prevent devotion, at least with persons who have but little; while those which are divinely fashioned excite even those who have little devotion or sensibility to contemplation and tears and by their austere beauty inspire them with greater reverence and fear.

FRANCISCO DE HOLLANDA

LEONARDO DA VINCI

For the Dominican monks of Santa Maria delle Grazie at Milan, he also painted a Last Supper, which is a most beautiful and admirable work; to the heads of the Apostles in this picture the master gave so much beauty and majesty that he was constrained to leave that of Christ unfinished, being convinced that he could not impart to it the divinity which should appertain to and distinguish an image of the Redeemer. But this work, remaining thus in its unfinished state, has been ever held in the highest estimation by the Milanese, and not by them only, but by foreigners also: Leonardo succeeded to perfection in expressing the doubts and anxiety experienced by the Apostles, and the desire felt by them to know by whom their Master is to be betrayed; in the faces of all appear love, terror, anger, or grief and bewilderment, unable as they are to fathom the meaning of their Lord. Nor is the spectator less struck with admiration by the force and truth with which, on the other hand, the master has exhibited the impious determination, hatred, and treachery of Judas. The whole work indeed is executed with inexpressible diligence even in its most minute part, among other things may be mentioned the table-cloth, the texture of which is copied with such exactitude, that the linen-cloth itself could scarcely look more real.

It is related that the Prior of the Monastery was excessively importunate in pressing Leonardo to complete the picture; he could in no way comprehend wherefore the artist should sometimes remain half a day together absorbed in thought before his work, without making any progress that he could see; this seemed to him a strange waste of time, and he would fain have had him work away as he could make the men do who were digging in his garden, never laying the pencil out of his hand. Not content with seeking to hasten Leonardo, the Prior even complained to the Duke, and tormented him to such a degree that the latter was at length compelled to send for Leonardo, whom he courteously entreated to let the work be finished, assuring him nevertheless that he did so because impelled by the importunities of the Prior. Leonardo, knowing the Prince to be intelligent and judicious, determined to explain himself fully on the subject with him, although he had never chosen to do so with the Prior. He therefore discoursed with him at some length respecting art, and made it perfectly manifest to his comprehension, that men of genius are sometimes producing most when they seem to be labouring least, their minds being occupied in the elucidation of their ideas, and in the completion of those conceptions to which they afterwards give form and expression with the hand. He further informed the Duke that there were still wanting to him two heads, one of which, that of the Saviour, he could not hope to find on earth, and had not yet attained the power of presenting it to himself in imagination, with all that perfection of beauty and celestial grace which appeared to him to be demanded for the due representation of the Divinity incarnate. The second head still wanting was that of Judas, which also caused him some anxiety, since he did not think it possible to imagine a form of feature that should properly render the countenance of a man who, after so many benefits received from his master, had possessed a heart so depraved as to be capable of betraying his Lord and the Creator of the world: with regard to that second, however, he would make search, and after all—if he could find no better, he need never be at any great loss, for there would always be the head of that troublesome and impertinent Prior. This made the Duke laugh with all his heart, he declared Leonardo to be completely in the right, and the poor Prior, utterly confounded, went away to drive on the digging in his garden, and left Leonardo in peace: the head of Judas was then finished so successfully, that it is indeed the true image of treachery and wickedness; but that of the Redeemer remained, as we have said, incomplete. The admirable excellence of this picture, the beauty of its composition, and the care with which it was executed, awakened in the King of France a desire to have it removed into his own kingdom, insomuch that he made many attempts to discover architects, who might be able to secure it by defences of wood and iron, that it might be transported without injury. He was not to be deterred by any consideration of the cost that might be incurred, but the painting, being on the wall, his Majesty was compelled to forego his desire, and the Milanese retained their picture.

GIORGIO VASARI

IMAGE AND REALITY

If, then, the beauties which with these dim eyes of ours we daily see in corruptible bodies (but which are naught but dreams and faintest shadows of beauty) seem to us so fair and gracious that they often kindle most ardent fire in us, and of such delight that we deem no felicity able to equal that which we sometimes feel at a single glance coming to us from a woman's beloved eyes,—what happy wonder, what blessed awe, shall we think is that which fills the souls that attain to the vision of divine beauty! What sweet flame, what delightful burning, must that be thought which springs from the fountain of supreme and true beauty, which never waxes nor wanes: ever fair, and of its own self most simple in every part alike; like only to itself, and partaking of none other; but fair in such wise that all other fair things are fair because they derive their beauty from it.

This is that beauty identical with highest good, which by its light calls and attracts all things to itself, and not only gives intellect to the intellectual, reason to the rational, sense and desire for life to the sensual, but to plants also and to stones communicates motion and that natural instinct of their quality, as an imprint of itself.

Therefore this love is as much greater and happier than the others, as the cause that moves it is more excellent; and hence, just as material fire refines gold, so does this most sacred fire in our souls destroy and consume that which is mortal there, and quickens and beautifies that celestial part which at first, by reason of the senses, was dead and buried in them. This is the Pyre whereon the poets write that Hercules was burned on the crest of Mount Œtna, and by such burning became divine and immortal after death. This is the Burning Bush of Moses, the Cloven Tongues of fire, the Fiery

Chariot of Elias, which doubles grace and felicity in the souls of those who are worthy to behold it, when they leave this earthly baseness and take flight towards heaven.

Let us, then, direct all the thoughts and forces of our soul to this most sacred light, which shows us the way that leads to heaven; and following after it, let us lay aside the passions wherewith we were clothed at our fall, and by the stairway that bears the shadow of sensual beauty on its lowest step, let us mount to the lofty mansion where dwells the heavenly, lovely and true beauty, which lies hidden in the inmost secret recesses of God, so that profane eyes cannot behold it. Here we shall find a most happy end to our desires, true rest from our toil, certain cure for our miseries, most wholesome medicine for our diseases, safest refuge from the boisterous storms of this life's tempestuous sea.

What mortal tongue, then, O most holy Love, can praise thee worthily? Most fair, most good, most wise, thou springest from the union of beauty and goodness and divine wisdom, and abidest in that union, and by that union returnest to that union as in a circle. Sweetest bond of the universe, joining things celestial to things terrestrial, thou with benignant sway inclinest the supernal powers to rule the lower powers, and turning the minds of mortals to their origin, joinest them thereto. Thou unitest the elements in concord, movest nature to produce—and that which is born, to the perpetuation of life. Thou unitest things that are separate, givest perfection to the imperfect, likeness to the unlike, friendship to the unfriendly, fruit to the earth, tranquillity to the sea, vital light to the heavens.

Thou art father of true pleasure, of grace, of peace, of gentleness and good will, enemy to rustic savagery and sloth—in short, the beginning and the end of every good. And since thou delightest to inhabit the flower of beautiful bodies and beautiful souls, and thence sometimes to display thyself a little to the eyes and minds of those who are worthy to behold thee, methinks that now thy abode is here among us.

Deign, then, O Lord, to hear our prayers, pour thyself upon our hearts, and with the splendour of thy most holy fire illumine our darkness and, like a trusted guide, in this blind labyrinth show us the true path. Correct the falseness of our senses, and after our long pursuit of vanities give us true and solid good; make us to inhale those spiritual odours that quicken the powers of the intellect, and to hear the celestial harmony with such accord that there may no longer be room in us for any discord of passion; fill us at that inexhaustible fountain of content which ever delights and never satiates, and gives a taste of true beatitude to all who drink of its living and limpid waters; with the beams of thy light purge our eyes of misty ignorance, to the end that they may no longer prize mortal beauty, and may know that the things which they seemed to see, are not, and that those which they saw not, really are.

BALDESAR CASTIGLIONE

ON THE HEIGHTS

I have this day climbed the highest mountain in this district—its name of *Ventosus* is not undeserved—guided only by a desire to behold what one could see from so extraordinary a height. The thought of such an expedition had been with me for many years. For, as you are aware, I have, by decree of the fate which governs the affairs of men, dwelt in these parts; and the mountain, visible from every point of vantage, is almost constantly before my eyes. At length an impulse seized me finally to put into action what I was daily doing in thought; and then also I happened to be reading yesterday Livy's history of Rome, and by chance my eye lighted on the passage which tells how Philip, King of Macedon (he who fought a war with the Roman people) ascended Mount Haemus in Thessaly.

But when I bethought myself of a suitable companion, scarcely any of my friends, strangely enough, seemed satisfactory in every respect. One seemed too inactive, another too easy-going; one too slow, and another too fast; one too sad, and another too cheerful. This one was more prudent than I could wish, and that one too rash. The silence of the one, the forwardness of another, this one's gravity and stoutness, that one's effervescence and leanness, deterred me. I was discouraged by the cool indifference of the one and the ardent enthusiasm of another. . . . At last I turned homeward for help, and related the affair to my only brother, who is younger than I and well-known to you. He listened with the greatest pleasure, being delighted at my considering him a friend as well as a brother.

On the appointed day we set out from home and arrived by evening at Malaucene, a place at the foot of the mountain, looking north. After staying there a day, we finally climbed the mountain today, with a servant apiece and not without difficulty, since it proved to be an almost inaccessibly steep mass of earth. But *labor omnia vincit improbus,* as the poet well says. The long day, the mild air, the strength and agility of our bodies, and everything else of the same sort aided us on. Our only obstacle was the terrain itself. We met an old shepherd in a valley below the mountain, who tried with many words to dissuade us from the climb. He himself (he said) had once climbed to the very top on an impulse of youthful enthusiasm, and had brought back nothing for his pains save pain and effort. His body and his clothes had been torn by the stones and briars. Never, before or since, had there been talk of anyone's doing as much. While he was shouting these things at us, our desire only grew with each of his warnings—the minds of young people are always incredulous of those who admonish them. Accordingly, when the old man saw that his endeavors were of no avail, he went ahead of us a little way and pointed with his finger to a steep path between the rocks, at the same time giving us a good deal of advice. This last he kept on repeating after we had left him. Having placed in his care whatever of our clothes and other possessions might prove an impediment, we dedicated ourselves vigorously to the ascent and mounted quickly with no other companions.

But, as usually happens, we had no sooner harnessed our energies than we suddenly grew weary. Having gone ahead a little way to the top of a cliff, we were compelled to halt. Then we started anew and pushed forward, though at a much slower pace. My brother, taking a path straight up the mountain, was making for the top; but I, less energetic, was turning downwards, and when called back by my brother and shown the right road I answered that I hoped to find the ascent easier on the other side and would not mind going a greater distance if only I could proceed with less difficulty. Thus I excused my own laziness; and meanwhile my brother was already quite a distance up the mountain, though I was meandering about in the valleys below, by no means finding an easier road and as a matter of fact growing weary by reason of my useless efforts. Then, exhausted and disgusted with myself for walking about aimlessly, I finally resolved to seek the heights and at length, tired and out of breath, joined my brother, who was waiting for me and was quite refreshed as a result. For a time we walked on, side by side. But ere long, forgetting what had happened before, I was straying downward again.

Then, my thoughts flitting suddenly from material to incorporeal things, I addressed these words (or others like them) to myself: "What thou has experienced today quite frequently while climbing this mountain, thou canst not help knowing is like what happens to thee and to many who enter into a life of blessedness; for the life which we term 'blessed' also lies in a high place. Narrow is the way which leads unto it, we are told. Many also are the hills which bar the way, and we must climb with mighty steps from virtue to virtue." I cannot tell you how elevating this thought was to my mind, and my body also seemed spurred on to make what remained of the ascent. . . .

At the top is a little level space on which we rested at last after so much effort. At first, deeply moved by a quality in the air to which I was unaccustomed and by the unrestricted view, I was like one stupified. I looked down; the clouds were under my feet. And now Athos and Olympus were become less incredible to me, beholding as I did in a mountain of lesser fame what I had heard and read of them. Then I turned my eyes towards Italy, which is dearest to my heart. The Alps themselves, stiff and snow-clad, through which the fierce enemy of the Roman name once crossed breaking (if we credit the story) the rocks with vinegar, seemed close to me even though they really were far away. I shall confess that I sighed for the skies of Italy, visible to my mind rather than to my eyes; and a boundless longing came upon me to see my friends and my native land again.

Then a different thought engrossed my mind, diverting it from places to times. I said to myself, "Today it is ten years since thou didst leave Bologna, having abandoned the studies of thy boyhood. O immortal God! O immutable Wisdom! How many changes, and what great ones, in thy character has the time which has passed since then witnessed. I pass over countless things, for I am not yet so safe in port that I can calmly recall the storms through which I passed. Perhaps the time will come when I shall run through them all in the order of their occurrence, prefacing them with the words of Thine Augustine, 'desire to recall my past foulness and the carnal corruptions of my soul, not because I love them, but because I would love Thee, O my God!' "

FRANCESCO PETRARCA

ELIZABETHAN SEMINARIANS

The English College is a house both large and fair, standing in the way to the Pope's Palace, not far from the Castle Sante Angello. In the College the scholars are divided by certain number into every chamber, as in some four, in some six, or so many as the Rector thinketh convenient, as well for the health of the scholars, as the troubling not much room. Every man hath his bed proper to himself, which is two little trestles, with four or five boards laid along over them, and thereon a quilted mattress, as we call it in England, which every morning after they are risen, they fold up their sheets handsomely, laying them in the midst of the bed, and so roll it up to one end, covering it with the quilt, that is their coverlet all the night time.

First in the morning, he that is the porter of the College ringeth a bell; at the sound whereof every student ariseth and turneth up his bed as I have said before. Not long after, the bell ringeth again, when as every one presently kneeling on his knees, prayeth for the space of half an hour; at which time, the bell being tolled again, they arise and bestow a certain time in study, every one having his desk, table and chair to himself very orderly, and all the time of study, silence is used of every one in the chamber, not one offering molestation in speech to another. The time of study expired, the bell calleth them from their chambers down into the Refectorium, where every one taketh a glass of wine and a quarter of a manchet, and so he maketh his collatione. Soon after, the bell is knolled again, when as the students, two and two together, walk to the Roman College, which is the place of school or instruction, where every one goeth to his ordinary lecture, some to Divinity, some to Physic, some to Logic, and some to Rhetoric. There they remain the lecture time, which being done, they return home to the College again, where they spend the time till dinner, in walking and talking up and down the gardens.

And an order there is appointed by the Rector and the Jesuits, and obeyed by all the students, that whosoever doth not in the morning turn up his bed handsomely, or is not on his knees at prayer time, or heareth not Mass before he go to school, or after he comes home, but forgetteth it, or else if he go forth and put not the peg at his name in the table; for there is a table hangeth by the door, which hath a long box adjoining to it, wherein lieth a great company of wooden pegs, and against the name of every scholar written in the table (which is observed by order of the alphabet) there is a hole made, wherein, such as have occasion to go abroad, must duly put a peg, to give knowledge who is abroad and who remaineth within, beside divers other orders they have for slight matters. The neglecting thereof is public penance at dinner time, when as all the students are placed at the tables, such as have so transgressed goeth up into the pulpit (which standeth there because one readeth all the dinner time) and there he sayeth: "Because I have not fulfilled this or that (whatsoever order it be that he hath broken), I am adjured such a penance"; either to kneel in the midst of the hall on his bare knees, and there to say his beads over, or to say certain Pater nosters and Ave Marias, or to stand upright and have a dish of pottage before him on the ground and so to bring up every spoonful to his mouth; or to lose either one or two or three of his dishes appointed for his dinner; or to stand there all the dinner time and eat no meat; and divers other, which according as it is, either afterward he hath his dinner or supper, or else goes without it. And all these penances I have been forced to do, for that I was always apt to break one order or other. . . .

As for their fare, trust me it is very fine and delicate, for every man hath his own trencher, his manchet, knife, spoon and fork laid by it, and then a fair white napkin covering it, with his glass and pot of wine set by him. And the first mess, or "antepast" (as they call it) that is brought to the table, is some fine meat to urge them to have an appetite, as sometime the Spanish anchovies, and sometime stewed prunes and raisins of the sun together, having such fine tart syrup made to them, as I promise you a weak stomach would very well digest them. The second is a certain mess of pottage of that country manner, no meat sod in them, but are made of divers things, whose proper names I do not remember, but me thought they were both good and wholesome. The third is boiled meat, as kid, mutton, chicken and such-like; every man a pretty modicum of each thing. The fourth is roasted meat of the daintest provision that they can get, and sometimes stewed and baked meat, according as pleaseth master cook to order it. The first and last is sometime cheese, sometime preserved conceits, sometime figs, almonds and raisins, a lemon and sugar, a pomegranate, or some such sweet gear; for they know that Englishmen loveth sweet meats.

And all the dinner while, one of the scholars, according as they take it by weekly turn, readeth; first a chapter of their Bible and then in their Martirologium, he readeth the martyrdom of some of the Saints, as Saint Francis, Saint Martin, Saint Longinus, that thrust the spear into Christ's side, Saint Agatha, Saint Barbara, Saint Cecilia, and divers others; among whom they have imprinted the martyrdom of Doctor Story, the two Nortons, John Felton and others calling them by the name of Saints, who were here executed at Tyburn for high treason.

The dinner done, they recreate themselves for the space of an hour, and then the bell calleth them to their chambers, where they stay a while, studying on their lectures given them in the forenoon; anon the bell summoneth them to school again, where they stay not past an hour, but they return home again and so soon as they be come in they go into the Refectorium, and there every one hath his glass of wine and a quarter of a manchet again, according as they had in the morning.

Then they depart to their chambers, from whence at convenient time they are called to exercise of disputation; the divines to a Jesuit appointed for them, and every study to a several Jesuit, where they continue the space of an hour, and afterward till supper time they are at their recreation.

After supper, if it be in winter time, they go with the Jesuits, and sit about a great fire, talking, and in all their talk they strive who shall speak worst of her Majesty, of some of her Council, of some Bishop here, or such-like; so that the Jesuits themselves will often take up their hands and bless themselves, to hear what abominable tales they will tell them. After they have talked a good while, the bell calleth them to their chambers, the porter going from chamber to chamber and lighteth a lamp in every one, so when the scholars come, they alight their lamps, lay down their beds, and go sit at their desks and study a little, till the bell rings, when every one falls on his knees to prayers. Then one of the priests in the chamber, as in every chamber there is some, beginneth the Latin Litany, all the scholars in the chamber answering him, and so they spend the time till the bell rings again, which is for every one to go to bed.

ANTHONY MUNDAY

A POPULAR PREACHER

It happened that for his sins Friar Gerund was favored with the attention and in due time with the intimate friendship of a *Predicator*

Major of the monastery, a gentleman of about the same standing as the lecturer, but of quite different ideas, taste and character. This *Predicator Major* was in the flower of his age, just past three-and-thirty. He was tall, robust and corpulent; his limbs were well set and admirably proportioned; his were a rather prominent belly, a straight neck and an erect gait. There was a bit of a foretop to his circle of hair, which was studiously and precisely rounded. His habit was unfailingly clean, and the folds hung long and even above a neat shoe. Above all his silk skull-cap was adorned with a great deal of comely needlework, which (together with the airy tassel raising itself in the center), was all the happy labor of certain blessed nuns, who were dying for their father *Predicator Major*. In short, he was a most gallant soul, and could boast in addition of a clear and resonant voice, something of a lisp, a special grace in telling a story, a famous talent for mimicry, easy and free movements, a quaint and fetching manner, a roaring style, and boldness of imagery. Nor did he ever forget to sprinkle his sermons with tales, jests, proverbs, and fire-side saws, most gracefully inserted into the discourse. He not only drew the multitudes to his pulpit, but bore the bell in all feminine conversation.

He was one of those polite preachers who never cite the Holy Fathers, nor even the Sacred Evangelists, by their proper names, because they deem that practice vulgar. He called Saint Matthew the "Historian Angel," and referred to Saint John as the "Eagle of Patmos." And so on.

But failure to place the two first fingers of his right hand, with a foppish air, between his neck and the collar of his habit, as if thereby to ease the ebb and tide of breath; neglect of the act of making a couple of affected tosses of the head while announcing his subject, and then of giving two or three little jumps, as it were, or risings upon his toes, at the same time puffing out both his cheeks with an enormous swallow of air, by way of clearing the passage and looking disdain on the little folks below the pulpit; indifference to being most properly trimmed and spruced up whenever he had to preach, which meant flattening his circle of hair and raising the foretop, or to making or not making his private short ejaculation as soon as he entered the pulpit, thereupon drawing airily a yard-wide silk handkerchief of a vivid color out of his left sleeve and shaking it as far as it would go, or to blow the trumpet of his nose sonorously, though nothing should emanate from it save air, and thereupon to tuck the handkerchief back into his sleeve with a series of regular, harmonious pauses, or to cast a haughty glance about him, heightened with a little frown, or to begin with "Blessed, praised and glorified be the Holy Sacrament above all things," etc., or to conclude with, "In the primitive instantaneous being of his natural animation"—no, the reverend father *Predicator Major* would have abhorred the neglect of a tittle of these things, though Saint Paul himself had strenuously maintained that they were all, to say the least, evidences of his not having a grain of gravity, a drop of devotion, a crumb of conscience, a morsel of marrow, or a pinch of penetration. Convince him, if you could! When he saw as plain as the nose on your face that with this preliminary apparatus alone he drew large throngs of people, gained volumes of applause, won hearts for himself, and that there was not a circle, soiree or party at which the topic of conversation first broached was aught else than the last sermon he had preached.

JOSEPH FRANCIS ISLA

THE ADVENTURE OF THE WINDMILLS

Engaged in this discourse, they came in sight of thirty or forty windmills, which are in that plain; and, as soon as Don Quixote espied them, he said to his squire:

"Fortune disposes our affairs better than we ourselves could have desired: look yonder, friend Sancho Panza, where thou mayest discover somewhat more than thirty monstrous giants, whom I intend to encounter and slay, and with their spoils we will begin to enrich ourselves; for it is lawful war, and doing God good service to remove so wicked a generation from off the face of the earth."

"What giants?" said Sancho Panza.

"Those thou seest yonder," answered his master, "with their long arms; for some are wont to have them almost of the length of two leagues."

"Look, sir," answered Sancho, "those which appear yonder are not giants, but windmills; and what seem to be arms are the sails, which, whirled about by the wind, make the mill-stone go."

"It is very evident," answered Don Quixote, "that thou art not versed in the business of adventures; they are giants: and, if thou art afraid, get thee aside and pray, whilst I engage with them in fierce and unequal combat."

So saying, he clapped spurs to his steed, notwithstanding the cries his squire sent after him, assuring him that they were certainly windmills, and not giants. But he was so fully possessed that they were giants, that he neither heard the outcries of his squire Sancho, nor yet discerned what they were, though he was very near them, but went on crying out aloud:

"Fly not, ye cowards and vile caitiffs; for it is a single knight who assaults you."

The wind now rising a little, the great sails began to move more rapidly; upon which Don Quixote called out:

"Although ye should have more arms than the giant Briareus, ye shall pay for it."

He recommended himself devoutly to his lady Dulcinea, beseeching her to succour him in the present danger, covering himself with his buckler, and setting his lance in the rest, he rushed on as fast as Rozinante could gallop, and attacked the first mill before him. Having run his lance into the sail, the wind whirled the latter about with so much violence that it broke the lance to shivers, dragging horse and rider after it, and tumbling them over and over on the plain, in very evil plight. Sancho Panza hastened to his assistance, as fast as the ass could carry him; and when he came up to his master, he found him unable to stir, so violent was the blow which he and Rozinante had received in their fall.

"God save me!" quoth Sancho, "did not I warn you to have a care of what you did, for that they were nothing but windmills? And nobody could mistake them, but one that had the like in his head."

"Peace, friend Sancho," answered Don Quixote: "for matters of war are, of all others, most subject to continual change. Now I verily believe, and it is most certainly the fact, that the sage Freston, who stole away my chamber and books, has metamorphosed these giants into windmills, on purpose to deprive me of the glory of vanquishing them, so great is the enmity he bears me! But his wicked arts will finally avail but little against the goodness of my sword."

"God grant it!" answered Sancho Panza; then helping him to rise, he mounted him again upon his steed, which was almost disjointed.

MIGUEL DE CERVANTES SAAVEDRA

THE BUSINESS OF POETRY

Though Poetry may challenge if not priority, yet equality with the best Sciences, both for antiquity and worth, I never set so high a rate upon it, as to give my selfe entirely up to its devotion. It hath too much ayre, and (if without offense to our next transmarine neighbour), wantons too much according to the French garbe. And when it is wholly employed in the soft straines of love, his soule who entertaines it loseth much of that strength which should confirm him man. The nerves of judgement are weakened most by its dalliance, and when woman (I mean only as she is externally faire) is the supreme object of wit, we soone degenerate into effeminacy. For the religion of fancie declines into a mad superstition, when it adores that Idol which is not secure from age and sicknesse. Of such heathens our times afford us a pitied multitude, who can give no nobler testimony of twenty yeares employment than some loose copies of lust happily exprest. Yet these the common people of wit blow up with their breath of praise and honour with the sacred name of Poets:—to which as I believe they can never have any just claime, so shall I not dare by this essay to lay any title, since more sweate and oil he must spend who shall arrogate so excellent an attribute. Yet if the innocency of a chaste Muse shall be more acceptable, and weigh heavier in the balance of esteeme than a fame begot in adultery of study, I doubte I shall leave them no hope of competition. For how unhappy soever I may be in the elocution, I am sure the Theme is worthy enough.

In all those flames in which I burnt, I never felt a wanton heate, nor was my invention ever sinister from the straite way of chastity. And when love builds upon that rocke, it may safely contemne the battery of the waves and threatnings of the wind. Since time that makes a mockery of the firmest structures shall itself be ruinated, before that be demolisht. Thus was the foundation laid. And though my eye in its survey was satisfied, even to curiosity, yet did not my search rest there. The Alabaster, Ivory, Porphyry, Jest, that lent an admirable beauty to the outward building entertained me with but a halfe pleasure, since they stood there only to make sport for ruine. But when my soule grew acquainted with the owner of that mansion, I found that Oratory was dumb when it began to speak her, and wonder (which must necessarily seize the best at that time) a lethargie that dulled too much the faculties of the mind, only fit to busie themselves in discoursing her perfections. Wisdom I encountered there, that could not spend it selfe since it affected silence, attentive only to instructions, as if all her senses had been contracted into hearing; Innocence, so not vitiated by conversation with the world that the subtle-witted of her sex would have termed it ignorance; Wit, which seated its self most in the apprehension, and if not enforced by good manners would scarce have gained the name of affability; Modesty, so timorous that it represented a besieged City, standing watchfully upon her guard, strongest in the loyalty to her Prince. In a word, all those vertues which should restore woman to her primitive state of beauty fully adorned her.

WILLIAM HABINGTON

SALADIN AND ROSADER

In this humor was Saladin, making his brother Rosader his foot-boy for the space of two or three years, keeping him in such servile subjection, as if he had been the son of any country vassal. The young gentleman bore all with patience, till on a day walking in the garden by himself, he began to consider how he was the son of John of Bordeaux, a knight renowned for many victories, and a gentleman famous for his virtues; how contrary to the testament of his father, he was not only kept from his land, and entreated as a servant, but smothered in such secret slavery, as he might not attain to any honorable actions. Alas, quoth he to himself (nature working these effectual passions), why should I, that am a gentleman born, pass my time in such unnatural drudgery? Were it not better either in Paris to become a scholar, or in the court a courtier, or in the field a soldier, than to live a foot-boy to my own brother? Nature hath lent me wit to conceive, but my brother denied me art to contemplate: I have strength to perform any honorable exploit, but no liberty to accomplish my virtuous endeavors: those good parts that God hath bestowed upon me, the envy of my brother doth smother in obscurity; the harder is my fortune, and the more his frowardness. With that casting up his hand he felt hair on his face, and perceiving his beard to bud, for choler he began to blush, and swore to himself he would be no more subject to such slavery. As thus he was ruminating of his melancholy passions, in came Saladin with his men, and seeing his brother in a brown study, and to forget his wonted reverence, thought to shake him out of his dumps thus: "Sir," quoth he, "what, is your heart on your halfpenny, or are you saying a dirge for your father's soul? what, is my dinner ready?" At this question —Rosader turning his head askance, and bending his brows as if anger there had ploughed the furrows of her wrath, with his eyes full of fire—he made this reply, "Dost thou ask me, Saladin, for thy cates? Ask some of thy churls who are fit for such office, I am thine equal by nature, though not by birth, and though thou hast more cards in the bunch, have as many trumps in my hand as thyself. Let me question with thee, why thou hast felled my woods, spoiled my manor houses, and made havoc with such utensils as my father bequeathed unto me? I tell thee, Saladin, either answer me as a brother, or I will trouble thee as an enemy."

At this reply of Rosader's, Saladin smiled as laughing at his presumption, and frowned as checking his folly: he therefore took him up thus shortly: "What, sir! Well I see early pricks the tree that will prove a thorn: hath my familiar conversing with you made you coy, or my good looks drawn you to be thus contemptuous? I can quickly remedy such a fault, and I will bend the tree while it is a want. In faith, sir boy, I have a snaffle for such a headstrong colt. You, sirs, lay hold on him and bind him, and then I will give him a cooling card for his choler." This made Rosader half mad, that stepping to a great rake that stood in the garden, he laid such load upon his brother's men that he hurt some of them, and made the rest of them run away. Saladin, seeing Rosader so resolute, and with his resolution so valiant, thought his heels his best safety, and took him to a loft adjoining the garden, whither Rosader pursued him hotly. Saladin, afraid of his brother's fury, cried out to him thus, "Rosader, be not so rash, I am thy brother, and thy elder, and if I have done thee wrong, I'll make thee amends: revenge not anger in blood, for so shalt thou stain the virtue of old Sir John of Bordeaux: say wherein thou art discontent and thou shalt be satisfied. Brothers' frowns ought not to be periods of wrath: what, man, look not so sourly; I know we shall be friends, and better friends than we have been; for, *amantium ira amoris redintegratio est.*"

These words appeased the choler of Rosader, for he was of a mild and courteous nature, so that he laid down his weapons, and upon the faith of a gentleman assured his brother he would offer him no prejudice: whereupon Saladin came down, and after a little parley, they embraced each other and became friends, and Saladin promising Rosader the restitution of all his lands, and what favor else, quoth he, anyways my ability or the nature of a brother may perform.

THOMAS LODGE

V

AN EXPANDING FAITH

Let us make use of a parable, Theotimus, seeing that this method was so agreeable to the sovereign Master of the love which we are teaching. A great and brave King, having espoused a most amiable young princess, and having on a certain day led her into a very retired cabinet, there to converse with her more at his pleasure, after some discourse saw her by a certain sudden accident fall down as dead at his feet. Alas! he was extremely disturbed at this, and it well nigh put him also into a swoon; for she was dearer to him than his own life. Yet the same love that gave him this assault of grief, gave him an equal strength to sustain it, and set him into action to remedy, with an incomparable promptitude, the evil which had happened to the dear companion of his life. Therefore rapidly opening a sideboard which stood by, he takes a cordial-water, infinitely precious, and having filled his mouth with it, by force he opens the lips and the set teeth of his well-beloved princess, then breathing and spurting the precious liquour, which he held in his mouth, into that of his poor lifeless one who lay in a swoon, and pouring what was left in the phial about the nostrils, the temples, and the heart, he made her return to herself and to her senses again; that done, he helps her up gently, and by virtue of remedies so strengthens and revives her, that she begins to stand and walk very quietly with him; but in no sort without his help, for he goes assisting and sustaining her by her arm, till at length he lays to her heart an epithem so precious and of so great virtue, that finding herself entirely restored to her wonted health, she walks all alone, her dear spouse not now sustaining her so much, but only holding her right hand softly between his, and his right arm folded over hers on to her bosom. Thus he went on treating her, and fulfilling to her in all this four most agreeable offices: for 1. He gave testimony that his heart was lovingly careful of her. 2. He continued ever a little nursing her. 3. If she had felt any touch of her former faintness he would have sustained her. 4. If she had lighted in any rough and diffcult place in her walking he would have been her support and stay: and in accidents, or when she would make a little more haste, he raised her and powerfully succoured her. In fine he stayed by her with this heartfelt care till night approached, and then he assisted to lay her in her royal bed.

The soul is the spouse of Our Saviour when she is just; and because she is never just but when she is in charity, she is also no sooner spouse than she is led into the cabinet of those delicious perfumes mentioned in the Canticles. Now when the soul which has been thus honoured commits sin, she falls as if dead in a spiritual swoon; and this is in good truth a most unlooked-for accident: for who would ever think that a creature could forsake her Creator and sovereign good for things so trifling as the allurements of sin? Truly the heavens are astonished at it, and if God were subject to passions he would fall down in a swoon at this misfortune, as when He was mortal He died upon the cross for our redemption. But seeing it is not necessary that He should employ His love in dying for us, when He sees the soul overthrown by sin He commonly runs to her succour, and by an unspeakable mercy, lays open the gates of her heart by the stings and remorses of conscience which come from the divers lights and apprehensions which He casts into our hearts, with salutary movements, by which, as by odorous and vital liquours, He makes the soul return to herself, and brings her back to good sentiments. And all this, Theotimus, God works in us without our action, by his all-amiable Goodness which prevents us with its sweetness. For even as our bride, having fainted, would have died in her swoon, if the King had not assisted her; so the soul would remain lost in her sin if God prevented her not. But if the soul thus excited add her consent to the solicitation of grace, seconding the inspiration which prevents her, and accepting the required helps provided for by God; He will fortify her, and conduct her through various movements of faith, hope and penitence, even till he restore her to her true spiritual health, which is no other thing than charity. And while He thus makes her walk in the virtues by which He disposes her to this holy love, He does not conduct her only, but in such sort sustains her, that as she for her part goes as well as she is able, so He on His part supports and sustains her; and it is hard to say whether she goes or is carried; for she is not so carried that she goes not, and yet her going is such that if she were not carried she could not go. So that, to speak apostolically, she must say: I walk, not I alone, but the grace of God with me.

But the soul being entirely restored to her health by the excellent epithem of charity which the Holy Ghost infuses into her heart, she is then able to walk and keep herself upon her feet of herself, yet by virtue of this health and this sacred epithem of holy love. Wherefore though she is able to walk of herself, yet is she to render the glory thereof to God, who has bestowed upon her a health so vigorous and strong: for whether the Holy Ghost fortify us by the motions which He enables our heart to make, or sustain us by the charity which He infuses into them, whether He succour us by manner of assistance in raising and carrying us, or strengthen our hearts by pouring into them fortifying and quickening love, we always live, walk, and work, in Him and by Him.

And although by means of charity poured into our hearts, we are able to walk in the presence of God, and make progress in the way of salvation, yet still it is the goodness of God which ever helps the soul to whom He has given His love, continually holding her with His holy hand; for so 1. He doth better make appear the sweetness of His love towards her. 2. He ever animates her more and more. 3. He supports her against depraved inclinations and evil habits contracted by former sins. 4. And finally, He supports her and defends her against temptations.

ST. FRANCIS DE SALES

COURTESY

We are only men by our reason, and yet it is a rare thing to find men really reasonable, inasmuch as self-love usually leads us astray from reason, conducting us insensibly into a thousand kinds of little but dangerous acts of injustice and wickedness, which, like the little foxes of whom mention is made in the Canticles, destroy the vines. For inasmuch as they are small, we do not take care of them; and because they are so numerous, they do not fail to do much damage. The things I am about to speak about to you, are they not unjust and unreasonable?

We accuse our neighbour for very little, and we excuse ourselves a great deal. We wish to sell at a high price and to buy at a low price. We wish to see justice rendered in the house of another, and mercy and indulgence at home. We wish our words to be taken in good part, and are froward and sensitive as to those of another. We would have our neighbour leave us his goods when we pay the money; is it not more just that he should keep them, and leave us our money? We take it in bad part that he will not accommodate us, has he not more reason to be angry because we will not accommodate him?

If we are attached to one practice, we despise all the rest, and criticise everything which is not to our taste. If there is one of our inferiors who has not shewn good grace, or against whom we have at some time shewn our teeth, whatever he does, we take it badly; we do not cease to vex him and are always quarrelling with him. On the other hand, if some one is agreeable to us in a manner pleasing to our senses there is nothing he does which we do not excuse. There are some children who are virtuous whom their fathers and mothers can scarcely ever see because of some bodily imperfection. There are some who are vicious, who are favourites because of some bodily grace. Upon the whole we prefer the rich to the poor, though they be not of better position or so virtuous. We prefer even those who dress best. We wish to exact our rights, but expect others to be courteous in the exaction of theirs. We assert our rank punctiliously, and wish that others should be humble and condescending. We complain lightly of a neighbour, and do not wish any one to complain of us. That which we do for another seems to us always a great deal, that which he does for us seems to us to be nothing. In short, we are like the partridges of Paphlagonia, who have two hearts; for we have one heart which is gentle, gracious, and courteous on our own behalf, and one heart which is hard, severe, and rigorous towards our neighbour. We have two weights, one to weigh our own convenience with greatest advantage to ourselves, the other to weigh that of our neighbour with the greatest disadvantage which is possible. Now, as the Scripture says, "Deceitful lips have spoken in one heart and one heart"; that is to say, they have two hearts. And to have two weights, the one heavy to receive, the other light to give, is a thing abominable before God.

Philothea, be equal and just in your actions. Place yourself always in the position of your neighbour, and place him in yours, and thus you will judge well. Make yourself a seller when you are buying, and a buyer when you are selling, and you will sell and buy justly. All this injustice is mean, because it does not oblige us to make restitution, inasmuch as we remain only within the limits of strictness in that which is favourable to ourselves. But it does not clear us of our obligation to make amends, for it is a great fault of reason and charity. And, when all is said, it is only treachery. For we lose nothing by living generously, nobly, courteously, and with a heart that is royal, equal, and reasonable. Remember then, dear Philothea, to examine your heart often, whether it has such regard for your neighbour as you would wish his to have for you if you were in his place; for here is the secret of true reason. Trajan being blamed by his advisers because in their opinion he rendered the imperial majesty too accessible: "Ought I not," said he, "to be such an emperor in regard to private people as I should desire to meet with as an emperor if I were myself a private person?"

ST. FRANCIS DE SALES

BROTHER LAWRENCE

The first time I saw Brother Lawrence was upon the third of August 1666. He told me that God had done him a singular favour, in his conversion at the age of eighteen.

That in the winter, seeing a tree stripped of its leaves and considering that within a little time the leaves would be renewed, and after that the flowers and fruit appear, he received a high view of the Providence and Power of God, which has never since been effaced from his soul. That this view had set him perfectly loose from the world, and kindled in him such a love for God, that he could not tell whether it had increased in above forty years that he had lived since.

That he had been footman to M. Fieubert, the treasurer, and that he was a great awkward fellow, who broke everything.

That he had desired to be received into a monastery, thinking that he would there be made to smart for his awkwardness, and the faults he should commit: but that God had disappointed him, he having met with nothing but satisfaction in that state.

That we should establish ourselves in a sense of God's Presence, by continually conversing with Him. That it was a shameful thing to quit His conversation to think of trifles and fooleries.

That we should feed and nourish our souls with high notions of God; which would yield us great joy in being devoted to Him.

That we ought to quicken, i. e., to enliven our faith. That it was lamentable that we had so little; and that instead of taking faith for the rule of their conduct, men amused themselves with trivial devotions, which changed daily. That the way of faith was the spirit of the Church, and that it was sufficient to bring us to a high degree of perfection.

That we ought to give ourselves up entirely to God, with regard both to things temporal and spiritual, and seek our satisfaction only in the fulfilling of His will, whether He lead us by suffering or by consolation; for all would be equal to a soul truly resigned. That there was need of fidelity in those times of dryness, or insensibility and irksomeness in prayer, by which God tries our love to Him: that then was the time for us to make good and effectual acts of resignation, whereof one alone would oftentimes very much promote our spiritual advancement.

That as for the miseries and sins he heard of daily in the world, he was so far from wondering at them, that, on the contrary, he was surprised that there were not more, considering the malice sinners were capable of: that for his part, he prayed for them; but knowing that God could remedy the mischiefs they did, when He pleased, he gave himself no further trouble.

That to arrive at such resignation as God requires, we should watch attentively over all the passions, which mingle as well in spiritual things as those of a grosser nature; that God would give light concerning those passions to those who truly desire to serve Him. That if this was my design, viz., sincerely to serve God, I might come to him (B. Lawrence) as often as I pleased, without any fear of being troublesome; but, if not, that I ought no more to visit him.

THE PRACTICE OF THE PRESENCE OF GOD

PRAYER

The devotion of the present day seems to me faulty in one point, namely, that people talk too much about their prayer, and its special conditions. Instead of dwelling so much upon the various stages of prayer, it would be better simply to pray as God leads one, without fidgeting one's self to analyse and discuss so much. I see nothing tending to show that one is always in the same condition, or that there is any fixed state of prayer: the Holy Spirit one while casts the soul down, at another time lifts it up—now He seems to be leading it to perfection, and the next moment He brings it back where it was. Our business is to conform in all such changes to His leading, and go whither He draws us.

When thoughts offer themselves, we should use them if good, and if a truth takes possession of the mind, we must fix our heart upon it, turn it into practical resolutions, and above all pray that God Who inspires us with it would enable us to bring it to good effect.

I think people make a great mistake in drawing so many fine distinctions concerning the Essence and Attributes of God. A prayer framed upon these definitions becomes very complex. In a word true prayer, and that which is best, lies in whatever unites us to God, whatever enables us to enjoy Him, to appreciate Him, to rejoice in His Glory, and to love Him as one's very own; so that, not satisfied with words or thoughts or affections or resolutions, one comes to a solid practice of detachment from self and from all creatures.

Above all, it is desirable not to perplex the brain or over-excite the feelings, but to take that which comes within our spiritual grasp, and to let ourselves be drawn gently to God, without the intervention of violent efforts, which are more the work of imagination than a substantial lasting good. If we feel a sensible delight, we may take it *en passant,* and as it flows by let one's self be drawn in the very depths of the soul into God, loving Him Himself, and not merely the pleasure we derive from Him;—His truth more than the satisfaction with which it fills us. . . . Follow the path God opens to you without hesitation; do not desire a higher kind of prayer in order to be more united to God, but desire a higher and closer union with Him, that He may fill and absorb you more and more, that you may be as wholly His by your own will, as you are in right of creation and redemption. . . .

JACQUES-BÉNIGNE BOSSUET

AT THE PROFESSION OF MADAME DE LA VALLIÈRE

Holy Spirit, Spirit of Peace, I have prepared the way for Thee by preaching Thy word. Perhaps my voice has been like unto the rushing sound which once announced Thy descending. Come upon us now, O Fire Invisible, and may the tongues of flame with which Thou speakest in the hearts of men fill them with heavenly heat. Give unto them a taste of life eternal, the business of which is to know God and to love Him. Show unto them a dim vision of what faith discovers, give them the savour of the possession of Thee in hope, serve unto them a drop from the torrent of delights which enchant the Blessed in the heavenly transports of Divine affection. And do you, my Sister, who have begun to taste of these chaste pleasures, rise from your seat. Go to the altar. Victim of penitence, hurry to consummate your sacrifice. The fire is kindled, the incense is ready, the knife has been drawn—that knife which is the word that sunders the soul from itself in order to attach it to its God alone. The Bishop awaits you with the mysterious veil which you have demanded of him. Wrap yourself in that veil. Live hidden even unto yourself, even as you will be hidden from all the world. Then, known to God, escape from your own self, rise from that self, and make so lofty a flight that you will henceforth find no resting place save in the eternal essence of the Father, the Son and the Holy Spirit.

JACQUES-BÉNIGNE BOSSUET

THE EDUCATION OF GIRLS

Nothing is more neglected than the education of girls. Custom and the caprice of mothers frequently decide everything: people suppose that they ought to give but little instruction to this sex. The education of boys passes for one of the principal concerns of life through its relation to the public weal; and although scarcely fewer mistakes are made than in the education of girls, people are at least persuaded that much intelligence is needed to succeed in it. The cleverest people have endeavored to give rules in this matter. How many teachers and colleges we see! What expense for the printing of books, for the researches of science, for methods of learning the languages, for the choice of professors! All this great preparation often has more superficiality than solidity; but it indicates the high conception people have of the education of boys. As for girls, they say, it is not necessary that they be learned, curiosity renders them vain and affected; it is enough if they know how to govern some day their households, and to obey their husbands without question. People do not fail to refer to many women whom science has rendered ridiculous: after which they believe themselves justified in blindly abandoning girls to the management of ignorant and indiscreet mothers.

It is true that we should fear making ridiculous scholars. Women ordinarily have minds weaker and more inquisitive than men; thus it is not expedient to engage them in studies that might turn their heads. They are not to govern the state, make war, or enter the secred ministry; accordingly they can dispense with certain branches of knowledge which belong to statecraft, the art of war, jurisprudence, philosophy, and theology. The greater part of the mechanic arts does not suit them: they are constituted for moderate exertion. Their bodies, as well as their minds, are less strong and robust than those of men; in return, nature has given them industry, neatness, and economy, to occupy them tranquilly in their homes.

But what follows from this natural weakness of women? The more they are weak, the more important is it to make them strong. Have they not duties to perform, even duties which form the foundation of all human life? Is it not women that ruin or uphold families, that regulate all the details of domestic life, and that decide, consequently, what touches most closely the whole human race? In that way they have the principal part in the good or the bad manners of almost the entire world. A judicious, diligent, and pious wife is the soul of a great household; she introduces order there for temporal welfare and future salvation. Even men, who have all authority in public, can not, by their deliberations, establish any efficient good, if women do not aid them to execute it.

The world is not a phantom; it is the union of all the families; and who can govern them with a nicer care than women who, besides their natural authority and their diligence in the household, have still the advantage of being born painstaking, attentive to details, industrious, winning, and persuasive? Can men themselves hope for any happiness in life, if their most intimate relation, which is that of marriage, turns to bitterness? And what will become of the children, who are later to constitute the human race, if their mothers spoil them from infancy?

These, then, are the occupations of women, which are scarcely less important to the public than those of men, since they have households to regulate, husbands to make happy, and children to bring up well. Add to this that virtue is no less for women than for men; without speaking of the good or ill they can do to the public, they are the half of the human race, redeemed by the blood of Jesus Christ, and destined to eternal life.

Finally, we must consider, besides the good which women do when they are well brought up, the evil which they cause in the world when they lack an education which inspires them with virtue. It is unquestionable that the bad education of women does more harm than that of men, since the disorders of men often come both from the evil training which they have received from their mothers, and from the passions which other women have inspired in them at a more advanced age. What intrigues are presented to us in history, what overturnings of laws and manners, what bloody wars, what innovations in religion, what revolutions in the state, caused by the profligacy of women! These are the considerations that prove the importance of giving girls a good education: let us seek the means of doing so.

FÉNELON

THE WAGER

Infinite—nothing.—Our soul is cast into a body, where it finds number, time, dimension. Thereupon it reasons, and calls this nature, necessity, and can believe nothing else.

Unity joined to infinity adds nothing to it, no more than one foot to an infinite measure. The finite is annihilated in the presence of the infinite, and becomes a pure nothing. So our spirit before God, so our justice before divine justice. There is not so great a disproportion between our justice and that of God, as between unity and infinity.

The justice of God must be vast like His compassion. Now justice to the outcast is less vast, and ought less to offend our feelings than mercy towards the elect.

We know that there is an infinite, and are ignorant of its nature. As we know it to be false that numbers are finite, it is therefore true that there is an infinity in number. But we do not know what it is. It is false that it is even, it is false that it is odd; for the addition of a unit can make no change in its nature. Yet it is a number, and every number is odd or even (this is certainly true of every finite number).

So we may well know that there is a God without knowing what He is. Is there not one substantial truth, seeing there are so many things which are not the truth itself?

We know then the existence and nature of the finite, because we also are finite and have extension. We know the existence of the infinite, and are ignorant of its nature, because it has extension like us, but not limits like us. But we know neither the existence nor the nature of God, because He has neither extension nor limits.

But by faith we know His existence; in glory we shall know His nature. Now, I have already shown that we may well know the existence of a thing, without knowing its nature.

Let us now speak according to natural lights.

If there is a God, He is infinitely incomprehensible, since, having neither parts nor limits, He has no affinity to us. We are then incapable of knowing either what He is or if He is. This being so, who will dare to undertake the decision of the question? Not we, who have no affinity to Him.

Who then will blame Christians for not being able to give a reason for their belief, since they profess a religion for which they cannot give a reason? They declare, in expounding it to the world, that it is a foolishness, *stultitiam;* and then you complain that they do not prove it! If they proved it, they would not keep their word; it is in lacking proofs, that they are not lacking in sense. "Yes, but although this excuses those who offer it as such, and takes away from them the blame of putting it forward without reason, it does not excuse those who receive it." Let us then examine this point, and say, "God is, or He is not." But to which side shall we incline? Reason can decide nothing here. There is an infinite chaos which separated us. A game is being played at the extremity of this infinite distance where heads or tails will turn up. What will you wager? According to reason, you can do neither the one thing nor the other; according to reason, you can defend neither of the propositions.

Do not then reprove for error those who have made a choice; for you know nothing about it. "No, but I blame them for having made, not this choice, but a choice; for again both he who chooses heads and he who chooses tails are equally at fault, they are both in the wrong. The true course is not to wager at all."

Yes; but you must wager. It is not optional. You are embarked. Which will you choose then? Let us see. Since you must choose, let us see which interests you least. You have two things to lose, the true and the good; and two things to stake, your reason and your will, your knowledge and your happiness; and your nature has two things to shun, error and misery. Your reason is no more shocked in choosing one rather than the other, since you must of necessity choose. This is one point settled. But your happiness? Let us weigh the gain and the loss in wagering that God is. Let us estimate these two chances. If you gain, you gain all; if you lose, you lose nothing. Wager, then without hesitation that He is.—That is very fine. Yes, I must wager; but I may perhaps wager too much.—Let us see. Since there is an equal risk of gain and of loss, if you had only to gain two lives, instead of one, you might still wager. But if there were three lives to gain, you would have to play (since you are under the necessity of playing), and you would be imprudent, when you are forced to play, not to chance your life to gain three at a game where there is an equal risk of loss and gain. But there is an eternity of life and happiness. And this being so, if there were an infinity of chances, of which one only would be for you, you would still be right in wagering one to win two, and you would act stupidly, being obliged to play, by refusing to stake one life against three at a game in which out of an infinity of chances there is one for you, if there were an infinity of an infinitely happy life to gain. But there is here an infinity of an infinitely happy life to gain, a chance of gain against a finite number of chances of loss, and what you stake is finite. It is all divided; wherever the infinite is and there is not an infinity of chances of loss against that of gain, there is no time to hesitate, you must give all. And thus, when one is forced to play, he must renounce reason to preserve his life, rather than risk it for infinite gain, as likely to happen as the loss of nothingness.

For it is no use to say it is uncertain if we will gain, and it is certain that we risk, and that the infinite distance between the certainty of what is staked and the uncertainty of what will be gained, equals the finite good which is certainly staked against the uncertain infinite. It is not so, as every player stakes a certainty to gain an uncertainty, and yet he stakes a finite certainty to gain a finite uncertainty, without transgressing against reason. There is not an infinite distance between the certainty staked and the uncertainty of the gain; that is untrue. In truth, there is an infinity between the certainty of gain and the certainty of loss. But the uncertainty of the gain is proportioned to the certainty of the stake according to the proportion of the chances of gain and loss. Hence it comes that, if there are as many risks on one side as on the other, the course is to play even; and then the certainty of the stake is equal to the uncertainty of the gain, so far is it from fact that there is an infinite distance between them. And so our proposition is of infinite force, when there is the finite to stake in a game where there are equal risks of gain and of loss, and the infinite to gain. This is demonstrable; and if men are capable of any truths, this is one.

"I confess it, I admit it. But, still, is there no means of seeing the faces of the cards?" Yes, Scripture and the rest, etc. "Yes, but I have my hands tied and my mouth closed; I am forced to wager, and am not free. I am not released, and am so made that I cannot believe. What, then, would you have me do?"

True. But at least learn your inability to believe, since reason brings you to this, and yet you cannot believe. Endeavour then to convince yourself, not by increase of proofs of God, but by the abatement of your passions. You would like to attain faith, and do not know the way; you would like to cure yourself of unbelief, and ask the remedy for it. Learn of those who have been bound like you, and who now stake all their possessions. These are people who know the way which you would follow, and who are cured of an ill of which you would be cured. Follow the way by which they began; by acting as if they believed, taking the holy water, having masses said, etc. Even this will naturally make you believe, and deaden your acuteness.—"But this is what I am afraid of."—And why? What have you to lose?

But to show you that this leads you there, it is this which will lessen the passions, which are your stumbling-blocks.

The end of this discourse.—Now, what harm will befall you in taking this side? You will be faithful, honest, humble, grateful, generous, a sincere friend, truthful. Certainly you will not have those poisonous pleasures, glory and luxury; but will you not have others? I will tell you that you will thereby gain in this life, and that, at each step you take on this road, you will see so great certainty of gain, so much nothingness in what you risk, that you will at last recognize that you have wagered for something certain and infinite, for which you have given nothing.

"Ah! This discourse transports me, charms me," etc.

If this discourse pleases you and seems impressive, know that it is made by a man who has knelt, both before and after it, in prayer to that Being, infinite and without parts, before whom he lays all he has, for you also to lay before Him all you have for your own good and for His glory, that so strength may be given to lowliness.

BLAISE PASCAL

PATIENCE

If you wish to pray for some length of time, for half an hour it may be, or even for a whole hour and more, you will join to your prayer the meditation on the Life and Passion of Jesus Christ, always applying His actions to that virtue which you desire.

For example, if you desire to obtain as a grace the virtue of patience, you will perchance take for meditation some points in the mystery of the scourging.

First, How, after the order given by Pilate, the Lord was dragged by the ministers of wickedness, with shouts and mockery, to the place appointed for the scourging.

Secondly, How He was stripped by them in haste and fury, and his flesh, in its spotless purity, left altogether exposed and naked.

Thirdly, How His innocent hands were bound together by a rough cord to the column.

Fourthly, How His body was altogether torn and lacerated by the scourges, so that streams of His divine blood ran down to the ground.

Fifthly, How blows upon blows falling in one and the same place, the wounds already made were always more and more irritated.

When you have thus set before you these or similar points of meditation that you may acquire patience, you will first of all apply your senses to feel as vividly as possible the most bitter anguish and the sharp pains which in each part of His most sacred Body, and in all together, your dear Lord endured.

Then you will pass to His most holy Soul, penetrating as far as possible the patience and meekness with which He bore so great afflictions, and yet not satisfying the hunger of suffering greater and more horrible torments for the honor of His Father and for our benefit.

Gaze then on Him, burning with a lively desire that you may bear your trouble, and see how, still turning to the Father, He prays for you that He may deign to give you grace to bear with patience the cross which is now tormenting you, and any other whatever.

And then, bending your will again and again that it may be willing to bear all with a patient mind, turn your mind again to the Father; and thanking Him first that of His pure love He has sent His only-begotten Son into the world to bear so many hard torments and to pray for us, ask of Him again the virtue of patience in virtue of the works and the prayers of His dear Son.

LORENZO SCUPOLI

THE DISCOVERY OF DIVINITY

Now, mark that God may be found in many ways in which the soul receives instruction. First, the soul finds God her Creator on the heights of penance or penitence. Therefore the soul must, above all things, exert all her strength to subdue her own free will, ready, for

God's sake, to learn to give up all things, both great and small, to do hard penance, and to punish herself for following the will she had forsaken. The more the soul exercises herself in these works, the more will she find God in her, and herself in God. This is shown in the Book of Love; for the Well-beloved says: "I will get me up to the mountain of myrrh, and will speak unto my love." The mountain of bitter myrrh is the height of the exalted spirit, which transforms into bitterness the desire for all personal gratification and deceitful delights in all things that are not according to God's will. Thus God speaks in spirit to the soul: "Thou art all fair my love, pure and undefiled, there is no spot in thee." But he who lives according to his own will, for his own pleasure, cannot thus find God, but will find Him as his adversary in all his works. Thus man will spoil all that he begins; for the works of the flesh will help but little, if the will and the affections of the heart are not first subdued. A Psalm, said by one who has subdued his will, is worth many Psalms: that is, the least work done by such a man is more pleasing to God than the greatest work done by a man who follows his own way.

At another time man finds God in the wilderness, in the burning bush, as Moses found Him. The bush in the wilderness signifies such a temper or spirit that, withdrawn and estranged from all creatures, puts forth leaves or blossoms on the heights of the Eternal Godhead. As the Divine Being comprises within Himself three Persons, so also this spirit has laid hold of God in His threefold powers, as the bush laid hold of the flames in its blossoming branches; and this is of grace. This putting forth of leaves causes the soul to grow steadily in light, in godlike virtues, day by day without ceasing, until she, with the vision of angels, beholds God in Zion. Now, mark, in the measure that thou hast found God, in that measure also wilt thou find in thyself the divine training and virtues—more today than yesterday. But he who will thus find God here, must cast off all carnal desires, and, with Moses, he must come under the dominion of self-restraint and the light of reason; for *flesh and blood cannot possess the Kingdom of God.* I believe, dear children, that nearly all your daily shortcomings proceed therefrom; that ye follow by word or deed the sudden impulses that thrust themselves into the heart from without, before the light of self-restraint can shine therein.

Thirdly, God may be found on the mountain, in the cloud; for the union (Testament) of Divine Light and of the commandment was written on the stone by the finger of God. The mountain is like a high-minded, large-hearted man, who has no pleasure in any of his works, neither can he find any rest in them, unless, like St. Paul, he is confirmed in all his works by an express sign of the Will of God; so that the will of the soul does not even carry on human actions according to his own will, but after the manner appointed by the Divine Will, divinely. Thus the soul by her works sanctifies the body, so that what the body does the soul does also; and again, on the other hand, the works of the Divine Will and the works of the soul are at one; so that the soul can say: *I Live, yet not I, but Christ liveth in me;* I work, yet not I, but the power of Divine Being worketh in me. This takes place in the cloud, in the eternal splendor of the Divine Light, for the light of all creatures is as night compared with the Divine Light.

JOHN TAULER

THE MISSIONARY IN PARAGUAY

You can well imagine, Monsieur, to what efforts an evangelical laborer must give himself up, if he would go in search of these savages in their mountains. "While I was in Europe," writes one of these missionaries, "I thought it would be sufficient to carry into this missionary field a great zeal for the conversion of souls; but, since I have had the happiness to be there, I have learned that it is necessary also to be exercised for a long while in the inward denial of self, in a complete separation from all things here below, in the mortification of the senses, in a contempt for life, and in the surrender of my whole self into the hands of Providence."

When the number of Indians at any settlement is great, two missionaries are ordinarily employed in civilizing and instructing the neophytes in Christian truths. Each year one of them makes excursions of thirty or forty leagues in length to the residence of the savage tribes, to win them for Jesus Christ and to draw them to the settlement. He departs with nothing except the breviary under his left arm and the large crucifix in his right hand, having no other provision than his confidence in God and what he can find along the way. He is accompanied by twenty or thirty Christian converts, who act as guides and interpreters, and who sometimes discharge the duty of preachers. With their aid, with a hatchet in his hand, he clears for himself a passage through the dense forests. If, as often happens, he finds himself on the borders of lakes or marshes which have to be crossed, he is always the one who marches ahead of the others, the water up to his waist, encouraging them by his example to follow him. He is the first to climb the steep rocky slopes and cliffs. He is the first to penetrate into caves, at the risk of finding wild beasts there, instead of the Indians he is seeking.

In the midst of these fatigues he often has, for his entire support, only some handfuls of Indian corn, some roots, or some of the wild fruits which they call *motaqui*. Often he can find nothing to quench his thirst save the dew gathered from the leaves of trees. At night he sleeps in a hammock suspended from the trees. I do not speak of the constant danger of losing his life by the hands of the Indians who sometimes lie in ambush, armed with arrows and clubs, ready to beat to death the unwary who come into their country and are looked upon by them as enemies.

We must acknowledge, however, the particular protection of God, who watched for their safety and for the wants of every missionary. It happened more than once that, when they found themselves reduced to extreme necessity, that the game and the fish came as it were of their own accord, to present themselves to the Indians who formed their party. At other times, when the savages were most hostile to the missionary who had placed himself in their power, they suddenly changed their cruel plans, or their strength left them at the moment and their enfeebled arms were unable to discharge the arrows which would have brought death.

But however painful and dangerous these journeys might be, the

Gospel laborer found himself fully recompensed for his pains and sufferings when he returned in triumph to the settlement, accompanied by three or four hundred Indians, with the hope of gaining the next year many more who, more defiant and fearing the missionary had come to deceive them and make them slaves, would not acquiesce before they had sent some of their people to the settlement to see what was taking place there and to return then with an account. What a consolation for him to find himself again in the midst of his dear neophytes, whose number had been increased by his solicitude, and to be once more in the place where, because of the pious liberality of persons who have interested themselves in the conversion of so many savage tribes, he has the opportunity to recruit his strength so that he may apply himself with renewed zeal to the task!

It is certain that these labors surpassed human strength, and that it would not have been possible to cope with them if one had not been sustained by a strength divinely given. It is not less astonishing that we can count among all the great number of missionaries who toiled for so many years in these laborious missions only three or four who were overcome by the fatigues incident to their work. The larger part, after having worked for twenty-five or thirty years, retained as much strength and vigor as those who in Europe enjoyed all the conveniences of life. Such a one was Father Jean Baptiste de Zea, who passed the greater part of his life in teaching these savage tribes and who, at the age of sixty-five years, did not appear to be more than forty.

FATHER JEROME HARRAN

DE SOTO AT THE MISSISSIPPI

Tuesday, April 26, in the year aforesaid, 1541, the Governor Hernando de Soto set out from the plain of Chicaca, and arrived at Limamu for the night; and there they searched for corn, because the Indians had hidden it, and they had to pass over a desert. And Thursday they came to another plain where the Indians had taken the position, having made a very strong barricade, and within it there were many Indian braves, painted red and decorated with other colours which appeared very fine (or rather, very bad, at least it meant harm to the Christians). And they entered the barricade by force, and with some loss by death and wounds on the part of the Commander and his army, and with a loss greater beyond comparison on the part of the conquered; and it would have been still more if the Indians had not taken flight.

Saturday, the last of April, the army set out from the place of the barricade and marched nine days through a deserted country and by a rough way, mountainous and swampy, until May 8, when they came to the first village of Quizqui, which they took by assault and captured much people and clothes; but the Governor promptly restored them to liberty and had everything restored to them for fear of war, although that was not enough to make friends of these Indians. A league beyond this village they came upon another with abundance of corn, and soon again after another league, upon another likewise amply provisioned. There they saw the great river. Saturday, May 21, the force went along to a plain between the river and a small village, and set up quarters and began to build four barges to cross over to the other side. Many of these conquerors said this river was larger than the Danube.

On the other side of the river, about seven thousand Indians had got together, with about two hundred canoes, to defend the passage. All of them had shields made of canes joined, so strong and so closely interwoven with such thread that a crossbow could hardly pierce them. The arrows came raining down so that the air was full of them, and their yells were something fearful. But when they saw that the work on the barges did not relax on their account, they said that Pacaha, whose men they were, ordered them to withdraw, and so they left the passage free. And on Saturday, June 8, the whole force crossed this great river in the four barges and gave thanks to God because in His good pleasure nothing more difficult could confront them. Soon, on Sunday, they came to a village of Aquixo. . . .

The next Thursday, they entered the land of Quarqui, and passed through small villages; and the next day, Friday, St. John's day, they came to the village of the Lord of Casqui, who gave food and clothing to the army. It was Saturday when they entered his village, and it had very good cabins, and, in the principal one, over the door, were many heads of very fierce bulls, just as in Spain, noblemen who are sportsmen mount the heads of wild boars or bears. There the Christians planted the cross on a mound, and they received it and adored it with much devotion, and the blind and lame came to seek to be healed. Their faith, says Rodrigo Ranjel, would have surpassed that of the conquerors if they had been taught, and would have brought forth more fruit than those conquerors did.

Sunday, June 26, they departed thence to go to Pacaha, an enemy of Casqui; and after passing several villages, they spent the night in one. And the following day they crossed a swamp over which the Indians had thrown a well-constructed bridge, broad and very cleverly built. On Wednesday they came to the village of Pacaha, a village and lord of wide repute and highly thought of in that country.

This town was a very good one, thoroughly well stockaded; and the walls were furnished with towers and a ditch round about, for the most part full of water which flows in by a canal from the river; and this ditch was full of excellent fish of divers kinds. The chief of Casqui came to the Christians when they were entering the village and they entertained him bravely. In Aquixo, and Casqui, and Pacaha, they saw the best villages seen up to that time, better stockaded and fortified, and the people were of finer quality, excepting those of Cofitachequi. The Commander and his soldiers remaining some days in Pacaha, they made some incursions further up country.

And the chief of Casqui, on one occasion, when he saw a chance for it, went off without seeking permission, on account of which the Governor tried to secure peace with Pacaha; and he came to the camp to recover a brother of his whom the Christians had taken when they entered the village; and an agreement was made with Pacaha that they should war against Casqui, which was very gratifying to Pacaha. But Casqui got wind of this resolve and came with fifty Indians of his in fine array, and he brought a clown for display, who said and did much that was amusing, making those who saw him laugh a good deal. The Governor assumed an air of irritation and sternness to please Paçaha, and sent word that Casqui should not come into the village. Casqui replied that he would not refrain from coming even if they cut off his head. Pacaha asked the Governor to allow him to give Casqui a slash in the face with a knife that he had in his hand, which the Christians had given him. But the Governor told Pacaha that he should do no such thing, nor do him any harm, for he would be angry at him; and he ordered Casqui to come so as to see what he wanted. . . . Casqui came and spoke to the Governor as follows—as it was reported by the interpreter Johan Ortiz and the other Indian interpreters that the Governor and the Christians had—: "How is it possible, my Lord, that after having given me the pledge of friendship, and without my having done any harm to you, or given any occasion, you desire to destroy me, your friend and brother? You gave me a cross for a defence against my enemies, and with it you seek to destroy me." (This he said because the Indians of Pacaha, his enemy, that went with the Christians, against him, wore crosses on their heads, high up, that they might be seen.) "Now, my Lord," said Casqui, "when God has heard us by means of the cross; when the women and boys and all those of my country threw themselves on their knees before it to pray for water to the God who you said suffered on it; and He heard us and gave us water in great abundance and refreshed our corn-fields and plantations; now, when we had the most faith in it and in your friendship, you desired to destroy these boys and women that are so devoted to you and your God. Why did you desire to use us with such cruelty without our deserving it from you? Why did you desire to destroy the faith and confidence which we had in you? Why did you desire to offend your God and us, when for Him, and in His name, you gave us assurances and received us for friends, and we gave you entire confidence and trust in the same God and His cross, and have it for our safeguard and protection, and hold it in the reverence and veneration which is proper?"

This said, he held his peace. The Governor, his eyes melting and not without trace of tears, considering the faith and words of this chief, replied to him, through the interpreters, in the presence of many of the Christian soldiers, who, attentively, and not without tears, overcome by such goodness and faith, had heard what was said, and spoke as follows: "Look you, Casqui, we are not come to destroy you, but to do for you what you know and understand is the work of the cross and our God, as you tell me. And these favours, which it has bestowed upon you, are a small thing in comparison with many others and very great ones, which it will secure for you if you love it and believe in it. . . . When you ran off without my permission I thought that you held the teaching we had given you of little account, and for that contempt that you had for it I wanted to destroy you; supposing that in pride you had gone off, for that is the thing which our God most abhors, and for which He punishes us the most. Now that you have come in humility, be assured that I wish you more good than you think; and if you have need of anything from me, tell me of it and you will see, since we do what our God commands us, which is not to lie."

GONZALO DE OVIEDO

WITNESSING A MORALITY PLAY

In the city of Gloucester the manner is (as I think it is in other like corporations), that when players of enterludes come to towne, they just attend the mayor, to enforme him what nobleman's servants they are, and so to get licence for their publike playing; and if the mayor like the actors, or would shew respect to their lord and master, he appoints them to play their first play before himself, and the alderman and common counsell of the city; and that is called the mayor's play: where every one that will, comes in without money, the mayor giving the players a reward as he thinks fit to shew respect unto them. At such a play, my father tooke me with him, and made me stand between his leggs, as he sate upon one of the benches, where we saw and heard very well. The play was called

"The Cradle of Security," wherein was personated a king or some great prince, with his courtiers of several kinds, among which three ladies were in special grace with him; and they keeping him in delights and pleasures, drew him from his graver counselors, hearing of sermons, and listening to good councell and admonitions, that in the end they got him to lye down in a cradle upon the stage, where these three ladies, joyning in a sweet song, rocked him asleep, that he snorted again; and, in the mean time, closely conveyed under the cloths wherewithall he was covered, a vizard, like a swine's snout, upon his face, with three wire chains fastened thereunto, the other end whereof being holden severally by those three ladies; who fall to singing againe, and then discovered his face, so that the spectators might see how they had transformed him, while going on with their singing.

Whilst all this was acting, there came forth of another doore at farthest end of the stage, two old men; the one in blue, with a serjeant at armes, his mace on his shoulder; the other in red, with a drawn sword in his hand, and leaning with the other hand upon the other's shoulder; and so they went along, with a soft pace, round about by the skirt of the stage, till at last they came to the cradle, when all the court was in the greatest jollity; and then the foremost old man, with his mace struck a fearful blow upon the cradle; wherewith all the courtiers, with the three ladies, and the vizard, all vanished; and the desolate prince, starting up bare-faced, and finding himself thus sent for to judgement, made a lamentable complaint of his miserable case, and so was carried away by wicked spirits. This prince did personate in the morall, the wicked of the world; the three ladies, Pride, Covetousness, and Luxury; the two old men, the end of the world and the last judgement. This sight took such an impression on me that when I came towards man's estate, it was as fresh in my memory as if I had seen it newly acted.

"A PENITENTIAL SINNER"

RELIGION AND ART

Were we even to grant, that our customs, combats, feasts, ceremonies, and religion, could not furnish a poet with such agreeable matter, as the subject of the Aeneid, still it would not follow, that it were less necessary to borrow the subjects of Epic poems from our own history. It would be indeed an inconveniency; but such an inconveniency as would prevent a much greater one; to wit, the defect of a particular interest. But this is far from being our case. The pomp of a carrousel, and the events of a tournament are much nobler subjects in themselves, than the games represented at the tomb of Anchises, of which Virgil had drawn so magnificent a picture. What superb descriptions would not this poet have made of the surprizing effects of gun-powder, that chief spring of our present military operations? The miracles of our religion have a kind of marvellous sublime, superior to any thing we meet with in the fables of paganism. With what success has not Corneille treated them in Polieuctes, and Racine in his Athalia? If Sannazarius, Ariosto, and some other poets are censured for their manner of handling the Christian religion; 'tis because they have not spoken of the sublime subject with a suitable dignity and decorum; 'tis because they have blended the fables of paganism with the truths of our religion; in fine, 'tis because, as Boileau says, they have foolishly idolatrized on Christian subjects. They are blamed for not having considered, how unreasonable it is, to say nothing worse, to usurp the same liberties in treating of our religion, as Virgil might have taken, in speaking of the pagan superstition. Let those, who will not consent to make such a choice of an epic subject, as has been here proposed, give the true reason of their refusal: 'tis because they stand in need of the assistance of the poetry of the ancients, to give a warmth and fecundity to their vein; and therefore they chuse to treat of such subjects as have been handled by the Greek and Latin poets, rather than any modern subjects, where they cannot be so easily assisted with the poetry, style, and invention of the former.

JEAN BAPTISTE DU BOS

UPON MODERNIZING CHAUCER

He must have been a man of a most wonderful comprehensive nature, because, as it has been truly observed of him, he has taken into the compass of his *Canterbury Tales* the various manners and humors (as we now call them) of the whole English nation in his age. Not a single character has escaped him. All his pilgrims are severally distinguished from each other; and not only in their inclinations, but in their very physiognomies and persons. Baptista Porta could not have described their natures better, than by the marks which the poet gives them. The matter and manner of their tales, and of their telling, are so suited to their different educations, humors, and callings that each of them would be improper in any other mouth. Even the grave and serious characters are distinguished by their several sorts of gravity; their discourses are such as belong to their age, their calling, and their breeding; such as are becoming of them, and of them only. Some of his persons are vicious, and some virtuous; some are unlearn'd, or (as Chaucer calls them) lewd, and some are learn'd. Even the ribaldry of the low characters is different: the Reeve, the Miller, and the Cook are several men, and distinguished from each other as much as the mincing Lady Prioress and the broad-speaking, gap-toothed Wife of Bath. But enough of this; there is such a variety of game springing up before me that I am distracted in my choice, and know not which to follow. 'Tis sufficient to say, according to the proverb, that *here is God's plenty*. We have our forefathers and great-grand-dames all before us, as they were in Chaucer's days: their general characters are still remaining in mankind, and even in England, though they are called by other names than those of Monks, and Friars, and Canons, and Lady Abbesses, and Nuns; for mankind is ever the same, and nothing lost out of Nature, though everything is altered. May I have leave to do myself the justice (since my enemies will do me none, and are so far from granting me to be a good poet that they will not allow me so much as to be a Christian, or a moral man), may I have leave, I say, to inform my reader that I have confined my choice to such tales of Chaucer as savor nothing of immodesty. If I had desired more to please than to instruct, the Reeve, the Miller, the Shipman, the Merchant, the Sumner, and, above all, the Wife of Bath, in the Prologue to her Tale, would have procured me as many friends and readers as there are beaux and ladies of pleasure in the town. But I will no more offend against good manners: I am sensible as I ought to be of the scandal I have given by my loose writings; and make what reparation I am able, by this public acknowledgment. If anything of this nature or of profaneness be crept into these poems, I am so far from defending it that I disown it. *Totum hoc indictum volo.* Chaucer makes another manner of apology for his broad speaking, and Bocace makes the like; but I will follow neither of them.

JOHN DRYDEN

A TRAGIC PASTORAL

I have a mind to fill the rest of this paper with an accident that happened just under my eyes, and has made a great impression upon me. I have just passed part of this summer at an old romantic seat of my Lord Harcourt's, which he lent me. It overlooks a common-field, where, under the shade of a haycock, sat two lovers, as constant as ever were found in romance, beneath a spreading beech. The name of the one (let it sound as it will) was John Hewet; of the other, Sarah Drew. John was a well set man about five and twenty, Sarah a brown woman of eighteen. John had for several months borne the labour of the day in the same field with Sarah; when she milked, it was his morning and evening charge to bring the cows to her pail. Their love was the talk, but not the scandal, of the whole neighbourhood; for all they aimed at was the blameless possession of each other in marriage. It was but this very morning that he had obtained her parents' consent, and it was but till the next week that they were to wait to be happy. Perhaps this very day, in the intervals of their work, they were talking of their wedding clothes; and John was now matching several kinds of poppies and field-flowers to her complexion, to make her a present of knots for the day.

While they were thus employed (it was on the last of July,) a terrible storm of thunder and lightning arose, that drove the labourers to what shelter the trees or hedges afforded. Sarah, frighted and out of breath, sunk on a haycock, and John (who never separated from her) sate by her side, having raked two or three heaps together to secure her. Immediately there was heard so loud a crack as if heaven had burst asunder. The labourers, all solicitous for each other's safety, called to one another: those that were nearest our lovers, hearing no answer, stepped to the place where they lay: they first saw a little smoke, and after, this faithful pair—John with one arm about his Sarah's neck, and the other held over her face, as if to screen her from the lightning. They were struck dead, and already grown stiff and cold in this tender posture. There was no mark or discolouring on their bodies, only that Sarah's eyebrow was a little singed, and a small spot between her breasts. They were buried the next day in one grave, in the parish of Stanton Harcourt in Oxfordshire; where my Lord Harcourt, at my request, has erected a monument over them.

ALEXANDER POPE

THE DEATH OF SCOTLAND'S QUEEN

The procession now set forward. It was headed by the sheriff and his officers; next followed Pawlet and Drury, and the earls of Shrewsbury and Kent; and, lastly, came the Scottish queen, with Melville bearing her train. She wore the richest of her dresses, that which was appropriate to the rank of a queen dowager. Her step was firm, and her countenance cheerful. She bore without shrinking the gaze of the spectators, and the sight of the scaffold, the block, and the executioner; and advanced into the hall with that grace and majesty which she had so often displayed in her happier days, and in the palace of her fathers. To aid her, as she mounted the scaffold, Pawlet offered his arm. "I thank you, sir," said Mary; "it is the last trouble I shall give you, and the most acceptable service you have ever rendered me."

The queen seated herself on a stool which was prepared for her. On her right stood the two earls; on the left, the sheriff, and Beal, the clerk of the council; in front, the executioner from the Tower, in a suit of black velvet, with his assistant also clad in black. The warrant was read, and Mary in an audible voice addressed the assembly. She would have them recollect, she said, that she was a sovereign princess, not subject to the Parliament of England, but brought there to suffer by injustice and violence. She, however, thanked her God that he had given her this opportunity of publicly professing her religion, and of declaring, as she had often before declared, that she had never imagined, nor compassed, nor consented to the death of the English queen, nor ever sought the least harm to her person. After her death, many things, which were then buried in darkness, would come to light. But she pardoned from her heart all her enemies, nor should her tongue utter that which might turn to their prejudice. Here she was interrupted by Dr. Fletcher, Dean of Peterborough, who, having caught her eye, began to preach, and under the cover, perhaps through motives, of zeal, contrived to insult the feelings of the unfortunate sufferer. He told her that his mistress, though compelled to execute justice on her body, was careful of the welfare of her soul, that she had sent him to bring her to the true fold of Christ, out of the communion of that Church, in which, if she remained, she must be damned; that she might yet find mercy before God, if she would repent of her wickedness, acknowledge the justice of her punishment, and profess her gratitude for the favors which she had received from Elizabeth. Mary repeatedly desired him not to trouble himself and her. He persisted: she turned aside. He made the circuit of the scaffold, and again addressed her in front. An end was put to this extraordinary scene by the Earl of Shrewsbury, who ordered him to pray. His prayer was the echo of his sermon; but Mary heard him not. She was employed at the time in her devotions, repeating with a loud voice, and in the Latin language, long passages from the Book of Psalms. When he had done, she prayed in English for Christ's afflicted Church, for her son James, and for Queen Elizabeth. At the conclusion, holding up the crucifix, she exclaimed: "As thy arms, O God, were stretched out upon the cross, so receive me into the arms of thy mercy, and forgive me my sins." "Madam," said the Earl of Kent, "you had better leave such popish trumperies, and bear him in your heart." She replied: "I cannot hold in my hand the representation of his sufferings, but I must at the same time bear him in my heart."

When her maids, bathed in tears, began to disrobe their mistress, the executioners, fearing to lose their usual perquisites, hastily interfered. The queen remonstrated, but instantly submitted to their rudeness, observing to the earls with a smile, that she was not accustomed to employ such grooms, or to undress in the presence of so numerous a company. Her servants, at the sight of their sovereign in this lamentable state, could not suppress their feelings; but Mary, putting her finger to her lips, commanded silence, gave them her blessing, and solicited their prayers. She then seated herself again. Kennedy, taking a handkerchief edged with gold, pinned it over her eyes; the executioners, holding her by the arms, led her to the block; and the queen, kneeling down, said repeatedly, with a firm voice, "Into thy hands, O Lord, I commend my spirit." But the sobs and groans of the spectators disconcerted the headsman. He trembled, missed his aim, and inflicted a deep wound in the lower part of the skull. The queen remained motionless, and, at the third stroke, her head was severed from the body. When the executioner held it up, the muscles of the face were so strongly convulsed, that the features could not be recognized. He cried as usual, "God save Queen Elizabeth."

"So perish all her enemies!" subjoined the Dean of Peterborough.

"So perish all the enemies of the Gospel!" exclaimed, in a still louder tone, the fanatical Earl of Kent.

Not a voice was heard to cry Amen. Party feeling was absorbed in admiration and pity.

JOHN LINGARD

THE JUDGMENT DAY

"Tell me now," says Baithin, "how Patrick will be troubled for Eire's men on the Judgment Day."

"I will tell you part thereof," says Columcille, "according as God shall allow me. Patrick will come to Clonmacnois to meet the men of Eire; and there he will order the bell to be struck on Cruachan Aigle—the bell that he broke upon the demons as he drove them from the Croagh. And the men and women of Eire will gather at the voice of that bell, and great will be the honour of Ciarán that the hosting shall be at his baile. But my own following will be mighty on that day, Baithin," says Columcille; "for the van of my host will be at Clonmacnois, and its rear at Dun Cuillin in Alba. Well for those who shall be followers of Patrick and the other saints of Eire on that day; and well for those who shall be able to boast to Patrick at that time touching the keeping of his feast-day with reverence and with prayer, and with alms-giving; . . . for it is he who will be the advocate and the judge of all Eire's men on the Day of Judgment.

"Then we will all go with Patrick to Crosa Cail in Meath, and there we will tarry for the last of our host; and thence we will go to Martin; and Martin and Patrick will go before us to Peter and Paul; and with them we will go to Slieve Olivet. There Patrick will bid Peter and Paul and Martin go before him to Slieve Zion to salute the Lord. And Patrick will sit upon a chair of gold above the men of Eire on that Slieve.

"Then Patrick will send Ailbe of Emly on the Yew and seven bishops with him to where Christ will be upon Slieve Zion to ask what He will have to say to him or to his hosts.

"The Lord will give Ailbe a feara-fáilte, and He will ask him where is the Lightning-flame of the West of the World, saying that he is long in coming.

" 'He will come to Thee,' Ailbe will say.

" 'There are many sinners and evil folk with him,' Christ will say.

" 'He'—says Ailbe—'counts these that he brought with him to be martyrs and penitents, since they were for seven years under the waves of the sea, even as he obtained from Thee that the ocean should cover Eire for seven years before the Judgment Day.'

"'Tell him,' says Christ, 'to leave behind him those of his host that are evil.'"

"'I think he will not do that,' says Ailbe, 'for a hasty and wrathful man is he yonder; and furthermore, I came not to carry Thy message to him, but to greet Thee and to bear his tidings. I think that other messengers will come to Thee from him.'

"Ailbe will come to Patrick and will salute him."

"'Didst thou not speak with the Lord?' says Patrick.

"'I did,' says Ailbe, 'and He bids thee leave behind those of thy host that are evil.'

"'That is no opening of welcome,' says Patrick, 'and so it shall not be,' says he.

"Then Patrick," says Columcille, "will send myself and Ciarán the Carpenter's Son and Canice O'Daly as messengers to Christ, and He will give us a feara-fáilte and thrice a fáilte to Canice, and He will send us to tell Patrick to desert his sinners.

"We will go to Patrick with that demand and will deliver it, and it is what he will say: 'I will not desert,' says he, 'one creature that came with me hither, and the men of Eire shall see clearly that I am their protector on this self-same day.' And he will tell us to go yet again to Christ and to call to mind how, on the day that He sent him to sow the Faith in Eire, He promised that it was Patrick who should be the brehon over the men of Eire on the Judgment Day, and moreover, that the Angel promised him the same when he made the long fast upon the Croagh in imitation of the fasts made by the Lord Himself and by Moses. And Patrick will send Munda mac Tulchain as a fourth man with us.

"We four will go then to Christ and will give Him Patrick's message, and will plead in respect of each of these promises.

"'Nothing slips out of your mind,' says Christ, as He remembers.

"'Why this unwelcome of Thine for Patrick?' says Munda mac Tulchain.

"'Thou wast a druid in thy youth,' says Christ.

" 'Then by my druidry,' says Munda, 'Patrick will not come from the slieve where he is until Thou dost consent to his conditions.'

" 'Maise, then,' says Christ, 'let Patrick and all his hosts come while We consult the nine grades of Heaven till We decide what is best to be done with him and with his people.' . . ."

Just then the mid-day bell struck in Armagh.

"Let us answer the bell," says Columcille; "for God has caused it to strike thus early to check me from telling more of this story; and more of these things I may not tell." And that revelation never was completed beyond that.

MANUS O'DONNELL

THE CHURCH AS AN INSTITUTION

There is not, and there never was on this earth, a work of human policy so well deserving of examination as the Roman Catholic Church. The history of that Church joins together the two great ages of human civilization. No other institution is left standing which carries the mind back to the times when the smoke of sacrifice rose from the Pantheon, and when camelopards and tigers bounded in the Flavian amphitheatre. The proudest royal houses are but of yesterday, when compared with the line of the Supreme Pontiffs. That line we trace back in an unbroken series from the Pope who crowned Napoleon in the nineteenth century to the Pope who crowned Pepin in the eighth; and far beyond the time of Pepin the august dynasty extends, till it is lost in the twilight of fable. The republic of Venice came next in antiquity. But the republic of Venice was modern when compared with the Papacy; and the republic of Venice is gone, and the Papacy remains. The Papacy remains, not in decay, but full of life and useful vigor. The Catholic Church is still sending forth to the farthest ends of the world missionaries as zealous as those who landed in Kent with Augustin, and still confronting hostile kings with the same spirit with which she confronted Attila. The number of her children is greater than in any former age. Her acquisitions in the New World have more than compensated for what she has lost in the Old. Her spiritual ascendancy extends over the vast countries which lie between the plains of the Missouri and Cape Horn, countries which, a century hence, may not improbably contain a population as large as that which now inhabits Europe. The members of her communion are certainly not fewer than a hundred and fifty millions; and it will be difficult to show that all other Christian sects united amount to a hundred and twenty millions. Nor do we see any sign which indicates that the term of her long dominion is approaching. She saw the commencement of all the governments and of all the ecclesiastical establishments that now exist in the world; and we feel no assurance that she is not destined to see the end of them all. She was great and respected before the Saxon had set foot on Britain, before the Frank had passed the Rhine, when Grecian eloquence still flourished in Antioch, when idols were still worshipped in the temple of Mecca. And she may still exist in undiminished vigor when some traveler from New Zealand shall, in the midst of a vast solitude, take his stand on a broken arch of London Bridge to sketch the ruins of St. Paul's.

THOMAS BABINGTON MACAULAY

VI

THE NINETEENTH CENTURY AND AFTER

Starting then with the being of a God (which, as I have said, is as certain to me as the certainty of my own existence, though when I try to put the grounds of that certainty into logical shape I find a difficulty in doing so in mood and figure to my satisfaction,) I look out of myself into the world of men, and there I see a sight which fills me with unspeakable distress. The world seems simply to give the lie to that great truth, of which my whole being is so full; and the effect upon me is, in consequence, as a matter of necessity, as confusing as if it denied that I am in existence myself. If I looked into a mirror and did not see my face, I should have the sort of feeling which actually comes upon me, when I look into this living busy world, and see no reflection of its Creator. This is, to me, one of those great difficulties of this absolute primary truth, to which I referred just now. Were it not for this voice, speaking so clearly in my conscience and my heart, I should be an atheist, or a pantheist, or a polytheist when I looked into the world. I am speaking for myself only; and I am far from denying the real force of the arguments in proof of a God, drawn from the general facts of human society and the course of history, but these do not warm me or enlighten me; they do not take away the winter of my desolation, or make the buds unfold and the leaves grow within me, and my moral being rejoice. The sight of the world is nothing else than the prophet's scroll, full of 'lamentations, and mourning, and woe.'

To consider the world in its length and breadth, its various history, the many races of man, their starts, their fortunes, their mutual alienation, their conflict; and then their ways, habits, governments, forms of worship, their enterprises, their aimless courses, their random achievements and acquirements, the impotent conclusion of longstanding facts, the tokens so faint and broken of a superintending design, the blind evolution of what turn out to be great powers or truths, the progress of final causes, the greatness and littleness of man, his far-reaching aims, his short duration, the curtain hung over his futurity, the disappointments of life, the defeat of good, the success of evil, physical pain, mental anguish, the prevalence and intensity of sin, the pervading idolatries, the corruptions, the dreary hopeless irreligion, that condition of the whole race, so fearfully yet exactly described in the Apostle's words "having no hope and without God in the world,"—all this is a vision to dizzy and appal; and inflicts upon the mind the sense of a profound mystery, which is absolutely beyond human solution.

What shall be said to this heart-piercing reason-bewildering fact? I can only answer, that either there is no Creator, or this living society of men is in a true sense discarded from His presence. Did I see a boy of good make and mind, with the tokens on him of a refined nature, cast upon the world without provision, unable to say whence he came, his birthplace or his family connexions, I should conclude that there was some mystery connected with his history, and that he was one, of whom, from one cause or other, his parents were ashamed. Thus only should I be able to account for the contrast between the promise and the condition of his being. And so I argue about the world;—if there be a God, since there is a God, the human race is implicated in some terrible aboriginal calamity. It is out of joint with the purposes of its Creator. This is a fact, a fact as true as the fact of its existence; and thus the doctrine of what is theologically called original sin becomes to me almost as certain as that the world exists, and as the existence of God.

And now, supposing it were the blessed and loving will of the Creator to interfere in this anarchical condition of things, what are we to suppose would be the methods which might be necessarily or naturally involved in his purpose of mercy? Since the world is in so abnormal a state, surely it would be no surprise to me, if the interposition were of necessity equally extraordinary—or what is called miraculous. But that subject does not directly come into the scope of my present remarks. Miracles as evidence involve a process of reason, or an argument. . . . I know that even the unaided reason, when correctly exercised, leads to a belief in God, in the immorality of the soul, and in a future retribution; but I am considering the faculty of reason actually and historically; and in this point of view, I do not think that I am wrong in saying that its tendency is towards a simple unbelief in matters of religion. No truth, however sacred, can stand against it, in the long run; and hence it is that in the pagan world, when our Lord came, the last traces of the religious knowledge of former times were all but disappearing from those portions of the world in which the intellect had been active and had had a career.

And in these latter days, in like manner, outside the Catholic Church things are tending—with far greater rapidity than in that old time from the circumstances of the age—to atheism in one shape or other. What a scene, what a prospect, does the whole of Europe present at this day! and not only Europe, but every government and every civilisation through the world, which is under the influence of the European mind! Especially, for it most concerns us, how sorrowful, in the view of religion, even taken in its most elementary, most attenuated form, is the spectacle presented to us by the educated intellect of England, France, and Germany! Lovers of their country and of their race, religious men, external to the Catholic Church, have attempted various expedients to arrest fierce wilful human nature in its onward course, and to bring it into subjection. The necessity of some form of religion for the interests of humanity, has been generally acknowledged; but where was the concrete representative of things invisible, which would have the force and the toughness necessary to be a breakwater against the deluge? Three centuries ago the establishment of religion, material, legal and social, was generally adopted as the best expedient for the purpose, in those countries which separated from the Catholic Church; and for a long time it was successful; but now the crevices of those establishments are admitting the enemy. Thirty years ago, education was relied upon; ten years ago there was a hope that wars would cease for ever, under the influence of commercial enterprise and the reign of the useful and fine arts; but will any one venture to say that there is anything anywhere on this earth, which will afford a fulcrum for us, whereby to keep the earth from moving onwards!

The judgment, which experience passes whether on establishments or on education, as a means of maintaining religious truth in this anarchical world, must be extended even to Scripture, though Scripture be divine. Experience proves surely that the Bible does not answer a purpose for which it was never intended. It may be accidentally the means of the conversion of individuals; but a book, after all, cannot make a stand against the wild living intellect of man, and in this day it begins to testify, as regards its own structure and contents, to the power of that universal solvent, which is so successfully acting upon religious establishments.

Supposing then it to be the Will of the Creator to interfere in human affairs, and to make provisions for retaining in the world a knowledge of Himself, so definite and distinct as to be proof against the energy of human scepticism, in such a case,—I am far from saying that there was no other way,—but there is nothing to surprise the mind, if He should think fit to introduce a power into the world, invested with the prerogative of infallibility in religious matters. Such a provision would be a direct, immediate, active, and prompt means of withstanding the difficulty; it would be an instrument suited to the need; and, when I find that this is the very claim of the Catholic Church, not only do I feel no difficulty in admitting the idea, but there is a fitness in it, which recommends it to my mind. And thus I am brought to speak of the Church's infallibility, as a provision, adapted by the mercy of the Creator, to preserve religion in the world, and to restrain that freedom of thought, which of course in itself is one of the greatest of our natural gifts, and to rescue it from its own suicidal excesses.

JOHN HENRY, CARDINAL NEWMAN

FAREWELL TO OXFORD

I left Oxford for good on Monday, February 23, 1846. On the Saturday and Sunday before, I was in my House at Littlemore simply by myself, as I had been for the first day or two when I had originally taken possession of it. I slept on Sunday night at my dear friend's,

Mr. Johnson's, at the Observatory. Various friends came to see the last of me; Mr. Copeland, Mr. Church, Mr. Buckle, Mr. Pattison, and Mr. Lewis. Dr. Pusey too came up to take leave of me; and I called on Dr. Ogle, one of my very oldest friends, for he was my private Tutor, when I was an Undergraduate. In him I took leave of my first College, Trinity, which was so dear to me, and which held on its foundation so many who have been kind to me both when I was a boy, and all through my Oxford life. Trinity had never been unkind to me. There used to be much snap-dragon growing on the walls opposite my freshman's rooms there, and I had for years taken it as the emblem of my own perpetual residence even unto death in my University.

On the morning of the 23rd I left the Observatory. I have never seen Oxford since, excepting its spires, as they are seen from the railway.

JOHN HENRY, CARDINAL NEWMAN

THE GENTLEMAN

Hence it is, that it is almost a definition of a gentleman, to say he is one who never inflicts pain. This description is both refined and, as far as it goes, accurate. He is mainly occupied in merely removing the obstacles which hinder the free and unembarrassed action of those about him; and he concurs with their movements rather than takes the initiative himself. His benefits may be considered as parallel to what are called comforts or conveniences in arrangements of a personal nature: like an easy chair or a good fire, which do their part in dispelling cold and fatigue, though nature provides both means of rest and animal heat without them. The true gentleman in like manner carefully avoids whatever may cause a jar or a jolt in the minds of those with whom he is cast;—all clashing of opinion, or collision of feeling, all restraint, or suspicion, or gloom, or resentment; his great concern being to make every one at their ease and at home. He has his eyes on all his company; he is tender towards the bashful, gentle towards the distant, and merciful towards the absurd; he can recollect to whom he is speaking; he guards against unseasonable allusions, or topics which may irritate; he is seldom prominent in conversation, and never wearisome. He makes light of favours while he does them, and seems to be receiving when he is conferring. He never speaks of himself except when compelled, never defends himself by a mere retort, he has no ears for slander or gossip, is scrupulous in imputing motives to those who interfere with him, and interprets everything for the best. He is never mean or little in his disputes, never takes unfair advantage, never mistakes personalities or sharp sayings for arguments, or insinuates evil which he dare not say out. From a long-sighted prudence, he observes the maxim of the ancient sage, that we should ever conduct ourselves towards our enemy as if he were one day to be our friend. He has too much good sense to be affronted at insults, he is too well employed to remember injuries, and too indolent to bear malice. He is patient, forbearing, and resigned, on philosophical principles; he submits to pain, because it is inevitable, to bereavement, because it is irreparable, and to death, because it is his destiny. If he engages in controversy of any kind, his disciplined intellect preserves him from the blundering discourtesy of better, though less educated minds; who, like blunt weapons, tear and hack instead of cutting clean, who mistake the point in argument, waste their strength on trifles, misconceive their adversary, and leave the question more involved than they find it. He may be right or wrong in his opinion, but he is too clear-headed to be unjust; he is as simple as he is forcible, and as brief as he is decisive.

JOHN HENRY, CARDINAL NEWMAN

SAINT PANCRATIUS

The mob were frantic, as they saw one wild beast after another careering madly round him, roaring and lashing its sides with its tail, while he seemed placed in a charmed circle, which they could not approach. A furious bull, let loose upon him, dashed madly forward, with his neck bent down, then stopped suddenly, as though he had struck his head against a wall, pawed the ground, and scattered the dust around him, bellowing fiercely.

"Provoke him, thou coward!" roared out, still louder, the enraged emperor.

Pancratius awoke as from a trance, and waving his arms, ran towards his enemy; but the savage brute, as if a lion had been rushing on him, turned round, and ran away towards the entrance, where, meeting his keeper, he tossed him high into the air. All were disconcerted except the brave youth, who had resumed his attitude of prayer; when one of the crowd shouted out, "He has a charm round his neck; he is a sorcerer!" The whole multitude re-echoed the cry, till the emperor, having commanded silence, called out to him, "Take that amulet from thy neck, and cast it from thee, or it shall be done more roughly for thee."

"Sir," replied the youth, with a musical voice, that rang sweetly through the hushed amphitheater, "it is no charm that I wear, but a memorial of my father, who in this very place made gloriously the same confession which I now humbly make: I am a Christian; and for the love of Jesus Christ, God and man, I gladly give my life. Do not take from me this only legacy, which I have bequeathed, richer than I received it, to another. Try once more, it was a panther which gave him his crown; perhaps it will bestow the same on me."

For an instant there was dead silence; the multitude seemed softened, won. The graceful form of the gallant youth, his now inspired countenance, the thrilling music of his voice, the intrepidity of his speech, and his generous self-devotion to his cause, had wrought upon that cowardly herd. Pancratius felt it, and his heart quailed before their mercy more than before their rage; he had promised himself heaven that day; was he to be disappointed? Tears started into his eyes, as stretching forth his arms once more in the form of a cross, he called aloud, in a tone that again vibrated through every heart:

"Today, oh yes, today, most blessed Lord, is the appointed day of

Thy coming. Tarry not longer; enough has Thy power been shown in me to them that believe not in Thee; show now Thy mercy to me who in Thee believe!"

"The panther!" shouted out a voice. "The panther," responded twenty. "The panther!" thundered forth a hundred thousand, in a chorus like the roaring of an avalanche. A cage started up, as if by magic, from the midst of the sand, and as it rose, its side fell down, and freed the captive of the desert. With one graceful bound the elegant savage gained its liberty; and, though enraged by darkness, confinement, and hunger, it seemed almost playful, as it leaped and turned about, frisked and gamboled noiselessly on the sand. At last it caught sight of its prey. All its feline cunning and cruelty seemed to return, and to conspire together in animating the cautious and treacherous movements of its velvet-clothed frame. The whole amphitheater was as silent as if it had been a hermit's cell, while every eye was intent, watching the stealthy approaches of the sleek brute to its victim. Pancratius was still standing in the same place, facing the emperor, apparently so absorbed in higher thoughts as not to heed the movements of his enemy. The panther had stolen round him, as if disdaining to attack him except in front. Crouching upon its breast, slowly advancing one paw after another, it had gained its measured distance, and there it lay for some moments of breathless suspense. A deep snarling growl, an elastic spring through the air, and it was seen gathered up like a leech, with its hind feet on the chest, and its fangs and fore claws on the throat of the martyr.

Pancratius stood erect for a moment, brought his right hand to his mouth, and looking up at Sebastian with a smile, directed to him, by a graceful wave of his arm, the last salutation of his life—and fell. His blood softened, brightened, enriched, and blended inseparably with that of his father, which Lucina had hung about his neck. The mother's sacrifice had been accepted.

NICHOLAS PATRICK WISEMAN

LIFE AMONG THE CONVICTS

Soon after my arrival at Sydney a venerable old man, who lived by splitting timber in the woods, came for his annual visit to go to his religious duties; for, like thousands of others, he lived in the bush a long way from any priest. He remembered the early days when Sydney was nothing but a penal settlement. He was a tall man, with white hair and a bowed head, with much refinement of speech and manner; an old insurrectionist of 1798. He spoke much of Father Flynn, and said with touching pathos: "If Father Flynn had been let remain, what would not have been done?" He had the sweetest and swiftest tongue of Irish I ever heard.

Another tall old man, with the same breadth of chest and shoulders, and the bearing of a chief, used to be led from the convict barracks every Saturday by a boy (for he was stone blind) to make his confession. And always, after concluding, he made a brief, but solemn, act of thanksgiving aloud for the gift of blindness, as it shut out half the wickedness in the midst of which he was compelled to live.

Bushranging, with its venturesome hazards, had an attraction to the Irish convicts, and some of the most desperate bushrangers were Irishmen. But it was a rule among bushrangers of all descriptions, English and Irish, never to touch a priest. They had a fixed idea that if they did they would never have luck again. So we always knew we were safe. Once, going on a sick call from Sydney to Liverpool, a man sprung out of the bush with a blunderbuss on his shoulders, and seized the horse's head. I was sitting in my gig, wrapped in a cloak, and at once disengaged my hands, whilst my servant prepared for a spring on him, when the bushman, seeing my face in the moonlight, ran off among the trees. The men in the condemned cells have told both the Bishop and the priests of particular times and circumstances when they passed them by, lying in wait in their hiding-places.

There were several soldiers in the 17th Regiment who went to their weekly Communion, and at least twenty-two who went once a fortnight. One young man I particularly remember, who was quite a contemplative. He had received the Carmelite scapular before he entered the army, and had persevered in a habit of prayer and fasting. He spent all his sentry watches in prayer. He had to stand sentry by the jail, close to the gibbet, one night after two men had been hung upon it; and such was his terror at the working of his imagination in that ghastly spot, with the shades of night around him, that, as he afterwards told me with a sense of gratitude, nothing but the earnestness with which he said his prayers, and so conquered his imagination, saved him from throwing down his musket and running away. The incidents of the barrack-room and the rigors of military discipline served him as subjects of self-mortification, and he certainly had a tender conscience and an habitual sense of the presence of God. He kept several of his comrades steady to their religious duties. I have often wondered what became of this young soldier, who had then gone on well and holily for several years.

There was a convict about thirty years old, far up the country on the Bathurst range, beyond the Blue Mountains, who was quite a contemplative. A shepherd, always following his sheep over extensive pastures, and except at lambing and shearing times, always alone, or nearly so, he spent his time in prayer and enjoyed his solitude. There was then no priest resident in all that country; and his master was so pleased with his steady, reliable conduct, and the care he took of his sheep, that he let him come down once a year to Sydney to receive the Sacraments, and gave him five shillings to buy food on the way. He walked upwards of a hundred miles for this purpose, praying by the way. He would stop a few days in Sydney, and I used to give him half-a-crown to help him back, and then he returned to his wilderness. He had the gentleness of manner which the habits of prayer and solitude give.

I was often struck with the injustice that men constantly commit in generalizing the habits of criminals, and leaving them not one virtue or humane quality. I have often sat at the table of lawyers and attendants at the criminal courts and have heard them discuss the criminals they had been engaged in trying, or hearing tried; and have observed how natural is the disposition, even of shrewd men, to apply the principle, "he who offends in one point is guilty of all," in a sense certainly never contemplated in the sacred Scriptures. There the sense intended undoubtedly is that the offender against one point of law is guilty against the principle on which all law is based, and against the God Whose command is disobeyed, and against that love of God which is the object and end of all law. But men of the world have a habit, fostered especially in law courts and among those who deal with criminals, of concluding that "once a criminal, always a criminal"; and that to have offended once implies a natural malignity ready on occasion to perpetrate every crime. Such monsters, however, are rare in human nature. I have often had the opportunity of comparing men, as from my scant knowledge I knew them inwardly, with the judgment passed upon them by those who knew the same criminals only by the outward evidence that is brought into the courts of justice. And I have seen the vast amount of practical truth embodied in the inspired sentence, "Man sees in the face, but God beholds the heart."

WILLIAM ULLATHORNE

GOSSIPS

"Noblest things find vilest using."And certainly it is a rigorous destiny that Gossipred should have come to signify the worst of social vices. There is something venerable in the pious confabulation of godfathers and godmothers over caudle-cups and postle-spoons: but there is something murderous in the conspiracy of Gossips. It may be that the christening of an infant may have usually let loose a flood of small talk, and volumes of charitable hopes that the son may be better than his father, and the daughter less intolerable than her mother. This mixture of detraction and prophecy is the original sin of gossiping: and it has descended with rapid propagation to all races and languages among Christian men.

There are many varieties in the Gossip kingdom. First, there is the Harmless Gossip, who, being good-hearted but empty-headed, talks incessantly in a kindly, bird-witted, scatter-brained way of all sorts and conditions of men. Such a one cannot talk of subjects scientific, literary, or historical, for he knows nothing about them; nor of things generally, for he is habitually unobservant; but his whole talk is of persons. What such a one has done, is doing, is about to do, would do, or will do: and what such another has said, or is saying, and so on, through all the moods and tenses: how Mr. Gladstone entered Parliament as a supralapsarian, but has gone over to the social democracy: and how no Duchess of Sutherland would ever have in her wardrobe less than one hundred forty-four pocket handkerchiefs, every one of which cost twenty-five guineas: how Sir Wilfred Lawson in early life tried to be a Dominican, but was sent away because of his hard drinking and contagious melancholy. Such gossips are, however, as free from guile or malice as they are from common sense or discernment of what in men or things is credible, probable, or possible. Nothing comes amiss to them. Gossip they must, by a second nature. If they have anything to say, they will say it: if nothing, it is all one: they buzz on amiably, *sicut chimaera bombitanes in vacua;* amiable buzzing creatures, the bluebottles of social life.

There is next the Unconscious Gossip, who repeats all he hears to all he meets, with no greater perception of the fitness of time, place, or person, than he has of colors in the dark. What somebody told him he tells to everybody; mostly to the person who ought last to hear it, and whom it most concerns. The unconscious gossip is an adult *enfant terrible*—a sort of *petroleur* or *petroleuse* on a large scale, sprinkling society with petroleum, believing it to be as harmless as salad-oils. Such innocents have not even the vice of curiosity. They have not sufficient perception of either the eternal or the transient relations of things to excite curiosity, or to make them conscious of the social explosions, earthquakes, conflagrations they are daily causing. The law against arson ought to be extended to such unconscious incendiaries. Their only plea at the bar is: "Who could have ever thought that the man I met in the train was accused of the crime or afflicted with the unhappiness of which I told him? I did not even know who he was."

To these must be added the Professional Gossip. This is the kind known to the Clubs. He knows everybody; is particularly intimate with the people you are talking of; he saw them yesterday; or is going to dine with them, to meet the Russian Ambassador, to-morrow. He puts no handle to any man's name: they are his familiars and clients, patients and penitents, Lords, Commons, and Lions. They all consult him; tell him everything, do nothing without him. He was called last night after twelve o'clock by telegram to Hawarden Castle or to Alnwick, but was not able to go, being sent for from Buckingham Palace. He knows the outline of the Bill of the Session; and how many Peers will be made to carry it; and who are to be made Peers. Such gossips have one fatality. Their prophecies never come to pass; and of their secrets, what is true is not new, and what is new is not true. Each day wipes them out; but they are like tales of fiction, a pleasant excitement for the moment. Such gossips are not malicious. They are too well pleased with themselves to bear ill-will. A quarrel, or even a duel now and then, they may create without meaning it; but they make it up by sacrificing themselves, which costs them nothing, and they begin again the old trade with new capital.

But Gossipdom has inner bolge or circles less innocuous. As we enter further, we encounter next the Malignant Gossip. Of this kind there are two sorts—men who murder the reputations of others, and women who throw vitriol over it. They have an ear always wide open to catch all evil that is said, truly or falsely in the world. Their ears are spread in the dark, like the nets of bat-folders; nothing escapes them. It is enough to be ten minutes in a room with them, to see the rent in every man's coat, or the wrinkle in every woman's temper. As a sponge sucks in water, so these malignant gossips draw in, by affinity, all malignant histories. They have, too, a laboratory in the brain, and a chemical acid by which all that is malignant is at once detected, and drawn out for use in a concentrated form.

Such men are man-slayers: for to a good man and an honorable man a fair name is dearer than life. And such women are domestic *vitrioleuses,* more guilty than the male malignities, as the nature and dignity of woman is mercy, tenderness, and compassion. The distortion of their nature is therefore more intense.

There remains one more kind—the Mendacious Gossip. We put him last, not because he is necessarily worse, but because he makes more havoc, and provides, both willingly and unwillingly, weapons and vitriol for the use of the malignants. For such gossips by no means are always conscious or intentional liars. They have gaping ears, and itching tongues, and wandering wits. They are never sure of what they hear, and never accurate in what they repeat. They magnify, and multiply, and put carts before horses, and all things upside down, first in their own minds, and next in their histories. They would not misrepresent if they knew it, nor do mischief if they were aware of it; but all their life long they do mischiefs of lesser or greater magnitudes. They are not false, for they have no intention to be untruthful; but they are not true, for a great part of what they say is false. With all their good intentions they are dangerous as companions, and still more dangerous as friends. But there is another kind of mendacious gossip, who knows that he is inventing, inverting, exaggerating, supplementing with theories and explanations of his own, the words and actions of other men. The Italians call such a man *uomo ficto.* He is a living fiction; and all he touches turns to fiction, as all that Midas touched turned to gold. He is reckless of the name, and fame, and feelings, and dignity of other men, having none of his own: and he is hardly conscious of the pain he inflicts, though he would still inflict it even if he could feel it himself: for in him the malignant and mendacious gossip meet in one brain—and a miserable brain it is. *Quisque suos patimur manes.* Self is our worst scourge.

HENRY EDWARD MANNING

MORAL EVIL

Let us renew our old picture. I am lying on a bed of illness, and looking back remorsefully on my shameful violation of my friend's confidence, and on a life of dishonest practices directed (as I myself knew) to the detriment of my country's highest interests. Not only I intue that a large number of my past acts have been morally evil, but I further intue that they violated the command of some living Personal Being. This is the further thesis, which we are now to advocate. The general axiom, we maintain, is cognizable, that all morally evil acts are prohibited by some living Personal Being.

Now, here let us distinctly explain our meaning. We by no means say—on the contrary, in an earlier part of our article we have denied—that the idea "morally evil" either includes or is equivalent with the idea "forbidden by some living Personal Being." The predicate of an axiom is not commonly included in, or equivalent with, the idea of its subject; for were it so, there would be no axioms except tautologies. Take the parallel case, on which we insisted in our last essay: "all trilaterals are triangular." So far is it from being true (as we there pointed out) that triangularity is included in the *idea* of trilateralness, that, on the contrary, I call a figure "trilateral" in the fullest sense of that word, before I have so much as considered any *question* as to the number of its angles. Nevertheless the proposition is axiomatic: because, to use F. Kleutgen's expression, "by merely considering the idea of the subject and predicate, I come to see that there exists between them that relation which the proposition expresses"; or (as we ourselves expressed the same thought) because, from my very conception of a trilateral, I know its triangularity.

This, then, is what we maintain in the present instance. If after such an ill-spent life as we have supposed, while lying on my sick-bed, I ponder in anguish of soul the idea "morally evil" as truly applicable to so many of my past acts,—I find myself to know, by my very conception of that attribute, that these acts have been acts of rebellion against some living personal authority, external to myself. We make this allegation, on the sole possible and the abundantly sufficient ground of an appeal to the indubitable facts of human nature. We say, "external to myself"; because to say merely that the lower part of my nature has rebelled against the higher, is absurdly inadequate to express my deep conviction. And we say "living personal authority," because it is still *more* absurd to suppose that there can be rebellion against an impersonal thing; least of all against an abstraction, which is in fact nothing at all. I intue, then, the axiom, that all morally evil acts are also forbidden me by some living personal authority external to myself.

WILLIAM GEORGE WARD

LOVE TRANSFIGURED

Love is rooted deeper in the earth than any other passion; and for that cause its head, like that of the Tree Igdrasil, soars higher into heaven. The heights demand and justify the depths, as giving them substance and credibility. "That He hath ascended—what is it but because He first also descended into the lower parts of the earth?" Love "reconciles the highest with the lowest, ordering all things strongly and sweetly from end to end." St. Bernard says that "divine love" (religion) "has its first root in the most secret of the human affections." This affection is the only key to the inner sanctuaries of that faith which declares, "Thy Maker is thy Husband"; the only clue by which searchers of the "secret of the King," in the otherwise inscrutable writings of prophet and apostle, discover, as Keble writes, "the loving hint that meets the longing guess," which looks to the future for the satisfying and abiding reality, the passage of whose momentary shadow forms the supreme glory of our mortality.

The whole of after-life depends very much upon how life's transient transfiguration in youth by love is subsequently regarded; and the greatest of all the functions of the poet is to aid in his readers the fulfilment of the cry, which is that of nature as well as religion, "Let not my heart forget the things mine eyes have seen." The greatest perversion of the poet's function is to falsify the memory of that transfiguration of the senses and to make light of its sacramental character. This character is instantly recognized by the initiated heart and apprehension of every youth and maiden; but it is very easily forgotten and profaned by most, unless its sanctity is upheld by priests and poets. Poets are naturally its prophets—all the more powerful because, like the prophets of old, they are wholly independent of the priests, and are often the first to discover and rebuke the lifelessness into which that order is always tending to fall. If society is to survive its apparently impending dangers, it must be mainly by guarding and increasing the purity of the sources in which society begins. The world is finding out, as it has often done before, and more or less forgotten, that it cannot do without religion. Love is the first thing to wither under its loss. What love does in transfiguring life, that religion does in transfiguring love: as any one may see who compares one state or time with another. Love is sure to be something less than human if it is not something more; and the so-called extravagances of the youthful heart, which always claims a character for divinity in its emotions, fall necessarily into sordid, if not shameful, reaction, if those claims are not justified to the understanding by the faith which declares man and woman to be priest and priestess to each other of relations inherent in Divinity itself, and proclaimed in the words "Let us make man in our own image" and "male and female created He them." Nothing can reconcile the intimacies of love to the higher feelings unless the parties to them are conscious—and true lovers always are—that for the season at least, they justify the words "I have said, Ye are gods." Nuptial love bears the clearest marks of being nothing other than the rehearsal of a communion of a higher nature. "Its felicity consists in perpetual conversion of phase from desire to sacrifice, and from sacrifice to desire, accompanied by unchangeable complaisance in the delight shining in the beauty of the beloved; and it is agitated in all its changes by fear, without which love cannot long exist as emotion." Such a state, in proportion to its fervor, delicacy, and perfection, is ridiculous unless it is regarded as a "great sacrament." It is the inculcation of this significance which has made love between man and woman what it is now—at least to the idea and aspirations of all good minds. It is time that the sweet doctrine should be enforced more clearly. Love being much more respected and religion much less than of old, the danger of profanation is not so great as it was when religion was revered and love despised. The most characteristic virtue of woman, or at least the most alluring of her weaknesses—her not caring for masculine truth and worth unless they woo her with a smile or a touch or some flattery of her senses—is the prevailing vice of most men, especially in these times. This general effeminacy is the poet's great opportunity. It is his pontifical privilege to feel the truth; and his function is to bridge the gulf between severe verity and its natural enemy, feminine sentiment, by speech which, without any sacrifice of the former, is "simple, sensuous, and passionate." He insinuates in nerve-convincing music the truths which the mass of mankind must feel before they believe. He leads them by their affections to things above their affections, making Urania acceptable to them by her praenomen Venus. He is the apostle of the Gentiles, and conveys to them, without any flavor of cant or exclusiveness, the graces which the chosen people have too often denied or disgraced in their eyes.

COVENTRY PATMORE

THE CHALLENGE OF DIVINE TRUTH

If Nature requires for her right interpretation "all" a man's virtues, the supernatural may certainly claim, as it has ever done, that of humility. It must require, however, many others also—the "single eye" of the Gospel, since neither moral nor Divine Truth has a meaning for sophisticated nature; zeal and perseverance, since the search is often arduous; purity, since it is the "clean of heart" that "see God": reverence, or else the inquirer will overrun and trample down truth in his quest after knowledge. Above all, it requires a devout heart; for as a heart seduced from the right leads the intellect into error, so a heart faithful to the right leads it to truth. Men sometimes imagine that such statements apply only to revealed religion. They are true not less in relation to Theism. To suppose that this principle applies to human knowledge on all moral subjects, and even on the highest and fairest material subjects, and yet that when cited in connection with man's appreciation of religion, whether natural or revealed, it is but a pretence and a pretext, this is to declaim, not to reason;—for there is a mental as well as a verbal form of declamation.

It is the whole vast and manifold being of man—his mind and his heart, his conscience and his practical judgment, his soul and his spirit—that Divine Truth challenges. The skeptic, when proud of his skepticism, insists upon the mighty and manifold problem being presented to his logical faculty alone, and wonders why he can make so little use of it. In place of dilating his being to embrace the largest of Truths, he contracts it to a lance's point, and pushes it forth in oppugnancy. He does not perceive that this mental attitude is one that violates not merely the philosophic conditions under which alone the knowledge he seeks could become his, but those under which only it professes to be cognisable. He makes this demand because he insists on gaining his knowledge of things divine in no degree by way of gift, but exclusively as his own discovery: that is, not as religion but as science. He assumes that because religion, like nature, *has* its science, it therefore *is* science, and nothing more. As well might he assume that nature is nothing more than natural philosophy. If he came forth to the threshold of his house, he would be bathed in the sunbeams. He has another way of ascertaining whether a sun can exist. He retires to the smallest and darkest chamber in his house, closes the shutter, and peers through a chink.

AUBREY DE VERE

DOM JOAM

Dom Joam de Castro had not money to rebuild the fortress of Dio, which was to save India and to be the foundation of his glorious renown. In this emergency he wrote from Dio to the Council of Goa stating his distress and concluding thus: "I earnestly beg of you to lend me 20,000 pardoas, which, as a gentleman I promise, and on the Holy Gospel swear, before a year's end, to see repaid to you. I commanded the taking up of my son, Dom Fernando, whom the Moors killed in this fortress (fighting for God and our Lord the King), to pawn to you his bones, but they were found so that it was without any other pawn but part of my beard, which I here send you by Diego Rodrigues de Azevedo. As you know I have neither gold, plate, nor anything of value to secure your property, only a plain and naked truth given me by God Almighty. I commend myself, Gentlemen, to your goodness. Dated at Dio, the 23d of November 1546." The merchants furnished him with more than he demanded. After his glorious triumph as Viceroy of India, he wrote to the King desiring leave to return to Portugal and begging for two acres of ground which rose into a hill above his country house at Cintra, which to this day is called the Mountain of Good News. The Infante Dom Luis in his letter to Dom Joam implies that he wanted these tops of the rocks of Cintra only that he might build chapels upon them. It was the King's wish, however, that he should stay for three years longer in India. But his long exertions and hardship caused him to sink suddenly under the pressure of so arduous a command. When seized with his mortal sickness, he summoned the bishop and the chancellor of the state and the chief magistrate of the city, the Guardian of the Franciscans, and St. Francis Xavier, before whom he made this speech: "I am not ashamed, gentlemen, to tell you that the Viceroy of India wants in his sickness those conveniences which the meanest soldier finds in the hospitals. I came to serve, not to traffic in the East. I would to yourselves have pawned the bones of my son, and did pawn the hairs of my beard, to assure you that I had no gold or plate. There was not this day money enough in the house to buy me a dinner; for in the fleets which I sent forth the soldiers fed upon the governor's salary before the King's pay, and it is no wonder for the father of so many children to be poor. I request of you during the time of this sickness to order me a becoming maintenance." Then asking for a missal he took his oath on the Gospel that he was not debtor one crusado to the King, or to any Christian, Jew, Moor, or pagan. As soon as he found that he was in danger he secluded himself with St. Francis Xavier who prepared him for his end. Having received the Sacraments of the Church, he gave up his soul to God on the 6th of June 1548 in the forty-eighth year of his age. In his study were found three pieces of small money, a discipline, and the locks of his beard which he had pawned. This was the sum of his riches after he had governed India with such glory and benefit to his King. So devoutly did he reverence the Cross of Christ that he rather chose to build a temple to its memory than raise a house to his posterity. So he left it, on his father's blessing, to his son Dom Alvaro, that, if he found in the King's favour any recompense for his father's services, he should with that build a convent for the Franciscans on the mountain of Cintra and name the house after the Holy Cross. His son faithfully carried out his injunction.

KENELM HENRY DIGBY

EPILOGUE TO HIS BOOK

O that the poet were not just in saying, that this is now an age of selfish men, that life is drest for a shew, while the great events which old story rings seem vain and hollow. O that some voice may raise us up again and give us virtue, that avarice and expense may be no more adored, but plain living and high thinking be again our glory. Had these rude and faint images of a faithful age been drawn by one who had indeed caught its simple spirit, he would not have let you depart without praying that you, who have followed him from the beginning to the ending would be pleased in charity to put him, who would rejoice to serve you, into your devout memento; that Almighty God might send him good deliverance while he was alive, and when he was dead and his body laid to the cold earth, when the darkness of age and death should have covered over both this book and him, through God's grace, his soule might enter Paradise. He would have prayed you all, if you heard never more of him, to pray for his soule.

KENELM HENRY DIGBY

A VIEW OF LONDON

Let us sit down upon the top of this fair hill. The clear sunshine and the bright air flow into us in streams of life and gladness, while our thoughts are lifted up to God, and our hearts quietly expand to love. Beneath us is that beautiful rolling plain, with its dark masses of summer foliage sleeping in the sun for miles and miles away, in the varying shades of blue and green, according to the distance or the clouds. There at our feet is the gigantic city, gleaming with an ivory whiteness beneath its uplifted but perpetual canopy of smoke. The villa-spotted hills beyond it, its almost countless spires, its one huge many-steepled palace, and its solemn presiding dome, its old bleached tower, and its squares of crowded shipping—it all lies below us in the peculiar sunshine of its own misty magnificence. There, in every variety of joy and misery, of elevation and depression, three million souls are working out their complicated destinies. Close around us, the air is filled with the songs of rejoicing birds, or the pleased hum of the insects that are drinking the sunbeams, and blowing their tiny trumpets as they weave and unweave their mazy dance. The flowers breathe sweetly, and the leaves of the glossy shrubs are spotted with bright creatures in painted surcoat or gilded panoply, while the blue dome above seems both taller and bluer than common, and is ringing with the loud peals of the unseen larks, as the steeples of the city ring for the nation's victory. Far off from the river-flat comes the booming of the cannon, and here, all unstartled, round and round the pond, a fleet of young perch are sailing in the sun, slowly and undisturbedly as if they had a very grave enjoyment of their little lives. What a mingled scene it is of God and man! and all so bright, so beautiful, so diversified, so calm, opening out such fountains of deep reflection, and of simple-hearted gratitude to our Heavenly Father.

FREDERICK WILLIAM FABER

MY BROTHERS

It is not only when He is about to send me some trial that Our Lord gives me warning and awakens my desire for it. For years I had cherished a longing which seemed impossible of realisation—to have a brother a Priest. I often used to think that if my little brothers had not gone to Heaven, I should have had the happiness of seeing them at the Altar. I greatly regretted being deprived of this joy. Yet God went beyond my dream; I only asked for one brother who would remember me each day at the Holy Altar, and He has united me in the bonds of spiritual friendship with two of His apostles. I should like to tell you, dear Mother, how Our Divine Master fulfilled my desire.

In 1898 our Holy Mother, St. Teresa, sent my first brother as a gift for my feast. It was washing day, and I was busy at my work, when Mother Agnes of Jesus, then Prioress, called me aside and read me a letter from a young Seminarist, in which he said he had been inspired by St. Teresa to ask for a sister who would devote herself specially to his salvation, and to the salvation of his future flock. He promised always to remember this spiritual sister when saying Mass, and the choice fell upon me. Dear Mother, I cannot tell you how happy this made me. Such unlooked-for fulfilment of my desire awoke in my heart the joy of a child; it carried me back to those early days, when pleasures were so keen, that my heart seemed too small to contain them. Years had passed since I had tasted a like happiness, so fresh, so unfamiliar, as if forgotten chords had been stirred within me.

Fully aware of my obligations, I set to work, and strove to redouble my fervor. Now and again I wrote to my new brother. Undoubtedly, it is by prayer and sacrifice that we can help our missionaries, but sometimes, when it pleases Our Lord to unite two souls for His Glory, He permits them to communicate their thoughts, and thus inspire each other to love God more. Of course an express command from those in authority is needed for this, otherwise, it seems to me, that such a correspondence would do more harm than good, if not to the missionary, at least to the Carmelite, whose manner of life tends to continual introversion. This exchange of letters, though rare, would occupy her mind uselessly; instead of uniting her to God, she would perhaps fancy she was doing wonders, when in reality, under cover of zeal, she was doing nothing but producing needless distraction.—And here am I, launched, not upon a distraction, but upon a dissertation equally superfluous. I shall never be able to correct myself of these lengthy digressions, which must be so wearisome to you, dear Mother. Forgive me, should I offend again.

Last year, at the end of May, it was your turn to give me my second brother, and when I represented that, having given all my merits to one future apostle, I feared they could not be given to another, you told me that obedience would double their value. In the depths of my heart I thought the same thing, and, since the zeal of a Carmelite ought to embrace the whole world, I hope, with God's help, to be of use to even more than two missionaries. I pray for all, not forgetting our Priests at home, whose ministry is quite as difficult as that of the missionary preaching to the heathen. . . . In a word, I wish to be a true daughter of the Church, like our holy Mother St. Teresa, and pray for all the intentions of Christ's Vicar. That is the one great aim of my life. But just as I should have had a special interest in my little brothers had they lived, and that, without neglecting the general interests of the Church, so now, I unite myself in a special way to the new brothers whom Jesus has given me. All that I possess is theirs also. God is too good to give by halves; He is so rich that He gives me all I ask for, even though I do not lose myself in lengthy enumerations. As I have two brothers and my little sisters, the novices, the days would be too short were I to ask in detail for the needs of each soul, and I fear I might forget something important. Simple souls cannot understand complicated methods, and, as I am one of their number, Our Lord has inspired me with a very simple way of fulfilling my obligations. One day, after Holy Communion, He made me understand these words of the Canticle of Canticles: "Draw me: we will run after Thee to the odour of Thy ointments." O my Jesus, there is no need to say: "In drawing me, draw also the souls that I love": these words, "Draw me," suffice. When a soul has let herself be taken captive by the inebriating odour of Thy perfume, she cannot run alone; as a natural consequence of her attraction towards Thee, the souls of all those she loves are drawn in her train.

Just as a torrent carries into the depths of the sea all that it meets on its way, so, my Jesus, does the soul who plunges into the shoreless ocean of Thy Love bring with it all its treasures. My treasures are the souls it has pleased Thee to unite with mine; Thou hast confided them to me, and therefore I do not fear to use Thy own words, uttered by Thee on the last night that saw Thee still a traveller on this earth. Jesus, my Beloved! I know not when my exile will have an end. Many a night I may yet sing Thy Mercies here below, but for me also will come the last night, and then I shall be able to say:

"I have glorified Thee upon earth: I have finished the work which Thou gavest me to do. I have manifested Thy name to the men whom Thou hast given me out of the world. Thine they were, and to me Thou gavest them; and they have kept Thy word. Now they have known that all things which Thou hast given me are from Thee: because the words which Thou gavest me I have given to them; and they have received them, and have known for certain that I came forth from Thee, and they have believed that Thou didst send me. I pray for them: I pray not for the world, but for them whom Thou hast given me, because they are Thine. And all mine are Thine, and Thine are mine; and I am glorified in them. And now I am no more in the world, and these are in the world, and I come to Thee. Holy Father, keep them in Thy name, whom Thou hast given me, that they may be one, as we also are one. And now I come to Thee, and these things I speak in the world, that they may have my joy fulfilled in themselves. I do not ask that Thou take them away out of the world, but that Thou preserve them from evil. They are not of the world, as I also am not of the world. And not for them only do I pray, but for those also who through their word shall believe in me. Father, I will that where I am they also whom

Thou hast given me may be with me, that they may see my glory which Thou hast given me, because Thou has loved me before the foundation of the world. And I have made known Thy name unto them, and will make it known, that the love wherewith Thou hast loved me may be in them and I in them."

ST. THÉRÈSE OF LISIEUX
(The Little Flower)

TO THE REV. DR. HYDE

I imagine you to be one of those persons who talk with cheerfulness of that place which oxen and wainropes could not drag you to behold. You, who do not even know its situation on the map, probably denounce sensational descriptions, stretching your limbs the while in your pleasant parlor on Beretania Street. When I was pulled ashore there one early morning, there sat with me in the boat two Sisters, bidding farewell (in humble imitation of Damien) to the lights and joys of human life. One of these wept silently; I could not withhold myself from joining her. Had you been there, it is my belief that nature would have triumphed even in you; and as the boat drew but a little nearer, and you beheld the stairs crowded with abominable deformations of our common manhood, and saw yourself landing in the midst of such a population as only now and then surrounds us in the horror of a nightmare—what a haggard eye would you have rolled over your reluctant shoulder toward the house on Beretania Street! Had you gone on; had you found every fourth face a blot upon the landscape; had you visited the hospital and seen the butt-ends of human beings lying there almost unrecognizable, but still breathing, still thinking, still remembering; you would have understood that life in the lazaretto is an ordeal from which the nerves of a man's spirit shrink, even as his eye quails under the brightness of the sun; you would have felt it was (even to-day) a pitiful place to visit and a hell to dwell in. It is not the fear of possible infection. That seems a little thing when compared with the pain, the pity, and the disgust of the visitor's surroundings, and the atmosphere of affliction, disease, and physical disgrace in which he breathes. I do not think I am a man more than usually timid; but I never recall the days and nights I spent upon that island promontory (eight days and seven nights), without heartfelt thankfulness that I am somewhere else. I find in my diary that I speak of my stay as "a grinding experience": I have once jotted in the margin, "Harrowing is the word"; and when the Mokolii bore me at last toward the outer world, I kept repeating to myself, with a new conception of their pregnancy, those simple words of the song——

'Tis the most distressful country
That ever yet was seen.

And observe: that which I saw and suffered from was a settlement, purged, bettered, beautified; the new village built, the hospital and the Bishop's-Home excellently arranged; the Sisters, the doctor, and the missionaries all indefatigable in their noble tasks. It was a different place when Damien came there, and made his great renunciation, and slept that first night under a tree amidst his rotting brethren: alone with pestilence; and looking forward (with what courage, with what pitiful sinkings of dread, God only knows) to a lifetime of dressing sores and stumps.

You will say, perhaps, I am too sensitive, that sights as painful abound in cancer hospitals and are confronted daily by doctors and nurses. I have long learned to admire and envy the doctors and the nurses. But there is no cancer hospital so large and populous as Kalawao and Kalaupapa; and in such a matter every fresh case, like every inch of length in the pipe of an organ, deepens the note of the impression; for what daunts the onlooker is that monstrous sum of human suffering by which he stands surrounded. Lastly, no doctor or nurse is called upon to enter once for all the doors of that gehenna; they do not say farewell, they need not abandon hope, on its sad threshold; they but go for a time to their high calling; and can look forward as they go to relief, to recreation, and to rest. But Damien shut to with his own hand the doors of his own sepulchre.

ROBERT LOUIS STEVENSON

FATHER DAMIEN REPORTS

By a special providence of Our Lord, who during His life revealed a special sympathy for lepers, I was able to trace my steps to Kalawao during May, 1873. I was then thirty-three years of age, robust, and in good health. A great many lepers had arrived not long before from the various islands. They numbered 816:—some of them were old acquaintances of mine from Hawaii, where I had previously been stationed as a missionary priest, but to the majority I was a stranger.

The Kalaupapa landing was at that time a quite deserted village of three or four wooden cottages and a few dilapidated grass houses. The lepers were permitted to go there only on days when a vessel docked. Most of them were living at Kalawao, about eighty being housed in the hospital, the buildings of which were the same one sees today. The others had, accompanied by a few kokuas (helpers), taken up their abode farther up the valley. They had cut down the old pandanus or puhala groves to build their houses, though a great many had only the branches of castor oil trees with which to construct their small shelters. These frail frames they covered with ki leaves or sugar cane leaves, the most fortunate using pili grass. I myself was sheltered during several weeks under the single pandanus tree which is still preserved in the church yard. Under such conditions lived these unfortunate outcasts of society, old and new "cases" alike—strangers for the most part to one another, they lived in pell-mell fashion, without distinction as to age and sex. They passed the time away playing cards, dancing the hula, drinking fermented ki-root beer or home-made alcohol, and with the sequel to all this. Because of the scarcity of water, which had to be carted at that time from a great distance, their clothes were far from being clean and decent.

The stench of their filth, mixed with the exhalation from their sores, was simply disgusting and unbearable to a new arrival. Many a time, carrying on my priestly duties in their domiciles, I was compelled not only to close my nostrils but to run outside for a breath of fresh air. In order to protect my legs from a peculiar itching experienced every evening after visiting them, I was obliged to request a friend to send me a pair of heavy boots. I also accustomed myself to the use of tobacco, in order to counteract the vile odor; and the smell of the pipe was really a help in disinfecting my clothes from the smell. At that time the progress of the disease was fearful and the rate of mortality very high.

DAMIEN DE VEUSTER

LIBERTY AND LAW

During this period, when science has given us countless new evidences of the inviolable order and harmony that pervade all things—of the "reign of law" in nature—man himself has claimed and won a larger liberty. The former restraints upon individual action have been loosened, the older and more rigid forms of government have yielded to the pressure of the democratic spirit, and this freedom, widening with the spread of knowledge, has apparently left to each man the shaping of his ideals and their attainment, the ordering of his life in the pursuit of happiness and fortune.

But this very assertion and recognition of personal rights has pointed out more forcibly than ever their natural and necessary mutual limitation. There is no real liberty without law, and there is no meaning or validity to law unless it be observed. The growth of democracy does not imply that each man shall become a law unto himself, but that he shall feel in himself the obligation to obey. If the enacting power has been transferred from the will of the ruler to the will of the people, the binding, coercive power has been laid, with greater stress than ever before, upon the individual conscience. Unless men be taught that obedience is right and honorable and necessary alike for private interest and the common weal, legislation will avail but little, the law-making power will become a mockery and the people themselves will be the first to complain that legislation has been carried to excess. They should learn that obedience is not an act of servility we pay to man but an act of homage we pay to God, whose representative he is.

Now conscience itself has need of a higher sanction, of a principle of direction, superior in wisdom to any merely human sense of justice. And the need becomes greater as the people, with reason or without reason, are led to the conviction that power, even in a democracy, can be abused, and that legislation is not always the surest remedy for wrong or the strongest safeguard of right.

But if education in its highest forms pay no attention to religious truth, then I ask by what means shall the conscience of the nation be developed? If men are taught that the laws of nature must be obeyed, yet learn nothing of a divine law-giver, what bound can be set or hindrance placed to the self-seeking tendencies, the passion of greed and the strife for domination that threaten to make life merely a struggle for existence? What guarantee of peace at home and abroad can we secure, what respect for the rights of a people, what confidence in an agreement among nations, if men are responsible to no higher tribunal, if force is the ultimate resort and the final arbiter?

JAMES, CARDINAL GIBBONS

DUELLING

Upon what ground can he who engages in a duel, through the fear of ignominy, lay claim to courage? Unfortunate delinquent! Do you not see by how many links your victim was bound to a multitude of others? Does his vain and idle resignation of his title to life, absolve you from the enormous claims which society has upon you for his services,—his family for that support, of which you have robbed them, without your own enrichment? Go, stand over that body; call back that soul which you have driven from its tenement; take up that hand which your pride refused to touch, not one hour ago. You have, in your pride and wrath, usurped one prerogative of God—you have inflicted death. At least, in mercy, attempt the exercise of another; breathe into those distended nostrils,—let your brother be once more a living soul! Merciful Father! how powerless are we for good, but how mighty for evil! Wretched man! he does not answer,—he cannot rise. All your efforts to make him breathe are vain. His soul is already in the presence of your common Creator. Like the wretched Cain, will you answer, "Am I my brother's keeper?" Why do you turn away from the contemplation of your own honorable work? Yes, go far as you will, still the admonition will ring in your ears: It was by your hand he fell! The horrid instrument of death is still in that hand, and the stain of blood upon your soul. Fly, if you will,—go to that house which you have filled with desolation. It is the shriek of his widow,—there are the cries of his children,—the broken sobs of his parent;—and amidst the wailings, you distinctly hear the voice of imprecation on your own guilty head! Will your honorable feelings be content with this? Have you now had abundant and gentlemanly satisfaction?

JOHN ENGLAND

THE QUEST OF TRUTH

If we take a survey of the classical authors, poets, philosophers, historians and orators, and note their most striking passages, we shall be impressed by the sameness of thought and sentiment which runs through them all, and thus we shall get a deeper insight into the narrowness of the circle in which even the noblest minds are condemned to move. Again and again, from age to age, from Greece to Italy, from Jerusalem, Athens, and Rome, the same truth emerges, clothed almost in the same words. Genius itself despairs of uttering anything really new, and the man of genius, while recognizing that the best has already been said, is tempted to lament his late appearance on earth. The more familiar we are with the world's literature, the more clearly do we perceive, that apart from new theories, resulting from new discoveries, inventions, and happenings, there is little any one can say which is new. But the soul of man, being infinite in its aspirations, capable of thoughts which transcend all bounds and penetrate eternity, is never weary of contemplating the spiritual facts which constitute its being, and which, like itself, are of unfathomable import; and therefore it never loses relish for the old truth, which is forever new in its applications to life, having power, like light, to remain itself, while it clothes the world with endless variety and beauty. Hence the works of genius never grow obsolete, but flourish from generation to generation, bearing fresh flowers and rich fruit; and as no truth is exactly the same for any two minds, so is truth modified to suit the changing environment in which the race lives, now emerging with diviner power and significance, and now obscured by the passions or the heedlessness of the age. But to him who has once perceived its real nature, its infinite worth is plain. He will abandon all, if need be, to follow it. It is the pearl above price; it is joy and love. It leads to the inner world where consciousness reveals God and the soul. It makes us meek and lowly, merciful and lovers of peace; it fills us with longing for righteousness; it enables us to bear patiently persecution, poverty, and obloquy, for these affect the outer man, not him who lives within, whom truth makes free and a citizen of unseen and higher worlds, capable of the spiritual worship, whereby he recognizes his kinship with the Eternal and with all the pure and loving souls for whom the universe is a temple and God is all in all.

JOHN LANCASTER SPALDING

CHARGE TO THE PRIESTHOOD

You are taught now that on the day when the Pontiff places his hands on your heads, and your fingers clasp the chalice, you are raised to the highest dignity on earth. That is true. You are taught that you are more than kings on their thrones, or ministers in their cabinets. That is true. You are taught that you are more than the angels or archangel. That is true. Furthermore, you are instructed that it is by no choice of yours, or your parents, that you are raised to the sacerdotal dignity. That is true. For you are instructed that the Divine Master applies to you the words He applied to His Apostles: "You have not chosen Me; but I have chosen you." You are also warned that no sanctity, however great, can be deemed commensurate with so high an office; and that your lives, and all that is connected with them, your talents, abilities, mental and spiritual faculties, are also placed in pledge with Christ for the fulfilment of your sublime vocation. Why do I insist on such patent and palpable truths? Because you will be tempted to deny them. Experience, so much lauded as a successful master, is also a most dangerous master. It teaches, we know; but often it teaches perilous and subversive doctrines. And the worst and most deadly temptation of your lives will come from experience the day that, looking around you and watching the ways and lives of men, you will utter that word of the Psalmist: *Omnis homo mendax!* or the more melancholy verdict of St. Paul: "All seek their own interests; not the interests of Jesus Christ!" Beware of that moment; for it is in that moment you will be tempted to forget, or deny, the sacred principles you have learned in these halls. You will be tempted to believe that your sacred office is not a mission and vocation, but a mere profession; and that you are at liberty to introduce the language, and the customs, and the principles of the world into that sanctuary, where the maxims of the Gospel alone should be recognised and accepted. You will stand for a moment half-paralysed with the spectacle of men rushing wildly into forbidden paths, and then, panic-stricken, you will be tempted to follow the herd with its treasonable cry: *Ego et rex Meus!* If you harbour that temptation for a moment, in that moment you have bartered and forfeited your birthright; you have cancelled the charter of your nobility; you have revoked your oath of ordination; and from being a *miles et amicus Christi* you have descended to be the slave and sycophant of self.

Hence the necessity of acquiring here, and developing hereafter, a certain phase of character, which I can only designate as "individualism." You must study to be self-centred, self-poised on the strong summits of conscience, not moving to left or right at every breath of opinion. This is quite compatible with that modesty, that humility, that gentleness which always characterize thoughtful minds—minds that move on a high plane, and that will not descend to the vulgarities or common-places of ordinary men. Priests of this class or calibre never forget their college lessons. But whilst striving in remote hamlets, as workhouse chaplains, or even in the slums of large cities, to develop themselves intellectually by wholesome and judicious studies, they are ever sensible of the gentle whispers of their Master, first heard here, never to be stifled in after life—"You are the light of the world! You are the salt of the earth." "You have not chosen Me; but I have chosen you!" "I do not any longer call you servant but friend." "*Filioli mei.*" Ah, these are the "burning and shining lights" of the Church of Christ, within whose rays men shelter themselves for warmth and illumination; who cannot be extinguished in life by envy or hatred or criticism; who even in death leave behind them in memory a certain twilight or aurora, for their words and works survive them; and many a soul, recalling them from the peace of eternity, justifies the presumption in the words of the Psalmist:—

> Thy Word was a lamp to my feet;
> And a light along my ways!

Here is what you have to strive after; here is what you have to attain, if you desire to maintain the traditions of the Irish Church; and to be, in very deed, the leaders of your people, the shepherds of your flock!

And so I, passing rapidly into the evening of life, say this farewell word to you in the morning of your days, and in the dawn of the century, where your life-work shall be placed. The intellectual and spiritual energies, gathered into this hall to-night, must exercise a tremendous influence in that future, when emancipated, they will have free play, and a boundless sphere of action. It is a pathetic, yet consoling thought that, when, far out in the century, our faces shall be upturned to the stars, you will be striving for the same eternal cause as that for which we shall have spent ourselves. Nor have I a moment's doubt, that when the torch falls from our feeble hands, you will take it up and carry it forward through all those years that are sweeping towards us from Infinity, and that come fraught with such solemn issues for the country we love, the Faith to which we cling, the Church, which is our Mistress and our Queen, and Him, who is our Captain and our King.

P. A. SHEEHAN

THE MYSTERY OF PAIN

Christianity, then, has, from the first, immensely deepened and widened, it has further revealed, not the "explanation"—which never existed for us men,—but the fact, the reality, the awful potency and baffling mystery of sorrow, pain, sin, things which abide with man across the ages. And Christianity has, from the first, immensely increased the capacity, the wondrous secret and force which issues in a practical, living, loving transcendence, utilisation, transformation of sorrow and pain, and even of sin. It is the literal fact, as demonstrable as anything that has happened or will happen to our human race can ever be, that Christianity, after some two centuries of the most terrific opposition, conquered—that it conquered in an utterly fair fight—a fight fair as regards the Christian success,—the philosophy of Greece and the power of Rome; indeed that it even conquered Gnosticism, that subtle New Paganism of the thousand elusive hues and forms, that Protean error so very dear to all over-ripe, blasé civilisations. It is the simple fact that Christianity conquered; and it is equally the simple fact that it did so, above all because of what it actually achieved with regard to suffering.

For Christianity, without ever a hesitation, from the first and everywhere, refused to hold, or even to tolerate, either the one or the other of the two only attempts at self-persuasion which, then as now, possess souls that suffer whilst they have not yet found the deepest. Christianity refused all Epicureanism,—since man cannot find his deepest by fleeing from pain and suffering, and by seeking pleasure and pleasures, however dainty and refined. And it refused all Stoicism,—since pain, suffering, evil are not fancies and prejudices, but real, very real; and since man's greatest action and disposition is not self-sufficingness or aloofness, but self-donation and love. Christianity refuted these theories, not by means of another theory of its own, but simply by exhibiting a Life and lives—the Life of the Crucified, and lives which continually re-live, in their endless various lesser degrees and ways, such a combination of gain in giving and of joy in suffering. Christianity thus gave to souls the faith and strength to grasp life's nettle. It raised them, in their deepest dispositions and innermost will, above the pitiful oscillations and artificialities of even the greatest of the Pagans in this central matter,—between eluding, ignoring pain and suffering, and, animal-like, seeking life in its fleeting, momentary pleasures; or trying the nobler yet impossible course, —the making out that physical, mental, moral pain and evil are nothing real, and the suppressing of emotion, sympathy and pity as things unworthy of the adult soul. Christianity did neither. It pointed to Jesus with the terror of death upon Him in Gethsemane; with a cry of desolation upon the Cross on Calvary; it allowed the soul, it encouraged the soul to sob itself out. It not only taught men frankly to face and to recognise physical and mental pain, death, and all other, especially all moral evils and sufferings as very real; it actually showed men the presence and gravity of a host of pains, evils and miseries which they had, up to then, quite ignored or at least greatly minimised. And yet, with all this—in spite of all such material for despair the final note of Christianity was and is still, one of trust, of love, of transcendent joy. It is no accident, but of the very essence of the mystery and of the power of faith, it springs from the reality of God and of His action within men's souls, that, as the nobly joyous last chapters of Isaiah (Chap. xl. to the end) contain also those wondrous utterances of the man of sorrows, so also the serenity of the Mount of the Beatitudes leads, in the Gospels, to the darkness of Calvary.

Pray believe me here: it is to Christianity that we owe our deepest insight into the wondrously wide and varied range throughout the world, as we know it, of pain, suffering, evil; just as to Christianity we owe the richest enforcement of the fact that, in spite of all this, God is, and that He is good and loving. And this enforcement Christianity achieves, at its best, by actually inspiring soul after soul, to believe, to love, to live this wondrous faith.

Hence all attempts to teach Christianity anything on this, central matter of pain and suffering would be, very literally, to "teach one's grandmother to suck eggs." For the very existence of the problem—I mean man's courage to face it, together with sensitiveness as to its appalling range and its baffling mystery—we owe, not to philosophy nor to science, still less to our own untutored hearts, but to religion—above all to the Jewish and Christian religion.

And note, please, that the alternative is not between "this or that non-religious view, denial, or scepticism which does explain suffering and evil," and "religious faith, especially Christianity, which does not explain them." No: this is a purely imaginary alternative: for there is no unbelief as there is no faith, there is no science as there is no popular tradition, which does or can explain these things. The real alternative is: "irreligion, which still oscillates between Epicureanism and Stoicism, systems which remain variously unreal and unhuman with regard to suffering, and which know only how to evade or to travesty pain and to deny sin," and "religion, which fully fronts, indeed extends and deepens indefinitely our sense of, suffering and sin, and which, nevertheless, alone surmounts and utilises them." Thus once again, not clearness, not any ready transferableness, but efficacious power and integrating comprehensiveness appear as the true, decisive tests.

You feel—this is your keenest, yet also your most fruitful suffering—that what has happened is cruel, cruel; is what yourself, you, imperfect as you are, would have given your life to prevent. How, then, you wistfully ask, can you possibly love and trust such a power, if it exist at all,—a power, which in this case, shows itself so deaf to the most elementary and legitimate, to the most sacred of your longings and your prayers? You possessed the darling, and you loved and served it with all you were; who possesses and tends it now?

How I understand! how keen, how cutting is this pang!

And I look around me, and again I see a similar bewildering contrast repeated upon an immense scale. I remember, in our own day, the earthquake at Messina, with its thousands of cases of seemingly quite undeserved, quite unmitigated anguish, when our own admittedly most imperfect, badly bungling humanity and governments appeared, as so many small dwarfs of pity, alone pitiful, against this awful background of grim havoc and blind fury and cruelty. And, of course, we could all of us add case upon case from history and from our own experience of souls.

But please note well. Where does the keenness of this our scandal come from? Why do we, in all such cases, suffer such feelings of shock and outrage? What makes us, in the midst of it all, persist in believing, indeed persist in acting (with great cost) on the belief, that love and devotedness are utterly the greatest things we know, and deserve the sacrifice of all our earthly gifts, of our very life? Whence comes all this?—The case is, I think, quite parallel with that as to trust in reality generally. Why is it, as to such trust and such reality, that even the most hardened of the sceptics continue to trouble themselves and to trouble us all, if not as to truth, at least as to truthfulness? Why is untruthfulness so very odious? Untruthfulness is certainly most convenient. Why indeed does every at all sane mind find it so intolerable to hold itself to be completely shut up within its own impressions, to admit that these impressions are nothing but illusions, or, at least, are utterly worthless as indications of realities other than its own? Whence springs the suffering—the most keen suffering—of the thought of being thus shut up, if we are, in fact, thus shut up within our own purely subjective impressions and fancies? The answer, surely, is that we thus suffer because, in fact, we are not thus shut up, because we do communicate with realities other than ourselves, and hence that these realities so impress and affect us that only by a painful effort can we, violently and artificially, treat those realities as mere fanciful projections of our own.

Similarly, if there is no source and standard of love, of pity, of giving, of self-donation,—a source and standing abiding, ultimate, distinct from, deeper than ourselves, a source Itself loving, Itself a Lover, and which, somehow profoundly penetrative of ourselves, keeps us poor things, rich with at least this sense of our poverty and with this our inability to abandon love (that very costly thing) as a chimera or a mere fleeting vibration of our nerves: if there is not such a more than human (deeper and higher than human) source and standard, then the real, actual situation becomes wholly rootless and unreasonable, precisely in what it has of admittedly greatest, of most precious and most significant.

Thus, both in the matter of Truth and Reality and in the matter of Love and a Lover, we suffer, when scepticism assails us, because we are not simply shut up within our own fancies, because (mysteriously yet most actually) we are penetrated and moved by God, the Ultimate Reality and Truth, the Ultimate Lover and Goodness. We are moved by Him Who is, Who is before ever we were, Who is with us from the beginning of our existence, Who is always the first in operation whenever there is interaction between Him and us. Because He is, we have our unconquerable sense of Reality; because He is Love and Lover, we cannot let love go. And it is He Who made the mother's heart; it is, not simply her love, but, in the first instance, His love, with just some drops of it fallen into the mother's heart, which produce the standard within her which cries out against all that is, or even looks like, blindness and cruel fate.

For remember, please, it is not Judaism, not Christianity, not any kind of Theism that bids us, or even allows us, to hold and to accept as good in themselves the several painful or cruel or wrong things that happen in this our complicated, difficult life. None of these convictions worship Nature, or the World-as-a-whole; they all, on the contrary, find much that is wrong in Nature as we know it, and in the World-as-a-whole as we actually find it. All such believers worship and adore not Nature but God—the love and the action of God within and from behind the world, but not as though this love and action were everywhere equally evident, not as though they directly willed, directly chose, all things that happen and as they happen. On the contrary: these great religions leave such a pure optimism to absolute Idealist philosophers, and to rhapsodising pantheists and poets; and these religions believe such views, wheresoever they are taken as ultimate, to be either shallow and unreal, or sorry travesties of the facts.

If, then, I be asked to whom I confide those I love when, after much utterly ineffectual-seeming devotion of my heart, I have seen them suffer fearfully and disappear from my own care and longing, I answer that I confide them to that Reality and Love, to that Real Lover, whose reality and lovingness and penetration of my heart alone make possible and actual my own poor persistent love. Thus my very bitterness and despair over the apparent insult flung at my love by the world as I know it, turns out to be but one more effect of the reality and operativeness of God, and one more reason (again not clear, not readily transferable, but rich and fruitful) for believing and trusting in Him, in Love, the Lover.

FRIEDRICH VON HÜGEL

PATRIOTISM

A country is no mere agglomeration of individuals or families living on the same soil, engaging more or less intimately in neighborly relations or commerce with one another, and recalling the same memories, whether joyful or sad. No, a country is an association of spirits in the service of a social organization which must be safeguarded and defended at all costs, even that of blood, as the one or the several entrusted with its destiny may direct. And it is because they are of one soul that fellow citizens live the same life in the past by reason of their traditions, just as they share in the prolongation of life into the future through common aspirations and hopes.

Patriotism, being the cardinal principal of domestic unity and order even as it is that which binds children of the fatherland together organically, was looked upon by the noblest thinkers of ancient Greece and Rome as the loftiest of the natural virtues. Aristotle, prince of pagan philosophers, thought that disinterestedness in the service of the city (that is, of the state) is the ideal *par excellence* here below. The religion of Christ, however, has made of patriotism a law. A perfect Christian must perforce be a perfect patriot, too. Christianity has ennobled the ideal visualized by pagan reason, at the same time making clear that this ideal cannot find its full realization save in the Absolute.

Whence, one may ask, is there derived this universal, irresistible movement of the soul which in an instant kneads all the urges of a people together in a single effort of cohesion and of resistance to hostile forces menacing its unity and independence? How shall one explain the manner in which all private interests are subordinated to the common interest once the tocsin sounds? Or why all the living offer themselves for immolation? It is not true that the state is essentially of greater worth than the family or the individual; for the state exists in order that the welfare of families and individuals may be served. Nor is it true that the fatherland is a god Moloch, on whose altar the lives of all may legitimately be sacrificed. The rudeness of pagan custom and the despotism of the Caesars had led to the erroneous assumption—which modern militarism has tended to revive—that the state is omnipotent and that its discretionary power creates the law.

No, says Christian theology, peace is the law—peace which is the nation with right order based on justice as its norm. But justice itself, in turn, is absolute only because it is the expression of the essential relationships of men with God and with each other. War for war's sake is therefore a crime. War can be justified only on the ground that it is a necessary means for keeping the peace, as defined, intact. "It is not lawful that peace should serve man to prepare for war," says St. Augustine. "Rather, war is lawful only if it makes peace secure."

In the light of this teaching, which St. Thomas made his own, patriotism take on a religious character. The interests of the individual (even his corporal existence), of the family, of the political party—all these are lower than the ideal of patriotism in the scale of values because this ideal is in fact the law, which is absolute. Or again, the ideal of patriotism is the public recognition of the law as it applies to nations. It is the national honor.

Yet in actuality there is no absolute save God alone.

God alone reigns above all interests and all aspirations by reason of His holiness and of the sovereignty of His dominion. Accordingly, when one affirms the absolute necessity for subordinating all things to law, to justice, to order and to truth, one is implicitly affirming the dependence of all things upon God. When our poor soldiers, hearing us commend them for their heroism, reply very simply, "We have only done our duty," or, "Honor demands these things of us," they profess in their own way the religious character of their patriotism.

Who does not feel that patriotism is "consecrated" and that an attack upon the national dignity is a sort of sacrilegious profanation?

Not long ago a staff officer asked me whether a soldier who falls in the service of a just cause—as ours manifestly is—can be called a "martyr." Now if one uses the word in its strict theological sense, the answer is negative. The soldier is not a martyr because he dies with a weapon in his hands, whereas the martyr delivers himself helpless unto the violence of his persecutors. But if you ask me for my opinion concerning the eternal welfare of a brave man who voluntarily lays down his life to defend the honor of his country and to rescue justice from the violence done to it, I do not hesitate to reply that one cannot doubt in the least that Christ will award the crown to military courage, and that death suffered in a Christian spirit will assure the salvation of the soldier's soul. "Greater love than this no man hath," said Our Lord, "that a man lay down his life for his friends."

The soldier who dies in order that his brethren may be saved, and that the hearthfires and the altars of his fatherland may be protected, has performed this nobler kind of charity. He will not, I grant, always have subjected to minute analysis the moral value of his sacrifice. But must one believe that God exacts of a brave soldier engaged in raging combat the methodical logic of the moralist or the theologian? We admire the heroism of the soldier. Who can doubt that God looks upon it with affection?

Christian mothers, be proud of your sons. Yours is, of all our sorrows, perhaps that most worthy of our respect. I seem to see you now, in mourning but erect nevertheless, standing beside the Mother of Sorrows at the foot of the Cross. Let us offer you our felicitations at the same time that we bring you our condolences. Not all your heroes and ours are mentioned by name in the communiqués, but we have the right to hope that to them will be given the immortal crown which graces the brows of the elect. For such is the virtue of a perfect act of charity that it may suffice to wipe out a lifetime of sin. In the twinkling of an eye it makes a saint of an erring soul.

It should be for us a source of Christian comfort to think that those in any fighting army, not ours alone, who follow in good faith the orders of their chiefs, thus serving a cause they deem just, can profit by the moral virtue of their sacrifice. How many there may be among these young men of twenty who, perhaps, would not have had the strength to live well but who, carried aloft by the sense of patriotic duty, find the courage to die well! Surely we see, my brethren, that God has the supreme ability to mingle mercy and wisdom with justice; and it is clear that we ought to bear in mind that although war is a scourge in so far as our life on earth is concerned—a scourge, indeed, of such destructive force that we cannot measure the range of its impact,—it is also an agent of purification for souls, a means of expiation, and a lever enabling many to climb the heights of patriotism and Christian disinterestedness.

CARDINAL MERCIER

FROM *SAPIENTIAE CHRISTIANAE*

Undoubtedly as they go through life, Catholics have more numerous and greater duties than those who are either wrongly informed upon or wholly destitute of the Catholic faith. . . . A man having embraced the Christian faith, as he ought to, is by that very act subject to the Church as to his mother and becomes a member of that greatest and most holy Society over which it is the function of the Roman Pontiff to wield supreme power under Jesus Christ, the invisible head. But if the law of nature bids us love particularly the city in which we were born and received into this world, and to defend it, so that the good citizen does not hesitate to lay down his life for his fatherland, it is the duty of Christians in like manner to be far more attached to the Church. For the Church is the city of the living God, born of God Himself and established by His authority, which is indeed a pilgrim here on earth, but is ever calling men, teaching them and leading them on to eternal happiness in heaven. So that fatherland deserves our love from which we receive the enjoyment of our mortal life; but needs must we with love maintain the Church, to whom we owe the everlasting life of the soul. For it is right to put the good of the mind before the good of the body, and much more sacred than our duties towards men are our duties towards God.

But, if we would form a true judgment, our supernatural love of the Church and our natural love of country are but twin forms of Charity springing from the same eternal principle, for of both the author and the cause is God; whence it follows that the one duty cannot conflict with the other. . . . And yet, because the days are veiled or the wills of men more than ever contrary, the order governing these two duties is from time to time overturned. Certainly cases occur when the State seems to demand one thing of its citizens and religion another of Christians; and that for no other reason than that the rulers of the State treat lightly the sacred power of the Church or want to make her subject to themselves. . . .

If the laws of the State are openly inconsistent with the rights of God, if they inflict any injury upon the Church, or are in contradiction to religious duties or do violence to the authority of Jesus Christ in the person of the Supreme Pontiff, then indeed is it a duty to resist, a crime to obey: and this involves an injury to the State itself, for every wrong that is committed in the sphere of religion is a transgression against the State.

POPE LEO XIII

TO THE LEADERS OF THE BELLIGERENT PEOPLES

Since the beginning of Our Pontificate, in the midst of the horrors of the terrible war which has burst upon Europe, We have considered three things among others:

To maintain an absolute impartiality toward all belligerents, as becomes him who is the common father, and who loves all his children with an equal affection;

To endeavour continually to do the utmost good to all without distinction of persons, nationality or religion, in accordance not only with the universal law of charity, but also with the supreme spiritual duty laid upon Us by Christ; and

Finally, as is demanded by Our pacific mission to omit nothing, as far as in Our power lies, to contribute to hasten the end of this calamity by trying to bring the peoples and their leaders to more moderate resolutions in the discussion of means that will secure a "just and lasting peace."

Whoever has followed Our work during these three sorrowful years that have just ended has been able easily to recognize that if We remained ever faithful to Our resolution of absolute impartiality and Our work of well-doing We have not ceased to exhort the belligerent peoples and Governments to become once again brothers, although publicity was not given to all that We have done in order to attain this noble end.

Towards the end of the first year of war, We addressed to the nations who were at grips the most earnest exhortations, and, further, We indicated the road to be followed in order to reach a peace which would be stable and honourable for all. Unhappily, Our appeal was not heard, and the war continued desperately for another two years, with all its horrors.

It became even more cruel, and spread upon the face of the earth, upon the sea, and even into the sky; and on defenceless cities, on tranquil villages, on their innocent populations, were seen to descend desolation and death.

And now any one can imagine how the sufferings of all would be multiplied and aggravated if yet more months, or worse still, more years, were to be added to this blood-stained time. Must the civilized world be nothing more than a field of death, and shall Europe, so glorious and flourishing, rush to the abyss, as if dragged by some universal madness, and lend a hand in her own destruction?

In a situation of so much anguish, in the presence of so terribly serious a situation, We—who have no private political aim, who listen not to the suggestions or interests of any of the belligerents, but are influenced only by the sentiment of Our supreme duty as the father of the faithful, by the solicitations of Our children who beg for Our intervention and Our mediatory word, and for the voice of humanity and reason—now again throw out a cry for peace, and We renew Our pressing appeal to those who hold in their hands the destinies of nations.

But that We may no longer limit ourselves to general terms, as circumstances counselled Us in the past, We desire now to put forward some more concrete and practical propositions, and invite the Governments of the belligerents to come to some agreement on the following points, which seem to offer the bases of a just and lasting peace, though leaving to them the duty of adjusting and completing them:

First of all, the fundamental point must be that the moral force of Right shall be substituted for the material force of arms; thence must follow a just agreement of all for the simultaneous and reciprocal diminution of armaments, in accordance with rules and guarantees to be established hereafter, in a measure sufficient and necessary for the maintenance of public order in each State; next, as a substitute for armies, the institution of arbitration, with its high peace-making function, subject to regulations to be agreed on and sanctions to be determined against the State which should refuse either to submit international questions to arbitration or to accept its decision.

Once the supremacy of Right is thus established, let all obstacles to the free intercourse of people be swept aside, in assuring, by means of rules, to be fixed in the same way, the true liberty of and common rights over the sea, which on the one hand would eliminate numerous causes of conflict, and, on the other, would open to all new sources of prosperity and progress.

As to the damage to be made good and the cost of the war, We see no other way of solving the question but to lay down, as a general principle, an entire and reciprocal condonation, justified moreover by the immense benefits which will accrue from disarmament—the more so as the continuation of such carnage solely for economic reasons would be inconceivable. If in certain cases there are, on the other hand, particular reasons, let them be weighed justly and equitably.

But these peaceful agreements, with the immense advantages which flow from them, are not possible without the reciprocal restitution of territories at the moment occupied—consequently, on the part of Germany, a total evacuation of Belgium, with a guarantee of her complete political, military, and economic independence, as against any other Power whatever; similar evacuation of French territory; on the part of other belligerent Powers a similar restitution of the German Colonies.

As regards territorial questions—as, for instance, those pending between Italy and Austria, and between Germany and France—there is ground for hope that in view of the immense advantages of a permanent peace with disarmament, the disputants would feel disposed to examine them in a conciliatory spirit, giving due weight, within the limits of justice and feasibility, as We have said previously, to the aspirations of the populations, and, on occasion, bringing their particular interests into harmony with the general welfare of the great community of mankind.

The same spirit of equity and justice must direct the examination of the remaining territorial and political questions, and particularly those which concern Armenia, The Balkan States, and the territories which form part of the former kingdom of Poland, which in particular, by reason of her noble historical traditions and the sufferings endured, especially during the present war, has a just claim on the sympathies of all nations.

Such are the principal foundations on which We believe that the future reorganization of the Peoples must be built. They are of a nature to make impossible the return of similar conflicts, and to prepare the solution of the economic question, which is so important for the material well-being of all the belligerent States.

In laying these proposals before you, who at this tragic hour are guiding the destinies of the belligerent nations, We are animated by a sweet hope—that of seeing them accepted, and thus of witnessing the speedy end of the terrible struggle which more and more seems to be a useless slaughter.

The whole world, on the other hand, recognizes that on one side as well as on the other the honour of their arms has been amply vindicated.

Lend an ear, therefore, to Our prayers, accept the paternal invitation which We address to you in the name of the Divine Redeemer, the Prince of Peace. Reflect on your very grave responsibility before God and before men; on your decision depend the repose and joy of unnumbered families, the lives of thousands of young men, the happiness, in a word, of the peoples, to secure whose welfare is our absolute duty.

May God inspire you with a decision in harmony with His most holy will. Heaven grant that in meriting the applause of your contemporaries you may assure to yourselves, in the sight of future generations, the noble name of peace-makers. For Us, in close communion in prayer and penitence with all the faithful souls who are sighing for peace, We implore for you from the Divine Spirit enlightenment and counsel.

POPE BENEDICT XV

JUSTICE AND CHARITY

Just as the unity of human society cannot be built upon class warfare, so the proper ordering of economic affairs cannot be left to free competition alone. From this source have proceeded in the past all the errors of the Individualistic school. This school, ignorant or forgetful of the social and moral aspects of economic questions, teaches that the state should refrain, in theory and in practice, from interfering in the processes involved, since these have in free competition and the open market a principle of self-direction which insures a better control than any created intellect could provide. Free competition, however, though within certain limits just and productive of good results, cannot be the ruling principle of the economic world.

This has been abundantly proved by the consequences that have followed from the free rein given to those dangerous individualistic ideals. It is therefore very necessary that economic affairs be once more subjected to and governed by a true and effective guiding principle. Still less can this function be exercised by the kind of economic autocracy which within recent times has taken the place of free competition, for this is a headstrong and vehement power which, if it is to prove beneficial to mankind, needs to be curbed strongly and ruled with prudence. It cannot be curbed and governed by itself. Therefore nobler and more lofty principles must be sought in order to bring that autocracy under stern and uncompromising control; and those principles are social justice and social charity.

To that end all the institutions of public and social life must be imbued with the spirit of justice, and that justice must above all be truly operative. It must build up a juridical and social order able to pervade all economic activity. Social charity should be, as it were, the soul of this order; and the duty of the state will be to protect and defend it effectively.

POPE PIUS XI

TO THE GERMAN PEOPLE

Whoever exalts race, or the people, or the State, or a particular form of State, or the depositories of power, or any other fundamental value of the human community—however necessary and honorable be their function in worldly things—whoever raises these notions above their standard value and divinizes them to an idolatrous level, distorts and perverts an order of the world planned and created by God: he is far from the true faith in God and from the concept of life which that faith upholds.

Beware, Venerable Brethren, of that growing abuse, in speech as in writing, of the name of God as though it were a meaningless label, to be affixed to any creation, more or less arbitrary, of human speculation. Use your influence on the Faithful, that they refuse to yield to this aberration. Our God is the Personal God, supernatural, omnipotent, infinitely perfect, one in the Trinity of Persons, tripersonal in the unity of divine essence, the Creator of all existence, Lord, King and Ultimate Consummator of the History of the world, who will not, and cannot, tolerate a rival god by His side.

This God, this Sovereign Master, has issued commandments whose value is independent of time and space, of country and race. As God's sun shines on every human face, so His law knows neither privilege nor exception. Rulers and subjects, crowned and uncrowned, rich and poor are equally subject to His word. From the fullness of the Creator's right there naturally arises the fullness of His right to be obeyed by individuals and communities, whoever they are. This obedience permeates all branches of activity in which moral values claim harmony with the law of God, and pervades all integration of the ever-changing laws of man into the immutable laws of God.

None but superficial minds could stumble into concepts of a national God, of a national religion; or attempt to lock within the frontiers of a single people, within the narrow limits of a single race, God, the Creator of the universe, King and Legislator of all nations before whose immensity they are as a drop of a bucket.

POPE PIUS XI

THOU DOST SMILE

Thou dost surely smile also, and lovingly, at Thy little saints, at the naïve confidence with which they approach Thee, at their fears little and great, and (yes) at their childish resistance as they flutter in the grasp of Thy hand, like so many captured birds.

One must smile at such serious matters,—smile tenderly, sympathetically, affectionately. But what about ludicrous things? For there are ludicrous things in Thy world, too. These are not found among the creatures which have remained what they were when they issued from Thy hand. Thou hast created nothing comical. But they exist among men, who have continued Thy creation in their fashion, who have made themselves into something else. Comedy is to be encountered among them and their works, their devices, their undertakings. Yes, there is so much comedy! I do not refer to the evil and the base which are likewise to be found there, but merely to the ludicrous. Often the underlying intention is very good. Only the whole thing is stupid, and stupid in a manner that can only be termed comical. It is not stupid in a way that arouses pity, as does, for example, the behaviour of a bird which seeks to fly straight through a glass pane, but in a stimulating, arousing way, concerning which one cannot even weep, or grow angry, because it is possible only to laugh,—to laugh bitterly. The human busybodies, the vain, the megalomaniacs, the foolish, the strutters, the posers, the devotees of bathos, the victims of ridiculous fantasies! What dost Thou say to these? There is much that is great and noble in Thy human creatures. Thou hast stationed them only a little below the angels. But what of all this silliness? Even the greatest spirits have their share of it. If one looks at them closely, seeing them at their domestic business, or in private . . . they are obviously fools. One can't help laughing at them.

How did they become thus? Since their ludicrousness is not wicked, it is not necessarily entirely their own fault. Thy nature, Thy cosmic laws, the sequences of the evolution Thou hast ordained, these may have something to do with the origins of the comedy. And even if a human being had made himself ridiculous solely through his own power and authority—the question would still remain, how did he do it? Thy lofty creature, Thy messenger, the Lord of Thy creation! I understand why he must be limited and even curbed in all his energies, and even why he must be a little stupid. But must he be so ridiculously stupid?

And since these human beings really cannot help being what they are, it is impossible to be severe with them. It would be unjust to treat them with ribald scorn. But it is just as impossible to weep; weep quietly and sadly, about their ridiculousness, in the same way one weeps over sin. I have no idea what one really ought to do. I should like to cry and laugh, strike and caress, denounce and comfort, be disconsolate and merry, all at the same time. That is the puzzle one confronts, so that there seems to be no way out except laughter, bitter laughter. But this cannot be said of Thee, because Thou art never puzzled. Thou canst do nothing except to overlook human banality and pass by it, quietly and reservedly, as if Thou didst not see it. If there is something Thou dost not wish to notice, surely it is the ludicrousness of Thy men and Thy nations. Thou passest over their presumptions and their pompousness as if they were not there. Thou leavest them alone for a time with their silly plaything, with which they make as much undecipherable racket as if they were all drunk. Then one day Thou takest it out of their hands, calmly and without a word, just as one takes from a silly child a toy it has not understood and has misused, without wasting an explanation.

PETER LIPPERT

THE LAST DAY

I tell myself that the Last Day will begin with a dawn of indescribable beauty. Throughout the previous night the tears of all who suffer or had suffered will have fallen, pure as the dew of Paradise's first spring-time. Then the sun will come up, like a pale Byzantine Virgin in her mosaic of gold. When the earth awakens, it will be all perfume. Men, intoxicated, beyond measure comforted, with the sources of delight about them, will look with wonder upon a resurrected Garden of Eden. They will walk among the flowers and sing merry songs which fill them with ecstasy. Stirred by a presentiment of the Coming of which no one dare speak, Nature will garb herself in her most magnificent accoutrements. Like unto a superb courtesan, she will bedeck herself with the jewels lost by so many condemned to die and with bewildering essences which induce forgetfulness of life.

Nothing, then, can be too beautiful, for this will be—at last—the day of God, awaited these thousands of years in the dens of iniquity, in the dungeons, in the tombs. And it shall be the day of derision, of that Derision vast as the heavens, which is called the divine Subsannation in Holy Writ. This shall be the true feast of charity, presided over by Charity in person—by that redoubtable Vagabond of whom it is written that no one knows His ways, that He giveth no accounting unto any, that He goeth wheresoever He wisheth to go. It shall be in all truth the feast of the poor, the feast for the poor, without delays or disappointments. In the twinkling of an eye, they shall themselves take without the help of any go-between, all that the rich can give them for the pleasure of giving. They shall take far, far more than this. They shall take prodigiously, forever.

LÉON BLOY

WHAT IS SCIENCE?

Pasteur, having been abruptly addressed by a colleague, who remarked that there were many yet unexplained facts in connection with fermentation, answered by thus apostrophizing his adversaries: "What is, then, your idea of the progress of Science? Science advances one step, then another, and then draws back and meditates before taking a third. Does the impossibility of taking that last step suppress the success acquired by the two others? Would you say to an infant who hesitated before a third step, having ventured on two previous ones, 'Thy former efforts are of no avail—thou shalt never walk'?

"You wish to upset what you are pleased to call my 'theory,' apparently in order to propose another. Permit me to tell you by what signs these theories are recognized: the characteristic of erroneous theories is that clinging to them it is impossible ever to foresee new facts, and one is therefore compelled to graft further hypotheses on them in order to account for those new facts; but correct theories, on the other hand, are the outcome of observed facts and are characterized by the ability of those who accept them to predict new facts which develop logically from those already known. In short, the characteristic of a correct theory is its fruitfulness."

"Science," he said further at the next meeting of the Academy, "ought not to concern itself in any way with the philosophical consequences of its discoveries. If through the development of my experimental studies I arrive at the demonstration that matter can organize itself of its own accord into a cell or into a living being, I would come here and proclaim it with the legitimate pride of a scientist conscious of having made a great discovery, and I would add, if provoked into doing so, "All the worse for those whose doctrines or systems do not fit in with the truth of the facts of nature."

"It was with similar pride that I defied my opponents to contradict me when I said, 'In the present state of science, the doctrine of spontaneous generation is a chimera.' And I add, with similar independence, 'So much the worse for those whose philosophical or political ideas are contradicted by my studies.'

"This must not be taken to mean that, in my beliefs and in the conduct of my life, I take account only of acquired science. Even if I wish to do so, I could not, for then I should have to strip myself of a part of myself. There are two men in each of us—the scientist, he who starts with a clear field and desires to rise to the knowledge of Nature through observation, experimentation and deduction, and the man of belief, the man who mourns his dead children, and who cannot, alas, prove that he will see them again, but who believes that he will, and lives in that hope, the man who would not die like a vibrio, but feels that the spirit that is within him cannot die. The two domains are distinct, and woe to him who tries to let them trespass on each other in the always so imperfect state of human knowledge."

RENÉ VALLERY-RADOT

THE MYSTERY OF SIMEON

And, behold, there was a man in Jerusalem named Simeon; and this man who was just and God-fearing, had waited for the consolation that was to be made manifest unto Israel. And the Holy Spirit was in him. He had received tidings from the Holy Spirit that he should not taste death until he had seen Christ the Lord.

He went into the Temple, and when the infant Jesus, borne by

His parents, entered in order that there might be done unto Him what the law prescribed, he himself took Him into his arms, blessed God, and said, "Now permit Thy servant to depart in peace, Lord, according to Thy promise. . . ."

But nobody knows if the old man, of that country of his, ever later on beheld anything else. And if he witnessed no other event, he was nevertheless happy. Happy, happier than anybody else. He knew of no other happening upon the earth. He could boast of having been at the right spot. For he had held, he had held in his arms, the greatest Dauphin of the world, the son of the greatest King —the very King, Jesus Christ. In his hands he had held and lifted up the King of Kings, the mightiest king of the world, the King above Kings, the King above all kings on earth.

He had held in his hands the greatest kingdom of the kingdoms of this world. And he did not know aught else that happened on the earth. For in the evening of his life, he had come to know the greatest story on earth. And likewise the greatest story of the heavens.

The greatest story of earth's history.

The greatest story ever told.

The only great story ever told.

The greatest story in the whole world.

The only interesting story that ever took place.

Then everybody could approach Thee. This old man, in the evening of his life, embraced Thee as if Thou wert an ordinary child. Most assuredly he embraced Thee. Just as an old man, as old people love to embrace infants, little ones, any little child.

CHARLES PÉGUY

SHALL BERLIN BE CHRISTIAN?

I had a telephone conversation. "O, Mr. Commissioner, what is meant by a 'small dwelling'?" "One or two rooms." "And a middle-sized dwelling?" "Three or four rooms." "Now what is a large dwelling?" "More than four rooms." "Now how many dwellings are there in Berlin? Old and new?" "1,210,602." "That means a million and a quarter, in round numbers. How many of these are small dwellings?" "The exact percentage is 69.5." "Therefore 70 per cent of all dwellings in Berlin consist of one or two rooms. Seventy per cent! Mr. Commissioner, let me ask another question. Are there families which have no dwelling? I don't mean single persons—I mean families." "There are 117,430 households which have no dwellings of their own." "Do I understand you correctly?" "Yes." "Which means that these people are like cuckoos, living in other people's nests. Perhaps that is possible in dwellings of medium or large size. But think of what it means in small dwellings, of two rooms or even one. That is incredible! How often does it happen?" "In exactly 51.9 per cent of the cases." "Do you really mean it? There are in Berlin 60,000 households which share two rooms or one with other people. One family fastened to another like a leech! As long as such conditions prevail, Mr. Commissioner, prisons will be necessary."

I should be ashamed of myself were I to go about preaching the Ten Commandments in the northern and eastern sections of Berlin were I not at the same time to work as hard as possible to see that those Commandments *can* be obeyed. To advocate family life in which children are welcome is impossible unless one advocates at the same time continuous social reform. The tenement is treason to the Commandments of God. The slums of the big city are areas from which Christian culture is kept by a blockade. The atmosphere of health and of Christian living is not to be found in damp flats and unlighted barracks. We are taught that the premiss of all supernatural life, of the life of grace, is the natural order. Therefore we must establish a new connection between religion and industrial activity. Therefore we must be interested in social welfare. Not as if it were a game. No, it is the never-ending duty of the whole people, especially of that part of it which believes in God, to help perform, directly or indirectly, the task of caring for souls in the world of our day. But if you would help fashion a contented people, interested in its destiny and willing to work loyally for the common good with God's blessing, give it a share in the rights and the goods the possession of which was entrusted by God to all men without exception and the stewardship over which is a responsibility for which He will ask an accounting from each and every one of us.

CARL SONNENSCHEIN

THE COMMANDMENT OF LOVE

Equal importance attaches to the neglect of the first part of the great Commandment—Love the Lord thy God above all things. For this neglect inevitably meant the drying up of those forces in European man which were central, governing, indicative of desirable goals to be reached. The historical significance of humanitarianism is, after all, this—that the Christian law of love was excluded from the public, visible business of life; that the efficacy of Christianity, taken in its religio-ecclesiastical forms, was impaired in the world of affairs and of the objective spirit alike; and that the energies of religion, of Christianity, could be made manifest only in the secret places of the individual heart. It is obvious now that the Age of Enlightenment had only to surmount the strongly over-emphasized, one-sided spiritualism of the early Protestant movements, with its dangerous repudiation of the wish to erect the Kingdom of God in this imperfect world of ours. All that was left was humanitarianism pure and simple; and this had no real objective other than that of a humanity without leadership and without a final goal. Having now been made dependent upon the fortuitous urges of natural instinct, this humanity had lost the most secure guaranty of its own unity at the same time that it had suffered its sense of dependence upon God to become obscure. For the idea of man is a theomorphic idea, as Augustine saw in his time.

The circumstance that a European anarchy analogous to that which followed the World War—the anarchy of humanitarianism which has definitely lost God—did not immediately appear, is due to the fact that during the Age of Enlightenment (also in the realm of the subconscious) the common traditions which a Christian culture that lasted many centuries and stood upon the fundament of antique achievement had created continued to exert their influence and so lingered on despite the fact that men had abandoned them, just as the afterglow survives past the hour of sunset. Just as musicians may keep on playing for a time, though their conductor may suddenly have dropped his baton, so the peoples of Europe seemed still to form a kind of symphony. Nevertheless it was obvious that disorder must finally set in. In that which the great thinkers of the Age of Enlightenment—Voltaire, Kant, Wolff, for example—termed the "autonomous" reason, which supposedly gave the principles of ethics, logic, economy, law and other subjects a validity transcending time and history, the Eternal Light still glowed in occasional flickers and remained, in so doing, Christian even though men might no longer realize what Christianity was.

The culture of the nineteenth century, increasingly one-sided and historical in character, gradually quenched even these traces of light. Following the humanitarian trend of thought to its strictly logical conclusions, this culture dissolved in particular that concept of the unity of reasoning human nature in which the Age of Enlightenment had embedded all its notions of truth and falsehood, good and evil, justice and injustice. Finally every idea which was supposed to serve as a common norm for mankind grew thinner and thinner, more abstract and more formalistic. The great masses could no longer discern any substance in the figments of the philosophers. And what remained? Only the idea of belligerent groups which fomented their interests or followed their instincts. Such groups might be races, nations, states, classes. There arose a mirage of struggle weaving to and fro, in which the only thing that mattered was brutal success. Everything which had been dubbed an idea, a norm, whether of morality or of law, was now looked upon only as if it were a club, knife or other weapon rendering useful service to some interested group.

MAX SCHELER

ACTION

Why then, we may ask, should not God raise up among ourselves also some great figure, like, for instance, St. Francis or St. Dominic, who through the miracle and grace of his character would bring about at one blow the great reaction, which the weakness of our hands and the poverty of our souls makes it impossible to effect by the natural way of isolated actions? It would surely be a mistake if we men of little faith denied the possibility of such an amazing intervention of Providence. But it would be equally mistaken to sit still and placidly await such a miracle of grace in order thereby to get rid of all personal responsibility. That would be as disastrous a fatalism as that described above. It is true, *spiritus ubi vult spirat;* we can never force the Spirit's miracle of grace; we must hope for it, wait for it, beg for it. But we must never make such a hope the pretext for sinking into a mystic lethargy, for shirking personal effort. We ourselves must begin to take action, and only then may we justly expect that God will act with us. We must ourselves try to prepare for the new outpouring of the Spirit.

PETER WUST

THE CATHOLIC CLAIM

I can understand the Catholic claim, but I cannot understand any other. The Church says to her children, you must believe these things because I tell you that I witnessed them myself, and you know that I am trustworthy. I do not refer you merely to written books, but to my continuous consciousness that is called Tradition. You can believe that Resurrection surely because I was there and I saw it. I saw with my own eyes the stone rolled away; I saw the Lord of Life come out; I went with the Maries to the tomb; I heard the footsteps on the garden path; I saw, through eyes blind with tears but clear with love, Him whom my companion thought to be the gardener.

WILLIAM HURRELL MALLOCK

PROVIDENCE AND HISTORY

In addition to the principle of free will in man, which rises above that law of nature which is necessity, there is another principle, higher and divine, in the historical progress of nations. This is the manifest guidance of an all-loving, all ruling Providence, displayed in the course of history and the march of human destiny, in great matters and small alike. The power of evil is, however, something more than a mere power of nature, being by comparison a power of a higher and more spiritual kind. Its influence is not only felt in the sensual inclinations of human nature, but it also, under the mask of a false liberty, unceasingly labors to rob man of his true freedom. Thus Providence is not a mere vague notion, a formula of belief, or a feeling of virtuous anticipation,—in short, a mere pious conjecture—but it is the real, effective, redeeming power of God in history, restoring lost freedom to the individual man and to the whole human race and, with that freedom, the effectual power to do good. The problem of human existence consists in this that man on the great stage of history as in the small details of private life has to choose and decide between a genuine, heavenly freedom, always steadfastly faithful to God, and the false, rebellious freedom of a will separated from God. The mere license of passion or of sensual appetite is not liberty but a stern bondage under the yoke of nature. But as that false and criminal freedom is spiritual, it is superior to nature; and it is strictly conformable with truth to regard as the author of this false liberty him whom revelation represents as the mightiest, the most potent and the most intelligent egotist among all created beings either in the visible or invisible world.

Were it not for this freedom of choice, innate in man or imparted to him, for this faculty of deciding between the divine impulse and the suggestions of the spirit of evil, there would be no history. And without faith in such a principle there could be no philosophy of history. If free-will were only a psychological illusion; if, consequently, man were incapable of sentiment or deliberate action; if everything in life were predetermined by necessity and subject, as nature is, to a blind, immutable destiny:—if these things were so, what we call history or the description of mankind would merely constitute a branch of natural science. But such notions are utterly repugnant to the general belief and the most intimate sentiments of mankind, according to which it is precisely the conflict between the good or divine principle, on the one hand, and the evil or adverse principle on the other, which constitutes the meaning of human life and human history, from the beginning to the end of time. Without the idea of a God-head regulating the course of human destiny, of an all-ruling Providence, and of the saving and redeeming power of God, the history of the world would be a labyrinth without an outlet—a confused pile of ages buried upon ages, a mighty tragedy without a proper beginning or a proper ending. Such is the tragic and melancholy impression produced on our minds by several of the ancient historians, particularly the profoundest of them all. Tacitus, who during the last days of antiquity, gazes so darkly, in retrospect, upon the past.

But the greatest historical mystery—the deepest and most complicated enigma of the world—is the fact that God permits evil; and the explanation and solution can only be found in the unfettered freedom of man, who is destined to lead a life of struggle, being exposed to the influences of two contending powers ever since the earthly mission of Adam began. Here, we see, is the real, the whole business of man—this divinely ordained trial of the faculty of freedom which was imparted to the firstling of creation, to God's image, and must continuously be tested in the conflict with and victory over temptation and all hostile spirits. Only the man who recognizes, in its, at first, inconceivably wide extent, the permission given by God to evil (the whole magnitude of the power given to the wicked principle, in accordance with God's inscrutable decrees, from the curse of Cain, and the sign of that curse, uninterruptedly transmitted through all the labyrinths of error and of grossly mishandled truth, through all the false religions of Heathenism and through all the ages of extreme moral corruption and of crime forever repeated and forever growing in malignancy, to the final period when the anti-Christian principle, the spirit of evil, shall usurp dominion over the whole world, and when mankind, sufficiently prepared for the ordeal, shall be summoned to the final decisive trial, the last great conflict with the enemy in all the fulness of his power), is able to understand the great phenomena of history, which are of a complexity often dark and strange, though he, too, can penetrate only a little way into the hidden and mysterious ways of Providence.

He who regards every thing in humanity and its progress from a merely natural or rationalist point of view and seeks to explain all in accordance with such views may not be without a certain instinctive feeling that an all-ruling Providence exists and entertain a kind of pious deference to its secret ways and high designs; but since he is without a deep insight into the ways of Providence and does not see clearly, manifestly and fully the power of evil, he must always rest on the surface of events and historical facts, content with outward appearances and neither comprehending the meaning of the whole nor understanding the import of any part. Yes, the matter of greatest moment is to observe the Spirit of God revealing itself in history, enlightening and directing the judgments of men, saving and guiding mankind, and, even here below, admonishing, judging and chastising nations and generations. This threefold law of the world, these three mighty principles which dominate the historical development of mankind,—the hidden ways of a Providence which delivers and emancipates the human race; the free-will of man, compelled to make a decisive choice in the struggle of life, in all of its acts and in the feelings to which it gives rise; and the power given by God to the evil principle—cannot be posited as absolutely necessary, as are the phenomena of nature or the laws of human reason. It is, rather, in the characteristic marks of particular events and historical facts that the visible traces of invisible power and design, of high and hidden wisdom, must be sought for.

FRIEDRICH SCHLEGEL

THE CHRISTIAN AGE OF GOLD

Times when Europe was a Christian realm were happy and illustrious times. Then this part of the earth, so diligently fashioned by mankind, was dwelt in by Christians foresworn to unity. A lofty bond of interest, which all sensed clearly, linked together even the most distant parts of this great spiritual kingdom. One ruler controlled and unified political energies, though he himself was without extensive territorial possessions. A populous gild to which anybody could gain admission was directly subject to this sovereign, doing his bidding and seeking to strengthen his beneficent reign. Every member of this company was everywhere honored; and when the common folk sought help or solace from the gild, or asked protection or counsel, they gladly offered whatever was necessary to sustain its multiform activities and received in return safety, respect and careful attention. The chosen men were endowed with miracle-working powers, and all trusted them as children of Heaven, whose presence and solicitude were productive of many blessings. When they spoke, the people listened with childlike confidence. How easy it was to perform one's daily tasks, when one had been assured of a safe future by these holy men. They forgave every sin; they blotted out and renewed every discolored spot in life. They were veteran pilots on the vast sea of the unknown, and while they watched one could laugh at the storms of life and hope for a safe landing on the shore of what was the true home of the human spirit.

Under their command the wildest, most voracious impulses were curbed by reverence and obedience. Always they preached love of the sacred, matchlessly beautiful Lady of Christendom, who had Divine powers at her beck and call and stood ready to rescue any believer from peril however dire. Folk talked also of heavenly persons, long since dead, who had been victorious over the lures of earth here below by reason of their devotion and loyalty to that Blessed Mother and her Divine and kindly Child. These persons had been honored by God, therefore, and become helpful, protecting patrons of their living brethren, to whom they eagerly gave assistance in hours of need. If some one had erred, they took his part; they were untiring friends of mankind at the Heavenly throne. And how much happiness was felt by those who came away from the beautiful assemblies in mysterious churches, all of them adorned with inspiring images, redolent of sweet odors, and vibrant with holy and uplifting music! In these shrines the blessed remains of those who had departed this world fearing the Lord were gratefully laid to rest in precious reliquaries. Round about these the Divine goodness and omnipotence —responsive to the generous bidding of the saintly dead—was made manifest in splendid signs and wonders. It all reminds us of the manner in which loving souls treasure the locks or the letters of their beloved dead, therewith nurturing the blissful glow of affection until death brings union once again. Yes, men in those ages gathered everywhere, with the most scrupulous care, whatever had belonged to these cherished, saintly souls. If one could own or, indeed, even touch, a comforting relic, one deemed oneself fortunate. Again and again the grace of Heaven seemed to have descended in a special way upon some particular image or grave. To such shrines men journeyed from all parts of the land, bringing gifts and taking with them in turn the Divine boons of peace of heart and health of body.

NOVALIS

MONASTICISM AND MANKIND

Transport yourself now to La Trappe, and contemplate those monks, dressed in sackcloth, digging their own graves! Behold them wandering like spectres in the extensive forest of Mortague and on the margin of the solitary lake! Silence walks by their side, or, if they speak when they meet, all they say to each other is, Brother, we must die. These rigorous orders of Christianity were schools of active morality, instituted in the midst of the pleasures of the age, and exhibiting continually to the eyes of vice and prosperity models of penance and striking examples of human misery.

And what a sight was that of an expiring monk of La Trappe! what sublime philosophy! what a warning to mankind! Extended upon a little straw and ashes in the sanctuary of the church, his brethren ranged in silence around him, he exhorts them to persevere in virtue while the funeral bell announces his last agonies. It is usually the task of the living to encourage their departing friends; but here is a spectacle much more sublime; it is the dying man who expatiates on death. Already stepping upon the threshold of eternity, he understands better than those around him what death is, and, with a voice which seems to issue from the sepulchre, he emphatically summons his companions and even his superiors to works of penance. Who does not shudder in perceiving that this religious, after a life of so much holiness, is yet penetrated with fear at the approach of his mortal dissolution? Christianity has drawn from the tomb all the morality that underlies it. By death has morality entered into the life of man. Had he remained immortal after the fall, he would never perhaps have been acquainted with virtue.

Thus religion everywhere presents scenes the most pleasing or the most instructive. Here holy men, like people enchanted by a magic spell, perform in silence the joyful operations of the harvest and the vintage; there the nuns of St. Clare tread with bare feet the ice-cold tombs of their cloister. Imagine not, however, that they are unhappy amid their austerities; their hearts are pure, and their eyes are directed toward heaven, indicative of desire and hope. A gray woollen robe is preferable to magnificent apparel purchased at the price of virtue, and the bread of charity is more wholesome than that of prostitution. From how many afflictions are not these females secured by the simple veil which separates them from the world? To give the reader an adequate idea of the objects which now suggest themselves to our contemplation would require a talent quite different from ours. The highest eulogy that we could present of the monastic life would be to exhibit a catalogue of the meritorious works to which it has been devoted. Religion, leaving the care of our joys to our own hearts, is like a tender mother, intent only on alleviating our sorrows; but in accomplishing this arduous task she has summoned all her sons and daughters to her aid. To some she has committed the care of those afflicted with disease, as to the multitude of monks and nuns dedicated to the service of hospitals; to others she has consigned the poor, as to the pious Sisters of Charity. The Redemptionist Father embarks at Marseilles; but whither is he bound alone, with his breviary and his staff? This conqueror is speeding to the deliverance of humanity, attended by invisible armies. With the purse of charity in his hand, he goes to brave pestilence, slavery, and martyrdom. He accosts the Dey of Algiers; he addresses him in the name of that heavenly king whose ambassador he is. The barbarian is astonished at the sight of this European stranger who ventures to come alone, across seas and through storms, to demand the release of his captive fellow-creatures. Impelled by an unknown power, he accepts the gold that is offered him, and the heroic deliverer, satisfied with having restored some unfortunate beings to their country, obscure and unknown, humbly sets out on foot to return to his monastery.

Wherever we look, a similar prospect presents itself. The missionary embarking for China meets, in the port, the missionary returning glorious and crippled from Canada; the Gray nun hastens to administer relief to the pauper in his cottage; the Capuchin flies to check the ravages of a conflagration; the friar Hospitaller washes the feet of the traveller; the brother of the Bona Mors Society consoles the dying Christian or conveys the body of the poor to the grave; the Sister of Charity mounts to the garret of indigence to distribute money and clothing and to light up the soul with hope; those women so justly denominated Filles-Dieu (daughters of God) are always carrying here and there food, lint, and medicaments; the Sister of the Good Shepherd extends her arms to the unhappy victim of crime, exclaiming, I am not come to call the just but sinners to repentance. The orphan finds a father, the lunatic a physician, the ignorant an instructor. All these doers of heavenly works encourage one another. Religion, meanwhile, attentive to their actions, and holding a crown of immortality, thus addresses them:—"Be of good heart, my children, go on! Quicken your pace; be more speedy than the evils which befall human life. Earn this crown which I have prepared for you, and which will secure you from every affliction, from every want."

Among so many pictures, each of which would require whole volumes to enter fully into its details and praises, on what particular scene shall we fix our view? We have already treated of those hospitable houses which religion has erected in the solitudes of the four quarters of the globe; let us now turn our eyes to objects of a different kind.

There are people in whom the mere name of Capuchin excites feelings of contempt. The monks of the order of St. Francis were, nevertheless, very often distinguished for simplicity and dignity. Which of us had not seen a couple of those venerable men journeying in the country, commonly toward All-Souls' day, at the approach of winter, about the time of the vintage? They went along soliciting hospitality at the ancient mansions which they passed in their way. At nightfall the two pilgrims reached a solitary edifice; they ascended the antique steps, laid down their long staves and their wallets at the top, knocked at the loud-resounding door, and applied for hospitality. If the master refused admittance to these guests of the Lord, they made a profound obeisance, silently retired, took up their wallets and their staves, and, shaking the dust from their sandals, proceeded, amid the shades of night, to seek the cabin of the husbandman. If, on the contrary, they were received, they were first supplied with water to wash, after the fashion of the days of Jacob and Homer, and then they went and seated themselves at the hospitable fire. As in times of old, they began to caress the children of their hosts, not merely to gain their favor, but because, like their divine Master, they were fond of children; they made them presents of relics and pictures. The young folks, who had at first run away affrighted, being now attracted by these curiosities, soon grew so familiar as to play between the knees of the good friars. The parents with a smile of tenderness beheld their innocent sports, and the interesting contrast between the infantine graces of their offspring, and the hoary age of their guests.

Meanwhile the rain poured in torrents; tempestuous winds swept through the leafless woods and howled among the chimneys and battlements of the Gothic mansion; the owl screeched from the top of the turret. Near a large fire, the family sat down to supper; the repast was cordial and the behavior friendly. The youthful daughter of the host timidly questioned her guests, who, with becoming gravity, commended her beauty and modesty. The good fathers entertained the whole family with their agreeable converse; they related some affecting story, for they had always met with many remarkable things in their distant missions among the savages of America or the tribes of ancient East, and the manner in which they came to ask for hospitality, revived the recollection of those times when a Thales and an Anacharsis thus travelled in Asia and Greece.

After supper the mistress called her servants, and one of the fathers was invited to perform the accustomed family devotions; the two monks then retired to rest, wishing their hosts every sort of prosperity. Next morning, upon inquiry for the aged travellers, it was found that they were gone, like those sacred visions which sometimes visit the habitations of the good.

Was there any thing calculated to harrow the soul, any errand which persons, averse to tears, durst not undertake for fear of compromising their pleasures; it was to the inmates of the convent that it was immediately consigned, and more particularly to the fathers of the order of St. Francis. It was supposed that men who had devoted themselves to suffering ought naturally to be the heralds of misfortune. One was obliged to carry to a family the disastrous intelligence of the loss of its fortune, another to inform the parent of the death of an only son. The great Bourdaloue himself performed this painful duty: he presented himself in silence at the door of the father, crossed his hands upon his breast, made a profound inclination, and retired mute as death, of which he was the interpreter.

Can we suppose that it afforded much pleasure (we mean what the world would deem such,) can we suppose that it was a very agreeable office, for a Carmelite or a Franciscan to go from prison to prison, to announce to the criminal his sentence, to hear his sad tale, to administer consolation to him, and to remain for entire days amid the most agonizing scenes? In the performance of these pious duties, the sweat has often been seen to flow from the brow of these sympathizing monks and to trickle upon their robes, making them forever sacred, in spite of the sarcasms of infidels. And yet what honor, what profit, accrued to these sons of charity from so many sacrifices, except the derision of the world, and, perhaps, the abuse of the very prisoners whom they went to console? Men, ungrateful as they are, at least acknowledged their own insufficiency in these important incidents of life, since they confided them to religion, the only effectual resource in the lowest depths of misfortune. O apostle of Christ! what scenes didst thou witness when, standing beside the executioner, thou wast not afraid of being sprinkled with the blood of the wretched culprit, and wast his last friend upon earth! Here is one of the most impressive sights that the world can exhibit! At the two corners of the scaffold human justice and divine justice are met face to face. The one, implacable, and supported by an avenging sword, is accompanied by despair; the sweet attendants of the other are pity and hope. The one has for her minister a man of blood, the other a man of peace. The one condemns, the other absolves. The former says to the victim, whether innocent or guilty, "Thou must die!" the latter cries, "Child of innocence or of repentance, speed thy flight to heaven!"

FRANÇOIS RENÉ DE CHATEAUBRIAND

THE MONKS OF THE WEST

From the middle of the fifth century the cenobitical institution, proceeding from the Thebaid, had occupied one by one all the provinces of the Roman Empire and encamped upon every frontier to await and win over the Barbarians. The immense services which this institution rendered to the Church, and the new and necessary force which it lent to society, lying inert between the avenging embrace of the Germans and the despicable languor of expiring imperialism, could already be appreciated.

The monks were, after the Papacy, the direct instruments of the salvation and honor of Europe. They rendered her capable of gigantic and supernatural effort against the inveterate paganism of the old world and the torrential impetuosity of the northern invaders. Contemporaries themselves perceived it; no one disputed the solemn testimony of the priest Rufinus, who was not himself a monk but had long studied and observed them: "There is no doubt that without these humble penitents the world could not have gone on existing."

Everything round about them was calculated to create terror and despair. On the one side, the savage hordes of a hundred hostile nations filled Gaul, Italy, Spain, Illyria, Africa, and all the provinces in their turn, with blood and horror; and after Alaric, Genseric and Attila, a well-founded presentiment of the final fall of Rome and the empire waxed stronger in all hearts every day. On the other hand, Arianism, with its implacable and growing obstinacy, and the many secondary heresies which succeeded each other uninterruptedly, rent the Church, disturbed consciences, and made men believe in impending universal upheaval. When the judgments of God appeared in the beginning of the fifth century, the world lost its senses. Some plunged into debauchery to enjoy like brutes the last remnant of bliss; others sank into incurable melancholy.

The lovers of solitude, the men of penitence, sacrifice, and voluntary humiliation, alone knew how to live, hope, resist and stand fast. To those who reproach the monastic spirit with enervating, debasing and making sluggards of men, let it suffice to recall what the monks were in those days of desolation and despair. They alone showed themselves equal to all needs and proof against all terrors. Human courage has never been more tried than among the monks; it has never displayed greater resources or a deeper constancy; and it has never shown itself more manly and unshakable.

The monks opposed to the successive waves of the invading Barbarians an insurmountable barrier of virtue, courage, patience and genius; and when all external resistance was found useless and impossible, it became apparent that they had formed, for all the germs of civilization and of the future, shelters which the floods might pass over but could not engulf. In the midst of the deluge which annihilated the Roman Europe and the world of antiquity, they concentrated themselves in a high and pure sphere which was destined to survive all that chaos and be the center from which new life would come into a new world.

Their courage was surpassed only by their charity—by their gentle and sympathetic compassion with all those whom, they saw, burdened with the miseries which overwhelmed the earth. They loved their neighbors passionately because they loved God more than themselves. They derived the secret of this love and this supernatural energy from Christian self-renouncement, from the voluntary expiation of their own faults and those of others. In opposing the three eternal bases of monastic life—poverty, chastity and obedience—to the orgies of luxury, debauchery and pride, they created a contrast which was also a remedy. By sacrificing in a spirit of penance all permitted privileges, such as marriage, property and the free disposition of their time and their lives, they became the guardians and saviors of those who lawfully desired to retain these legitimate possessions, and who saw no way in which such things could be safeguarded from irremediable outrage in a social order so desperate.

But we must not be under a misapprehension on this matter. They never dreamed of making their exceptional life the common rule. They knew that it could only be the privilege of certain souls, more completely transfixed than others by the blood of Christ. They did not presume to compel all to accept their evangelical counsels as precepts. They remained faithful to the interpretations of the sacred texts which has been unchanged from the time of the first Popes until the present day. Their leaders always resisted the excesses of intemperate zeal which characterized the Gnostics and others, who would have rendered what was possible for some obligatory upon all. No doubt one could cite certain events, or certain lives, which appear to lean towards excess. But there are excesses which was inseparable from the force and vigor of all great movements of the spirit, and which only serve to reveal the existence of a vital and fertile current. In their hearts, on the whole, they remained aloof from all unregulated exaltation, and firmly attached alike to apostolic traditions and to the infallible prudence of the Church. They had no tendency to transform the whole world into a cloister, though this accusation has been brought against them. They wanted only to create and maintain, despite all the storms and defeats which characterized the world they knew, the home, the place of refuge, the school of a peace and power mightier than the world.

This is why they brought so great an influence to bear upon the world thereafter. They had fled from men in vain, for men followed them. Everything of the good heart, the lofty mind and the clear intellect which survived in this broken-down society rallied round the monks, as if to escape from universal ruin. Their spirit breathed from the far places of the desert upon towns, upon schools, and even upon palaces, lighting them anew with some rays of vigor and reason. The distraught people sought them out, listened to them, and admired them, understanding them little, to be sure, and imitating them even less. Yet their mere existence was the most energetic protest against pagan materialism, which had ended by depraving all souls and undermining the social constitution of the ancient world. They aroused in man all those intellectual and moral forces which could help him to bear up under the unparalleled catastrophies of the age. They taught him to struggle against that reign of sensuality which was to be so painfully expiated under the yoke of the Barbarians. They showed him at one and the same time the road to heaven and the way to a future in this world—the sole future open to these long enervated races, namely regeneration by suffering voluntarily accepted and courageously borne.

CHARLES, COUNT DE MONTALEMBERT

IN DARK DAYS

We believe great evil has been done, grave wrongs committed, but we do not believe it all over with the church or with humanity. In the darkest day "the old God," as say the Germans, "still lives," and his providence is as young, as fresh, as vigorous, and as worthy of reliance as ever. We are among those who believe it never wise to sit down and waste our energies in sighing over the sins we have committed, but to look out for the virtue, and engage with redoubled vigilance in the performance of the virtue, of which we are still capable. As long as God lives we will never believe in the permanent triumph of evil, or in the impossibility of repairing the greatest wrongs that may have been committed. The church is as present, is today as powerful as she was when she went forth with the apostles from that "upper room" in Jerusalem to conquer the world. The loss of temporal sovereignty by the successor of Peter, the loss of all her temporal goods, the reduction of her ministers to mere staff and script will not make her weaker than she was when Peter erected his chair in the capital of the pagan world. Perhaps this loss would even prove to be a gain. Woe to him who despoils the church, but not therefore woe to the church despoiled. What the church has once done she can do again, and perhaps could do more without than with the worldly trappings with which she has so long been encumbered.

We by no means despair of the future; we by no means despair of seeing religion again recovering its hold on men's hearts and on men's consciences; we by no means despair of seeing again peoples and nations, sovereign princes and states recognizing the authority of Peter, and acknowledging the supremacy of the spiritual over the temporal; we by no means despair of seeing reestablished that system of Christian politics and international right which the church, through her sovereign pontiffs, labored so long and earnestly to introduce and establish among Christian nations. Political atheism is a falsehood, and no falsehood can live. Its triumph can be but temporary, and last no longer than the heated passions which have given it birth. The church will regain her power and her rightful supremacy, but probably not in a society modelled after that of the middle ages. She then worked through princes and nobles, hereafter she must work through the people; she then operated by diplomacy and force, she must hereafter operate through the intelligence and conscience of the people elevated to an effective power in the management of their own public affairs.

ORESTES A. BROWNSON

GOVERNMENT

Government exists in heaven as well as on earth, and in heaven in its perfection. Its office is not purely repressive, to restrain violence, to redress wrongs, and to punish the transgressor. It has something more to do than to restrict our natural liberty, curb our passions, and maintain justice between man and man. Its office is positive as well as negative. It is needed to render effective the solidarity of the individuals of a nation, and to render the nation an organism, not a mere organization—to combine men in one living body, and to strengthen all with the strength of each, and each with the strength of all—to develop, strengthen, and sustain individual liberty, and to utilize and direct it to the promotion of the common weal—to be a social providence, imitating in its order and degree the action of the Divine Providence itself; and, while it provides for the common good of all, to protect each, the lowest and meanest, with the whole force and majesty of society. It is the minister of wrath to wrongdoers, indeed; but its nature is beneficent, and its action defines and protects the right of property, creates and maintains a medium in which religion can exert her supernatural energy, promotes learning, fosters science and arts, advances civilization, and contributes as a powerful means to the fulfilment by man of the Divine purpose in his existence. Next after religion, it is man's greatest good; and even religion without it can do only a small portion of her work. They wrong it who call it a necessary evil; it is a great good, and instead of being distrusted, hated, or resisted, except in its abuses, it should be loved, respected, obeyed, and, if need be, defended at the cost of earthly goods, and even of life itself.

ORESTES A. BROWNSON

COLUMBUS

Columbus, after gazing in silence on this foremost shore of the land so often determined by his calculations, and so magnificently coloured by his imagination, found it to exceed even his own expectations. He burned with impatience to be the first to set foot on the sand, and to plant the Cross and the flag of Spain. But he restrained the eagerness of himself and his crew, being desirous of giving the act of taking possession of a new world a solemnity worthy of the greatest deed, perhaps, ever accomplished by a seaman; and to call God and his angels, sea, earth, and sky, as witnesses of his conquest of an unknown hemisphere.

He put on all his insignia as admiral and viceroy, wrapped himself in his purple cloak, and, taking a flag embroidered with a cross, in which the initials of Ferdinand and Isabella were interlaced, and surmounted by a crown, he entered his boat, and pulled toward shore, followed by Alonzo and Yanés Pinzon. On landing, he fell on his knees to acknowledge the greatness of God. He kissed the ground, and, with his face on the earth, wept tears of a double import and a double meaning—tears of joy for Columbus; the overflowing of a proud spirit, grateful and pious—tears of sadness for this virgin soil, seeming to foreshadow the devastation, with fire and sword, which the strangers were to bring with their pride, their knowledge, and their power.

"Almighty and eternal God," said Columbus, as he raised his forehead from the dust, with a Latin prayer which his companions have handed down to us, "who, by the energy of Thy creative word, hast made the firmament, the earth, and sea, blessed and glorified be Thy name in all places! May Thy majesty and dominion be exalted for ever, as Thou has permitted Thy Holy Name to be made known and spread by the most humble of Thy servants in this hitherto unknown portion of Thy empire."

He then baptized this land with the name of Christ—the Island of San Salvador.

ALPHONSE DE LAMARTINE

THE CATHOLIC IDEA OF THE STATE

When, therefore, in the political shipwreck of modern Europe, it is asked which political form of party is favoured by the Church, the only answer we can give is, that she is attached to none; but that though indifferent to existing forms, she is attached to a spirit which is nearly extinct. Those who, from a fear of exposing her to political animosity, would deny this, forget that the truth is as strong against political as against religious error, and shut their eyes to the only means by which the political regeneration of the modern world is a possibility. For the Catholic religion alone will not suffice to save it, as it was insufficient to save the ancient world, unless the Catholic idea equally manifests itself in the political order. The Church alone, without influence on the State, is powerless as a security for good government. It is absurd to pretend that at the present day France, or Spain, or Naples, are better governed than England, Holland, or Prussia. A country entirely Protestant may have more Catholic elements in its government than one where the population is wholly Catholic. The State which is Catholic *par excellence* is a byword for misgovernment, because the orthodoxy and piety of its administrators are deemed a substitute for a better system. The demand for a really Catholic system of government falls with the greatest weight of reproach on the Catholic states.

Yet it is important to remember that in the ages of faith the same unity prevailed in political ideas, and that the civil as well as the religious troubles of our time are in great measure due to the Reformation. It is common to advise Catholics to make up their minds to accept the political doctrines of the day; but it would be more to the purpose to recall the ideas of Catholic times. It is not in the results of the political development of the last three centuries that the Church can place her trust; neither in absolute monarchy, nor in the revolutionary liberalism, nor in the infallible constitutional scheme. She must create anew or revive her former creations, and instill a new life and spirit into those remains of the mediaeval system which will bear the mark of the ages when heresy and unbelief, Roman law, and heathen philosophy, had not obscured the idea of the Christian state. These remains are to be found, in various stages of decay, in every state that grew out of the mediaeval civilization. Above all they will be found in the country which, in the midst of its apostasy, and in spite of so much guilt towards religion, has preserved the Catholic forms in her establishment more than any other Protestant nation, and the Catholic spirit in her political institutions more than any Catholic nation. To renew the memory of the times in which this spirit prevailed in Europe, and to preserve the remains of it, to promote the knowledge of what is lost, and the desire of what is most urgently needed,—is an important service and an important duty which it behooves us to perform. We are greatly mistaken if these are not reflections which force themselves on every one who carefully observes the political history of the Church in modern Europe.

LORD ACTON

CHRISTIANITY AND THE CHURCH

It would be presumptuous if I attempted to indicate the numberless channels by which Christian influence gradually penetrated the State. The first striking phenomenon is the slowness with which an action destined to be so prodigious became manifest. Going forth to all nations, in many stages of civilisation and under almost every form of government, Christianity had none of the character of a political apostolate, and in its absorbing mission to individuals did not challenge public authority. The early Christians avoided contact with the State, abstained from the responsibilities of office, and were even reluctant to serve in the army. Cherishing their citizenship of a kingdom not of this world, they despaired of an empire which seemed too powerful to be resisted and too corrupt to be converted, whose institutions, the work and the pride of untold centuries of paganism, drew their sanctions from the gods whom the Christians accounted devils, which plunged its hands from age to age in the blood of martyrs, and was beyond the hope of regeneration and foredoomed to perish. They were so much overawed as to imagine that the fall of the State would be the end of the Church and of the world, and no man dreamed of the boundless future of spiritual and social influence that awaited their religion among the race of destroyers that were bringing the empire of Augustus and of Constantine to humiliation and ruin. The duties of government were less in their thoughts than the private virtues and duties of subjects; and it was long before they became aware of the burden of power in their faith. Down almost to the time of Chrysostom, they shrank from contemplating the obligation to emancipate the slaves.

Although the doctrine of self-reliance and self-denial, which is the foundation of political economy, was written as legibly in the New Testament as in the Wealth of Nations, it was not recognized until our age. Tertullian boasts of the passive obedience of the Christians. Melito writes to a pagan Emperor as if he were incapable of giving an unjust command; and in Christian times Optatus thought that whoever presumed to find fault with his sovereign exalted himself almost to the level of a god. But this political quietism was not universal. Origen, the ablest writer of early times, spoke with approval of conspiring for the destruction of tyranny.

After the fourth century the declarations against slavery are earnest and continual. And in a theological but yet pregnant sense, divines of the second century insist on liberty, and divines of the fourth century on equality. There was one essential and inevitable transformation in politics. Popular governments had existed, and also mixed and federal governments, but there had been no limited government, no State the circumference of whose authority had been defined by a force external to its own. That was the great problem which philosophy had raised, and which no statesmanship had been able to solve. Those who proclaimed the assistance of a higher authority had indeed drawn a metaphysical barrier before the governments, but they had not known how to make it real. All that Socrates could effect by way of protest against the tyranny of the reformed democracy was to die for his convictions. The Stoics could only advise the wise man to hold aloof from politics, keeping the unwritten law in his heart. But when Christ said: "Render unto Caesar the things that are Caesar's, and unto God the things that are God's," those words, spoken on His last visit to the Temple, three days before His death, gave to the civil power, under the protection of conscience, a sacredness it had never enjoyed, and bounds it had never acknowledged; and they were the repudiation of absolutism and the inauguration of freedom. For our Lord not only delivered the precept, but created the force to execute it. To maintain the necessary immunity in one supreme sphere, to reduce all political authority within defined limits, ceased to be an aspiration of patient reasoners, and was made the perpetual charge and care of the most energetic institution and the most universal association in the world. The new law, the new spirit, the new authority, gave to liberty a meaning and a value it had not possessed in the philosophy or in the constitution of Greece or Rome before the knowledge of the truth that makes us free.

LORD ACTON

LIBERTY

By liberty I mean the assurance that every man shall be protected in doing what he believes his duty against the influence of authority and majorities, custom and opinion. The State is competent to assign duties and draw the line between good and evil only in its immediate sphere. Beyond the limits of things necessary for its well-being, it can only give indirect help to fight the battle of life by promoting the influences which prevail against temptation—religion, education, and the distribution of wealth.

Now liberty and good government do not exclude each other; and there are excellent reasons why they should go together. Liberty is not a means to a higher political end. It is itself the highest political end. It is not for the sake of a good public administration that it is required, but for security in the pursuit of the highest objects of civil society, and of private life. Increase of freedom in the State may sometimes promote mediocrity, and give vitality to prejudice; it may even retard useful legislation, diminish the capacity for war, and restrict the boundaries of empire.

A generous spirit prefers that his country should be poor, and weak, and of no account, but free, rather than powerful, prosperous and enslaved. It is better to be the citizen of a humble commonwealth in the Alps, without a prospect of influence beyond the narrow frontier, than a subject of the superb autocracy that overshadows half of Asia and of Europe.

LORD ACTON

MARIE LANGLOIS: A HEROINE OF THE REVOLUTION

In the village of Levi there lived a young milkmaid who had been born in Normandy and was known as Marie Langlois. She was an ignorant girl of twenty-two years, who had finished only the first two grades at school, was not acquainted with any priests or religious, and was employed by a master interested in nothing save work in the fields. It so happened that during May, 1793, she was denounced as a "fanatic" by the village pastor, who had taken the oath of loyalty to the revolutionary Constitution. She was arrested and sent to Versailles.

"Do you know whether Monsieur le Curé of Levi has taken the oath prescribed by law?" demanded the inquisitor.

"Yes, he has."

"Do you approve of what he has done?"

"No."

"Why do you disapprove?"

"Those who crave the right to make law governing the temporal welfare do not have the right to regulate the spiritual welfare."

"Who has so completely misinformed you?"

"The Lord instructs me."

"Who has told you not to trust priests who have taken the oath?" the inquisitor continued.

"Nobody. That has come to me from God."

"Do you believe in God?"

"Yes, I do believe. Are we not His children? If you do not believe this, in what do you believe? I believe also in the Blessed Virgin and all the saints of Heaven."

"Is it true that you are not a good citizeness?"

"No, sir. I am for religion," she added quickly, "and for helping everyone."

"A good citizeness obeys the law."

"I do so, except when there is question of my religion."

Thus the young girl spoke, with a lucidity of mind which would have been surprising even if she had been a person of the most subtle intelligence. She also revealed a faith so ardent that it seemed not that of a believer merely but almost that of one inspired.

"Has God spoken to you?" she was asked.

"He is the master of all that. My soul is made according to His image and likeness. He is the master of my body and my soul."

"Does God make use of human creatures in order to manifest His will?"

"Yes."

"Of whom does He make use?"

"Those who seek to know His will."

"And so you think that you have had inspiration from above?"

"Yes."

The magistrate continued to probe, trying to find out who her accomplices were. But Marie Langlois had no intimate friends, received no letters, did not converse with those round about her. Her parents were far away. The only money she possessed was a sum of forty francs which her employers owed her. She could hardly write her name, and her only devotional objects were two pious leaflets and a rosary. How could such a person be transformed into a conspirator against the state?

"Has some priest made you believe that you would earn the crown of martyrdom?" she was asked.

"No."

"Do you think that those who obey the law are enemies of God?"

"There is no harm in the law, in so far as it is not opposed to the dictates of conscience and is not concerned with spiritual matters."

"Do you obey the law?"

"I do, in so far as my conscience and my faith are not involved."

The hearing was nearly ended. "Why have you spoken publicly

in favor of priests who have not taken the oath?" demanded the magistrate.

"Yes, I have stood for them in public. Those are the things of God, all of which must be made known."

"Did you not do so with the intention of fomenting a disturbance?"

"No."

"Have you heard whether or not people approved of what you said?"

"I have not heard that anybody approved. Some laughed and made fun of me."

"Have you told me the truth?"

"Yes."

"Do you wish to change, add to, or subtract from anything you have said?"

"No."

I have cited this testimony almost in its entirety. The hearing took place nearly eleven months before the law rendering this sort of procedure unnecessary was passed. Marie remained a prisoner in Versailles for a long while. . . . She was then questioned for the last time.

"Have you not spoken in a manner unbecoming a citizen?"

"No."

"You are certainly accused of having boasted that you were an aristocrat."

"I am on trial only because of my religion."

When the hearing was finished, this note was written in the *dossier:* "This is a *sans-culotte* who has been in custody for a year. It would be well to dispose of the case." And as a matter of fact it was disposed of quickly. On the 24th Prairial, the poor servant appeared before a tribunal assembled in the Hall of Equality, in company with some drunkards accused of having toasted the King's health. Two witnesses had been summoned, one of whom was the priest who had reported her to the authorities. The Revolution, however, had completed its cycle. Since no dastardly deed is profitable, the bad priest had in the mean time been brought to the same Versailles prison where Marie Langlois was held captive; and now he was escorted to the witness stand by the gendarmes, so that he could play the final scene in his role of informant. The accused girl aroused interest by reason of her youth, her flaming sincerity, and her humble station, of which no one could be envious. If Dumas, the president of the tribunal, had instructed the jury to consider whether she had acted in criminal intent, he would doubtless have saved her. He abstained from that suggestion of clemency; and before night fall the young martyr (can one call her aught else?) appeared before the Master in whom she had professed to believe.

PIERRE DE LA GORCE

SAINT BERNARD AND THE BLESSED VIRGIN

The century in which Bernard lived was in a very special way the century of the Virgin. Vast throngs were attracted by the pilgrimage to Puy:—the "great pardons" which God and the Madonna offered there in the rare years when Good Friday coincided with the feast of the Annunciation had, since the year 992, given the "Virgin of Mount Anis" renown throughout the whole of Christendom; and when Louis VII returned from the Orient he brought to Puy the image of the Dark Virgin. More and more books dealt with the miracles she performed—miracles identified with the church of Coutances, with Notre-Dame de Rocamadour, with Notre-Dame de Chartres. These volumes revive before our eyes the far-flung movement of the crowds having these mighty sanctuaries for their destination.

Along the highways the silence of these masses was such that "one did not suspect that a single human being was there;" and whenever a halt was made, the voice of preachers was heard, bidding men do penance and forgive whomsoever had been his enemy. Those who did not heed these exhortations were expelled from the pious caravan, and their offerings were not accepted. The atmosphere seemed charged with prodigies. Loaves of bread were multiplied, and empty casks were filled anew. There were ambulances bearing the sick and the infirm, who sometimes cried out that they had been cured even before they had reached the shrine. Once arrived in the presence of the Virgin, the crowds carried on a "blockade of the heavenly Jerusalem." They gave themselves over to flagellations—their prayers sought to do violence. The chroniclers, on the look-out for miracles, confessed to the slowness of their pens; and the canon who kept the record at Coutances declared that he knew of twice as many as he had entered into his books.

The shrine of Chartres gave rise to a kind of literary *genre*—those short dramatic poems which in subsequent centuries were known as *Miracles of Our Lady*. The Dark Virgin of Puy, she whom Bishop Adhemar of Monteil had celebrated in 922 for the whole of Christendom in the *Salve Regina,* took as her interpreter a pious carpenter of the town, and so had herself multiplied in countless places everywhere in France during 1182 and 1183. Her object was reputed to be the establishment of social peace by the suppression of brigandage; and she was served by strange hooded confraternities, having for their badge a plaque of tin bearing the likeness of the Virgin and her Child. Yet ere long these groups, having directed their forces against the tyranny of certain knights, came to be looked upon as trouble makers and were stamped out cruelly.

All this devotion to wonder-working local Madonnas was only the popular expression of the ardent desire of the Church in France to honor more fulsomely the Mother of Christ. Even though the feast of the Immaculate Conception, which was observed in England during the eleventh century and was then, in the twelfth, solemnly adopted by the canons of Lyons, had found an adversary in Saint Bernard, it was nevertheless from his writings that Christendom gained its knowledge of Mary as the daily, universal mediatrix of every grace. By piecing together several fragments of prayers which had been on the lips of Bernard, popular fervor elaborated, during the fifteenth century, the petition which is known as the *Memorare.* It seems likely also that the posthumous influence of the Abbot of Clairvaux was felt in the movement which little by little led the bishops and the Councils of the Church to prescribe for the faithful, about the close of the twelfth century, the recitation, along with the

Our Father and the *Creed,* of the greeting addressed by the Archangel Gabriel to the Virgin Mary: "Hail Mary, full of grace, the Lord is with thee, blessed art thou among women," and in addition of the words of welcome spoken by Saint Elizabeth, "Blessed is the fruit of thy womb." One finds the teaching of this prayer ordered for the first time in Paris during 1198, and Orleans followed suit about the same time. Enriched finally with words added by the Church, this prayer became, during the fifteenth century, our *Ave Maria.*

Thus the century of Saint Bernard, before drawing to a close, began to invite the Christian world to greet Our Lady in the same phrases which had been used in greeting her by the two earliest witnesses of her vocation; and this invitation, which was destined to teach human lips the *Ave Maria* throughout the whole of Christendom, was extended by Eudes de Sully, Archbishop of Paris.

GEORGES GOYAU

A JESUIT MISSIONARY

The perils which beset the missionaries did not spring from the fury of the Iroquois alone, for Nature herself was armed with terror in this stern wilderness of New France. On the thirtieth of January, 1646, Father Anne de Nouë set out from Three Rivers to go to the fort built by the French at the mouth of the River Richelieu, where he was to say Mass and hear confessions. De Nouë was sixty-three years old, and had come to Canada in 1825. As an indifferent memory disabled him from mastering the Indian languages, he devoted himself to the spiritual charge of the French, and of the Indians about the forts, within reach of an interpreter. For the rest, he attended the sick, and, at times of scarcity, fished in the river or dug roots in the woods for the subsistence of his flock. In short, though sprung from a noble family of Champagne, he shrank from no toil, however humble, to which his idea of duty or his vow of obedience called him.

The old missionary had for companions two soldiers and a Huron Indian. They were all on snowshoes, and the soldiers dragged their baggage on small sledges. Their highway was the St. Lawrence, transformed to solid ice, and buried, like all the country, beneath two or three feet of snow, which, far and near glared dazzling white under the clear winter sun. Before night they had walked eighteen miles, and the soldiers, unused to snowshoes, were greatly fatigued. They made their camp in the forest, on the shore of the great expansion of the St. Lawrence called the Lake of St. Peter,—dug away the snow, heaped it around the spot as a barrier against the wind, made their fire on the frozen earth in the midst, and lay down to sleep. At two o'clock in the morning De Nouë awoke. The moon shone like daylight over the vast white desert of the frozen lake, with its bordering fir-trees bowed to the ground with snow; and the kindly thought struck the Father, that he might ease his companions by going in advance to Fort Richelieu, and sending back men to aid them in dragging their sledges. He knew the way well. He directed them to follow the tracks of his snowshoes in the morning; and, not doubting to reach the fort before night, left behind his blanket and his flint and steel. For provisions, he put a morsel of bread and five or six prunes in his pocket, told his rosary, and set forth.

Before dawn the weather changed. The air thickened, clouds hid the moon, and a snow-storm set in. The traveler was in utter darkness. He lost the points of the compass, wandered far out on the lake, and when day appeared could see nothing but the snow beneath his feet, and the myriads of falling flakes that encompassed him like a curtain, impervious to the sight. Still he toiled on, winding hither and thither, and at times unwittingly circling back on his own footsteps. At night he dug a hole in the snow under the shore of an island, and lay down, without fire, food, or blanket.

Meanwhile the two soldiers and the Indian, unable to trace his footprints, which the snow had hidden, pursued their way to the fort; but the Indian was ignorant of the country, and the Frenchmen were unskilled. They wandered from their course, and at evening encamped on the shore of the island of St. Ignace, at no great distance from De Nouë. Here the Indian, trusting to his instinct, left them and set forth alone in search of their destination, which he soon succeeded in finding. The palisades of the feeble little fort, and of the rude buildings within, were whitened with snow, and half buried in it. Here, amid the desolation, a handful of men kept watch and ward against the Iroquois. Seated by the blazing logs, the Indian asked for De Nouë, and, to his astonishment, the soldiers of the garrison told him that he had not been seen. The captain of the post was called; all was anxiety; but nothing could be done that night.

At daybreak parties went out to search. The two soldiers were readily found; but they looked in vain for the missionary. All day they were ranging the ice, firing their guns and shouting; but to no avail, and they returned disconsolate. There was a converted Indian, whom the French called Charles, at the fort, one of four who were spending the winter there. On the next morning, the second of February, he and one of his companions, together with Baron, a French soldier, resumed the search; and, guided by the slight depressions in the snow which had fallen on the wanderer's footprints, the quick-eyed savages traced him through all his windings, found his camp by the shore of the island, and thence followed him beyond the fort. He had passed near without discovering it,—perhaps weakness had dimmed his sight,—stopped to rest at a point a league above, and thence made his way about three leagues farther. Here they found him. He had dug a circular excavation in the snow, and was kneeling in it on the earth. His head was bare, his eyes open and turned upwards, and his hands clasped on his breast. His hat and his snowshoes lay at his side. The body was leaning slightly forward, resting against the bank of snow before it, and frozen to the hardness of marble.

Thus, in an act of kindness and charity, died the first martyr of the Canadian mission.

FRANCIS PARKMAN

FALLEN AMONG THE IROQUOIS

Even from the ranks of the Church Triumphant, the five Jesuit missionary priests and two devoted laymen now declared Blessed by

Papal decree, and who will always be known as the "Jesuit Martyrs of North America," stand forth as a challenge to any standard of success which the world has erected, and by which profane history judges the commensurateness of effort with result. The record of the world is littered with ruined causes and lives that seem to have been given in vain; and of this mass of apparently wasted heroism, the cause of God, as is natural, has taken particularly heavy toll. Even so, without paying tribute for one moment to any of the standards by which the world assesses gain and loss, we feel instinctively that within martyrdom a deeper martyrdom can subsist.

To feel the knife at one's throat, or the flames creeping up one's limbs, and to know that every drop of blood which sinks into the ground, and every grain of ashes dispersed upon the air, is destined in God's providence to bear fruit a thousandfold, is a tragic and heroic fate. But to die, not only in torture whose recital chills the blood at a distance of three centuries, but in utter dereliction of spirit as well—to be the ruined leader of a lost cause, conscious that, as the shepherd is being stricken, the sheep are dispersing—to have led a nation to the Cross only to see them fastened to it before one's eyes—this is to taste the bitterness of martyrdom as few men, and these the very elect of Christ's Passion, have been predestined to taste it.

It is this extremity in their martyrdom which lends so spectral a quality to the story of Blessed Isaac Jogues and his companions. It is not because their lives were so comfortless, and their deaths so terrible—though few men have suffered more—that historians, of alien religion and race, have bowed their heads when these noble names were mentioned. It is because the forlornness, the divine insanity of the task which they had imposed upon themselves, consecrates them and sets them apart from a world which has hardly ever dared to stake all on love. Like the scapegoat of the Israelites, loaded down with the sins of the people and driven forth into the alkaline desert to perish of thirst, these wild emissaries of the Cross pass out ahead of the great migration that is to build up a nation from Atlantic to Pacific, bearing upon their foredoomed heads the burden, not only of wrongs that have been accomplished, but of those whose perpetration is in the womb of time. They become more than the glory of the Catholic Church and the Jesuit order. They are the reparation, offered by Christianity in advance, for all that Christianity will have to forget and forgive.

HENRY LONGAN STUART

ST. JOAN AT ORLEANS

Orleans had been under siege since October, 1428. The place was particularly strong for that time: it had an unbroken wall and thirty-five towers. Situated on the right bank of the Loire, it was in touch with the left, towards Sologne, by means of a great bridge. If its garrison was not strong in regular soldiers, it was yet well manned by the townspeople; it was commanded by Dunois.

For the English Orleans was of great importance, since it lay on the road from Guyenne, and it could serve as a base of operations against the King of Bourges. It was, in one way, the last link in their line. So that having won over the smaller places in the district, the English, with strategy and much strength, laid siege upon it from the 12th of October, 1428. They were firmly settled upon the left bank of the Loire at St. Jean-le-Blanc in Fort Augustins and in Fort Tourelles, thus cutting off communication with Blois and Bourges.

In spite of a gallant resistance, Orleans, ever more closely hedged in, was in danger of succumbing to famine in the spring of 1429 if immediate help were not at hand.

Two roads led from Blois to Orleans; one on the right bank, the Beauce road, overlooked by many places in English hands; the other on the left, the Sologne road, quite plainly easier of access, and yet leaving the Loire to be crossed when Orleans was reached. The left bank was chosen, and on the 27th of April began the march on Orleans.

Difficulties were greater than had been foreseen. Having marched by the Loire and come to the Loiret, the army had to board pontoons to cross to the other bank. But the place was overlooked by an English stronghold. Moreover, the river was swollen and the wind blew contrary. The English could take advantage of this to attack the relief force. The French leaders wondered if they would do well to withdraw to Blois and cross the river there.

Here Joan showed herself. She had unsuccessfully pleaded for the right bank, which led directly to the English, but the left had been chosen, and now they had to keep to it. Obstacles are never materially impassable. It would be morally disastrous to retire to Blois. As it happened, the wind changed suddenly, the pontoons were loaded, and on Friday the 29th the river was crossed and the army established on the right bank. Joan came into Orleans and the whole town acclaimed her. She wanted to attack the English forthwith, but she submitted to the advice of Dunois and waited. Her mission was not to make men act in spite of themselves, but to place herself totally at the service of whoever had need of her.

On the 2nd of May she reconnoitred the English position. She observed that they lay on both banks of the river, inactive. The crossing of the Loire became every day an easier matter for the people of Orleans. She must take advantage of this, and from that time she considered shameful any hesitation or delay, strengthened as she was by knowing that she must fulfil her mission, by these first successes, and by the enthusiastic support of the populace.

On the 4th of May a new convoy coming from Blois along the right bank entered Orleans, and the garrison successfully attacked the stronghold of Saint-Loup to the east of the town, which had so sorely hindered the embarkation of the first relief force.

A council of war held on the 5th, Ascension Day, decided for an attack against the forts of Augustins and Saint-Laurent. In the event the greatest confusion reigned at first. The attack on Saint-Laurent took a long time to develop. Joan made for the Burgundy Gate, and was followed by the townspeople, a crossing to the left bank was effected by boats and by fords, and a disorderly advance on Augustins was repulsed. Joan went again to the attack, stormed Augustins, and set it on fire, and then surrounded Tourelles, while the English from Saint-Pryvé withdrew from the left bank.

The night of the 6th and 7th was without quiet for the French camp. An English counter-attack on the morrow was feared. The officers with Joan were afraid to attack Tourelles, but for her part she did not hesitate. "In the name of God I shall go, and whoever loves me will follow me." Not a man held back. They made for the rampart that joined Tourelles to the ruined Augustins.

At mid-day the issue was still uncertain. In the early afternoon Joan was wounded, and at evening the officers were considering the prospect of leaving off the fight until the following day. But Joan came amongst them once more and implored them to carry on the attack. She went forth herself, and when her standard fluttered above the rampart at the head of the French columns the English retired in disorder. By now the drawbridge connecting the ramparts with Tourelles was afire. Only a few could cross it. Tourelles still stood, and thus for a whole day the fighting on the left bank continued. Meanwhile the men of Orleans, who were on the right bank, had undertaken the repair of the bridge which crossed the river by Tourelles. Soon they had set fire to the barricade which covered the fort on this flank. Attacked from two directions, the fort at length capitulated, and in the evening of that day Joan crossed over the newly-repaired bridge and entered Orleans once again. The whole town acclaimed her.

On the 8th and 9th the English withdrew all along the line. Thus ended in a few days the six-months' siege on which they had concentrated all their strength—for success there meant the final surrender of the very heart of France.

The set-back was complete; and in achieving it Joan's part had been the greatest. From the start she had seen how much hinged on Orleans, how vitally important it was to force the action there. With all her being she had pleaded for the enterprise, and once it had been undertaken, she had carried it through with her own strength, using to the full her power upon her followers. The professional soldiers about her had been hesitant before difficulties and dismayed at losses, they had procrastinated and would have wanted to rest before their end was attained, even at the risk of thus forewarning the enemy, of losing the benefit of sacrifices already made, of hurting the men's morale. But her vision had gone beyond theirs; she had shown them a way, and made them feel an impulse stronger than their own: it had real strategy behind it, it did not engage but with good reason, and then it slackened only when the end was achieved, when all energy was spent and the ultimate consequences of the action had been worked out to the full.

For Joan, inspired by her mission as she was, the springs of her action seemed to lie simply in the situation as each new day presented it: there was the enemy reserved and cautious, and shortly not a little troubled, in spite of his power and his resources; and here were her own followers, both soldiers and townspeople, with a dash and devotion and a great hope doubling their own value, and adding to their strength more surely than could an actual reinforcement. It were folly to slacken in such circumstances, and a crime to let an action drag.

From beginning to end Joan had been the moving spirit in the fight and prime factor of that tremendous force that brought the great victory to the French. And this she had been by using to the full the magnificent energy of the mass, never falsely buoying it up, though it was delicate in its way and inexperienced. Wholly vowed to her mission, she had fought for, and won, the freedom of the people by means of the people, showing all the powers of a great commander at every crisis of the fight.

FERDINAND FOCH

CHRISTIAN HUMANISM

To the question, What is man, whence comes and whither goes he? humanism by its own lights is powerless to reply; the individual is free to solve these problems by his own philosophy or theology. Hence the two groups into which fall all genuine disciples of the Renaissance, the one Christian Humanism, the only one that interests us here; the other, "Natural" Humanism. Over against the two groups looms the Protestant Reformation.

Christian Humanism easily adapts to the dogmas and the spirit of the Church the two mottoes mentioned above; with Terence and better and more markedly than Terence, it holds that nothing in human nature should be foreign to it, because in all humanity it recognizes the image of God and in every man a brother; with Shakespeare, and in a higher sense than Shakespeare, it cries: How beauteous is mankind! since mankind has been redeemed by God made Man, and raised by Grace above its natural perfection. Indeed! Can it show nothing newer and more original? But what more is wanted? For its theology, Christian Humanism accepts purely and simply that of the Church. Is it taken for a sect? It is nothing but a temper of mind. Without neglecting any of the essential truths of Christianity, it brings forward by preference those which appear the most consoling, encouraging, in a word human, which to it seem the most divine and the most conformed to Infinite Goodness. Thus it does not hold that the central dogma is Original Sin, but the Redemption. "Redemption," it is true, implies fault, but a fault thrice-blessed, since it has procured mankind so great and lovely a Redeemer. O felix culpa! Again, it does not question the necessity of Grace, but far from Grace being parsimoniously measured out to some few elect, it sees it liberally offered to all, more anxious to be received by man than man can be to receive it. The manhood praised by Christian Humanism is in a sense, though not the only or the chief sense, that of the natural man with the simply human gifts bestowed upon him in the state of pure nature and still retained by him, more or less injured by the Fall, but not vitiated, corrupted to the core, incapable of goodness. On all these points, the Church condemns exaggerations, those of Pelagians and semi-Pelagians on the one hand, of Calvin, Baïus, and Jansenius on the other. Between these two extremes she permits theologians to interpret the common dogma to their taste, to lay the stress where they will, to incline the balance in favour either of rigour or of humanity. Christian Humanism instinctively favours the latter, as for instance in the case of infants dying unbaptized. The system it opposes, it condemns as false, because it is unhuman. The word frequently occurs on the humanist's lips.

HENRI BRÉMOND

WHEN THE POPES LEFT ROME

The removal of the Holy See to Avignon was most disastrous to the Eternal City, which thereby lost not only its historic position as the capital of Christendom, but also the material benefits which the presence of the Popes conferred on the community at large and on many of the individual inhabitants. When the Popes were in residence in Rome and its environs, they were able, during periods of varying length, to maintain order as well as peace between the barons and the burghers. Their Court and the numerous foreign guests it attracted brought great wealth into the city; and when the Pontiff was in their midst, it was easy for Romans to secure lucrative ecclesiastical positions. Now this state of affairs had changed completely. Rome, left to herself, had fewer resources of her own than did any of the larger cities of central Italy. She fell a victim to increasing isolation and anarchy. The longer the Popes were absent the greater did the desolation become. The churches were so dilapidated and neglected that cattle grazed even at the foot of the altar in St. Peter's and the Lateran. Many sacred edifices were roofless; others were almost in ruins. The monuments of pagan antiquity fared even worse than did those of Christian Rome, and were mercilessly destroyed. A Legate sold marble blocks from the Colosseum to a lime-burner. The materials of which the ancient buildings were constructed were even carted out of the city. The archives regarding the erection of the Cathedral of Orvieto contain a number of documents which show that the overseers in charge of the work brought a great deal of the marble used from Rome, that they sent agents thither almost more frequently than to Carrara, and that they repeatedly received presents of huge blocks of marble because they feared that the greater part of the subsidies they paid would fall into French hands. The Papal financiers adopted measures for covering deficits which were highly questionable. From the time of John XXII especially, the baneful system of Annates, Reservations and Expectancies came into use, and a multitude of abuses resulted. Alvaro Pelayo, the most devoted and perhaps even over-zealous defender of Papal power during the fourteenth century, rightly considers recourse to measures likely to arouse the cupidity of the clergy one of the wounds which then afflicted the Church. His testimony is all the more worthy of consideration because, as an official of many years' standing at the Court, he describes the state of affairs at Avignon from his own most intimate knowledge. In his famous book "On the Lamentation of the Church," he says, "Whenever I entered the chambers of the ecclesiastics of the Papal Court, I found brokers and clergymen, engaged in weighing and reckoning the money which lay in heaps before them."

This system of taxation and the abuses consequent upon it soon aroused passionate resentment. Dante, "consumed with zeal for the House of God," expressed in burning words his deep indignation at the cupidity and nepotism of the Popes. But he always distinguished carefully between the Pope and the Papacy, the person and the office. It was not long, however, before an opposition arose which made no such distinctions and attacked not only the abuses which had crept in but the ecclesiastical authority itself. The Avignon financial system, which contributed more than has been generally supposed to the undermining of Papal authority, greatly facilitated the attacking party's efforts.

From what has been said it will be clearly seen that the long-continued sojourn of the Popes in France, occasioned as it was by the confusion rampant in Italian affairs, was an important turning point in the history of the Papacy and the Church. The development which had been in progress during many centuries was quite abruptly halted, and a completely new state of affairs was substituted for it. No one who has any idea of the nature and necessity of historical continuity can fail to perceive the danger latent in this transference of the center of ecclesiastical unity to southern France. It was inevitable that the Papal power and the general interests of the Church, which at that time needed quiet progress and thorough reform of many things, should be adversely affected.

LUDWIG PASTOR

A TRIBUTE

Among the many tributes called forth by the death of Cardinal Mercier, possibly none is more touching than the story contributed to the *Tageblatt,* of Berlin, by a Dr. Heinemann, a veteran of the War. He relates that he stood in the cathedral of Malines, wearing the German uniform and feeling disconsolately alone. Two churchmen crossed the aisle and whispered something in Latin. The soldier turned promptly and answered in the same language. He was speaking to Cardinal Mercier. An invitation to dinner followed, with more Latin and a blessing from the venerable host, who said, "An old man who has always tried to do his duty blesses a young man who is going to do the same. May God watch over your young life!" Dr. Heinemann concludes with this memento: "The old man is dead now, at five-and-seventy. He was Germany's relentless but honorable foe. In our country perhaps only one man is sorrowful over his parting hence—a man of thirty, whom a hard life has made old before his time, and who was once a little subaltern bidden to a birthday dinner by an old man, during years of blood and hate."

ANONYMOUS

VII

MODERN CREATIVE AND CRITICAL WRITING

If any one asks how Father Cristoforo had so quickly at his disposal these means of transport by land and water, it will show that he does not know the influence and power of a Capuchin held in reputation as a saint.

"Before you go," said the father, "let us pray all together that the Lord may be with you in this your journey, and forever; and, above all, that He may give you strength, and a spirit of love, to enable you to desire whatever He has willed." So saying, he knelt down in the middle of the church, and they all followed his example. After praying a few moments in silence, with a low but distinct voice he pronounced these words: "We beseech Thee, also, for the unhappy person who has brought us to this state. We should be unworthy of Thy mercy, if we did not, from our hearts, implore it for him; he needs it, O Lord! We, in our sorrow, have this consolation, that we are in the path where Thou hast placed us; we can offer Thee our griefs, and they may become our gain. But he is Thine enemy! Have mercy on him, O Lord; touch his heart; reconcile him to Thyself, and give him all those good things we could desire for ourselves."

Rising then in haste, he said, "Come, my children, you have no time to lose; God defend you; His angel go with you;—farewell!" And while they set off with that emotion which cannot find words, and manifests itself without them, the Father added, in an agitated tone, "My heart tells me we shall meet again soon."

Certainly, the heart, to those who listen to it, has always something to say on what will happen; but what did his heart know? Very little, truly, of what had already happened.

Without waiting a reply, Father Cristoforo retired with hasty steps; the travellers took their departure; and Father Fazio shut the door after them, bidding them farewell with even his voice a little faltering.

The trio slowly made their way to the shore they had been directed to; there they espied the boat, and exchanging the pass-word, stepped in. The waterman, planting one oar on the land, pushed off; then took up the other oar, and rowing with both hands, pulled out and towards the opposite beach. Not a breath of wind was stirring; the lake lay bright and smooth, and would have appeared motionless but for the tremulous and gentle undulation of the moon-beams, which gleamed upon it from the zenith. No sounds were heard but the muffled and slowly-measured breaking of the surge upon the pebbly shore, the more distant gurgling of the troubled waters dashing among the piles of the bridge, and the even plash of the light sculls, as, rising with a sharp sound of the dripping blade, and quickly plunged again beneath, they cut the azure surface of the lake. The waves, divided by the prow, and re-uniting behind the little bark, tracked out a curling line, which extended itself to the shore. The silent travellers, with faces turned backwards, gazed upon the mountains and the country, illumined by the pale light of the moon, and diversified here and there with vast shadows. They could distinguish the villages, the houses, and the little cabins: the palace of Don Rodrigo, with its square tower, rising above the groups of huts at the base of the promontory, looked like a savage standing in the dark, and meditating some evil deed, while keeping guard over a company of reclining sleepers. Lucia saw it and shuddered; then drawing her eye along the declivity till she reached her native village, she fixed her gaze on its extremity, sought for her own cottage, traced out the thick head of the fig tree which towered above the wall of the court-yard, discovered the window of her own room; and, being seated on the bottom of the boat, she leaned her elbow onto the edge, laid her forehead on her arm, as if she were sleeping, and wept in secret.

Farewell, ye mountains, rising from the waters, and pointing to the heavens! ye varied summits, familiar to him who has been brought up among you, and impressed upon his mind as clearly as the countenance of his dearest friends! ye torrents, whose murmur he recognizes like the sound of the voices of home! ye villages, scattered and glistening on the declivity, like flocks of grazing sheep! How mournful is the step of him who, brought up amidst your scenes, is compelled to leave you! Even in the imagination of one who willingly departs, attracted by the hope of making a fortune elsewhere, the dreams of wealth at this moment lose their charms; he wonders he could form such a resolution, and would even now turn back, but for the hope of one day returning with a rich abundance. As he advances into the plain, his eye becomes wearied with its uniform extent; the atmosphere feels heavy and lifeless; he sadly and listlessly enters the busy cities, where houses crowded upon houses, and streets intersecting streets, seem to take away his breath; and, before edifices admired by the stranger, he recalls with restless longing the fields of his own country, and the cottage he had long ago set his heart upon, and which he resolves to purchase when he returns enriched to his own mountains.

But what must he feel who has never sent a passing wish beyond these mountains, who has arranged among them all his designs for the future, and is driven far away by an adverse power! who, suddenly snatched away from his dearest habits, and thwarted in his dearest hopes, leaves these mountains to go in search of strangers whom he never desired to know, and is unable to look forward to a fixed time of return!

Farewell! native cottage, where, indulging in unconscious thought, one learnt to distinguish from the noise of common footsteps, the approach of a tread expected with mysterious timidity! Farewell! thou cottage, still a stranger, but so often hastily glanced at, not without a blush, in passing, in which the mind took delight to figure to itself the tranquil and lasting home of a wife! Farewell! my church, where the heart was so often soothed while chanting the praises of the Lord; where the preparatory rite of betrothal was performed; where the secret sighing of the heart was solemnly blessed and love was inspired, and one felt a hallowing influence around; farewell! He who imparted to you such gladness is everywhere; and He never disturbs the joy of his children, but to prepare them for one more certain and durable.

Of such a nature, if not exactly these, were the reflections of Lucia;

and not very dissimilar were those of the two other wanderers, while the little bark rapidly approached the right bank of the Adda.

ALESSANDRO MANZONI

A PEASANT DIES

The poor child was at the point of death. A candle had been lighted in honor of the sacred Host, and also to permit a little sight within that black cavern. Those present knelt upon the damp earth. My eyes became imperceptibly used to the darkness, and I could at length discern the objects around me. The little cow-herd lay upon a trestle-bed of badly joined boards; a truss of straw served for his pillow; a tattered packing-cloth was his sheet; his waistcoat, his breeches, and I know not what formless rags, formed his coverlet. Never in all my life had I encountered such misery. Amid all these hideous surroundings, the child beamed with resignation and innocence. Nothing was white save his face and the surplice of the priest; everything else appeared tawny or livid in that hut, where the timid light of the torch was overpowered by palpable shadows. And I bent my knee; then, rising, I poured forth the words of absolution upon the gentle patient; then approaching, and bending down, I laid upon his lips, already growing cold, the God of all consolation. At that moment, the clank of chains resounded, and the head of an animal emerged from an opening in the wall near the pallet, then another quite different head. . . . It was a cow and an ass, who stretched out their necks lovingly towards the bed, to the barely covered feet of him who had formerly led them to pasture; and this sight suddenly made me shiver, and the tears rose to my eyes; and, as Christmas was at hand, I thought I had been transported to Bethlehem, during that great night: all was there,—the stable, the manger, the infant Jesus, for the poor are all Jesuses; that woman, his mother, represented the Divine Mother; those men, Saint Joseph, the shepherds, the magi; those two humble beasts the ass and the ox; that light, the miraculous star; I, the minister of salutation, the Angel sent to announce the great joy. . . .

As he breathed his last sigh, I exclaimed, "God descended from heaven into a manger, do thou, child, mount from this manger into heaven! . . ." This is an unforgettable memory.

JOSEPH ROUX

ABI! ANIMA CHRISTIANA

And yet it was the fact, again, that the vision of men and things, actually revealed to him on his way through the world, had developed, with a wonderful largeness, the faculties to which it addressed itself, his general capacity of vision; and in that too was a success, in the view of certain very definite, well-considered, undeniable possibilities. Throughout that elaborate and lifelong education of his receptive powers, he had ever kept in view the purpose of preparing himself towards possible further revelation some day—towards some ampler vision, which should take up into itself and explain this world's delightful shows, as the scattered fragments of a poetry, till then but half-understood, might be taken up into the text of a lost epic, recovered at last. At this moment, his unclouded receptivity of soul, grown so steadily through all those years, from experience to experience, was at its height; the house ready for the possible guest; the tablet of the mind white and smooth for whatsoever divine fingers might choose to write there. And was not this precisely the condition, the attitude of mind, to which something higher than he, yet akin to him, would be likely to reveal itself; to which that influence he had felt now and again like a friendly hand upon his shoulder, amid the actual obscurities of the world, would be likely to make a further explanation? Surely, the aim of a true philosophy must lie, not in futile efforts towards the complete accommodation of man to the circumstances in which he chances to find himself, but in the maintenance of a kind of candid discontent, in the face of the very highest achievement; the unclouded and receptive soul quitting the world finally, with the same fresh wonder with which it had entered the world still unimpaired, and going on its blind way at last with the consciousness of some profound enigma in things, as but a pledge of something further to come. Marius seemed to understand how one might look back upon life here, and its excellent visions, as but the portion of a race-course left behind him by a runner still swift of foot: for a moment he experienced a singular curiosity, almost an ardent desire to enter upon a future, the possibilities of which seemed so large.

And just then, again amid the memory of certain touching actual words and images, came the thought of the great hope, that hope against hope, which, as he conceived, had arisen—Lux sedentibus in tenebris—upon the aged world; the hope Cornelius had seemed to bear away upon him in his strength, with a buoyancy which had caused Marius to feel not so much that by a caprice of destiny, he had been left to die in his place, as that Cornelius was gone on a mission to deliver him also from death. There had been a permanent protest established in the world, a plea, a perpetual afterthought, which humanity henceforth would ever possess in reserve, against any wholly mechanical and disheartening theory of itself and its conditions. That was a thought which relieved for him the iron outline of the horizon about him, touching it as if with soft light from beyond; filling the shadowy, hollow places to which he was on his way with the warmth of definite affections; confirming also certain considerations by which he seemed to link himself to the generations to come in the world he was leaving. Yes! through the survival of their children, happy parents are able to think calmly, and with a very practical affection, of a world in which they are to have no direct share; planting with a cheerful good-humor, the acorns they carry about with them, that their grand-children may be shaded from the sun by the broad oak-trees of the future. That is nature's way of easing death to us. It was thus too, surprised, delighted, that Marius, under the power of that new hope among men, could think of the generations to come after him. Without it, dim in truth as it was, he could hardly have dared to ponder the world which limited all he really knew, as it would be when he should have departed from it. A strange lonesomeness, like physical darkness, seemed to settle upon the thought of it; as if its business hereafter must be, as far as he was concerned, carried on in some inhabited, but distant and alien, star. Contrariwise, with the sense of that hope warm about him, he seemed to anticipate some kindly care for himself, never to fail even on earth, a care for his very body—that dear sister and companion of his soul, outworn, suffering, and in the very article of death, as it was now.

For the weariness came back tenfold; and he had finally to abstain from thoughts like these, as from what caused physical pain. And then, as before in the wretched, sleepless nights of those forced marches, he would try to fix his mind, as it were impassively, and like a child thinking over the toys it loves, one after another, that it may fall asleep thus, and forget all about them the sooner, on all the persons he had loved in life—on his love for them, dead or living, grateful for his love or not, rather than on theirs for him—letting their images pass away again, or rest with him, as they would. In the bare sense of having loved he seemed to find, even amid this foundering of the ship, that on which his soul might assuredly rest and depend. One after another, he suffered those faces and voices to come and go, as in some mechanical exercise, as he might have repeated all the verses he knew by heart, or like the telling of beads one by one, with many a sleepy nod between-whiles.

For there remained also, for the old earthly creature still within him, that great blessedness of physical slumber. To sleep, to lose one's self in sleep—that, as he had always recognized, was a good thing. And it was after a space of deep sleep that he awoke amid the murmuring voices of the people who had kept and tended him so carefully through his sickness, now kneeling around his bed: and what he heard confirmed, in the then perfect clearness of his soul, the inevitable suggestion of his own bodily feelings. He had often dreamt he was condemned to die, that the hour, with wild thoughts of escape, was arrived; and waking, with the sun all around him, in complete liberty of life, had been full of gratitude for his place there, alive still, in the land of the living. He read surely, now, in the manner, the doings, of these people, some of whom were passing out through the doorway, where the heavy sunlight in very deed lay, that his last morning was come, and turned to think once more of the beloved. Often had he fancied of old that not to die on a dark or rainy day might itself have a little alleviating grace or favor about it. The people around his bed were praying fervently—Abi! Abi! Anima Christiana! In the moments of his extreme helplessness their mystic bread had been placed, had descended like a snow-flake from the sky, between his lips. Gentle fingers had applied to hands and feet, to all those old passage-ways of the senses, through which the world had come and gone for him, now so dim and obstructed, a medicinable oil. It was the same people who, in the gray, austere evening of that day, took up his remains, and buried them secretly, with their accustomed prayers; but with joy also, holding his death, according to their generous view in this matter, to have been of the nature of a martyrdom; and martyrdom, as the church had always said, is a kind of sacrament with plenary grace.

WALTER PATER

PORTRAIT OF A LADY

But while Owen lived, and while his garden flourished, he and his neighbours were as merry together as if death could never reach the one, nor desolation waste the other. Among those frequenters of his little retreat whom he distinguished with an especial favour and attention, the foremost was the handsome daughter of an old man who conducted the business of a ropewalk in his neighbourhood, and who was accustomed on a fine Saturday evening to sit under the shade of a yellow osier that stood by his door and discourse of the politics of the day—of Lord Halifax's administration—of the promising young patriot, Mr. Henry Grattan—and of the famous Catholic concession of 1773. Owen, like all Irishmen, even of the humblest rank, was an acute critic in female proportions, and although time had blown away the thatching from his head, and by far the greater portion of blood that remained in his frame had colonized about his nose, yet the manner in which he held forth on the praises of his friend's daughter was such as to put to shame her younger and less eloquent admirers. It is true, indeed, that the origin of the suburban beauty was one which, in a troubled country like Ireland, had little of association to recommend it; but few even of those to whom twisted hemp was an object of secret terror, could look on the exquisitely beautiful face of Eily O'Connor and remember that she was a rope-maker's daughter; few could detect beneath the timid, hesitating, downcast gentleness of manner, which shed an interest over all her motions, the traces of a harsh and vulgar education. It was true that she sometimes purloined a final letter from the King's adjectives, and prolonged the utterance of a vowel beyond the term of prosodiacal orthodoxy, but the tongue that did so seemed to move on silver wires, and the lip on which the sound delayed

"long murmuring, loth to part,"

imparted to its own accents an association of sweetness and grace, that made the defect an additional allurement. Her education in the outskirts of a city had not impaired the natural tenderness of her character; for her father, who, all rude as he was, knew how to value his daughter's softness of mind, endeavoured to foster it by every indulgence in his power. Her uncle, too, who was now a country parish priest, was well qualified to draw forth any natural talent with which she had been originally endowed. He had completed his theological education in the famous university of Salamanca, where he was distinguished as a youth of much quietness of temper and literary application, rather than as one of those furious gesticulators, those "figures Hibernoises," amongst whom Gil Blas, in his fit of logical lunacy, could meet his only equals. At his little lodging, while he was yet a curate at St. John's, Eily O'Connor was accustomed to spend a considerable portion of her time, and in return for her kindness in presiding at his simple tea-table, Father Edward undertook to bestow a degree of attention on her education, which rendered her, in a little time, as superior in knowledge as she was in beauty to her female associates. She was remarked likewise at this time, as a little devotee, very regular in her attendance at chapel, constant in all the observances of her religion and grave in her attire and discourse.

On the coldest and dreariest morning in winter she might be seen gliding along by the unopened shop windows to the nearest chapel, where she was accustomed to hear an early mass, and return in time to set everything in order for her father's breakfast. During the day she superintended his household affairs while he was employed upon the adjacent ropewalk; and, in the evening, she usually slipped on her bonnet, and went across the street to Father Edward's, where she chatted away until tea was over; if he happened to be engaged in reading his daily office, she amused herself with a volume of moral entertainment, such as Rasselas, Prince of Abyssinia, or Mr. Addison's Spectator, until he was at leisure to hear her lessons. An attachment of the purest and tenderest nature was the consequence of those mutual attentions between the uncle and niece, and it might be said that if the former loved her not as well, he knew and valued her character still better than her father. Father Edward, however, was appointed to a parish, and Eily lost her instructor. It was for her a severe loss, and most severe in reality when its effects upon her own spirits began to wear away. For some months after his departure, she continued to lead the same retired and unobtrusive life, and no eye, save that of a consummate observer, could detect the slightest alteration in her sentiments, the least increase of toleration for the world and worldly amusements. That change, however, had been silently affected in her heart. She was now a woman—a lovely, intelligent, full grown woman—and circumstances obliged her to take a part in the little social circle which moved around her. Her spirits were naturally light, and, though long repressed, became readily assimilated to the buoyant tone of the society in which she happened to be placed. Her father who, with a father's venial vanity, was fond of showing his beautiful child among his neighbours, took her with him to Owen's garden, at a time when it was unusually hot and crowded, and from that evening might be dated the commencement of a decided and visible change in the lovely Eily's character.

As gradual as the approach of a spring morning was the change from grave to gay in the costume of this flower of the suburbs. It dawned at first in a handsome bowknot upon her head-dress, and ended in the full noontide splendour of flowered muslin, silks and sashes. It was like the opening of the rose-bud, which gathers around it the winged wooers of the summer meadow. "Lads, as brisk as bees," came thronging in her train, with proffers of "Honourable love, and rites of marriage"; and even among the youths of a higher rank, whom the wild levity of Irish blood and high spirits sent to mingle in the festivities of Owen's garden, a jealousy prevailed respecting the favour of the rope-maker's handsome daughter. It was no wonder that attentions paid by individuals so much superior to her ordinary admirers, should render Eily indifferent to the sighs of those plebeian suitors. Dunat O'Leary, the hair-cutter, or Foxy Dunat, as he was named in allusion to his red-head, was cut to the heart by her utter coldness. Myles Murphy, likewise a good-natured farmer from Killarney, who travelled through the country selling Kerry ponies, and claiming a relationship with every one he met, claimed kindred in vain with Eily, for his claim was not allowed. Lowry Looby, too, the servant of Mr. Daly, a wealthy middleman who lived in the neighbourhood, was suspected by many to entertain delusive hopes of Eily O'Connor's favour—but this report was improbable enough, for Lowry could not but know that he was a very ugly man; and if he were as beautiful as Narcissus, Mihil O'Connor would still have shut the door in his face for being as poor as Timon. So that though there was no lack of admirers, the lovely Eily, like many celebrated beauties in a higher rank, ran, after all, a fair chance of becoming what Lady Mary Montague has elegantly termed "a lay nun." Even so a book-worm, who will pore over a single volume from morning till night, if turned loose into a library, wanders from shelf to shelf, bewildered amid a host of temptations, and unable to make any selection until he is surprised by twilight, and chagrined to find, that with so much happiness within his grasp, he has spent, nevertheless, an unprofitable day.

GERALD GRIFFIN

PORTRAIT OF A TRANSCENDENTALIST

A transcendentalist is one who had keen sight, but little warmth of heart; who has fine conceits, but is destitute of the rich glow of love. He is en rapport with the spiritual world, unconscious of the celestial one. He is all nerve and no blood—colorless. He talks of self-reliance, but fears to trust himself to love. He never abandons himself to love, but is always on the lookout for some new fact. His nerves are always tight-stretched, like the string of a bow; his life is all effort. In a short period he loses his tone. Behold him sitting on a chair; he is not sitting, but braced upon its angles, as if his bones were of iron and his nerves steel; every nerve is drawn, his hands are closed like a miser's—it is the lips and head that speak, not his tongue and heart. He prefers talking about love to possessing it, as he prefers Socrates to Jesus. Nature is his church, and he is his own god. He is a dissecting critic—heartless, cold. What would excite love and sympathy in another, excites in him curiosity and interest. He would have written an essay on the power of the soul at the foot of the cross.

ISAAC THOMAS HECKER

A PROTESTANT'S CONFESSION

Still gliding onward, Hilda now looked up into the dome, where the sunshine came through the western windows, and threw across long shafts of light. They rested upon the mosaic figures of two evangelists above the cornice. These great beams of radiance, traversing what seemed the empty space, were made visible in misty glory, by the holy cloud of incense, else unseen, which had risen into the middle dome. It was to Hilda as if she beheld the worship of the priest and people ascending heavenward, purified from its alloy of earth, and acquiring celestial substance in the golden atmosphere to which it aspired. She wondered if angels did not sometimes hover within the dome, and show themselves, in brief glimpses, floating amid the sunshine and the glorified vapor, to those who devoutly worshipped on the pavement.

She had now come into the southern transept. Around this portion of the church are ranged a number of confessionals. They are small tabernacles of carved wood, with a closet for the priest in the centre; and, on either side, a space for a penitent to kneel, and breathe his confession through a perforated auricle into the good father's ear. Observing this arrangement, though already familiar to her, our poor Hilda was anew impressed with the infinite convenience—if we may use so poor a phrase—of the Catholic religion to its devout believers.

Who, in truth, that considers the matter, can resist a similar impression: in the hottest fever-fit of life, they can always find, ready for their need, a cool, quiet, beautiful place of worship. They may enter its sacred precincts at any hour, leaving the fret and trouble of the world behind them, and purifying themselves with a touch of holy water at the threshold. In the calm interior, fragrant of rich and soothing incense, they may hold converse with some saint, their awful, kindly friend. And, most precious privilege of all, whatever perplexity, sorrow, guilt, may weigh upon their souls, they can fling down the dark burden at the foot of the cross, and go forth—to sin no more, nor be any longer disquieted; but to live again in the freshness and elasticity of innocence.

"Do not these inestimable advantages," thought Hilda, "or some of them at least, belong to Christianity itself? Are they not a part of the blessings which the system was meant to bestow upon mankind? Can the faith in which I was born and bred be perfect, if it leave a weak girl like me to wander, desolate, with this great trouble crushing me down?"

A poignant anguish thrilled within her breast; it was like a thing that had life, and was struggling to get out.

"Oh, help! Oh, help!" cried Hilda; "I cannot, cannot bear it!"

Only by the reverberations that followed—arch echoing the sound to arch, and a Pope of bronze repeating it to a Pope of marble, as each sat enthroned over his tomb—did Hilda become aware that she had really spoken above her breath. But, in that great space, there is no need to hush up the heart within one's own bosom, so carefully as elsewhere; and if the cry reached any distant auditor, it came broken into many fragments, and from various quarters of the church.

Approaching one of the confessionals, she saw a woman kneeling within. Just as Hilda drew near, the penitent rose, came forth, and kissed the hand of the priest, who regarded her with a look of paternal benignity, and appeared to be giving her some spiritual counsel, in a low voice. She then knelt to receive his blessing, which was fervently bestowed. Hilda was so struck with the peace and joy in the woman's face, that, as the latter retired, she could not help speaking to her.

"You look very happy," said she. "Is it so sweet, then, to go to the confessional?"

"Oh, very sweet, my dear signorina!" answered the woman, with moistened eyes and an affectionate smile; for she was so thoroughly softened with what she had been doing, that she felt as if Hilda were her younger sister. "My heart is at rest now. Thanks be to the Saviour, and the Blessed Virgin and the saints, and this good father, there is no more trouble for poor Teresa!"

"I am glad for your sake," said Hilda, sighing for her own. "I am a poor heretic, but a human sister; and I rejoice for you!"

She went from one to another of the confessionals, and, looking at each, perceived that they were inscribed with gilt letters: on one, PRO ITALICA LINGUA; on another, PRO FLANDRICA LINGUA; on a third, PRO POLONICA LINGUA; on a fourth, PRO ILLYRICA LINGUA; on a fifth, PRO HISPANICA LINGUA. In this vast and hospitable cathedral, worthy to be the religious heart of the whole world, there was room for all nations; there was access to the Divine Grace for every Christian soul; there was an ear for what the overburdened heart might have to murmur, speak in what native tongue it would.

When Hilda had almost completed the circuit of the transept, she came to a confessional—the central part was closed, but a mystic rod protruded from it, indicating the presence of a priest within—on which was inscribed, PRO ANGLICA LINGUA.

It was a word in season! If she had heard her mother's voice from within the tabernacle, calling her, in her own mother-tongue, to come and lay her poor head in her lap, and sob out all her troubles, Hilda could not have responded with a more inevitable obedience. She did not think; she only felt. Within her heart was a great need. Close at hand, within the veil of the confessional, was the relief. She flung herself down in the penitent's place; and, tremulously, passionately, with sobs, tears, and the turbulent overflow of emotion too long repressed, she poured out the dark story which had infused its poison into her innocent life.

NATHANIEL HAWTHORNE

DAYS IN ROME

We entered Rome after a long, wet, cold carriage journey that would have disillusionized a Doré. As we jolted along, my mother held me in her arms, while I slept as much as I could; and when I could not, I blessed the patient, weary bosom upon which I lay exhausted. It was a solemn-faced load of Americans which shook and shivered into the city of memories that night. In "Monte Beni," as he preferred to call "The Marble Faun," my father speaks of Rome with mingled contempt for its discomforts and delighted heartiness for its outshining fascinations. "The desolation of her ruin" does not prevent her from being "more intimately our home than even the spot where we were born." A ruin or a picture could not satisfy his heart, which accepted no yoke less strong than spiritual power. Rome supplies the most telling evidence of human failure, because she is the theatre of the greatest human effort, both in the ranks of Satan and of God; and she visibly mourns her sins of mistake at the feet of spiritual victory, Saints Peter and Paul. (As a Catholic, I could hardly win the respect of the gentle reader if I were so unAmerican as to fear to stand by my belief.) And while the observer in Rome may well feel sad in the midst of reminders of the enormous sins of the past, there is an uplifting, for the soul eager to perceive the truth, in all her assurances of that mercy which is the cause of religion. If the Holy See was established in Rome because it was the city where the worst wickedness upon earth, because the most intelligent, was to be found, we may conclude that the old emperors, stormy and grotesque, are responsible for its melancholy "atmosphere of sin," to which Hilda alludes as a condition of the whole planet; and not the Popes who have prayed in Rome, nor the people who believed there. In printed remarks about Italy both my parents say that she most reminds them of what is highest.

But, whether chilly or warm, the Eternal City did not at once make a conquest of my father's allegiance, though before he bade it farewell, it had painted itself upon his mind as sometimes the sunniest and most splendid habitation for a populace, that he knew. In the spring my sister wrote:——

We are having perfectly splendid weather now, unclouded Italian skies, blazing sun, everything warm and glorious. But the sky is too blue, the sun is too blazing, everything is too vivid. Often I long for the more cloudy skies and peace of that dear, beautiful England. Rome makes us all languid. We have to pay a fearful price for the supreme enjoyment there is in standing on the very spots made interesting by poetry or by prose, imagination, or (which is still more absorbing) truth. Sometimes I wish there had never been anything done or written in the world! My father and I seem to feel in this way more than the rest. We agree about Rome as we did about England.

ROSE HAWTHORNE LATHROP

PÈRE FIDELIS

How fresh seems the memory of this journey! yet its place is with the archives of the past. I seem to breathe the incense of orange-flowers and to hear the whisper of distant waterfalls as I write.

It must have been toward sunset,—we were threading the eastern coast, and a great mountain filled the west,—but I felt that it was the hour when day ends and night begins. The heavy clouds looked as though they were still brimful of sunlight, yet no ray escaped to gladden our side of the world.

Finally, on the brow of what seemed to be the last hill in this life, I saw a cross,—a cross among the palms. Hoké saw it, and quickened his pace: he was not so great an ass but he knew that there was provender in the green pastures of Père Fidelis, and his heart freshened within him.

A few paces from the grove of palms I heard a bell swing jubilantly. Out over the solemn sea, up and down that foam-crested shore, rang the sweet Angelus. One may pray with some fervor when one's journey is at an end. When the prayer was over I walked to the gate of the chapel-yard, leading the willing Hoké, and at that moment a slender figure, clad all in black, his long robes flowing gracefully about him, his boyish face heightening the effect of his grave and serene demeanor, his thin, sensitive hands held forth in hearty welcome,—a welcome that was almost like a benediction, so spiritual was the love which it expressed,—came out, and I found myself in the arms of Père Fidelis, feeling like one who has at least been permitted to kneel upon the threshold of his Mecca.

Why do our hearts sing jubilate when we meet a friend for the first time? What is it within us that with its life-long yearning comes suddenly upon the all-sufficient one, and in a moment is crowned and satisfied? I could not tell whether I was at last waking from a sleep or just sinking into a dream. I could have sat there at his feet contented; I could have put off my worldly cares, resigned ambition, forgotten the past, and, in the blessed tranquillity of that hour, have dwelt joyfully under the palms with him, seeking only to follow in his patient footsteps until the end should come.

Perhaps it was the realization of an ideal that plunged me into a luxurious revery, out of which I was summoned by *mon père,* who hinted that I must be hungry. Prophetic father! hungry I was indeed.

Mon père led me to his little house with three rooms, and installed me host, himself being my ever-watchful attendant. Then he spoke: "The lads were at the sea, fishing: would I excuse him for a moment?"

Alone in the little house, with a glass of claret and a hard biscuit for refreshment, I looked about me. The central room, in which I sat, was bare to nakedness: a few devotional books, a small clock high up on the wall, with a short wagging pendulum, two or three paintings, betraying more sentiment than merit, a table, a wooden form against the window, and a crucifix, complete its inventory. A high window was at my back; a door in front opening upon a veranda shaded with a passion-vine, beyond it a green, undulating country running down into the sea; on either hand a little cell containing nothing but a narrow bed, a saint's picture, and a rosary. Kahèle, having distributed the animals in good pasturage, lay on the veranda at full length, supremely happy as he jingled his spurs over the edge of the steps and hummed a native air in subdued falsetto, like a mosquito.

Again I sank into a revery. Enter *mon père* with apologies and a plate of smoking cakes made of eggs and batter, his own handiwork, enter the lads from the sea with excellent fish, knotted in long wisps of grass; enter Kahèle, lazily sniffing the savory odors of our repast with evident relish; and then supper in good earnest.

How happy we were, having such talks in several sorts of tongues, such polyglot efforts toward sociability,—French, English, and native in equal parts, but each broken and spliced to suit our dire necessity! The candle flamed and flickered in the land-breeze that swept through the house,—unctuous waxen stalactites decorated it almost past recognition; the crickets sang lustily at the doorway; the little natives grew sleepy and curled up on their mats in the corner; Kahèle slept in his spurs like a born muleteer. And now a sudden conviction seized us that it was bedtime in very truth; so *mon père* led me to one of the cells, saying, "Will you sleep in the room of Père Amabilis?" Yea, verily, with all humility; and there I slept after the benediction, during which the young priest's face looked almost like an angel's in its youthful holiness, and I was afraid I might wake in the morning and find him gone, transported to some other and more lovely world.

But I didn't. Père Fidelis was up before daybreak. It was his hand that clashed the joyful Angelus at sunrise that woke me from my happy dream; it was his hand that prepared the frugal but appetizing meal; he made the coffee, such rich, black, aromatic coffee as Frenchmen alone have the faculty of producing. He had an eye to the welfare of the animals also, and seemed to be commander-in-chief of affairs secular as well as ecclesiastical; yet he was so young!

There was a day of brief incursions mountainward, with the happiest results. There were welcomes showered upon me for his sake; he was ever ministering to my temporal wants, and puzzling me with dissertations in assorted languages.

By happy fortune a Sunday followed when the Chapel of the Palms was thronged with dusky worshippers; not a white face present but the father's and mine own, yet a common trust in the blessedness of the life to come struck the key-note of universal harmony, and we sang the Magnificat with one voice. There was something that fretted me in all this admirable experience. Père Fidelis could touch neither bread nor water until after the last mass. Hour by hour he grew paler and fainter, in spite of the heroic fortitude that sustained his famishing body.

"Mon père," said I, "you must eat, or go to heaven betimes." He would not. "You must end with an earlier mass," I persisted. It was impossible: many parishioners came from miles away; some of these started at daybreak, as it was, and they would be unable to arrive in season for an earlier mass. Excellent martyr! thought I, to offer thy body a living sacrifice for the edification of these savage Christians! At last he ate, but not until appetite itself had perished. Then troops of children gathered about him clamoring to kiss the hand of the priestly youth; old men and women passed him with heads uncovered, amazed at the devotion of one they could not hope to emulate.

CHARLES WARREN STODDARD

MADAME CÉLESTIN

Madame Célestin always wore a neat and snugly fitting calico wrapper when she went out in the morning to sweep her small gallery. Lawyer Paxton thought she looked very pretty in the gray one that was made with a graceful Watteau fold at the back: and with which she invariably wore a bow of pink ribbon at the throat. She was always sweeping her gallery when lawyer Paxton passed by in the morning on his way to his office in St. Danis Street.

Sometimes he stopped and leaned over the fence to say good-morning at his ease; to criticise or admire her rosebushes; or when he had time enough, to hear what she had to say. Madame Célestin usually had a good deal to say. She would gather up the train of her calico wrapper in one hand, and balancing the broom gracefully in the other, would go tripping down to where the lawyer leaned, as comfortably as he could, over her picket fence.

Of course she had talked to him of her troubles. Every one knew Madame Célestin's troubles.

"Really, madame," he told her once, in his deliberate, calculating, lawyer-tone, "it's more than human nature—woman's nature—should be called upon to endure. Here you are, working your fingers off"—she glanced down at two rosy finger-tips that showed through the rents in her baggy doeskin gloves—"taking in sewing; giving music lessons; doing God knows what in the way of manual labor to support yourself and those two little ones"—Madame Célestin's pretty face beamed with satisfaction at this enumeration of her trials.

"You right, Judge. Not a picayune, not one, not one, have I lay my eyes on in the pas' fo' months that I can say Célestin give it to me or sen' it to me."

"The scoundrel!" muttered lawyer Paxton in his beard.

"An' *pourtant,*" she resumed, "they say he's making money down roun' Alexandria w'en he wants to work."

"I dare say you haven't seen him for months?" suggested the lawyer.

"It's a good six month' since I see a sight of Célestin," she admitted.

"That's it, that's what I say; he has practically deserted you; fails to support you. It wouldn't surprise me a bit to learn that he has ill treated you."

"Well, you know, Judge," with an evasive cough, "a man that drinks—w'at can you expec'? An' if you would know the promises he has made me! Ah, if I had as many dolla' as I had promise from Célestin, I would n' have to work, *je vous garantis*."

"And in my opinion, madame, you would be a foolish woman to endure it longer, when the divorce court is there to offer you redress."

"You spoke about that befo', Judge; I'm goin' think about that divo'ce. I believe you right."

Madame Célestin thought about the divorce and talked about it, too; and lawyer Paxton grew deeply interested in the theme.

"You know, about that divo'ce, Judge," Madame Célestin was waiting for him that morning. "I been talking to my family an' my frien's, an' it's me that tells you, they all plumb agains' that divo'ce."

"Certainly, to be sure; that's to be expected, madame, in this community of Creoles. I warned you that you would meet with opposition, and would have to face it and brave it."

"Oh, don't fear, I'm going to face it! Maman says it's a disgrace like it's neva been in the family. But it's good for Maman to talk, her. W'at trouble she ever had? She says I mus' go by all means consult with Père Duchéron—its my confessor, you undastan'—Well, I'll go, Judge, to please Maman. But all the confessor' in the worl' ent goin' make me put up with that conduc' of Célestin any longa."

A day or two later, she was there waiting for him again. "You know, Judge, about that divo'ce."

"Yes, yes," responded the lawyer, well pleased to trace a new determination in her brown eyes and in the curves of her pretty mouth. "I suppose you saw Père Duchéron and had to brave it out with him, too."

"Oh, fo' that, a perfec' sermon, I assho you. A talk of giving scandal an' bad example that I thought would neva en'! He says, fo' him, he wash' his hands; I mus' go see the bishop."

"You won't let the bishop dissuade you, I trust," stammered the lawyer more anxiously than he could well understand.

"You don't know me yet, Judge," laughed Madame Célestin with a turn of the head and a flirt of the broom which indicated that the interview was at an end.

"Well, Madame Célestin! And the bishop!" Lawyer Paxton was standing there holding to a couple of the shaky pickets. She had not seen him. "Oh, it's you, Judge?" and she hastened towards him with an empressement that could not but have been flattering.

"Yes, I saw Monseigneur," she began. The lawyer had already gathered from her expressive countenance that she had not wavered in her determination. "Ah, he's a eloquent man. It's not a mo' eloquent man in Natchitoches parish. I was fo'ced to cry, the way he talked to me about my troubles; how he undastan's them, an' feels for me. It would move even you, Judge, to hear how he talk' about that step I want to take; its danga, its temptation. How it is the duty of a Catholic to stan' everything till the las' extreme. An' that life of retirement an' self-denial I would have to lead,—he tole me all that."

"But he hasn't turned you from your resolve, I see," laughed the lawyer complacently.

"For that, no," she returned emphatically. "The bishop don't know w'at it is to be married to a man like Célestin, an' have to endu' that conduc' like I have to endu' it. The Pope himse'f can't make me stan' that any longer, if you say I got the right in the law to sen' Célestin sailing."

A noticeable change had come over lawyer Paxton. He discarded his work-day coat and began to wear his Sunday one to the office. He grew solicitous as to the shine of his boots, his collar, and the set of his tie. He brushed and trimmed his whiskers with a care that had not before been apparent. Then he fell into a stupid habit of dreaming as he walked the streets of the old town. It would be very good to take unto himself a wife, he dreamed. And he could dream of no other than pretty Madame Célestin filling that sweet and sacred office as she filled his thoughts, now. Old Natchitoches would not hold them comfortably, perhaps; but the world was surely wide enough to live in, outside of Natchitoches town.

His heart beat in a strangely irregular manner as he neared Madame Célestin's house one morning, and discovered her behind the rosebushes, as usual plying her broom. She had finished the gallery and steps and was sweeping the little brick walk along the edge of the violet border.

"Good-morning, Madame Célestin."

"Ah, it's you, Judge? Good-morning." He waited. She seemed to be doing the same. Then she ventured, with some hesitancy, "You know, Judge, about that divo'ce. I been thinking,—I reckon you betta neva mine about that divo'ce." She was making deep rings in the palm of her gloved hand with the end of the broom-handle, and looking at them critically. Her face seemed to the lawyer to be unusually rosy; but maybe it was only the reflection of the pink bow at the throat. "Yes, I reckon you nedd n' mine. You see, Judge, Célestin came home las' night. An' he's promise me on his word an' honor he's going to turn ova a new leaf."

KATE CHOPIN

MARZIO'S CRUCIFIX

For some minutes he rested his head in his hand in deep thought. At last he rose and went to a corner of the workshop in which stood a heavily ironed box. Marzio fumbled in his pocket till he found a key, bright from always being carried about with him, and contrasting oddly with the rusty lock into which he thrust it. It turned with difficulty in his nervous fingers, and he raised the heavy lid. The coffer was full of packages wrapped in brown paper. He removed one after another till he came to a wooden case which filled the whole length and breadth of the safe. He lifted it out carefully and laid it on the end of the bench. The cover was fastened down by screws, and he undid them one by one until it moved and came off in his hands. The contents were wrapped carefully in a fine towel, which had once been white, but which had grown yellow with age. Marzio unfolded the covering with a delicate touch as though he feared to hurt what was within. He took out a large silver crucifix, raising it carefully, and taking care not to touch the figure. He stood it on the bench before him, and sat down to examine it.

It was a work of rare beauty, which he had made more than ten years before. With the strange reticent instinct which artists sometimes feel about their finest works, he had finished it in secret, working at night alone, and when it was done he had put it away. It was his greatest feat, he had said to himself, and as from time to time he took it out and looked at it, he gradually grew less and less inclined to show it to any one, resolving to leave it in its case, until it should be found after his death. It had seemed priceless to him, and he would not sell it. With a fantastic eccentricity of reasoning he regarded it as a sacred thing, to part with which would be a desecration. So he kept it. Then, taking it out again, it had seemed less good to him, as his mind became occupied with other things, and he had fancied he should do better yet. At last he screwed it up in a wooden case and put it at the bottom of his strong box, resolving never to look at it again. Many years had passed since he had laid eyes on it.

The idea which had come to him when Paolo had communicated the order to him on the previous evening, had seemed absolutely new. It had appeared to him as a glorification of the work he had executed in secret so long ago. Time, and the habit of dissatisfaction had effaced from his mind the precise image of the work of the past, and the emotions of the present had seemed something new to him. He had drawn and modeled during many hours, and yet he was utterly disappointed with the new result. He felt the innate consciousness of having done it before, and of having done it better.

And now the wonderful masterpiece of his earlier years stood before him—the tall and massive ebony cross, bearing the marvelous figure of the dead Saviour. A ray of sunlight fell through the grated window upon the dying head, illuminating the points of the thorns in the crown, the falling locks of hair, the tortured hands, and casting a shadow of death beneath the half-closed eyes.

For several minutes Marzio sat motionless on his stool, realizing the whole strength and beauty of what he had done ten years before. Then he wanted to get a better view of it. It was not high enough above him, for it was meant to stand upon an altar. He could not see the face. He looked about for something upon which to make it stand, but nothing was near. He pushed away his stool, and turning the cross a little, so that the sunlight should strike it at a better angle, he kneeled down on the floor, his hands resting on the edge of the bench, and he looked up at the image of the dead Christ.

FRANCIS MARION CRAWFORD

IN THE REIGN OF CHARLES I

Affairs in England at this time were in a very strange condition. First, the Duke of York, who was heir to the throne, was a declared Catholic; and then the King himself was next door to one, in heart at any rate. Certainly he had never been reconciled to the Church, though the report among some was that he had been, during his life in Paris; but in heart, as I have said, he was one, and waited only for a favorable occasion to declare himself. For he had been so bold, seventeen years before, as to send to Rome a scheme by which the Church of England was to be reunited to Rome under certain conditions, as that the mass, or parts of it, should be read in English, that the Protestant clergy who would submit to ordination should be allowed to keep their wives, and other matters of that kind. His answer from Rome, sent by word of mouth only, was that no scheme could be nearer to the heart of His Holiness; but that he must not be too precipitate. Let him first show that his subjects were with him in his laudable desires; and then perhaps the terms of the matter might be spoken of again. For the King himself, and even the Duke too at this time (though later he amended his life), Catholic in spirit, were scarce Christian in life. The ladies of the Court then must not be overlooked, for they as much as any statesman, and some think, more, controlled the King and his brother very greatly at this time.

But this was not all. Next, the King was embroiled in a great number of ways. The more extreme of his Protestant subjects feared and hated the Catholic Church as much as good Catholics hate and fear the Devil; and although for the present our people had great liberty both at Court and elsewhere, no man could tell when that liberty might be curtailed. And, indeed, it had been to a great part already curtailed five years before by the Test Act, forbidding the Catholics to hold any high place at the Court or elsewhere, though this was largely evaded. There was even a movement among some of them, and among the most important of them too, in the House of Lords and elsewhere, to exclude the Duke of York from the succession; and they advanced among themselves in support of this the fear that a French army might be brought in to subdue England to the Church. And, worst of all, as I learned privately in Rome, there was some substance in their fear, though few else knew it; since the King was in private treaty with Louis for this very purpose. Again, a further embroilment lay in the propositions that had been made privately to the King that he should rid himself of his Queen—Catherine—on the pretext that she had borne no child to him, and could not, and marry instead some Protestant princess. Lastly, and most important of all, so greatly was Charles turned towards the Church, that he begged more than once, and again lately, that a priest might be sent to him to be always at hand, in the event of his sudden sickness, whom none else knew to be a priest; and it was this last matter, I think, that had determined the Holy Father to let me go, as I had wished, though I was no priest, to see how the King would bear himself to me; and then, perhaps, afterwards a priest might be sent as he desired.

ROBERT HUGH BENSON

CHILDREN IN MIDWINTER

Children are so flowerlike that it is always a little fresh surprise to see them blooming in winter. Their tenderness, their down, their colour, their fulness—which is like that of a full rose or of a tight grape—look out of season. Children in the withering wind are like the soft golden-pink roses that fill the barrows in Oxford Street, breathing a southern calm on the north wind. The child has something better than warmth in the cold, something more subtly out of place and more delicately contrary; and that is coolness. To be cool in the cold is the sign of a vitality quite exquisitely alien from the common conditions of the world. It is to have a naturally, and not an artificially, different and separate climate.

We can all be more or less warm—with fur, with skating, with tea, with fire, and with sleep—in the winter. But the child is fresh in the wind, and awakes cool from his dreams, dewy when there is hoar-frost everywhere else; he is "more lovely and more temperate" than the summer day and than the winter day alike. He overcomes both heat and cold by another climate, which is the climate of life; but that victory of life is more delicate and more surprising in the tyranny of January. By the sight and the touch of children, we are, as it were, indulged with something finer than a flower or a fruit in untimely bloom. The childish bloom is always rare. The fruit and the flower will be common later on; the strawberries will be a matter of course anon, and the asparagus dull in their day. But a child is a perpetual *primeur.*

Or rather he is in truth always untimely. Some few days in the year are his own season—unnoticed days of March or April, soft, fresh and equal, when the child sleeps and rises with the sun. Then he looks as though he had his brief season, and ceases for a while to seem so strange.

It is no wonder that we should try to attribute the times of the year to children; their likeness is so rife among annuals. For man and woman we are naturally accustomed to a longer rhythm; their metre is so obviously their own, and of but a single stanza, without repetition, without renewal, without refrain. But it is by an intelligible illusion that we look for a quick waxing and waning in the lives of young children—for a waxing that shall come again another time, and for a waning that shall not be final, shall not be fatal. But every winter shows us how human they are, and how they are little pilgrims and visitants among the things that look like their kin. For every winter shows them free from the east wind; more perfectly than their elders, they enclose the climate of life. And, moreover, with them the climate of life is the climate of the spring of life; the climate of a March that is sure to make a constant progress, and of a human

April that never hesitates. The child "breathes April and May"—another April and his own May.

The winter child looks so much the more beautiful for the season as his most brilliant uncles and aunts look less well. He is tender and gay in the east wind. Now more than ever must the lover beware of making a comparison between the beauty of the admired woman and the beauty of a child. He is indeed too wary ever to make it. So is the poet. As comparisons are necessary to him, he will pay a frankly impossible homage, and compare a woman's face to something too fine, to something it could never emulate. The Elizabethan lyrist is safe among lilies and cherries, roses, pearls, and snow. He undertakes the beautiful office of flattery, and flatters with courage. There is no hidden reproach in the phrase. Pearls and snow suffer, in a sham fight, a mimic defeat that does them no harm, and no harm comes to the lady's beauty from a competition so impossible. She never wore a lily or a coral in the colors of her face, and their beauty is not hers. But here is the secret: she is compared with a flower because she could not endure to be compared with a child. That would touch her too nearly. There would be the human texture and the life like hers, but immeasurably more lovely. No color, no surface, no eyes of woman have ever been comparable with the color, the surface, and the eyes of childhood. And no poet has ever run the risk of such a defeat. Why, it is defeat enough for a woman to have her face, however well-favored, close to a child's even if there is no one by who should be rash enough to approach them still nearer by a comparison.

ALICE MEYNELL

THE MAMMA OF SAMPIETRO

Seeing a chance of changing the subject, I remarked that it would be nice to know what sort of a mamma Madonna had given to Sampietro.

"Well, sir, you must know that the mamma of Sampietro was the meanest woman that ever lived—scraping and saving all the days of her life, and keeping Sampietro and his two sisters (the nun and the other one, of whom I will tell you another time), for days together with nothing to eat except perhaps a few potato peelings and a cheese rind. As far as acts of kindness and charity to her neighbours, I don't believe she knew the names of the said virtues, though of course I cannot be certain; and whatever good there was in Sampietro, he must have picked up elsewhere. As soon as he was old enough to work he became a fisherman, as you know; because, when Il Santissimo Salvatore wanted a Santo Padre to govern the Church, He went down to the seaside and chose Sampietro; knowing that Sampietro, being a fisherman, was just the right man to bear all kinds of hardships, and to catch people's souls and take them to paradise, just as he had been used to catch fish and take them to the market. So Sampietro went to Rome, and He reigned there for many years. And at last the pagans settled that all the Christians were to be killed. And the Christians thought that, though they had no objections to being killed in their proper persons, it would be a pity to waste a good Pope like Sampietro, who had been chosen and given to them by the Signor Iddio Himself. Therefore they persuaded Sampietro to run away on a night of the darkest, and to hide Himself for a time in a lonely place outside the gates of the City. After He had gone on a little way along the Via Appia—and the night was very dark—He was aware of a grey light on the road in front of Him, and in the light there was Il Santissimo Himself; whereat Sampietro was astonished, for La Sua Maesta' was walking towards Rome. To whom Sampietro said: 'O Master, where do you go?' Then the face of Il Santissimo became very sad, and He said: I am going to Rome to ride the Cross a second time. And then Sampietro knew it was not a noble thing that He was doing, running away all on the sly like this; because no shepherd leaves his sheep when wolves come—at least, no shepherd worth a baiocco. Then Sampietro turned round and went back to Rome, where He was crucified with much joy midway between the goals in the Circus of Nero; but He would not let Himself be crucified in the manner consecrated by Il Santissimo, because He wished to make amends for His weakness in trying to run away; wherefore He begged and prayed to be crucified with His head where His feet should be. The pagans said most certainly, if He preferred it that way, it was all the same to them. And so Sampietro made no more ado, but simply went straight to heaven. And, of course, when He was arrived His angel-guardian clothed Him in a new cope and a tiara and handed Him the Keys; and the Padre Eterno put Him to look after the gate, which is a very great honour, but only His due, because He had been of such high rank when He lived in the world.

"Now after He had been there a little while, His mamma also left the world, and was not allowed to come into paradise: but because her meanness amounted to mortal sin she was sent to hell. Sampietro did not like this at all, and when some of the other gods chaffed Him about it He would grow angry. At last He went to the Padre Eterno, saying that it was by no means suitable that a man of His quality should be disgraced in this way; and the Padre Eterno, Who is so good, so full of pity and of mercy that He would do anything to oblige you if it is for the health of your soul, said He was sorry for Sampietro, and He quite understood His position. He graciously suggested that perhaps the case of Sampietro's mamma had been decided hurriedly, and He ordered her angel-guardian to bring the book in which had been written down all the deeds of her life, good or bad.

" 'Now,' said the Padre Eterno, 'We Carefully Will Go Through This Book, And, If We Can Find Only One Good Deed That She Has Done, We Will Add To That One Good Deed The Merits Of Our Son And Of Hers, So That She May Be Delivered From Eternal Torments.'

"Then the angel read out of the book; and it was found that, in the whole of her life, she had only done one good deed; for a poor starving beggar-woman had once prayed her, per'l Amor di Dio, to give her some food; and she had thrown her the green top of an onion which she chanced to be peeling for her own supper.

"And the Padre Eterno instructed the angel-guardian of Sampietro's mamma to take that identical onion-top from the Treasury of Virtuose Deeds, if indeed he could find so insignificant a thing;

and to go and hold it over the pit of hell; so that if, by chance, she should boil up with the other damned souls to the top of that stew, then she might grasp the onion-top and by it be dragged up to Heaven.

"The angel-guardian did as he had been commanded. He hovered in the air over the pit of hell. He held out the onion-top with his right hand. The furnace flamed. The burning souls boiled and writhed like pasta in a copper pot, and presently Sampietro's mamma came up thrusting out her hands in anguish. And when she saw the onion-top she gripped it, for she was a very covetous woman; and the angel-guardian began to soar into the air, carrying her up to Heaven.

"Now when the other damned souls saw that Sampietro's mamma was leaving them, they also desired to escape; and, clutching of the skirts of her gown, they hung thereon, hoping to be delivered from their pain. And still the angel-guardian rose, and Sampietro's mother held the onion-top, and many tortured souls held her skirts, and others held the feet and skirts of those, and again others held the last, and you surely would have thought that hell was about to be emptied straight away. And still the angel-guardian rose higher, and the long stream of people all hanging to the onion-top rose too, nor was the onion-top too weak to bear the strain: so great is the virtue of one good deed,—of but one small good deed! But when Sampietro's mamma became aware of what was going on, and of what a perfect godsend she was becoming to the numbers who were escaping from hell along with her, she was annoyed: and, because she was a nasty, selfish and cantankerous woman, she kicked and struggled, and even took the onion-top in her teeth, so that she might use her hands to beat off those who were hanging to her skirts. And she fought so violently that she bit through the onion-top, and tumbled back once more into hell flame.

"So you see, sir, that it is sure to be to your own advantage, if you are kind to other people and let them have their own way, always supposing that they will not interfere with you."

FREDERICK BARON CORVO

REMORSE

"I am rightly served—most rightly served!" he repeated to himself at times, with savage pleasure, wallowing in his own torments and in the recognition of the state he was in and of the evil he had done. At length he mastered himself, and got the better of his thoughts. But it was a bitter victory, which had cost him such extremity of effort that he would not go home, but drove to his office, locked himself in, sent away Matthew, who had been there in attendance, and remained quite alone.

"Oh, mine has been a wasted life!" he said presently, starting up from the ottoman he had sat down upon. The thought had worked its way out of the dark recesses of his brain, rent him with tormenting certitude, and cast a dazzling but excruciating ray into his very soul.

He peered about the dusky room, as if he had suddenly come to himself, and saw all things in a new light.

"And why wasted?" he asked himself. And, opening the window, he set himself to reflect.

The street noises sounded fainter and fainter as the town sank to rest in that pleasant night of spring. It was a greenish darkness, save for the twinkling gleams of starlight, and enveloped all the town as in a winding-sheet. From his window the huge bulk of the town was seen, dimly spread out far and wide. Here and there a few lights were visible in those factories that worked by night; and their hum, wafted to his ears by the wind, came like the dull leafy rustling of a forest.

"Why wasted?" he asked himself once again, nerving himself with might and main to the impending struggle with his soul; for it began to make reply with the reminiscences of all his past, weaving together all these threads of memory that had fallen into oblivion, but now had unrisen again and were present. He resisted, he fought them, but unavailingly. He was compelled to see them; compelled, too, to hear all the voices of the past. Submitting to the inevitable, he looked down into himself with terrible and sorrowful interest. He reviewed his past and present life—forty years all told—which, like a thread dangling from the spindle of time, let its strands float loose before him; and he could look into each of them. And into each of them did he look.

The town slumbered in deep shadow, stretched over the ground like an octopus with factories for tentacles; the far-off widely scattered electric suns—a flock of cranes with heads of fire—looked out into the night with sparkling eyes, and watched over the rest of that sleeping Moloch of a town.

"Well, well. After all, I am what I am—what I had to be," he said, with a note of haughty challenge in his voice. But he could not gag his conscience, which by this time was thoroughly awakened, nor still the cries of his beliefs, long set at naught, of his ideals, long forsworn, of his life itself, long contaminated by self-seeking. All these cried aloud within him: "Thou hast lived for thyself alone, thou hast trampled everything down to please thy vanity, to satisfy thy pride, and to become a man of millions!"

"Quite true. Yes, I have sacrificed all things to my career—to my career!" He repeated the words, like a self-inflicted blow in the face; he was overwhelmed with a flood of shame and humiliation.

All had indeed been sacrificed—and to what end? To the raking together of a heap of useless money! He had no friend, no peace, no pleasure, no happiness, no desire even to live; nothing. Nothing!

"Man cannot live for himself alone; if he does, he must needs be unhappy." This saying he had heard before, and knew well, but he had never yet realized its profound truth.

LADISLAS REYMONT

BROTHER SIMEON

"I have not noticed Brother Anacletus or old Brother Simeon among these monks," exclaimed Durtal suddenly.

"They are not occupied on the farm; Brother Anacletus is employed in the chocolate factory, and Brother Simeon looks after the pigs; both are working in the immediate neighborhood of the monastery. If you like, we will go and wish Simeon good-morning."

And the oblate added, "You can tell them, when you go back to Paris, that you have seen a real saint, such as existed in the eleventh century; he carries us back to the time of St. Francis of Assisi; he is in some sense the reincarnation of that astonishing Juniper whose innocent exploits the *Fioretti* celebrate for us. You know that work?"

"Yes. After the *Golden Legend* it is the book on which the soul of the Middle Ages is most clearly impressed."

"But to return to Simeon. This old man is a saint of uncommon simplicity. Here is one proof out of a thousand. Several months ago I was in the prior's cell when Brother Simeon appeared. He made use of the ordinary formula in asking permission to speak—'*Benedicite.*' Father Maximin replied '*Dominus,*' and on this word, which permitted him to speak, the brother showed his glasses and said he could no longer see clearly.

" 'That is not very surprising,' said the prior, 'you have been using the same glasses for nearly ten years, and since then your eyes may well have become weaker. Never mind, we will find the number which suits your sight now."

"As he spoke, Father Maximin mechanically moved the glass of the spectacles between his hands, and suddenly he laughed, showing me his fingers, which were black. He turned round, took a cloth, cleaned the spectacles, and replacing them on the brother's nose, said to him, 'Do you see, Brother Simeon?'

"And the old man, astonished, cried, 'Yes. . . . I see!'

"But this is only one side of this good man. Another is the love of his beasts. When a sow is going to bring forth, he asks permission to pass the night by her, and delivers her, looking after her like a child. He weeps when they sell his little pigs or when the big ones are sent to the slaughter-house. And how all the animals adore him!"

"Here is the piggery," continued M. Bruno, showing a tumbledown old place in front of the left wing of the cloister, surrounded by palisades. "I warn you, the old man grunts like a pig, but he will not answer your questions except by signs."

"But he can speak to his animals?"

"Yes, to them only."

The oblate opened a small door, and the lay brother, all bent, lifted his head with difficulty.

"Good-day, brother," said M. Bruno. "Here is a gentleman who would like to see your pupils."

There was a grunt of joy on the lips of the old man. He smiled and invited them by a sign to follow him.

He introduced them into a shed, and Durtal recoiled, deafened by horrible cries, suffocated by the pestilential heat of the liquid manure. All the pigs jumped up behind their barrier, and howled with joy at the sight of the brother.

"Peace, peace," said the old man, in a gentle voice; and lifting an arm over the paling, he caressed the snouts which, on smelling him, were almost suffocated by grunting.

He drew Durtal aside by the arm, and making him lean over the trellis work, showed him an enormous sow with a snub nose, of English breed, a monstrous animal surrounded by a company of sucking pigs which rushed, as if mad, at her teats.

"Yes, my beauty; go, my beauty," murmured the old man, stroking her bristles with his hand.

The sow looked at him with little eyes, and licked his fingers. She ended by screaming abominably when he went away.

And Brother Simeon showed off other pupils, pigs with ears like the mouth of a trumpet and corkscrew tails, sows whose stomachs trailed and whose feet seemed hardly outside their bodies, new-born pigs which sucked ravenously at the teats, larger ones, who delighted in chasing each other about and rolled in the mud, snorting.

Durtal complimented him on the beasts, and the old man was jubilant, wiping his face with his great hand; then, on the oblate inquiring about the litter of some sow, he felt his fingers in a row.

Replying to the observation that the animals were very greedy, he stretched his arms to heaven, showed the empty troughs, lifted ends of wood, and tore up tufts of grass which he carried to his lips.

Then he took them into the courtyard, placed them against the wall, opened a door beyond, and hid himself. A formidable boar passed him like a waterspout, upset a wheelbarrow, scattering everything round him with a noise like a shell bursting; then he broke into a gallop all round the courtyard, and ended by taking a header into a sea of liquid manure. He wallowed, turned head over heels, kicked about with his four feet in the air, and got up black and disgusting as the inside of a chimney.

After this he halted, grunted a cheerful note, and wished to fawn on the monk, who checked him with a gesture.

"Your boar is splendid!" said Durtal.

And the lay brother looked on Durtal with moist eyes as he rubbed his neck with his hand, sighing.

"That means they are going to kill him soon," said the oblate.

And the old man acquiesced with a melancholy shake of his head.

They left him, thanking him for his kindness.

"When I think of how this being, who is devoted to the lowest duties, prays in church, I long to kneel before him and, like his pigs, kiss his hands!" exclaimed Durtal after a silence.

"Brother Simeon is an angelic being," replied the oblate. "He lives the Unitive life, his soul plunged, drowned in the Divine essence. Under a rough exterior an absolutely white soul, a soul without sin, lives in this poor body. It is right that God should spoil him! As I have told you, He has given him all power over the Demon; and in certain cases He allows him also the power of healing by the imposition of hands. He has renewed here the wonderful cures of the ancient saints."

They ceased speaking, and warned by the bells which were ringing for Vespers, they moved towards the church.

JORIS-KARL HUYSMANS

MAN IN NEED

"It was exactly twelve yeares ago," he began. "I was returning from Italy and had stopped at Monte Carlo to see some friends. I was to spend a week in that abominable place, which has only one good thing about it; but it has that—those wonderful terraced gardens. By the way, I have often been surprised that some essayist has not written a page on the palm trees of those terraces. They ennoble the immoral compost which is heaped up at their feet, as the work of a degraded artist—a Byron, an Edgar Poe, a Baudelaire, a Verlaine—ennobles the vices from which it springs. I give you this comparison just as it presented itself to my mind while I was walking in those alleys with that view before me, one of the finest in the world! I was enjoying it much, but, as usual, with a secret remorse. I attended the concerts, which are excellent, and you know whether I love music; and this pleasure also caused me remorse. Behind this orchestra, as behind these groups of trees and flowers, I saw too distinctly the detestable money of the gaming table. I employed, to tranquillize my scruples in some degree, a procedure, not original with me, which I recommend to you. I have it from a Boston woman, devout and music-mad. It consists in estimating as nearly as possible what sum of money represents, for each visitor, the keeping up of these gardens and this theatre, and then systematically losing that sum at the tables. Try it, when next you are there, and you will find your conscience much relieved.

"One evening, then, I was at the Casino for the purpose of paying this new kind of tithe—that is to say, I amused myself with playing, having the fixed intention of leaving the table as soon as the croupier's rake should have drawn in the amount which I had decided to lose; but it will not surprise you that, having decided to lose, I gained instead, at first. I had taken out of my *porte-monnaie* a hundred-franc note. It was shortly transformed into some fifteen hundred-franc gold pieces, and I now amused myself by throwing these down by handfuls upon the green cloth until the luck should turn—it always does turn! I ended by losing all that I had won except ten louis. I risked these two last pieces upon the black—we were playing *trente et quarante*—which had just won thirteen consecutive times. It won a fourteenth time. I was about to pick up my new gains, almost regretfully, and had leaned forward in this intention over the shoulder of the seated player behind whom I stood, when I saw opposite me a hand extend itself and grasp the four gold pieces. I looked at the thief who had just ventured this astonishing act, and who was a very young man, and involuntarily, —decided to lose though I was,—so strong in us is the instinct of ownership, I cried out,

"But, sir, those twenty louis are mine!" I repeated it, "They are mine!" And, as I had instinctively called out in a loud voice, one of the players, who had chanced to notice me laying down the gold pieces, confirmed what I had said:—

" 'Those twenty louis certainly belonged to this gentleman,' he said, addressing the croupier, who stopped paying the bank's losses to ask:—

" 'Who is the person who took up those twenty louis?' and, addressing me, 'Should you recognize him?'

" 'Certainly,' I replied, and I was just going to point to the spot where my thief had stood half a minute before; but he was no longer there! Though questions and answers had passed with the greatest rapidity, and I had but for a moment turned my eyes toward the croupier, that moment had sufficed for the young man to disappear and to be lost in the crowd, which stood deep around the table. I glanced rapidly over this crowd, saying, as I did so, 'But he was there!' And, at the instant, surprise choked my voice. I had just recognized him standing close beside me. Having committed the theft and finding himself on the point of being seized, he had slipped around the table, in some inconceivable way, and here he was, in the place where it was most unlikely that he would be, at the very elbow of the man whom he had robbed. My amazement at seeing him close to me was now increased by something even more unexpected: I felt the same hand, which just before had so rapidly snatched up my four gold pieces, now grasp me by the arm and hold it tight in a grip that trembled. Our eyes had met. He had become aware that I recognized him, and he had to make this sudden movement in order to stop me if I had meant to strike him. I have told you that he was a very young man. In an instant's flash, with that inconceivable rapidity of sensations which accompanies a crisis like this, I read in his pallid face a desperate entreaty; and I also divined that he was, like myself, an American. By what sign did I know this? I shall not try to explain it to you. Nor shall I try to explain the irresistible pity for the suffering stamped upon this face, still so young, which overmastered me to such a degree that I felt myself incapable of denouncing him—which was, however, my duty in this case. It is always a duty to have a thief arrested, whoever or wherever he is! Instead of that, however, I can hear now how I blundered out to the croupier: 'I shall have to lose it. I ought to have kept a better watch. I don't see him now.' 'Then you make no further claim?' the croupier asked; and I replied that I made no further claim.

"When I had said these words, the hand upon my arm relaxed its grasp; and what happened next on my part I can explain even less than my previous conduct. I had yielded just before, as I tell you, to an emotion of pity, very spontaneous and really very excusable, for a poor young fellow whose imprudent distress showed plainly that he was not hardened in crime. It followed naturally, you know, that I should now complete my charitable act by talking with him and seeking to know what motives were hidden behind this theft, which might even, perhaps, excuse it. Well! I did nothing of the kind. I had no sooner let the words fall, that secured immunity to that young man, than I was ashamed of my leniency as of the most culpable weakness, as of complicity, I will even say, though I had practiced it to my own detriment. I no longer felt, in respect to him whom, however, I had just saved from a very serious peril, anything but a kind of wrathful indignation; and as, after releasing my arm, he lingered near me, evidently upset and wishing, but not daring, to speak to me, I turned abruptly toward him and, in a low voice, but with the most contemptuous and insulting tone, I said to him, in English, 'Get away, get away, you rascal!'

"He made no reply. The blood rushed to his face, just now so pallid. His lips quivered, as if trying in vain to speak. His eyes filled with tears. He seemed to hesitate a moment, then bending his head under the disgrace, he obeyed my brutal injunction, and I saw him cleave a path through the rows of spectators crowded around the table, and disappear—on his way to what new act of villainy, to what crimes, perhaps, or to what repentance? His shameless action, on the one hand, and on the other, his strange attitude; the impudence of the theft, followed by his emotion at my insulting words, have scope to all sorts of conjectures. I felt this so deeply that I now wanted to follow him; and I, in turn, pushed through the crowd, seeking to find him and to learn his story. It was labour lost. He had disappeared completely.

"Did you ever have the singular feeling of having been anyone's fate—I mean to say, of having met a man, at some decisive moment of his life, and of having, by some act of yours, insignificant in itself, thrown the switch for him to one track or another? If you never have, I shall hardly be able to make you understand the disproportionate place that this Casino episode began to occupy in my mind. No sooner had I left the hall than the distressed face of the young thief began haunting me with singular force. Do you know this thing—the retrospective scrutiny of a face that has been seen briefly, in circumstances too striking to be forgotten, and whose secret we mentally strive to decipher, but always without success?"

PAUL BOURGET

AN ACCIDENT

Saint Médard, the old church of the Rue Mouffetard, once well known as the scene of the Convulsionnaires, is a very poor parish. The "Faubourg Marceau," as they call it there, has not much religion, and the vestry-board must have hard work to make both ends meet.

On Sundays, at the hours of service, there are but few there, and they are for the most part women: some twenty of the folk of the quarter and some servants in their round caps. As for the men, there are not at the most more than three or four—old men in peasant jackets, who kneel awkwardly on the stone floor, near a pillar, their caps under their arms, rolling a great chaplet of beads between their fingers, moving their lips, and raising their eyes towards the arched roof, with an air as if they had given the stained-glass windows. On week days, nobody. On Thursdays, in the winter, the aisles resounded for an instant with the clang of wooden shoes, when the students of the catechism came and went. Sometimes a poor woman, leading one or two children and carrying a baby in her arms came to burn a little candle on the stand at the chapel of the Virgin, or perhaps one heard by the baptismal font the wailing of a new-born babe; or, more often, the funeral of some poor wretch: a deal box, covered with a black cloth and resting on two trestles, hastily blessed by the priest, before a little group of women, the men being free-thinkers, and waiting the conclusion of the ceremony in the drinking-shop across the way, where they played bagatelle for drinks.

Therefore, the old Abbé Faber, one of the vicars of the parish, is sure that twice out of three times he will find no penitent before his confessional, and has only to hear, for the most part of the time, the uninteresting confession of some good women. But he is conscientious, and on Tuesdays, Thursdays and Saturdays, at seven o'clock precisely, he betakes himself regularly to the chapel of St. John, only to make a short prayer and return should there be nobody there.

II

One day last winter, struggling against a heavy wind with his open umbrella, the Abbé Faber toiled painfully up the Rue Mouffetard, on the way to his parish, and, almost certain that his toil was useless, he regretted to himself the warm fire he had just quitted in his little room in the Rue D'homond, and the folio *Bollandiste* which he had left lying on the table, with his eye-glasses on its open pages. But it was Saturday night, the day when certain old widows, who earned their scant income in the neighboring boarding-houses, sometimes sought absolution for the morrow's communion. The honest priest could not, therefore, excuse himself from entering his oak box and opening, with the punctuality of a cashier, that wicket where the devotees, for whom the confessional is a spiritual savings-bank, make a weekly deposit of their venial sins.

III

A male penitent! a rare and exceptional thing at Saint Médard. But distinguishing by the red light of the lamp hanging from the roof of the chapel the short white jacket and the heavy nailed shoes of the kneeling man, the Abbé Faber believed him to be some workman who had kept his rustic faith and his early habits of religious observance. Without doubt the confession that he was about to hear would be as stupid as that of the cook of the Rue Monge, who, after having accused himself of petty thefts, exclaimed loudly against a single word of restitution. The priest even smiled to himself as he remembered the formal confession of one of the inhabitants of the faubourg, who came to ask for a billet of confession that he might marry. "I have neither killed or robbed. Ask me about the rest." And so the vicar entered very tranquilly into his confessional, and, after having taken a copious pinch of snuff, opened without emotion the little green curtain of serge which closed the wicket.

"Monsieur le curé," stammered a rough voice, which was making an effort to speak low.

"I am not a curé, my friend. Say your *confiteor* and call me father."

The man, whose face the abbé could not see among the shadows, stumbled through the prayer, which he seemed to have great difficulty in recalling, and he began again in a hoarse whisper:

"Monsieur le curé—no—my father—excuse me if I do not speak properly, but I have not been to confession for twenty-five years—no, not since I quitted the country—you know how it is—a man in Paris, and yet I have not been worse than other people, and I have said to myself, 'God must be a good sort of fellow.' But today what I have on my conscience is too heavy to carry alone, and you must hear me, monsieur le curé: I have killed a man!"

The abbé half rose from his seat. A murderer! There was no longer any question of his mind wandering from the duties of his office, of half annoyance at the garrulity of the old women, to whom he listened with a half attentive ear, and whom he absolved in all confidence. A murderer! That head which was so near his had conceived and planned such a crime! Those hands, crossed on the confessional, were perhaps still stained with blood! In his trouble, perhaps not unmixed with a certain amount of fear, the Abbé Faber could only speak mechanically.

"Confess yourself, my son. The mercy of God is infinite."

"Listen to my whole story," said the man, with a voice trembling with profound grief. "I am a workingman, and I came to Paris more than twenty years ago with a fellow-countryman, a companion from childhood. We robbed birds'-nests, and we learned to read in school together—almost a brother, sir. He was called Philip; I am called Jack, myself. He was a fine big fellow; I have always been heavy and ill-formed. There was never a better workman than he—while I am only a 'botcher'—and so generous and good-natured, wearing his heart on his sleeve. I was proud to be his friend, to walk by his side—proud when he clapped me on the back and called me a clumsy fellow. I loved him because I admired him, in fact. Once here, what an opportunity! We worked together for the same employer, but he left me alone in the evenings more than half the time. He preferred to amuse himself with his companions—natural enough, at his age. He loved pleasure, he was free, he had no responsibilities. All this was impossible for me. I was forced to save my money, for at that time I had an invalid mother in the country, and I sent her all my savings. As for me, I stayed at the fruiterer's where I lodged, and who kept a lodging-house for masons. Philip did not dine there; he used to go somewhere else, and, to tell the truth, the dinners were not particularly good. But the fruiterer was a widow, far from happy, and I saw that my payments were of help to her; and then, to be frank, I fell at once in love with her daughter. Poor Catherine! You will soon know, monsieur le curé, what came from it all. I was there three years without daring to tell her of the love I had for her. I have told you that I am not a good workman, and the little that I gained hardly sufficed for me and for the support of my mother. There could be no thought of marrying. At last my good mother left this world for a better. I was somewhat less pressed for money, and I began to save, and when it seemed to me that I had enough to begin with, I told Catherine of my love. She said nothing at first—neither yes or no. Well, I knew that no one would fall upon my neck; I am not attractive. In the mean time Catherine consulted her mother, who thought well of me as a steady workman, and a good fellow, and the marriage was decided upon. Ah, I had some happy weeks! I saw that Catherine barely accepted me, and that she was by no means carried away with me; but as she had a good heart, I hoped that she would love me some day—I would make her love me. As a matter of course, I told everything to Philip, whom I saw every day at the work-yard, and as Catherine and I were engaged, I wanted him to meet her. Perhaps you have already guessed the end, monsieur le curé. Philip was handsome, lively, good-tempered—everything that I was not; and without attempting it, innocently enough, he fascinated Catherine. Ah, Catherine had a frank and honest heart, and as soon as she recognized what had happened she at once told me everything. Ah, I can never forget that moment! It was Catherine's birthday, and in honor of it I had bought a little cross of gold which I had arranged in a box with cotton. We were alone in the back shop, and she had just brought me my soup. I took my box from my pocket, and, opening it, I showed her the jewel. Then she burst into tears.

" 'Forgive me, Jack,' she said, 'and keep that for her whom you will marry. As for me, I can never become your wife. I love another—I love Philip.'

IV

"Believe me, I had trouble enough then, monsieur le curé; my soul was full of it. But what could I do, since I loved them both? Only what I believed was for their happiness—let them marry. And as Philip had always lived freely, and spent as he made, I lent him my hoard to buy the furniture.

"Then they were married, and for a while all went well. They had a little boy, and I stood sponsor for him and named him Camille, in remembrance of his mother. It was a little after the birth of the baby that Philip began to go wrong. I was mistaken in him—he was not made for marriage; he was too fond of frivolity and pleasure. You live in a poor quarter, monsieur le curé, and you must know the sad story by heart—the workman who glides little by little from idleness into drunkenness, who is off on a spree for two or three days, who does not bring home his week's wages, and who only returns to his home, broken up by his spree, to make scenes and to beat his wife. In less than two years Philip became one of these wretches. At first I tried to reform him, and sometimes, ashamed of himself, he would attempt to do better; but that did not last long. Then my remonstrances only irritated him; and when I went to his house, and he saw me look sadly around the chamber made bare by the pawn-shop, at poor Catherine, thin and pale with grief, he became furious. One day he had the audacity to be jealous of me on account of his wife, who was as pure as the blessed Virgin, reminding me that I was once her lover and accusing me of still being so, with slanders and infamies that I should be ashamed to repeat. We almost flew at each other's throats. I saw what I must do. I would see Catherine and my godson no more; and as for Philip, I would only meet him when by chance we worked on the same job.

"Only, you will understand, I loved Catherine and little Camille too well to lose sight of them entirely. On Saturday evenings, when I knew that Philip was drinking up his wages with his comrades, I used to prowl about the quarter, and chat with the boy when I found him; and if it was too miserable at home, he did not return with empty hands, you know. I believe that the wretched Philip knew that I was helping his wife, and that he closed his eyes to the fact, finding it rather convenient. I will hurry on, for the story is too miserable. Some years have passed; Philip plunging deeper into vice; but Catherine, whom I had helped all I could, has educated her son, who is now a fellow of twenty years, good and courageous like herself. He is not a workman; he is educated; he has learned to draw at the evening schools, and he is now with an architect, where he gets good wages. And though the house is saddened by the presence of the drunkard, things go fairly well, for Camille is a great comfort to his mother; and for a year or two, when I see Catherine—she is so changed, the poor woman!—leaning on the arm of her manly son, it warms my heart.

"But yesterday evening, coming out of my cook-shop, I met Camille; and shaking hands with him—oh, he is not ashamed of me, and he doesn't blush at a blouse covered with plaster—I saw that something was the matter.

"'Let's see—what's the matter now?'

"'I drew the lot yesterday,' he replied, 'and I drew the number ten —a number that sends you to die with fever in the colonies with the marines. That will, at all events, send me there for five years, to leave mother alone, without resources, with father, who has never been drinking so much, who has never been so wicked. And it will kill her—it will kill her! How cursed it is to be poor!'

"Oh, what a horrible night I passed! Think of it, monsieur le curé, that poor woman's labor for twenty years destroyed in a minute by an unhappy chance; because a child, rummaging in a sack, has drawn an unfortunate number! In the morning I was broken as by age when I went to the house we were building on the Boulevard Arago. Of what use is sorrow? We must work all the same. So I mounted the scaffolding. We had already built the house to the fourth story, and I began to place my mortar. Suddenly I felt some one strike me on the shoulder. It was Philip. He only worked now when the inclination seized him, and he was apparently putting in a day's work to get something to drink; but the builder, having a forfeit to pay if the building was not finished by a certain date, accepted the first-comers.

V

"I had not seen Philip for a long time, and it was with difficulty that I recognized him. Burned and fevered by brandy, his beard gray, his hands trembling, he was more than an old man—he was a ruin.

" 'Well,' I said to him, 'the boy has drawn a bad number.'

" 'What of it?' he replied, with an angry look. 'Are you going to worry me about that, too, like Catherine and Camille? The boy will do as others have done: he will serve his country. I know what worries them, both my wife and son. If I were dead he would not have to go. But, so much the worse for them, I am still solid at my post, and Camille is not the son of a widow.'

" 'The son of a widow! Ah, monsieur le curé, why did he use that unhappy phrase? The evil thought came to me at once, and it never quitted me all the morning that I worked at the wretch's side. I imagined all that she was about to suffer—poor Catherine!—when she no longer had her son to care for and protect her, and she must be alone with the miserable drunkard, now completely brutalized, ugly, and capable of anything. A neighboring clock struck eleven, and the workmen all descended to lunch. We remained until the last, Philip and I, but in stepping on the ladder to descend, he turned to me with a leer, and said, in his hoarse, dissipated voice:

" 'You see, steady as a sailor; Camille is not nearly the son of a widow.'

"The blood mounted to my head. I was beside myself. I seized with both hands the rounds of the ladder to which Philip clung shouting 'Help!' and with a single effort I toppled it over.

"He was instantly killed—by an accident, they said—and now Camille is the son of a widow and need not go.

"That is what I have done, monsieur le curé, and what I want to tell to you and to the good God. I repent, I ask pardon, of course; but I must not see Catherine in her black dress, happy on the arm of her son, or I could not regret my crime. To prevent that I will emigrate —I will lose myself in America. As to my penance—see, monsieur le curé, here is the little cross of gold that Catherine refused when she told me that she was in love with Philip. I have always kept it, in memory of the only happy days that I ever knew in my life. Take it and sell it. Give the money to the poor."

Jack arose absolved by the Abbé Faber.

One thing is certain, and that is that the priest never sold the little cross of gold. After having paid its price into the Treasury of the Church, he hung the jewel, as an *ex voto,* on the altar of the chapel of the Virgin, where he often went to pray for the poor mason.

FRANÇOIS COPPÉE

THE GLOOMY SUNDAY

Easter was late that year. It was the twenty-second of April, and the bells were ringing for the high mass of Quasimodo Sunday. The sacristan, Padovan, formerly the lock-keeper of the Nivernais canal, infirm and fat, pulled the rope in the left transept, gazing at the six porcelain vases which he had just placed on the altar, and from which arose six gold palms with roses of gold. He noticed that he had turned one of the palms wrong side forward, and he shrugged his shoulders higher than was necessary, letting the cord of the bell slip as he abused himself. "Idiot, the one time that you take them from the cupboard, not to place them facing right! Are any of the parishioners of Monsieur le Curé coming today? At Easter I counted ninety-two. Yes, and some famous unbelievers among them! They come at Easter, All-Saints', and to funerals. But for Quasimodo Sunday! Ah! Monsieur le Curé may as well delay his mass and let me ring. I see him making signs to me. Courage, Padovan! What good does it do? There are seven in the church. Poor Curé."

The chorister buttoned his short red cassock slowly in the sacristy; Abbé Roubiaux put on his vestments; the flame of the wax tapers ascended in the daylight, and they would have been hardly visible if the wind, slipping through the crannies of the windows, through the doors, through the holes of the vaulted roof, had not blown down their tongues of yellow light, and made a little whirlwind of smoke at their ends which showed the presence and the life of fire. "Good people," sang the bells, "Christ has risen! He has suffered, He has returned to life! Follow His example—come, ye who are looked down upon, ye of humble station, ye who are sad, come all the world, and find the new life over which death shall have no sway. Come! I called your fathers and they came. I now call you."

But the men did not come. When the curé left the sacristy and approached the altar he had, as his entire congregation, four women and one child (little Elié Gombaud, son of the socialist lock-keeper), Père Dixneuf, retired sergeant of Zouaves, Michel de Meximieu, his valet, and the sacristan Padovan, who chanted: *"Quasi modo geniti infantes, alleluia, rationabile, sine dolo lac concupiscite, alleluia, alleluia, alleluia."*

Where were those who did not sing alleluia? Some were working, as if their fatigue of six days did not necessitate the holy rest of the seventh. They were breaking clods in a field, or working at a carpenter's bench, or heating red hot the iron hoop of a cart wheel. Others—the greater number—had already gone to the taverns, those in the village or those in neighboring towns, and were drinking bad alcohol which burned in their veins. The remarks they exchanged had no joy or healthy comfort in them—were only complaints, threats, bits of gossip, jokes that reeked of hatred, vulgarity or wantonness. Others sat in their houses before the fire with nothing to do, waiting for meal time to arrive, or hoping that the father or master of the house would come back so that they could go out and drink in turn. Young girls were dressing for the dance, braiding or curling their hair, thinking of the merriment of past Sundays, and enjoying the excitement which the memory brought with it. The schoolteacher, who was also secretary to the Mayor, was trying to estimate the number of geese, hens, ducks, pigs and turkeys of the region for the official statistics; and he changed the figures cheerfully after consulting those of previous years, thus diminishing or increasing, with an amused smile, the animal wealth about him. A farm hand—a former miner from Calvados, who had left home after a quarrel with his father over extravagance—was saying at that very hour to his master, the farmer of Semelin, "Give me twenty-five francs. I need to go and buy some boots at Saint-Saulge." And he set out, resolved not to buy the boots but to spend the francs. It was the fourth pair of boots he had purchased in this way since the start of the year. Four young men, carrying a fish net and lines, were on their way to poach in the pond; a lock-keeper, exhausted from having opened the lock five times during the night between Saturday and Sunday for the boats which came up the Nivernais canal from Berri, lay snoring on the sheets of his unmade bed, while his wife, bloodless, worn by fever and tired out by a weary life without rest or hope, was dressing, washing and scolding five children who were crying in the foul air of the room. Other men were going off on their bicycles to see women. Everybody in the hamlet, unemployed for a day, was trying to escape from the ordinary routine; and, making little progress, envied wealth as the sovereign power—the wealth represented by the forest and the chateau as well as that described in the newspaper serial or the story book. The envy grew keener as one sat alone or talked with others. The innermost nature of the human beast, vain and violent, betrayed itself in the words, gestures and glances of people. They hated everything, in greater or lesser degree. Had an unknown passer-by crossed the market place at that moment he would have been hated. Legendary names were pronounced and greeted with curses and contempt—names of noblemen, Louis XIV, Rothschild; and all denounced the government which paid poorly, and which (they were beginning to feel) must be replaced by another government ready to pay better for less work and, possibly, willing to supply money for expenses, comforts and pleasures in the town, the province and everywhere, without demanding any work at all. Homely girls surmised that a thirty-franc hat would make them beautiful. Such gross and fantastic dreams debased the souls of many who would have been proud and strong had they been properly educated.

Such was the rural Sunday, a masterpiece of ennui when worship has gone out of it. The curé said Mass and he suffered indescribably, feeling the silence that was everywhere behind him, around him. The loneliness of the church, empty of the faithful; the loneliness of souls without the grace of God. And this was a spot in France! When he had finished, Abbé Roubiaux was so pale that old Perrine, the last spinner in the town, seeing him reenter the sacristy tottering, his eyes cast down, said half aloud, "They've sent us a curé who is like my wool—he can't stand. I thought these Morvandians had more backbone!"

RENÉ BAZIN

PARADISE

The poet looked at his friends, his relatives, the priest, the doctor, and the little dog, who were in the room. Then he died.

Some one wrote his name and age on a piece of paper. He was twenty-eight years.

As they kissed his forehead his friends and relatives found that he was cold, but he could not feel their lips because he was in heaven. And he did not ask as he had done when he was on earth, whether heaven was like this or like that. Since he was there, he had no need of anything else.

His mother and father, whether or not they had died before him, came to meet him. They did not weep any more than he, for the three had really never been separated.

His mother said to him:

"Put out the wine to cool, we are about to dine with the Bon Dieu under the green arbor of the Garden of Paradise."

His father said to him:

"Go down and cull of the fruits. There is none that is poisonous. The trees will offer them to you of their own accord, without sufferance either to their leaves or their branches, for they are inexhaustible."

The poet was filled with joy in being able to obey his parents.

When he had returned from the orchard and submerged the bottles of wine in the water, he saw his old dog. It too had died before him, and it came gently running toward him, wagging its tail. It licked his hands, and he patted it. Beside it were all the animals he had loved best while on earth: a little red cat, two little gray cats, two little white cats, a bullfinch, and two goldfish.

Then he saw that the table was set and about it were seated the Bon Dieu, his father and mother, and a lovely young girl whom he had loved here-below on earth. She had followed him to heaven even though she was not dead.

He saw that the Garden of Paradise was none other than that of his own birthplace here on earth, in the high reaches of the Pyrenees, all filled with lilies and pomegranates and cabbages.

The Bon Dieu had laid his hat and stick on the ground. He was garbed like the poor on the great highways, those who have only a morsel of bread in their wallet, and whom the magistrates arrest at the town gates, and throw into prison, since they know not how to write their name. His beard and hair were white like the great light of day, and his eyes profound and black like the night. He spoke, and his voice was very soft:

"Let the angels come and minister unto us, for to serve is their happiness."

Then from all corners of the heavenly orchard legions were seen to hasten. They were the faithful servitors who here on earth had loved the poet and his family. Old Jean was there, he who drowned while saving a little boy, old Marie who had fallen dead under a sunstroke, and lame Pierre was there and Jeanne and still another Jeanne.

Then the poet rose to do them honor, and said unto them:

"Sit down in my place, it is meet that you should be near God."

And God smiled because he knew in advance what their answer would be.

"Our happiness is service. This puts us close to God. Do you not serve your father and mother? Do they not serve Him who serves us?"

And suddenly he saw that the table had grown larger and that new guests were seated about it. They were the father and mother of his mother and father, and the generations that had gone before them.

Evening fell. The older of the people slumbered. Love held the poet and his sweetheart. But God to whom they had done honor, took up his way again like the poor on the great highways, those who have only a morsel of bread in their wallet, and whom the magistrates arrest at the town gates, and throw into prison, since they know not how to write their name.

FRANCIS JAMMES

THE CHARITY CHILDREN

One day the souls of the charity children cried out to God. It was on a stormy evening when their fevers and wounds made them suffer more than ever. They lay white with grief in their rows of beds, above which ignoble science had hung the placards of their maladies.

They were sad, very sad, for it was a day of festival. Their tiny arms were stretched out on the coverlets, and with their transparent hands they touched the meager toys that pious grand ladies had brought them. They did not even know what to do with these playthings. A President of the Republic had visited them, but they had not understood what it meant.

Their souls cried out toward God. They said:

"We are the daughters of misery, of scrofula, and of syphilis. We are the daughters of daughters of shame."

"I," said one, "was dragged out of a cesspool where in her distraction my mother, the servant of an inn, had thrown me." Another said: "I was born a child with an enormous head that had a red gap in the forehead. My father killed my mother, and he killed himself."

Still others said:

"We are the survivors of abortions and infanticides. Our mothers are on the lists. Our fathers, cigar in mouth, saunter smiling amid the tumult of business and the markets. We are born like kings with a crown on our heads, a crown of red rash."

And God, hearing their cry, came down toward these souls. He entered the hospital of more than human sorrows. At His approach the fumes rose from the medicaments which the good sisters had prepared, as though from censers by the side of the child martyrs, who sat up in their narrow cots like white, weary flowers.

The sovereign Master said to them:

"Here I am. I heard your call, and am waiting to condemn those that caused you to be born. What torment do you implore for them?"

Then the souls of the children sang like the bindweed of the hedges.

They sang:

"Glory to God! Glory to God! Pardon those who gave us birth. Lead us some day to Heaven by their side."

FRANCIS JAMMES

PAN MICHAEL AT KAMENYETS

Pan Michael sat there leaning against the masonry. Basia nestled up to him, like a child to its mother. The night was in August, warm and fragrant. The moon illuminated the niche with a silver light; the faces of the little knight and Basia were bathed in its rays. Lower down, in the court of the castle, were groups of sleeping soldiers and the bodies of those slain during the cannonade, for there had been no time yet for their burial. The calm light of the moon crept over those bodies, as if the hermit of the sky wished to know who was sleeping from weariness merely, and who had fallen into the eternal slumber. Farther on was outlined the wall of the main castle, from which fell a black shadow on one half of the courtyard. Outside the walls, from between the bulwarks, where the janissaries lay cut down with sabres, came the voices of men. They were camp followers and those of the dragoons to whom booty was dearer than slumber; they were stripping the bodies of the slain. Their lanterns were gleaming on the place of combat like fireflies. Some of them called to one another; and one was singing in an undertone a sweet song not beseeming the work to which he was given at the moment:

"Nothing is silver, nothing is gold to me now,
Nothing is fortune.
Let me die at the fence, then, of hunger,
If only near thee."

But after a certain time that movement began to decrease, and at last stopped completely. A silence set in which was broken only by the distant sound of the hammers breaking the cliffs, and the calls of the sentries on the walls. That silence, the moonlight, and the night full of beauty delighted Pan Michael and Basia. A yearning came upon them, it is unknown why, and a certain sadness, though pleasant. Basia raised her eyes to her husband; and seeing that his eyes were open, she said,

"Michael, you are not sleeping."

"It is a wonder, but I cannot sleep."

"It is pleasant for you here?"

"Pleasant. But for you?"

Basia nodded her bright head. "Oh, Michael, so pleasant! ai, ai! Did you not hear what that man was singing?"

Here she repeated the last words of the little song:

"Let me die at the fence, then, of hunger,
If only near thee."

A moment of silence followed, which the little knight interrupted,—

"But listen, Basia."

"What, Michael?"

"To tell the truth, we are wonderfully happy with each other; and I think that if one of us were to fall, the other would grieve beyond measure."

Basia understood perfectly that when the little knight said "if one of us were to fall," instead of *die,* he had himself only in mind. It came to her head that maybe he did not expect to come out of that siege alive, that he wished to accustom her to that termination; therefore a dreadful presentiment pressed her heart, and clasping her hands, she said,

"Michael, have pity on yourself and on me!"

The voice of the little knight was moved somewhat, though calm.

"But see, Basia, you are not right," said he; "for if you only reason the matter out, what is this temporal existence? Why break one's neck over it? Who would be satisfied with tasting happiness and love here when all breaks like a dry twig,—who?"

But Basia began to tremble from weeping, and to repeat, "I will not hear this! I will not! I will not!"

"As God is dear to me, you are not right," repeated the little knight. "Look, think of it: there above, beyond that quiet moon, is a country of bliss without end. Of such a one speak to me. Whoever reaches that meadow will draw breath for the first time, as if after a long journey, and will feed in peace. When my time comes—and that is a soldier's affair—it is your simple duty to say to yourself: 'That is nothing! Michael is gone. True, he is gone far, farther than from here to Lithuania; but that is nothing, for I shall follow him.' Basia, be quiet; do not weep. The one who goes first will prepare quarters for the other; that is the whole matter."

Here there came on him, as it were, a vision of coming events; for he raised his eyes to the moonlight and continued,—

"What is this mortal life? Grant that I am there first, waiting till some one knocks at the heavenly gate. Saint Peter opens it. I look; who is that? My Basia! Save us! Oh, I shall jump then! Oh, I shall cry then! Dear God, words fail me. And there will be no tears, only endless rejoicing; and there will be no Pagans, nor cannon, nor mines under the walls, only peace and happiness. Ai, Basia, remember, this life is nothing!"

"Michael, Michael!" repeated Basia.

And again came silence, broken only by the distant, monotonous sound of the hammers.

"Basia, let us pray together," said Pan Michael, at last.

And those two souls began to pray. As they prayed, peace came on both; and then sleep overcame them, and they slumbered till the first dawn.

Pan Michael conducted Basia away before the morning kindya to the bridge joining the old castle with the town. In parting, he said,—

"This life is nothing! Remember that, Basia."

HENRYK SIENKIEWICZ

THICK WEATHER

We had just gone down below for a moment to commune in a battened-down cabin, with a large white chart lying limp and damp upon a cold and clammy table under the light of a smoky lamp. Sprawling over that seaman's silent and trusty adviser, with one elbow upon the coast of Africa and the other planted in the neighborhood of Cape Hatteras (it was a general track-chart of the North Atlantic), my skipper lifted his rugged, hairy face, and glared at me in a half-exasperated, half-appealing way. We had seen no sun, moon, or stars for something like seven days. By the effect of the West Wind's wrath the celestial bodies had gone into hiding for a week or more, and the last three days had seen the force of a southwest gale grow from fresh, through strong, to heavy, as the entries in my log-book could testify. Then we separated, he to go on deck again, in obedience to that mysterious call that seems to sound forever in the ship-master's ears, I to stagger into my cabin with some vague notion of putting down the words "Very heavy weather" in a log-book not quite written up to date. But I gave it up, and crawled into my bunk instead, boots and hat on, all standing (it did not matter; everything was soaking wet, a heavy sea having burst the poop skylights the night before), to remain in a nightmarish state between waking and sleeping for a couple of hours of so-called rest.

The southwesterly mood of the West Wind is an enemy of sleep, and even of a recumbent position, in the responsible officers of a ship. After two hours of futile, light-headed, inconsequent thinking upon all things under heaven in that dark, dank, wet and devastated cabin, I arose suddenly and staggered up on deck. The autocrat of the North Atlantic was still oppressing his kingdom and its outlying dependencies, even as far as the Bay of Biscay, in the dismal secrecy of the thick, very thick, weather. The force of the wind, though we were running before it at the rate of some ten knots an hour, was so great that it drove me with a steady push to the front of the poop, where my commander was holding on.

"What do you think of it?" he addressed me in an interrogative yell.

What I really thought was that we both had just about enough of it. The manner in which the great West Wind chooses at times to administer his possessions does not commend itself to a person of peaceful and law-abiding disposition, inclined to draw distinctions between right and wrong in the face of every force, whose standard, naturally, is that of might alone. But, of course, I said nothing. For a man caught, as it were, between his skipper and the great West Wind, silence is the safest sort of diplomacy. Moreover, I knew my skipper. He did not want to know what I thought. Ship-masters hanging on a breath before the thrones of the winds ruling the seas have their psychology, whose workings are as important to the ship and those on board of her as the changing moods of the weather. The man, as a matter of fact, under no circumstances, ever cared a brass farthing for what I or anybody else in his ship thought. He had had just about enough of it, I guessed, and what he was at really was a process of fighting for a suggestion. It was the pride of his life that he had never wasted a chance, no matter how boisterous, threatening, and dangerous, of a fair wind. Like men racing blindfold for a gap in a hedge, we were finishing a splendidly quick passage from the antipodes, with a tremendous rush for the Channel in as thick a weather as any I can remember, but his psychology did not permit him to bring the ship to with a fair wind blowing—at least not on his own initiative. And yet he felt that very soon indeed something would have to be done. He wanted the suggestion to come from me, so that later on, when the trouble was over, he could argue this point with his own uncompromising spirit, laying the blame upon my shoulders. I must render him the justice that this sort of pride was his only weakness.

But he got no suggestion from me. I understood this psychology. Besides, I had my own stock of weaknesses at the time (it is a different one now), and among them was the conceit of being remarkably well up in the psychology of the Westerly Weather. I believed —not to mince matters—that I had a genius for reading the mind of the great ruler of high latitudes. I fancied I could discern already the coming of a change in his royal mood. And all I said was:

"The weather shall clear up with the shift of wind."

"Anybody knows that much," he snapped at me, at the highest pitch of his voice.

"I mean before dark," I cried.

This was all the opening he ever got from me. The eagerness with which he seized upon it gave me the measure of the anxiety he had been laboring under.

"Very well," he shouted, with an affectation of impatience, as if giving way to long entreaties. "All right. If we don't get a shift by then we'll take that foresail off her and put her head under the wing for the night."

I was struck by the picturesque character of the phrase as applied to a ship brought-to in order to ride out a gale with wave after wave passing under her breast. I could see her resting in the tumult of the elements like a sea-bird sleeping in wild weather upon the raging waters with its head tucked under its wing. In imaginative force, in true feeling, this is one of the most expressive sentences I have ever heard on human lips. But as to taking the foresail off that ship before we put her head under her wing, I had my grave doubts. They were justified. That long-enduring piece of canvas was confiscated by the arbitrary decree of the West Wind, to whom belongs the lives of men and the contrivances of their hands within the limits of his kingdom. With the sound of a faint explosion it vanished into the thick weather bodily, leaving behind of its stout substance not so much as one solitary strip big enough to be picked into a handful of lint for, say, a wounded elephant. Torn out of its boltropes, it faded like a whiff of smoke in the smoky drift of clouds shattered and torn by the shift of wind. For the shift of wind had come. The unveiled, low sun glared angrily from a chaotic sky upon a confused and tremendous sea dashing itself upon a coast. We recognized the headland, and looked at each other in the silence of dumb wonder.

Without knowing it, we had run up alongside the Isle of Wight, and that tower, tinged a faint evening red in the salt wind-haze, was the lighthouse on St. Catherine's Point.

My skipper recovered first from his astonishment. His bulging eyes sank back gradually into their orbits. His psychology, taking it all round, was really very creditable for an average sailor. He had been spared the humiliation of laying his ship to with a fair wind; and at once that man, of an open and truthful nature, spoke up in perfect good faith, rubbing together his brown, hairy hands—the hands of a master craftsman upon the sea:

"Humph! that's just about where I reckoned we had got to."

JOSEPH CONRAD

MARIA VISITS HER BROTHER

Having eaten at noonday, Maria walked to the Und gate in order to visit her brother, the Capuchin friar. When she reached the cloister she saw with astonishment that the building was much larger than the one she remembered from youth. She did not know there had been a fire and that the Countess Werda had rebuilt the cloister more beautifully. She had not chosen a good day for her visit. It was very difficult even to get into the monastery, since all the entrances were guarded by policemen who had come from the city because a murderer had taken refuge with the monks. And how long she had to wait in the sacristy for her brother! When he finally came, she did not recognize him. Where was his shining curly hair? He was covered with nothing but stubble. And where were his great brown eyes, as beautiful as a woman's? They were lustreless now and stared almost wildly at one from beneath craggy brows. The once red cheeks were yellow, and the man had a beard worthy of a father of the desert. His body was plump and his hands and feet—how large they were now! How old could he be? Certainly not more than thirty-five, but he looked sixty. And how raw and old his voice sounded as he muttered the Capuchin greeting, *Ave Maria!*

"Ignatius—don't you know me?"

"Yes—it's Marie," he said with utter unconcern. What was she doing there and what did she want of him? Besides she should have called him by his name in the Holy Order. He scarcely glanced at his sister, but looked over her head through the window of the sacristy and appeared to be observing the guards.

"I've been in Krems on business. And so I did want to come and see how you're getting along, Ignatius dear."

"Camillus a Krems is my name.'"

"Dear Cam-millus," she said to please him. She had always been so fond of him when they were both youngsters. "Do you remember when we went to Gottweig together the last time? It was such a fine day—the birds were singing."

How she did remember things! He recalled nothing.

"Oh, Igna—Camillus! How pale you are," she said, drawing him out with her melancholy voice. "Perhaps you are sick—you have a cough. You should eat honey on an empty stomach. That's good for the cough. . . . And is it healthy for you to be so fat?" she queried, remembering that her father had been bloated—with the dropsy, which caused his death.

"It makes no difference whether the ass is sick or well," he said reprovingly. "The main thing is that the soul be healthy—that is, have God's grace!"

"And your clothes are so torn and patched," she continued, looking at his shabby habit and torn sandals. "Must they be so? Even on a holiday?"

"Certainly, certainly. . . . A Capuchin ought to be rigged out like you are," he said almost ironically. "How well was Our Lord dressed on the Cross, eh?" He did not mean to be offensive: he was still new in the Order and overzealous, wherefore every kind of tenderness or comfort which was customary in the world aroused his opposition. "I ought to take it easy . . . guzzle honey," he grumbled on. "And after that put on a silk habit and let my hood be lined with satin. . . . Oh, Father in Heaven! And she once wanted to go to the convent!" He clapped his swollen hands together and added, to the accompaniment of laughs and coughs, "It was really luck

Schinnagel got you before you could make such a stupid move. You'd have been a nun fit for God to have mercy on. Ha, ha, ha, huh, huh, huh!"

Maria appeared to have been hurt. And so he looked at her good-naturedly through eyes which swam with tears brought on by his fit of coughing and changed the conversation. "Well, how are you and your husband getting on? Any children?"

"Three little boys," she began to explain, seeing that he knew absolutely nothing about her. "There would have been four, but one died."

"Do they behave?"

"Peter is a mischief, but Paul is very good and all three are very dear. Little Joseph just came last Lent."

As she spoke about the children his eyes took on the old mischievous look of which she had been so fond when he was still in the world. And so she poured out her heart to him, describing her mother's fortune in charming words. He listened patiently until she began to draw a comparison between little Peter and the boy Ignatius of long ago.

"One child's like another," he growled savagely. "All have two eyes, noses in the middle of their faces and yellow hair—excepting when it's brown . . . but if you're so fond of your children, why are you sailing around the world and leaving them alone?"

"I have to do it," she answered and began to tell him about Jesse's attack on the holy image and about how she had come to get a ransom for the Blessed Mother, how this had then fallen into her lap miraculously,—and how, in addition, she had succeeded in getting the Father Rector of the Jesuits to send a Commission which would restore the faith in their land and punish the wicked Velderndorff.

Stroking his anchoritic beard, the Capuchin gazed at the excited woman with a somewhat contemptuous smile. When she had finished he said dryly, "When it's all over with you'll weep and mourn."

"I? What for?" she asked in amazement.

"You will weep and mourn for this same man—this Lutheran—

what did you say his name was?—when they punish him. I can see you now!"

The woman stared at him with wide-open eyes and the expression on her face became unattractive. Then she laughed impetuously and said almost angrily, "I'll save my tears for something more becoming to them! Indeed. . . . Do you think I left my husband and my children, and that I went down on my knees before the Father Rector to beg him for help, in order to cry when help comes and the monster gets his due?— You must think I'm a fool. You don't know your sister!"

"I have known a girl with such a tender heart that she couldn't watch them take any villain, robber or murderer to gaol, or whip a thief, without shedding such bitter tears they chapped her cheeks badly. Then mother had to put salve on them!" he said, emphasizing the effective words and maintaining his stolid gaze unchanged. "This same little girl, Marie, sobbed over every beetle and toad that was stepped on; and once when a litter of little kittens had been thrown into the River, she followed them into the water trying to rescue them. . . . The name of this little girl was Marie Aichinger, and now she's called Frau Schinnagel. Could she have changed her heart with her name? I don't believe it!"

She turned as red as a flame, and, quite as if she were warding off an unjust accusation, cried firmly: "If all that was really so—I don't remember it any more—I do believe a married woman can be a little more sensible than a school girl and still not change her heart. . . . And it's something else entirely to sympathize with poor sinners going to their death, or with innocent animals suffering, than to have pity on one who goes about stealing the faith and salvation of poor folk, and desecrating the Mother of God herself and her image. . . . May God punish me and separate me from all just souls," she cried tempestuously, "if I should ever so far forget myself as to feel pity for this devilish fellow!"

"Silence!" said Camillus, putting a finger upon his lips. "The Blessed Sacrament is next door."

Now she was ashamed of her outburst and tried to explain that she had not been herself here of late—all these trials had been more than a human being could bear. He listened without stirring; and when she had finished he asked, "Do you pray earnestly? And reverence the Holy Eucharist?"

Marie saw that he was subtly giving her counsel. She replied somewhat snappily, "I should say I do!"

"But rightly? You pray rightly?" he continued to probe. Then both he and she were silent, and he asked, "Am I right? Have we finished?"

"Yes," she retorted coolly.

"Well, then—let us say *vale*—I've got to look after that Viennese murderer. He broke his foot as he fled. I'll bandage it now to relieve the pain."

"You care more for that murderer than you do for your own sister!" she said bitterly. "Anyone who had listened to us today wouldn't have imagined we are brother and sister . . . and that we haven't seen each other for seven years."

Her lips trembled.

"Don't you know," he said with a quiet earnestness that was not quarrelsome now but peaceful, "that we men of religion have no brothers and sisters according to the flesh, but only in Christ? All men are our brothers. . . . It is all the same whether they are good or bad, saints or murderers, Christians or—heretics. Marie! The heretic of whom you have spoken is your brother, too. . . . You must forgive me if I tell you that. . . ."

She wanted to protest. But she could not because his eyes looked at her so benevolently. And so she hung her head. "Pray for me, Ignatius," she murmured. "And God bless you—Camillus!" she added, sobbing because she had suddenly been overwhelmed by tenderness.

"Ave Maria," he answered solemnly but unemotionally, withdrew the hand for which she had reached, and instead offered her the crucifix on his rosary to kiss. Then he shuffled away, coughing.

ENRICA VON HANDEL-MAZZETTI

THE ART OF CHRISTMAS GIVING

The business of expressing one's personality by one's gifts has been carried to extraordinary lengths of late years. There are people who actually select for all their friends and relatives things that they themselves would like. If they consider themselves to be dainty—as all women do—they give dainty presents, disregarding the fact that the recipient may suffer acute physical pain at the mere thought of daintiness.

They wish their beneficiaries to say on Christmas morning, "How characteristic of Mrs. Slipslop to give me this exquisite Dresden china chewing-gum holder," instead of "How generous and discerning of Mrs. Slipslop to give me this pair of rubber boots or this jar of tobacco or this hypodermic syringe!" But what every child and every grown person wants to receive is a gift suited to his tastes and habits; it is a matter of indifference whether or not it expresses the personality of the giver. Perhaps it will in his eyes supply the giver with a new and charming personality.

You have hitherto regarded Mr. Blinker, the notorious efficiency engineer, with disfavor. You have regarded him as a prosaic theorist, a curdled mass of statistics. On Christmas morning you find that he has presented you, not with an illuminated copy of "Rules for Eliminating Leisure," or a set of household ledgers or an alarm clock, but with a cocktail set or a pool table or an angora kitten or some other inefficient object.

At once your opinion of Mr. Blinker changes for the better. He assumes a new and radiant personality. Your Sunday school teacher has always exhibited to you virtues which you respect but do not enjoy; she has seemed to you lacking in magnetism. If she gives you for Christmas a Bible or a tale of juvenile virtue, you will write her a graceful letter of thanks (at your mother's dictation), but your affection for the estimable lady will not be materially increased. But if your Sunday school teacher gives you a bowie knife or a revolver or a set of the Deadwood Dick novels! then how suddenly will the nobility of your Sunday school teacher's nature be revealed to you!

To elevator men, janitors, domestic servants, newspaper deliverers, and other necessary evils we always give something appropriate—money. And money does not express the personalities of most of us. We—that is, the general public, the common people, the populace, the average man, the great washed and the rest of us—do our duty in this matter, following religiously the admirable tradition of the Christmas box. But our retainers—if they will permit us thus picturesquely to address them—do not. They serve us during the year, and are duly paid for it, but they do nothing picturesque or extraordinary at Christmas time to justify our gifts to them.

As a matter of fact, they are not upholding their part of the tradition. It is not enough for them to bow and say, "Thank you," while they feverishly count the money. They should revel romantically, as did their predecessors who established the custom by which they profit. The elevator boys should sing West Indian carols under our windows—especially if our apartment is in the twentieth story. The janitor and his family should enact in the basement a Christmas miracle play.

It is pleasant to think of the janitor attired as a shepherd or as a Wise Man, with his children as angels or sheep, to picture the Yule log on the janitorial hearth, and to hear in fancy, rising up the dumbwaiter shaft, the strains of "The Carnal and the Crane," or of the excellent carol which begins,

The shepherd upon a hill he sat;
He had on him his tabard and his hat,
His tarbox, his pipe and his flagat;
His name was called Joly Joly Wat,
For he was a gude herdes boy.
Ut hoy!
For in his pipe he made so much joy.

In some places the newspaper deliverers and the telegraph boys feebly support this tradition by writing, or causing to be written, a "carrier's address" and leaving printed copies of it with their customers. It would be better, of course, if they were to sing or to recite these verses, but even the printed address is better than nothing. It is a pity to see even this slight concession to tradition disappearing. In bygone days some of the most distinguished of our poets were glad to write these addresses—the late Richard Watson Gilder wrote one for the newspaper carrier of Newark.

And then there are the numerous public servants who nowadays receive from the public no special Christmas benefaction— How gracefully they might obtain it by infusing into their occupations a little Yuletide pageantry! As it is, the subway guards celebrate the golden springtime by donning white raiment. Let them on Christmas day be wreathed with mingled holly and mistletoe, and let them chant, in mingled chorus,

> God rest you, merry gentlemen!
> Let nothing you dismay:
> Please slip us some coin, you've got money to boin,
> And this is Christmas day.

JOYCE KILMER

HUNTING A HAIR SHIRT

Let it be distinctly understood that I do not want a hair shirt. I have no idea that I ever shall want one. But if I should—I say impressively—if I ever should want one, I think the getting of it should be a simpler matter than it is. As the White Knight said of the mouse-trap that he carried on his saddle, you never know when you may need a thing. Think of it! Suppose, in some perfectly unforeseen moment, it was brought home to you that a hair shirt you must have. How on earth would you get it?

For a long time I pondered the subject deeply. I would not ask anyone. I was too proud. I supposed everyone else knew and that I was in a lonely depth of ignorance. So I was very stealthy about it. I sought secretly and eagerly for signs or advertisements that might read "Spring Novelties in Hair Shirtings" or "Custom-Made Hair Shirts," so that I might at least learn whether you bought them by the yard or had them tailored for you. It even occurred to me that they might be found ready-to-wear in a department store. I pictured myself approaching a haughty saleslady and asking her timidly if she could direct me to the section where they sell hair shirts. I am brave and I might have brought myself to do this, if I had really wanted that shirt. But, you see, I didn't. And the signs failed me. I never saw a sign that even remotely hinted at hair shirts.

I became discouraged. Life is so unnecessarily complicated and outrageously artificial. If I had wanted a piece of wood painted to represent a basket of flowers and weighted for its homely duty of holding the door open, I should have had no trouble. I could easily have found rubbers for dogs and elaborately upholstered bassinets for cats who prefer to sleep in the cellar by the furnace. But a simple, mediaeval garment like a hair shirt seemed to be out of reach.

"Can it be," I thought despairingly, "that the demand for them has decreased so that there is no longer any incentive to anyone to make them?" But in happier moments I was more sane and put thoughts like that determinedly from me. Penitence must be as sincere as ever, though it may be less general in its severity. The rarity of its severe forms should not stop the manufacture of hair shirts. Carters, I know it to my sorrow, are extremely rare, yet smocks blossom on every hand.

So I decided that more direct methods must be tried. But my spirit quailed at the thought of asking people. It happens that I have had to ask for so much useful information in my life that I am ashamed to do it. I never know where to go to pay taxes or to vote. I don't know the difference between the North River and the Hudson—and that I shall never have the courage to ask. Even simple things like getting a carpenter to mend the lattice under the porch where the children went through after the rabbit are utterly beyond me.

Keeping in mind this failing of mine and the reputation I am fast acquiring of being an idiot, I hoped I might manage it by indirect discourse, so to say. I would be very wily, tactfully lead the conversation in the desired direction and watch the result. I found it unexpectedly difficult to steer conversation in the direction of hair shirts without using force. But I waited, hungrily watching for a chance. At last it came.

It was at dinner at the house of Amaryllis. Amaryllis lives next door to me. This evening she seemed somewhat distrait. I enquired the reason of this, as she usually keeps up the dinner conversation with a hectic eagerness that speaks volumes for her early training.

"It's my Belgian andirons," she said readily. "I can't get anyone to make tails for them."

It appeared that she had been looking for a blacksmith to complete the almost-Belgian andirons bought from an almost-Belgian refugee. "But blacksmiths are almost extinct since motors came in," she ended sadly. I took no heed of her sorrow. My chance had come.

"So many things are hard to get," I broke in feverishly. "Now, hair shirts, for instance."

I said it with great earnestness, but everybody seemed to think that I had made a joke. They laughed in a way that would have delighted me if I had really made one. But no one volunteered a suggestion, and I realized that that way wouldn't work.

So, a few days later, I gathered myself together and asked Amaryllis in private. "Amaryllis," I said, somewhat timidly, "if you wanted a hair shirt, where would you go to get it?"

"I'd buy an old sofa and cut it down," said Amaryllis just like that. And she would, too. But this seemed to me extreme.

"You know I can't sew," I said crossly, "and besides, I couldn't afford it." But Amaryllis was now hot on the trail.

"I never really thought about it before," she said with deep and, to me, gratifying interest. "There should be hair shirt emporiums or factories or something. We'll ask everyone until we find out."

I consented, as there seemed no other way for me to get one in case of need, unless I sat up nights and wove my own hair, that being the only hair available. There was, I remembered, an old lady in a fairy tale who wove her own hair into cloth. It always grew again by morning. Mine wouldn't, so I did not like this idea. Also, I had no loom.

As time went on our quest assumed almost national proportions. I went travelling and asked people in all walks of life, but received no sensible replies. Then at home the table talk usually drifted automatically into a discussion of ways and means. Sometimes I almost wished I had not started it.

"They are woven in convents," once mused some gentle and dreamy soul, "of the hair of nuns, which is cut four times a year."

The thought of the nuns I knew engaged in weaving shirts of hair made me giggle.

"Nonsense!" I exclaimed wildly. "The best ones are made of horse hair."

"They are made of camel's hair," said the beardless cousin of Amaryllis with an air of omniscience. Amaryllis upheld me stoutly.

"They aren't. I know they're made of horse hair. Don't you remember?

> And a shirt of the roughest and coarsest hair
> For a year and a day, Sir Ingoldsby, wear.

That proves it. Horse hair *is* the roughest and coarsest." Amaryllis proves most things by the Ingoldsby Legends. "But they must be woven on hand looms?" she went on thoughtfully.

"Hairlooms," said some flippant person in the background.

But light came at last. Father Agrippa came to dinner at my house. I had not seen him for a long time. He *does* know everything. So I asked him. He beamed.

"You get them from the monasteries of the penitential orders, of course. Franciscans, for instance. Where you get the chains, you know."

"The chains!" we exclaimed in chorus, aghast.

"Yes. The chains with the points turned in that you wear on your arm or waist. I'll be glad to send you one. The simplest thing in the world. But it would never do for it to be opened in the post office. It must be marked 'Private'—yes, 'Private and Penitential' would be better." He smiled happily.

"But, Father Agrippa," I said meekly, but with desperate firmness, "I don't want"— He contemplated me rather sadly.

"No," he admitted. "No, I don't suppose you do. And I'm afraid it wouldn't do you any good, anyhow. But"—he brightened up and turned around hopefully—"I shall send one to Amaryllis tomorrow."

ALINE KILMER

TWO DAYS

August 16.—We rose at four, when it was stormy and I saw duncoloured waves leaving trailing hoods of white breaking on the beach. Before going I took a last look at the breakers, wanting to make out how the comb is morselled so fine into string and tassel, as I have lately noticed it to be. I saw big smooth flinty waves, carved and scuppled in shallow grooves, much swelling when the wind freshened, burst on the rocky spurs of the cliff at the little cove and break into bushes of foam. In an enclosure of rocks the peaks of the water romped and wandered and a light crown of tufty scum standing high on the surface kept slowly turning round: chips of it blew off and gadded about without weight in the air. At eight we sailed for Liverpool in wind and rain. I think it is the salt that makes rain at sea sting so much. There was a good-looking young man on board that got drunk and sung "I want to go home to Mamma." I did not much look at the sea: the crests I saw ravelled up by the wind into the air in arching whips and straps of glassy spray and higher broken into clouds of white and blown away. Under the curl shone a bright juice of beautiful green. The foam exploding and smouldering under water makes a chrysoprase green. From Blackburn I walked: infinite stiles and sloppy fields, for there had been much rain. A few big shining drops hit us aslant as if they were blown off from eaves or leaves. Bright sunset: all the sky hung with tall tossed clouds, in the west with strong printing glass edges, westward lamping with tipsy bufflight, the colour of yellow roses. Parlick ridge like a pale goldish skin without body. The plain about Clitheroe was sponged out by a tall white storm of rain. The sun itself and the spot of "session" dappled with big laps and flowers-in-damask of cloud. But we hurried too fast and it knocked me up. We went to the College, the seminary being wanted for the secular priests' retreat: almost no gas, for the retorts are being mended; therefore candles in bottles, things not ready, darkness and despair. In fact being unwell I was quite downcast: nature in all her parcels and faculties gaped and fell apart, *fatiscebat,* like a clod cleaving and holding only by strings of root. But this must often be.

September 6.—With Wm. Kerr, who took me up a hill behind ours (ours is Mynefyr), a furze-grown and healthy hill, from which I could look round the whole country, up the valley towards Ruthin and down to the sea. The cleave in which Bodfari and Caerwys lie was close below. It was a leaden sky, braided or roped with cloud, and the earth in dead colours, grave but distinct. The heights by Snowdon were hidden by the clouds but not from distance or dimness. The nearer hills, the other side of the valley, shewed a hard and beautifully detached and glimmering brim against the light, which was lifting there. All the length of the valley the skyline of hills was flowingly written all along upon the sky. A blue bloom, a sort of meal, seemed to have spread upon the distant south, enclosed by a basin of hills. Looking all round but most in looking far up the valley I felt an instress and charm of Wales. Indeed in coming here I began to feel a desire to do something for the conversion of Wales. I began to learn Welsh too but not with very pure intentions perhaps. However on consulting the Rector on this, the first day of the retreat, he discouraged it unless it were purely for the sake of labouring among the Welsh. Now it was not and so I saw I must give it up. At the same time my music seemed to come to an end. Yet, rather strangely, I had no sooner given up these two things (which disappointed me and took an interest away—and at that time I was very bitterly feeling the weariness of life and shed many tears, perhaps not wholly into the breast of God but with some unmanliness in them too, and sighed and panted to Him), I had no sooner given up the Welsh than my desire seemed to be for the conversion of

Wales and I had it in mind to give up everything else for that; nevertheless weighing this by St. Ignatius' rules of election I decided not to do so.

GERARD MANLEY HOPKINS

MY CONVENT SCHOOL

Everything about the convent was very old-fashioned. The nuns entered the convent usually from the schoolroom—or but a little later. No newspapers were allowed to disturb the convent atmosphere, no magazines; nothing of what was happening outside in the world unless it came by word of mouth. The nuns talked, as doubtless they do to-day, of "out in the world," as though it was the other side of the world. The aloofness was never more justified. There was something mediaeval about that convent. The nuns were excellent musicians and linguists. They taught the ordinary subjects with ordinary success, I imagine. But the progress of the world had stopped for them some ten or twenty or thirty or forty years before. Their books were old-fashioned. I well remember the intense indignation of the most capable of all the teachers, when, on her telling her class that the source of the Nile had never been discovered, Ten Years' Old, fresh from the newspapers of her vacation, cut in with: "Oh, yes, Dr. Livingstone discovered its source in Lake Victoria Nyanza." "And pray who is Dr. Livingstone?" Mother Alphonsus asked, shaking her veil and in contemptuous indignation moving on to something else.

A very simple curriculum indeed! But what was it they did teach that was better than much learning? What was it that brought the gentlest, tenderest, loveliest of their pupils flying back to that white peace of the Convent from a rough and coarse world? What was it that made the most unworthy of their pupils, one with a keen eye for their simplicities, resolve that a girl of hers should go nowhere else but to a convent school?

It was the heavenliness of the convent atmosphere. I can find no other word.

I do not intend to convey that all the nuns were saints, although the very choice of the convent life carries with it, to my mind, a great measure of sanctity. One nun in my time, Mother Imelda, was such a saint I believe in the supernatural order as the Church loves to honor and set the seal of sainthood upon. Many of the nuns had their human defects, their weaknesses. Impossible to conceal them from the sharp eyes of school-girls. But if one laughs, one laughs tenderly. There were exquisite women among the nuns—beautiful women often. I used to think there never was such beauty as Sister Teresa's with her delicate classic profile, her face as finely moulded, as purely coloured as a Madonna lily, or Mother Joseph's with her opulent golden colouring, the magnificent intense blue of her eyes. Perhaps the white coif and habit and the black veil made the fittest frame for beauty. We might laugh at their simplicities, their innocencies. We might even discuss their little jealousies and preferences. But we left school in floods of tears: and doubtless a good many of those who left not to return found the change a hard one.

Many outsiders have remarked on the grace, the beauty, the refinement of Irish girls of the shop-keeping and farming classes, qualities not always shared by their brothers. Something, of course, is explained by the ups and downs of Irish history which have reduced the descendants of the old families to the cabins and placed the sons of the freebooters in the castles. But the convent schools afford the fullest explanation needed. Whatever of ladyhood is in a girl the convent school fosters and brings to perfection.

The convent school remains in my mind as a place of large and lofty rooms, snow-white, spotless, full of garden airs: of long corridors lit by deep windows, with little altars here and there—statues of Our Lord or the Blessed Virgin or the Saints, each with its flowers. A blue lamp burned at Our Lady's feet. The Sacred Heart had its twinkling red lamp. The corridors seem always in my thoughts of them full of quietness. The rustling of the nun's habit as she came only added to the sense of quietness.

The floors were polished and beeswaxed as you see it in convents of to-day but seldom anywhere else. I imagine that housecraft was rarer among Irish women of all classes then than it is to-day. But housecraft is seen in its perfection in a convent. What was it that made the girls who would have been slovenly at home fit in with the life so exquisitely neat and feat? Perhaps those of them who went back leavened the lump of indifference and unthrift. Certainly, coming back to Ireland after twenty years' absence I find in the Irish households an order, an efficiency, which were rare in my young days. The ramshackle, the topsy-turvy, seem to be gone out of fashion.

At the convent school we slept in dormitories which contained long lines of little iron beds curtained in blue and white check. The curtains went completely round the beds, and when they were drawn at night there was a sense of isolation which had its charm for one of an overflowing family who could appreciate dimly how many ills come from not being sufficiently alone.

The long dormitory, with its thirty or forty beds, was lit and aired by a lunette at either end. That these were open at night I very much doubt. We had not yet got away from the superstition that night air was deadly. "You ought not to be out in the night air" was always said if you had a cold or weakness. Florence Nightingale had swept it away in the Crimea some fifteen years earlier by her simple reply to a doctor's expostulation upon her admitting the enemy—"But the only air you can get at night is night-air." That reply had not yet reached Ireland. But—stay—I have a memory of revolving ventilators in the lunette above my head. They were highly scientific and advanced in those days, however our age might despise them.

I can remember no lack of air as I lay between my check curtains with a feeling akin to George Herbert's when he made his thanksgiving—

Lord, Thou hast given me a little cell
Wherein to dwell.

I remember summer evenings there when we went to bed at 8:30 with the sun hardly yet below the horizon, or he had left his pinks and primroses and faint greens in the sky. At 9 everyone was in bed and quiet. At 9:30 a bell rang "Profound Silence" in the convent. Except for urgent reasons the silence must not be broken till 4 in the morning, when a lay sister entered the nun's cell, offering the holy water from a dripping finger with the wake-word—"Praise be to Jesus!" to which the other would respond "Amen!"

They sang the Divine Office every day in that convent, an obligation laid only upon a limited number of orders of women. What is the order? Matins, Lauds, Prime, Tierce, Sext, None, Vespers, and Compline. It necessitated a very early rising. The nuns used the Gregorian Chant, and at the hours of Office you might meet them hurrying through the corridors, chanting as they went.

It was not always so easy to fall asleep in the summer evenings when you could hear, lying between the check curtains, the shouting from a distance which showed that the world was yet up and living and doing. I remember standing up in bed and peeping through the window. The thing in view was the graveyard of the nuns, an enclosed walled space with a wicket gate. From the high dormitory window you could see over the walls to the white marble slab at the head of the cemetery, on which was a list of the dead nuns. Of winter nights it used to glimmer whitely in the dark. There is always a chill feeling about the memory which makes me imagine that the beautifully coloured evening must have been May's and a cold May's.

KATHARINE TYNAN HINKSON

SHELLEY

Coming to Shelley's poetry, we peep over the wild mask of revolutionary metaphysics, and we see the winsome face of the child. Perhaps none of his poems is more purely and typically Shelleian than *The Cloud,* and it is interesting to note how essentially it springs from the faculty of make-believe. The same thing is conspicuous, though less purely conspicuous, throughout his singing; it is the child's faculty of make-believe raised to the *nth* power. He is still at play, save only that his play is such as manhood stoops to watch, and his playthings are those which the gods give their children. The universe is his box of toys. He dabbles his fingers in the day-fall. He is gold-dusty with tumbling amidst the stars. He makes bright mischief with the moon. The meteors nuzzle their noses in his hand. He teases into growling the kennelled thunder, and laughs at the shaking of its fiery chain. He dances in and out of the gates of heaven: its floor is littered with his broken fancies. He runs wild over the fields of ether. He chases the rolling world. He gets between the feet of the horses of the sun. He stands in the lap of patient Nature, and twines her loosened tresses after a hundred wilful fashions, to see how she will look nicest in his song.

This it was which, in spite of his essentially modern character as a singer, qualified Shelley to be the poet of *Prometheus Unbound,* for it made him, in the truest sense of the word, a mythological poet. This child-like quality assimilated him to the child-like peoples among whom mythologies have their rise. Those Nature myths which, according to many, are the basis of all mythology, are likewise the very basis of Shelley's poetry. The lark that is the gossip of heaven, the winds that pluck the grey from the beards of the billows, the clouds that are snorted from the sea's broad nostril, all the elemental spirits of Nature, take from his verse perpetual incarnation and reincarnation, pass in a thousand glorious transmigrations through the radiant forms of his imagery.

Thus, but not in the Wordsworthian sense, he is a veritable poet of Nature. For with Nature the Wordsworthians will admit no tampering: they exact the direct interpretative reproduction of her; that the poet should follow her as a mistress, not use her as a handmaid. To such following of Nature, Shelley felt no call. He saw in her not a picture set for his copying, but a palette set for his brush; not a habitation prepared for his inhabiting, but a Coliseum whence he might quarry stones for his own palaces. Even in his descriptive passages the dream-character of his scenery is notorious; it is not the clear, recognizable scenery of Wordsworth, but a landscape that hovers athwart the heat and haze arising from his crackling fantasies. The materials for such visionary Edens have evidently been accumulated from direct experience, but they are recompensed by him into such scenes as never mortal eye beheld.

FRANCIS THOMPSON

"PARD-LIKE SPIRIT"

Enchanted child, born into a world unchildlike; spoiled darling of Nature, playmate of her elemental daughters; 'pard-like spirit, beautiful and swift,' laired amidst the burning fastnesses of his own fervid mind; bold foot along the verges of precipitous dream; light leaper from crag to crag of inaccessible fancies; towering Genius, whose soul rose like a ladder between heaven and earth with the angels of song ascending and descending it;—he is shrunken into the little vessel of death, and sealed with the unshatterable seal of doom, and cast down deep below the rolling tides of Time.

Mighty meat for little guests, when the heart of Shelley was laid in the cemetery of Caius Cestius! Beauty, music, sweetness, tears—the mouth of the worm has fed them all. Into that sacred bridal-gloom of death where he holds his nuptials with eternity let not our rash speculations follow him; let us hope rather that as, amidst material nature, where our dull eyes see only ruin, the finer eye of science has discovered life in putridity and vigour in decay, seeing dissolution even and disintegration, which in the mouth of man symbolize disorder, to be in the works of God undeviating order, and the manner of our health,—so, amidst the supernatural universe, some tender undreamed surprise of life in doom awaited that wild nature, which, worn by warfare with itself, its Maker, and all the world, now

Sleeps, and never palates more the dug,
The beggar's nurse, and Caesar's.

FRANCIS THOMPSON

THE PERSONALITY OF NEWMAN

It is hard now to represent adequately the extraordinary personal charm which so many of his contemporaries felt in John Henry Newman. The letters convey much of it, but not all. Yet the tradition of this charm is a fact which must be set down in his biography. It was a charm felt by intellectual minds and even sceptical minds, and by simple and practical men. Blanco White, Mark Pattison, Henry Wilberforce, Frederick Rogers, R. W. Church, and Ambrose St. John were all among his most intimate friends. The almost unique combination of tenderness, brilliancy, refinement, wide sympathy, and holiness doubtless went for much. He had none of the repellent qualities which sometimes make asceticism forbidding. He had an ample allowance of those human sympathies which are popularly contrasted with asceticism. Again, he seemed able to love each friend with a peculiarly close sympathy for his mind and character and thoughtfulness for the circumstances of his life. The present writer's father—never one of the most intimate of the circle which surrounded Newman at Oxford—used to say that his heart would beat as he heard Newman's step on the staircase. His keen humor, his winning sweetness, his occasional wilfulness, his resentments and anger, all showed him intensely alive, and his friends loved his very faults as one may love those of a fascinating woman; at the same time many of them revered him almost as a prophet. Only a year before his death, after nearly twenty years of misunderstandings and estrangement, W. G. Ward told the present biographer of a dream he had had—how he found himself at a dinner party next to a veiled lady, who charmed him more and more as they talked. At last he exclaimed, "I have never felt such charm in any conversation since I used to talk with John Henry Newman, at Oxford." "I am John Henry Newman," the lady replied, and raising her veil showed the well-known face.

A very human and attractive side was visible in his love for music, of which I have already spoken, and a few words may here be added on this subject.

From the days when he played the violin as a young boy, his brother Frank playing the bass, down to the Littlemore period when he played in company with Frederick Bowles and Walker, string quartets and trios were his favourite recreation. Mr. Mozley, in his

Reminiscences of the Oxford Movement, thus describes his playing of Beethoven with Blanco White in 1826: "Most interesting was it to contrast Blanco White's excited and indeed agitated countenance with Newman's Sphinx-like immobility, as the latter drew long rich notes with a steady hand." When the gift of a violin from Rogers and Church in 1864 made him renew acquaintance with his old love after a long interval, the manner of his playing was somewhat different. "Sphinx-like immobility," writes Mr. Edward Bellasis, "had made way for an ever varying expression upon his face as strains alternated between grave and gay. Producing his violin from an old green baize bag, bending forward, and holding it against his chest, instead of under the chin in the modern fashion, most particular about his instrument being in perfect tune, in execution awkward yet vigorous, painstaking rather than brilliant, he would often attend the Oratory School Sunday practices between two and four of an afternoon, Father Ryder and Father Norris sometimes coming to play also."

When Canon McNeile, the Liverpool anti-Popery speaker, challenged him to a public dispute, Newman replied that he was no public speaker, but that he was quite ready for an encounter if Mr. McNeile would open the meeting by making a speech, and he himself might respond with a tune on the violin. The public would then be able to judge which was the better man.

His favourite composer was Beethoven, to whom he was passionately devoted. Once, when Mr. Bellasis said of the Allegretto of the Eighth Symphony, that it was like a giant at play, Newman replied, "It is curious you should say that. I used to call him the gigantic nightingale. He is like a great bird singing. My sister remembers my using the expression long ago." He had reached this preference gradually. "I recollect," he writes to a friend in 1865, "how slow I was as a boy to like the School of Music, which afterwards so possessed me that I have come to think Haydn almost vulgar." He impressed the cult of Beethoven on all the young Oratorians who played in his company. "They might start with Corelli, and go on to Romberg, Haydn, and Mozart," writes Mr. Bellasis. "Their ultimate goal was Beethoven." As with literature so with music, Newman was on the whole true to his early loves—indeed, he was resolutely old-fashioned. Beethoven already possessed him in the twenties, and later masters never quite won his heart.

WILFRID WARD

PORTRAIT OF HURRELL FROUDE

Coleridge remarked, in summing up his old friend Charles Lamb, that he had more totality and universality of character than any man he had ever known. In some such terms must be couched the eulogy of Hurrell Froude. He is all of a piece. "From his very birth," as his mother put it, "his temperament has been peculiar." He knew his mind, and went his way. He, at least, did not

—half-live a hundred different lives.

He paid for such concentration of purpose with long oblivion. Biography, a purblind creature, took him at his own valuation, as we have seen, and gathered him not to her bosom. The history of all the other Tractarians was written, the history of the men who lived very long, long enough to see as Cardinal Manning once said, the polarity of England changed, when the one among them who died young was given his chance. Until Dean Church, abetted by Lord Blachford, made his worth plain, in the beautiful subduing art of a book where all is charity and serene wisdom, Froude had inhabited shadow-land, and was less than the phantom of his brother's brother. Eventually no mystic, but a wide-awake, matter-of-fact person, he yet had always a sort of seal upon him of the objective, the remote, the unearthly. Now that he has his station and we have our perspective, these qualities increase rather than diminish. The enfranchised vision of him now is his inner self, more like a harper than a trumpeter. We seem to see the thin tender face 'shine' out of night air, as it shone at parting on his friend at Dartington, fifty-four years before it smiled again at him out of the Light. Time is the only crystal which gives us the souls of men and things. Whatever looks like idealisation there must be the literal truth.

Hurrell Froude's poet-friend Williams calls him

> Like to himself alone, and no one else.

But he is unique without being isolated. His habitual mood was a country of far distances, not unlike his own Devon, where the rote is audible from a stern coast, and the desolate tors stand up abrupt and sharp against the white February horizon: a country which gets, in due season, its own merriment of interlying verdure, and builds a most delicate overhanging opal sky. There is in him, though unexpressed, a wholeness and relativity as of this landscape. His saliency and roguery, his affection, his wistful oddity, his extraordinary intensity of life, the endearing charm which has served to keep his memory bright as racing sea-fire, only remind us the more how fully he belongs to the issues to which he gave himself of old. The temptation to think him a good deal like the sworded poets of the Civil Wars, with their scarcely exerted aptitudes for the fine arts, whose names leave a sort of star-dust along the pages of the anthologies, need not blind us to his severer aspect: he is also a good deal like the more militant among the Saints. His first Editors thought so, and say so in that most fragrant and touching Preface of theirs to his volumes printed in 1839. He was wing and talon to them and to their holy hope. "Froude of the Movement": he is that, first and last. Great as is to the mere humanist eye his individual interest, he cannot fairly be separated for a moment from the ideal to which all that was in him belonged; to which he belongs in its present and its yet unrevealed phases; to which he will belong when, as the very vindication of his foregone career, helping to breathe into successive generations the spirit of cleansing scrutiny and renewing faith, Catholicism shall triumph in England.

To a Catholic, Froude has something yet finer than his "totality and universality of character." He has the grace of God. He stands in a mysterious place,

> Beautiful evermore, and with the rays
> Of dawn on his white shield of expectation,

and it would be covetous indeed, it might be even impious, to wish to dislodge him. Such as he is, and where he is, he stands pledge enough for Reunion. Meanwhile, let him enjoy the irony for what it is worth, that to compensate for many of his own who esteem him not, many "swallowers of the Council of Trent as a whole" esteem him well. The English Oratory has for him a sort of veneration, as for a little brother lost who had Saint Philip's very brow and mouth; the Benedictine monks at Buckfast Abbey, near his old home, familiarly remember him, on birthdays, with prayer which is both a gift and a petition; and there are lay hearts which cannot think of his lonely burial-place, in snow-time or in rose-time, without the sense of hearing over it a solemn music from the Purgatorio:

Qui sarai tu poco tempo silvano;
E sarai meco senza fine cive
Di quella Roma onde CRISTO e Romano.

That wonderful prophetic strain, meant for eternity, must linger in the ear of every "Roman" who has learned to love Hurrell Froude.

LOUISE IMOGEN GUINEY

FREDERICK GOES TO A LITERARY TEA

The ladies, all whose faces wore rapt aesthetic expressions, proceeded to sit down under the aegis of the lady of the house, who began with infinite graciousness to pour tea. There was a sprinkling of men. Little by little the company took on the air of a platoon arrayed for battle, and commenced to lay down a barrage of conversation. Frederick was amazed at the agility with which these women disposed of the latest literary phenomena, the very names of which he did not, in many instances, know; and he was a little taken aback when poets to whom he was accustomed to refer with wonder and awe were disposed of as if they were so many trifles light as air. Among the guests was a young man with a sardonic stare who seemed to be regarded by everyone with special confidence and respect. Whenever one of the ladies found herself on the verge of expressing an opinion, she cast a glance in his direction, as if hoping that his eyes would predict approval or dissent in advance, so that she might not be caught prostituting herself with something which lacked distinction. This young man had gone on any number of exciting voyages, seemed to have cavorted on the main streets of many cities quite as he pleased, had once bluntly spoken his mind to Kotzebue at a soiree, and had lunch or gone for a stroll with nearly all the famous writers of the time. Apparently, however, he belonged to no school—tranquilly surveyed the whole literary scene, found the contradictory trends and manifestos amusing, and laughed at the battles waged by philosophers and poets. He was the point at which these varying refractions came into focus. Whenever he delivered a verdict, it was tossed off casually, as if in fun, with a sort of nonchalant mystical gesture. The ladies marveled not so much at what he said as at what he seemed to keep to himself because he was not sure it would be understood.

But ever and anon, when he appeared to be reigning calmly over the opinions of the company, another guest would speak up sonorously. He was a young and athletically moulded gentleman of excellent health, with a face which gleamed and glistened with comfortable self-satisfaction. He had a fine phrase for everything, distributed blame and praise alike without measure, and spoke rapidly in a piercing, bellowing voice. He appeared to be a frenzied enthusiast by profession and gladly suffered the ladies, to whom he seemed deeply attached, to call him the sacred guardian of the Thyrsus stave. At the same time he did not lack a certain canny air, which he donned whenever there was occasion to douse low and bloodless personages with irony. Frederick could not imagine what creature was the target for his incessant amorous glances until he realized that the young man was sitting directly across the room from a large mirror. The enthusiast needed little prodding to induce him to read some of his verses. He delivered a long dithyramb having to do with God, Heaven, Hell and the *carbunculus,* the whole being ejected with the most hectic violence, and ending with such a roar of emphasis that the poet was quite blue in the face. The ladies, however, were quite beside themselves with admiration for the heroic power of the ditty and the declamation.

JOSEPH VON EICHENDORFF

THE IDEAL POET

The great poet who will some day arise in our midst will keep himself aloof from the school which claims to serve the cause of beauty alone, though it has only an imperfect understanding of what beauty is. He will be no less sensitive than are its devotees of the loveliness revealed to the senses, but he will be superior to them in awareness of spiritual and moral grace. He will hear the voice of the spirit of beauty as Shelley heard it, and more clearly than he. In his *Hymn to Intellectual Beauty* Shelley sang of a mysterious power whose invisible rays strike us now and then, giving the indescribable feeling that a supernatural, living reality has somehow touched the deepest places of our hearts—a reality which is the very essence of beauty, communicating itself to us, setting our minds aflame, enrapturing us, moving us to tears of joy and love.

No, beauty does not lie in things but in the spirit. Here on earth, the images of things color themselves in beauty's light, and the shadows which give them comeliness are cast by its radiance. The soul of man can no more evoke those lights and shadows from within itself than it can produce truth, which is the being of things. Beauty comes from above. It is spirit, of Divine origin; and so it colors the pictures of the world of the spirit—namely, ideas and feelings—just as it does the images of the physical world. But it does not give itself without reserve to every one. It is withdrawn almost wholly from those souls who either because they lack insight or culture or because they are not attuned to beauty remain captives of the world of the senses. They merely catch a glimpse of it in the mutual attraction of the sexes. It is more beholden to others, whose intelligence develops and whose hope it is to live by their higher faculties. It favors in unequal fashion, according to an unfathomable plan, souls whom it makes receptive to certain combinations of lines and colors, or sounds, or words, to certain external impressions of the world, to these or those states of mind, or to particular relationships between human actions and the laws of ethical consciousness. The painter, the composer, the writer and their admirers; the scholar, who recognizes a secret rhythm in nature; the thoughtful person, fascinated by a landscape or by the play of light on the things around him; the magnanimous man, who dedicates himself to a good and noble cause:—all these share in the enjoyment of one and the same beauty in differing ways.

But beauty gives itself entirely only to the great artist, the great poet. It shines upon the depths of his spirit as if that were a mirror in which the images of the spiritual and the physical worlds appear side by side in their divine clarity. The impressions he forms of sensuous and moral beauty are the same in character. Humbler poets, to whom this gift of God is denied, fail miserably if they are not ready to be content with their more modest lot, often, indeed, far from negligible, and venture to approach the beauty which smiles on them not as platonic lovers but as lords and masters. The poet who will some time arise will free her from such annoying suitors with a single blow, even as in the legend Tristan freed Isoldè from the gross flatterers who carried her off into the depths of a wood. Beauty will belong to him completely. She will be a bride to him, and their children will be worthy of her—will guide the souls of men into ways whereon the highest reason, which is the eternal fundament of beauty, will be better understood and loved. And when he shall leave the world, he shall have the right to say to his immortal beloved what Leconte de Lisle addressed to her:

Telle que le Naïade en ce bois écarté
Dormant sous l'onde diaphane,
Fuis toujours l'oeil impur et la main du profane,
Lumière de l'âme, ô Beauté!

Just as the Naiad in this distant wood
Slumbers under the diaphanous wave,

Do thou flee always the impure eye, the hand of the profaner,
O Beauty, light of the soul.

ANTONIO FOGAZZARO

THE SEARCH FOR THE BEAUTIFUL

A sense of quality stirred in me—of that quality which is independent of personal whims: it was self-sufficient and had no need of relationships with me, nor did it ask for my approval or that of others; it rested in itself, obedient to its own laws, indefinable by us but laying bounds to itself. Now for the first time I felt again that there was a Power over me, and I knew that with reference to that Power a human being could conduct himself only as a servant. For simultaneously with the idea of quality and my growing concern with it, there appeared a set of standards:—the meaning of worth and of worthlessness came home to me, and seemed something ordained for me to follow, something that paid no attention to my notions but presided by reason of its own majesty. A ladder was immovably present: transitory appearances gave way to form, change was halted, and permanence was manifest to me, was almost within reach of my hand. It was permanence unmoved by time and bringing to me in the midst of the stream of flitting things a pledge of the eternal. Now for the first time my life had a meaning, and dwelt in the morning glow of a way to live.

HERMANN BAHR

THE SEARCH FOR TRUTH

Before the outbreak of that ghastly malady of the spirit which is known as rationalism, no man would have hit upon the bottomless idea that he could think through his fingertips. Kant is the physician who cured the Western world of that malady. I had been trained too thoroughly in Kant from my boyhood to dream of pulling my own head out of the swamp. My vehement craving for authority, without which beauty, goodness and truth, so vitally necessary to my life, must remain unattainable, could not be satisfied with purely human theories. . . .

The mere historical circumstance that God once appeared on earth and died for us was also of no assistance to me, so long as He simply left me alone. I was only then to be rescued when He Himself would lift me up, give Himself to me, and make me certain that gradually I should lessen my attachment to myself and strengthen my love for Him. . . .

Of all the religions which I know, only the Catholic Church makes possible this certainty. The others do not even dare to propose it. Then, too, my spirit is much too proud to be obedient to a church which in any way grants that salvation might be found without its assistance. If a church admits to me that I might perhaps be able to get along without it, my self confidence will never permit me to refrain from the attempt to try. Only the Church *extra quam nulla salus* is at all worth a trial. If one can reach the goal otherwise, why the added complication? A church which regards itself, so to speak, as one among many variants of a text can offer me no certitude; and of uncertainties I have quite enough of my own.

HERMANN BAHR

GREAT ART

Great art is never out of date, nor obsolete: like the moral law of Sophocles, "God is great in it and grows not old"; like the moral law of Kant, it is of equal awe and splendour with the stars. . . . In our day, many men of admirable powers love to think of themselves as alone in the world, homeless in the universe; without fathers, without mothers; heirs to no inheritance, to no tradition; bound by no law, and worshippers at no shrine; without meditation, without reverence, without patience, they utter, and would have us hear, their hasty and uncertain fancies. . . . It is the office of art to disengage from the conflict and the turmoil of life the interior virtue, the informing truth, which compose the fine spirit of its age; and to do this, with no pettiness of parochial pride in the fashions and the achievements of its own age, but rather with an orderly power to connect what is, with what has been, looking out prophetically to what will be.

LIONEL JOHNSON

ART AND TRUTH

Contempt for art is one of the commonest of sentiments, not only among ordinary men but among artists and critics. To permit art to lie is to have contempt for it. The artist despises art when he aims at anything else than the realization of truth. The critic despises art when he pardons it for having served an ideal which is not truly ideal. Every day we hear this absurd expression with reference to some error clothed in brilliant language: "It is poetry." When the mediocre man, speaking of a lie, has declared that it is poetry, he believes that he has excused the liar. On the contrary. He has brought a fresh accusation against him. For if the liar has lied *poetically,* he has laid hold on the loftiest form of language and forced it to utter an untruth.

ERNEST HELLO

THE STAGE DIRECTOR

Just what does a director do? He is like the leader of an orchestra, except for the important fact that when it comes to the performance, he must step aside and let the orchestra play without him. He must give sufficient impetus in rehearsal to last for weeks to come. How does he do this? He will probably start by soaking himself in the play. Then he will take the cast provided, give them his general idea of the play, and allow them, for a short time, to work out their own interpretations. This gives him a chance to sense the abilities of each actor. He may find one whose diction and manner are strident, another who plays everything in an ultra-restrained key, and still others who gallop through their lines as if making a recitation. If the play is to have unity of effect, he must pick the one actor who comes nearest to his own idea of the play, and begin, by slow processes, to tune the others to the same key. This may mean long private conversations with each actor, much coaxing and coaching, much explanation of character, much tedious, tactful effort. Or frank public brutality may be needed. A director must be a master psychologist if he is to bring out the best unity from his actors without necessarily wounding their feelings or discouraging their ambition.

The mere routine of directing is no child's play. The director must know how to place his actors on the stage for the best effect in each scene—one grouping for pictorial effect, another for dramatic contrast, another to give the sense of swift action, another to give the illusion of complete naturalness and ease. They must not cross each other at awkward moments. At the right instant they must be standing where they can be heard and seen from all parts of the house. The lighting effects must bring out the important points in the action. All this the director must determine in relation to the human material he is using. The personal eccentricities of a certain star may demand the rearrangement of an entire scene. And then, when all these matters have been attended to, all experiments made and either adopted or rejected, the director must generally give the actors much of their important "business"—that is, the use of their hands or of properties, telling pantomime and a hundred and one minor perfections all tending to complete the illusion of the play. An orchestral leader has only tonal effect to consider. The stage director must think of voice, of visual effect, of characterization, of group movement, and all conditioned by the personalities, sensitiveness, physical appearance, vocal equipment and "temperament" of the particular actors with whom he is asked to work. As a last straw, when the fatal opening evening comes, he must step aside, with the knowledge that the audience will applaud the cleverness of the playwright, the genius of certain actors, and hardly notice the program line "staged by ——." An orchestra leader takes the public's applause. The stage director, on the contrary, gives his child the glory!

RICHARD DANA SKINNER

THE HAND OF HEROD

A news despatch from Paris says that the authorities have decided that midnight Masses may not be celebrated in any of the churches of the city during the Christmas season. It is explained that it would be impossible to keep the light from filtering out through the great stained glass windows of a cathedral. A candle by a shrine sheds a beam which is too broad for the warring world in which we live. If the figure of the Christ child were illuminated, it might serve as a beacon for the way of wise flying men from out of the East. And their gifts would not be gold and frankincense and myrrh.

Once again the hand of Herod is raised for the slaughter of the innocents. But those things which were are with us now. I have seen men and women moved by devotion into such a mood that they felt themselves not only followers but contemporaries in the life of Jesus. To them His death was a present tragedy and Easter morning marked a literal triumph. And to those who are like-minded there lies reassurance in the revelation of the past. Herod was a ruler who for a little time had might and power vested in himself. His word was absolute and his will was cruel. As captain over thousands he commanded his messengers to find and kill the newborn king. An army was set in motion against an infant in a manger.

But though the hand of Herod fell heavily upon Bethlehem and all the coasts thereof, Joseph, the young child and his mother escaped into Egypt. "In Rama was there a voice heard, lamentation and weeping and great mourning, Rachel weeping for her children, and would not be consoled, because they are not." The blood of the young was spilled upon the ground even as it is being shed today. And it may well have seemed, some two thousand years ago, that there was no force which could stay the ravages of the monarch and his minions.

Around the child there stood on guard only Joseph and Mary, three wise men and shepherds from the field who had followed the course set for them by a bright star. Death came to Herod, and the bright star was a portent of the perfect light which was to save the world from darkness. The light of the world was not extinguished then, and it lives today and will again transfix the eyes of men with its brilliance.

In the dark streets of Paris on Christmas Eve, even as in the little town of Bethlehem, a star will animate the gloom. The call comes once more to kings and shepherds to journey to the manger and worship at the shrine of the Prince of Peace. Quite truly the civil authorities of Paris have said that it is impossible to blackout the light which shines from the altar.

And if I were in France I would go at midnight to the little island on the Seine and stand before Notre Dame de Paris. At first the towers of that great Gothic structure might seem to be lost in the blackness of the night. And it has been ruled that no congregation shall raise its voice to welcome the tidings of great joy. But then I think all the windows will take on magnificence, and that the air will resound with the message which has been given to the sons of men and will be offered again to the fellowship of all mankind. "Glory to God in the highest and on earth peace to men of good will." And that choral cry will rise above the hum of Herod's grim messengers. It will be much louder than the crash of guns and the roar of cannon. No hymn of hate can prevail if we only heed the eternal cadence of the Christmas Carol.

HEYWOOD BROUN

CONVERSION

It is impossible to be just to the Catholic Church. The moment men cease to pull against it they feel a tug toward it. The moment they cease to shout it down they begin to listen to it with pleasure. The moment they try to be fair to it they begin to be fond of it. But when that affection has passed a certain point it begins to take on the tragic and menacing grandeur of a great love affair. The man has exactly the same sense of having committed or compromised himself; of having been in a sense entrapped, even if he is glad to be entrapped. But for a considerable time he is not so much glad as simply terrified. It may be that this real psychological experience has been misunderstood by stupider people and is responsible for all that remains of the legend that Rome is a mere trap. But that legend misses the whole point of the psychology. It is not the Pope who has set the trap, or the priests who have baited it. The whole point of the position is that the trap is simply the truth. The whole point is that the man himself has made his way toward the trap of truth, and not the trap that has run after the man. All steps, except the last step, he has taken eagerly on his own account, out of interest in the truth; and even the last step, or the last stage, only alarms him because it is so very true. If I may refer once more to a personal experience, I may say that I for one was never less troubled by doubts than in the last phase [of conversion], when I was troubled by fears. Before that final delay I had been detached and ready to regard all sorts of doctrines with an open mind. Since that delay has ended in decision, I have had all sorts of changes in mere mood; and I think I sympathize with doubts and difficulties more than I did before. But I had no doubts or difficulties just before. I had only fears; fears of something that had the finality and simplicity of suicide. But the more I thrust the thing into the back of my mind, the more certain I grew of what Thing it was. And by a paradox that does not frighten me now in the least, it may be that I shall never again have such absolute assurance that the thing is true as I had when I made my last effort to deny it.

GILBERT KEITH CHESTERTON

JOY AND THE CHRISTIAN

It is said that Paganism is a religion of joy and Christianity of sorrow; it would be just as easy to prove that Paganism is pure sorrow and Christianity pure joy. Such conflicts mean nothing and lead nowhere. Everything human must have in it both joy and sorrow; the only matter of interest is the manner in which the two things are balanced or divided. And the really interesting thing is this, that the pagan was (in the main) happier and happier as he approached the earth, but sadder and sadder as he approached the heavens. The gaiety of the best Paganism, as in the playfulness of Catullus or Theocritus, is, indeed, an eternal gaiety never to be forgotten by a grateful humanity. But it is all a gaiety about the facts of life, not about its origin. To the pagan the small things are as sweet as the small brooks breaking out of the mountain; but the broad things are as bitter as the sea. When the pagan looks at the very core of the cosmos he is struck cold. Behind the gods, who are merely despotic, sit the fates, who are deadly. Nay, the fates are worse than deadly; they are dead. And when rationalists say that the ancient world was more enlightened than the Christian, from their point of view they are right. For when they say "enlightened" they mean darkened with incurable despair. It is profoundly true that the ancient world was more modern than the Christian. The common bond is in the fact that ancients and moderns have both been miserable about existence, about everything, while mediaevals were happy about that at least. I freely grant that the pagans, like the moderns, were only miserable about everything—they were quite jolly about everything else. I concede that the Christians of the Middle Ages were only at peace about everything—they were at war about everything else. But if the question turn on the primary pivot of the cosmos, then there was more cosmic contentment in the narrow and bloody streets of Florence than in the theatre of Athens or the open garden of Epicurus. Giotto lived in a gloomier town than Euripides, but he lived in a gayer universe.

The mass of men have been forced to be gay about the little things, but sad about the big ones. Nevertheless (I offer my last dogma defiantly) it is not native to man to be so. Man is more himself, man is more manlike, when joy is the fundamental thing in him, and grief the superficial. Melancholy should be an innocent interlude, a tender and fugitive frame of mind; praise should be the permanent pulsation of the soul. Pessimism is at best an emotional half-holiday; joy is the uproarious labour by which all things live. Yet according to the apparent estate of man as seen by the pagan or the agnostic, this primary need of human nature can never be fulfilled. Joy ought to be expansive; but for the agnostic it must be contracted, it must cling to one corner of the world. Grief ought to be a concentration; but for the agnostic its desolation is spread through an unthinkable eternity. This is what I call being born upside down. The skeptic may truly be said to be topsy-turvy; for his feet are dancing upward in idle ecstacies, while his brain is in the abyss. To the modern man the heavens are actually below the earth. The explanation is simple; he is standing on his head; which is a weak pedestal to stand on. But when he had found his feet again he knows it. Christianity satisfies suddenly and perfectly man's ancestral instinct for being the right way up; satisfies it supremely in this; that by its creed joy becomes something gigantic and sadness something special and small. The vault above us is not deaf because the universe is an idiot; the silence is not the heartless silence of an endless and aimless world. Rather the silence around us is a small and pitiful stillness like the prompt stillness in a sick-room. We are perhaps permitted tragedy as a sort of merciful comedy: because the frantic energy of divine things would knock us down like a drunken farce. We can take our own tears more lightly than we could take the tremendous levities of the angels. So we sit perhaps in a starry chamber of silence, while the laughter of the heavens is too loud for us to hear.

Joy, which was the small publicity of the pagan, is the gigantic secret of the Christian. And as I close this chaotic volume I open again the strange small book from which all Christianity came; and I am again haunted by a kind of confirmation. The tremendous figure which fills the Gospels towers in this respect, as in every other, above all the thinkers who ever thought themselves tall. His pathos was natural, almost casual. The Stoics, ancient and modern, were proud of concealing their tears. He never concealed His tears; He showed them plainly on His open face at any daily sight, such as the far sight of His beloved city. Yet He concealed something. Solemn supermen and imperial diplomatists are proud of restraining their anger. He never restrained His anger. He flung furniture down the front steps of the Temple, and asked men how they expected to escape the damnation of Hell. Yet He restrained something. I say it with reverence; there was in that shattering personality a thread that must be called shyness. There was something that He hid from all men when He went up a mountain to pray. There was something that He covered constantly by abrupt silence or impetuous isolation. There was some one thing that was too great for God to show us when He walked upon our earth; and I have sometimes fancied that it was His mirth.

GILBERT KEITH CHESTERTON

BIOGRAPHICAL NOTES

Acton, John E. E. Dalberg-Acton, First Baron (1834–1902), was born in Naples. He succeeded Cardinal Newman as editor of the *Rambler,* a Catholic monthly periodical. He was often the center of controversy. Appointed professor of modern history at Cambridge in 1895, he planned the *Cambridge Modern History* and edited the first volume. The selections are from *The History of Freedom and Other Essays* (London: Macmillan & Company. 1913).

Acts of the Apostles, The. This Book, the original of which is in Greek, tells the story of Christianity for a period of about thirty years after the first Pentecost. Catholic tradition declares that St. Luke was the author.

Alan, of Auxerre, Bishop, was a contemporary of Saint Bernard, and wrote down anecdotes concerning him gathered from Godfrey, Bishop of Langres. The selection is from Migne, *Patrologia Latina,* as quoted from *Life in the Middle Ages,* edited by G. G. Coulton (New York: The Macmillan Company. 1930).

Alfred, the Great, King (849–899?), was the heroic ruler of the West Saxons, and victor over the invading Danes. He was an ardent lover of learning and religion, following in what he did for both the example of Charlemagne. The selection is from Alfred's preface to his translation of St. Gregory's *Pastoral Care,* the English version being that of P. V. D. Shelly (*English Prose and Verse,* selected and edited by Henry S. Pancoast. New York: Henry Holt and Company).

Anonymous. The selection is from *The Commonweal,* New York, March 10, 1926 (Vol. III, Nr. 18).

Apocalypse, The. According to Catholic tradition, this Book was written in Greek about sixty-four years after the Ascension of the Saviour. The author is held to have been St. John; the place where it was written, the island of Patmos.

D'Arc, Jeanne, Saint, was born in Domremy about 1412, and was burned at the stake in Rouen in 1431. Obeying the voices of saints, she rode to the assistance of the Dauphin, Charles VII, raised the siege of Orleans, and conducted Charles to Rheims, where he was crowned. Later, in an attempt to raise the siege of Compiègne, she was captured, turned over to the English, and tried by an international court. The death sentence was imposed. Saint Jeanne was canonized in 1919. The selection is from *The Trial of Jeanne d'Arc,* translated by W. P. Barrett (New York: Gotham House. 1931).

Augustine, Saint, Bishop of Hippo, was born in Tagaste (354) and died during the siege of Hippo by the Vandals (430). The *Confessions* tell the story of his return to Christianity after a time of association with the Manicheans. *The City of God* is a great treatise on the relation between the Heavenly Kingdom and the Earthly State, written at the time when the Roman Empire was crumbling. Saint Augustine was likewise a busy controversialist, refuting the doctrines of the Manicheans, the Donatists and the Pelagians. In philosophy and theology he was the founder of Christian Platonism. The first selection is from the *Confessions,* and is based on the translation by Sir Tobie Matthew. The second is from the *City of God.*

Bacon, Roger, Friar (1214?–1294), is also known as the "Admirable Doctor." He studied in Paris, returned to Oxford as a member of the Franciscan Order, and became a famous though sometimes unpopular professor. He was an advocate of textual criticism and of scientific method, both of which aroused the suspicions of the mystical theologians. The selections are from *Compendium Studii Philosophiae,* as quoted by G. G. Coulton (*Op. cit.,* New York: The Macmillan Company).

Bahr, Hermann (1863–1934), was an Austrian playwright and essayist who played an important part in Viennese literary history. Educated by the Benedictines, he drifted away from religion but returned to the Catholic fold shortly before the outbreak of the first World War. His better-known works include *Das Konzert,* a comedy (1909); *Ueberwindung des Naturalismus,* a critical essay (1891), and *Himmelfahrt,* a novel (1916). The selections are from *Selbstbildnis,* an autobiography (Berlin: S. Fischer. 1923).

Bazin, René (1853–1932), was born in Angers, and devoted a good part of his busy life to Catholic causes. Thus he was an ardent advocate of religious education, deplored the trend from the country to a city life exposed to corrupting influences, supported the resistance of Pope Pius X to Modernism, and wrote in praise of missionary activity. His greatest book is probably *Père Foucauld,* translated as *A Saint of the Desert* (1921), which tells the inspiring story of a great modern missionary and martyr. Bazin's novels are characterized by a Milletlike ability to describe the

French peasant and his environment. In all of them religion plays a dominant part. *La Terre qui Meurt* (*Autumn Glory*) is probably the most notable. The selection is from *The Coming Harvest,* translated by Edna K. Hoyt (New York: Charles Scribner's Sons. 1908). Here a different translation is used, and the passage has been condensed.

Bede, the Venerable (often called Saint Bede) (673–735), was a Benedictine scholar most of whose life was spent in the monasteries of Wearmouth and Jarrow. He was a man of vast learning and critical insight, who may be termed the father of historical writing. The selection is from the most important of his books, *The Ecclesiastical History of the English Nation,* in the admirable translation of J. A. Giles (London. 1843 ff.).

Benedict, Saint, was born in Nursia, Italy, about 480. Disgusted with the sensualism of life in Rome, he retired to a hermitage at Subiaco. There he was joined by a considerable number of young men; and in 529 the Abbey of Monte Cassino, mother abbey of all Benedictines, was founded. *The Rule of Saint Benedict* is notable for its moderate spirit, based on experience and love of culture. The selection follows the translation by Cardinal Gasquet (London: Chatto & Windus. 1925).

Benedict XV, Pope (Giacomo della Chiesa), was born in 1854, was elected Pope in 1914, and died in 1922. His pontificate is remembered for several notable achievements, particularly the Papal Peace Plan of 1917. The present selection is from the "Peace Note" of August 1, 1917.

Benson, Robert Hugh, Monsignor (1871–1914), was the youngest son of the Archbishop of Canterbury. He came into the Catholic fold in 1903, and was ordained a priest during the following year. Though he was a noted preacher, he is best remembered for his novels, notably *Initiation, The Lord of the World, Come Rack, Come Rope,* and *The Sentimentalists.* The selection is from *Oddsfish* (New York: Dodd, Mead and Company. 1914. New edition: New York: P. J. Kenedy and Sons).

Bernard, of Clairvaux, Saint, was born in 1091 and died in 1153. He was of good family and, together with his brothers and many friends, entered the Abbey of Citeaux. Later he withdrew to Clairvaux with a few companions, in quest of a more austere life. As abbot and teacher, Saint Bernard became the most influential man of his time. He was the defender of the Papacy, the preacher of the Second Crusade, the advocate of reform, and above all the preacher of devotion to the Blessed Virgin. The selections are well-known passages, often quoted in religious literature.

Bernardino, da Siena, Saint (1380–1444), was a Franciscan whose preaching was so effective that Pope Pius II called him "a second Saint Paul." He fostered devotion to the Holy Name of Jesus, and labored to bring about the union of Eastern with Western Christendom. The selection is from *Le Prediche volgari di San Bernardino da Siena,* edited by L. Banchi (Siena, 1880), as quoted by G. G. Coulton (*Op. cit.* New York: The Macmillan Company).

Bloy, Léon (1846–1917), was born in Perigueux and died near Paris. He was a great religious visionary and satirist, whose works were read only by the elect. Most of his books are in part autobiographical. They include *Le déséspére* (1886) and *La femme pauvre* (1897). The selection is from *Le sang du pauvre* (1909).

Bonaventure, Saint (1221–1274), called the "Seraphic Doctor," was the General of the Franciscans, the biographer of Saint Francis, and in his time the leading opponent of Aristotelianism. He was born near Viterbo, studied in Paris, and died while in attendance at the Council of Lyons. He wrote a great Commentary on the Sentences of Peter Lombard; and his *Breviloquium* and *Collationes de donis Spiritus Sancti* are notable expositions of mediaeval mystical theology. The selections are taken from the *Meditationes Vitae Christi,* attributed to Saint Bonaventure, as translated into English by Nicholas Lowe. A memorable edition of Lowe's version, by Laurence Powell, was published by the Oxford University Press (New York) in 1928. The translations used here were supplied by Granger Ryan and the editor's thanks are therefore specially due him.

Bossuet, Jacques-Bénigne, Bishop of Meaux (1627–1704), was one of the greatest pulpit orators of France, a controversialist whose views on theological issues were of far-reaching influence, and the author of important treatises on history and government. The *Discours sur l'histoire universelle,* long since translated into English, is doubtless his most famous work. The first of the selections is an extract from his correspondence, and is part of a letter to a penitent; the second is from the sermon preached at the profession of Madame de la Vallière.

Bourdeille, Pierre de, Seigneur de Brantôme (c. 1540–1614), was born in Périgord, was educated for the priesthood, but turned instead to a military career. He accompanied Mary Stuart to Scotland, and later on saw Queen Elizabeth. Though he was for a time won over to Protestantism, he returned to the Catholic faith. His *Memoirs* are among the most realistic portraits of the age with which they are concerned. The translation is by Barrett H. Clark, for a volume entitled *Great Short Biographies of the World* (New York: Robert M. McBride and Company. 1928).

Bourget, Paul (1852–1935), continued but clarified the work of Balzac, the object of both novelists being to "demonstrate" that life is the logical consequence of the moral principles adopted by an individual or a society. Bourget avoided, however, the objectionable obscenity of Balzac. In *Le Disciple* (*The Disciple*), published in 1889, he dealt with the effect of philosophic skepticism on the mind and conduct of a young man. A later novel, *Le Démon de Midi,* studied the triumph of temptation over a man of middle age who has lost his sense of the values of religion. Bourget was also a great literary critic, his principal collection of essays—*Essais de psychologie contemporaine* (1883)—being still a model in this *genre.* The present selection is from *Monica,* translated by William Marchant (New York: Charles Scribner's Sons. 1902).

Brémond, Henri (1865–1938), is above all the historian of French mysticism in the seventeenth century. After having spent twenty-two years as a member of the Society of Jesus, he became a secular priest. He was elected to the French Academy in 1924, accepting the honor as a tribute to the thousands of "poor curés" in France. The selection is from Vol. I of *A Literary History of Religious Thought in France,* translated by K. L. Montgomery (New York: The Macmillan Company. London: Society for Promoting Christian Knowledge).

Broun, Heywood (1888–1941), was born in Brooklyn, New York, and was educated at Harvard. His career as a newspaperman was marked by successful writing for a series of New York dailies, including the *World* and the *World-Telegram.* He wrote also for the *New Republic* and the *Commonweal.* Long noted as an advocate of social reform, he entered the Catholic Church not long before his death. His books include *Pieces of Hate* and *The Boy Grew Older* (1922). The selection is from *Collected Edition of Heywood Broun,* edited by Heywood Hale Broun (New York: Harcourt, Brace and Company. 1941).

Brownson, Orestes Augustus (1803–1876), was successively a Presbyterian, a Universalist, a Unitarian, and a convert to the Catholic faith.

An account of his religious experience is supplied in *The Convert* (1857). Brownson's *Quarterly Review* was the first great venture in American Catholic intellectual journalism, and it not infrequently encountered rough sailing. The selections are from *The American Republic,* a noteworthy treatise on the American form of government.

Caesarius of Heisterbach, a Cistercian monastery in Germany, appears to have been born in the Rhineland. For the novices under his direction he wrote the *Dialogus Miraculorum* from which the selection is taken. The translation is that used by G. G. Coulton (*Op. cit.* New York: The Macmillan Company).

Castiglione, Baldesar, Count (1478–1529), served the Dukes of Milan and Urbino. The selection is from *The Courtier,* as translated by Leonard E. Opdycke from the *Libro del Cortegiano* of 1518 (New York: Charles Scribner's Sons. 1903). Castiglione not only provides comment on etiquette and education but expounds the doctrine of Christian Platonism.

Catherine, of Siena, Saint (1340–1380), was born in Siena and died in Rome. She was both a mystic and a reformer, who labored indefatigably to elevate and ennoble the spirit of the Dominican Order, to which she belonged. As the spokesman for the reform of ecclesiastical rule during the Great Schism she exerted greater influence on the policy of the Church than has any other woman. Most of her writings were dictated. They are collected in the *Dialogo* and the *Lettere.* The selections are quoted from *Saint Catherine of Siena as Seen in Her Letters,* translated by Vida D. Scudder (New York: E. P. Dutton and Company. 1927).

Cervantes Saavedra, Miguel de (1547–1616), is known principally as the author of *Don Quixote de la Mancha,* published in 1605. He fought in the battle of Lepanto, losing the use of his left hand as the result of a wound received in that engagement. Captured by the Turks four years later, he was ransomed. The selection is from *Don Quixote,* as translated by David Urquhart.

Chateaubriand, François René de (1768–1848) was born in Saint-Malo, France, and died in Abbaye-aux-Bois. Having entered the army prior to the Revolution, he was compelled to go into exile. He traveled in North America, then resided in England, and returned to France during 1800. Much of his subsequent life was spent on diplomatic missions. Chateaubriand was a master of melodious, sonorous French prose, with an undertone of melancholy. In his books the Catholic revival in France after the Revolution found expression. They suffer by reason of a too personal attitude towards religious verity, but manifest deep faith and enthusiasm. Chateaubriand's greatest work is the twelve-volume *Mémoires d'outre-tombe* (1850). The most influential was *La génie du Christianisme* (1802) from which the selection is taken. The translation is based on that of Charles I. White (Baltimore: John Murphy Company).

Chaucer, Geoffrey, was born in London (c. 1300) and died in 1400. He served in France with the army of Edward III, embarked on a career at the Court, traveled on diplomatic missions to Italy, and thereafter held various official positions. Chaucer's work as a poet began with translations and adaptations of French poetry. Soon he was deeply interested in Italian literature, and his work reflected the influence of Dante, Petrarch and Boccaccio. Finally he began the composition of the immortal *Canterbury Tales,* one of the most illustrious contributions to English poetry. See R. D. French, *A Chaucer Handbook*. The selection is from Chaucer's translation of Boethius's *De Consolatione Philosophiae.*

Chesterton, Gilbert Keith (1874–1926), was a great humorist, artist, poet, thinker and Catholic apologist. His best-known books include *The Man Who Was Thursday* (1908), *Magic* (1913), *Poems* (1915), and *The Everlasting Man* (1925). The selections are from *Orthodoxy* (London: John Lane. 1908, New York: Dodd Mead), and *The Catholic Church and Conversion* (New York: The Macmillan Company. 1926).

Chopin, Kate O'Flaherty (1851–1894), was the author of stories illustrative of Creole life. The selection is taken from her best-known book, *Bayou Folk* (Boston: Houghton, Mifflin Company. 1894).

Chrysostom, Saint John (c. 347–407), was the greatest of the Greek Fathers and, perhaps, the greatest of Christian classical orators. Made bishop of Constantinople in 398, he dedicated himself to the reform of the Church. As a result he soon became popular with the people but distasteful with the favorites of the Court. The intrigues against him caused his death but earned him a secure place in the heart of the Church. Eutropius, who had once been hostile to the Saint, profited by his friendship when in disfavor. It is with Eutropius that the selection, from the "Homily on the Fall of Eutropius," is concerned. The translation is that of Father Gerard Manley Hopkins, and is quoted from *The Note-Books and Papers of Gerard M. Hopkins* (New York: Oxford University Press. 1937).

Cloud of Unknowing, The, was written in England during the fourteenth century. It shows the influence of Dionysius, the pseudo-

Areopagite, and has had a profound effect upon modern mystical literature. The selection is based on the admirable edition prepared by Dom Justin McCann (New York: Benziger Brothers. 1924).

Conrad, Joseph—Teodor Jozef Konrad Korzeniowski—(1857–1924), was the son of a Polish political exile. He entered the British merchant service, learned English, and acquired British citizenship. His books include *Almayer's Folly* (1895), *The Nigger of the Narcissus* (1897), and *Lord Jim* (1900). The selection is from *Rulers of the East and West* (New York: Doubleday Doran and Company).

Coppée, François Edouard Joachim (1842–1908), is remembered for verse and short stories, though he was also a novelist and playwright. His later work shows the influence of the Catholic faith, to which he returned after years of skepticism. The poor of Paris—those with scarce a place to lay their heads, and those of modest means whose lives were beset by trouble—aroused Coppée's compassion, and most of his writing is concerned with them. The present selection is from *Ten Tales by François Coppée,* translated by Walter Learned (New York: Harper and Brothers. 1890).

Corvo, Frederick Baron (1860–1913), was born in London and died in Venice. An amateur in the arts and possibly also in theology, he is satirized in Monsignor R. H. Benson's *Sentimentalists.* His most beguiling work is *Hadrian VII.* The selection is from *In His Image* (London: John Lane. 1901).

Crawford, Francis Marion (1854–1909), was born and buried in Italy, though he was an American citizen and had for a time been a newspaperman in India. His novels, which were very successful, include *Saracinesca, Mr. Isaacs,* and *The White Sister.* Crawford was also interested in historical writing and is the author of *Ave Roma Immortalis.* The selection is from *Marzio's Crucifix* (New York: The Macmillan Company).

Cyril, Saint (c. 315–386), was the Bishop of Jerusalem and the associate of Saint Basil the Great. By most students, he is believed to have been the author of the Nicene Creed. The selection appears frequently in religious literature.

Damien de Veuster, J., Father (1840–1889), was born in Belgium. In 1864 he went to Hawaii as a missionary, was ordained a priest, and went to the lepers' colony at Molokai in 1873. There he contracted the dread disease. The selection is from a letter addressed to Dr. E. C. Hall and dated March, 1866. It is reprinted from *History of the Catholic Mission in the Hawaiian Islands,* by the Reverend Reginald Yzendoorn (Honolulu, 1927).

Dante Alighieri (1265–1321), greatest of Italian poets and no doubt the most illustrious writer of Catholic verse, was born in Florence and exiled thence by the political faction which opposed his views of government. After wandering through Italy, he settled in Ravenna and died there. *La Commedia* (which we know as the *Divine Comedy*), judged the times in which Dante lived in the light of the Thomistic philosophy. Its heroine, Beatrice Portinari, is probably a real person as well as a symbol. Dante's meeting with her is described in *La Vita nuova* (*The New Life*), written in 1292. A section of this is reprinted here, in the translation of Dante Gabriel Rossetti. The Latin prose writings of Dante were concerned with literature and political theory. There are several good English translations of the *Divine Comedy,* among them that by J. B. Fletcher.

De Vere, Aubrey (1814–1902), was born in Ireland and died in London. Converted to the Catholic faith, he wrote successfully in both prose and verse. De Vere was a genial person and the friend of many eminent literary men. The selection is from an essay entitled "Subjective Difficulties in Religion," which appears in Vol. II of *Essays Chiefly on Poetry* (London: Macmillan and Company. 1887).

Digby, Kenelm Henry (1800–1880), was educated at Cambridge. Induced by study and travel to explore the life of the Middle Ages, he was converted to the Catholic faith. The selections are from *The Broad Stone of Honour* (1822: enlarged edition, 1826). Digby's most pretentious work is *Mores Catholici* (1831–1842).

Douai Version of the Holy Bible, the, from which the selections used in this volume are taken, is a translation which was supervised by Cardinal Allen. He was assisted by Gregory Martin, Richard Bristow and Richard Worthington. The Old Testament was published at Douai, home of a Catholic college for English students, in 1609. The New Testament had been published earlier (1582) at Rheims. The Douai Version is more rugged than the King James Version, but follows the Vulgate carefully and is, in the opinion of many students, a highly meritorious translation.

Dryden, John (1631–1700), was born in Aldwinkle, Northamptonshire, and died in London. He entered the Catholic Church during 1686, his sincerity being often but quite unjustly questioned. Dryden's comedies are usually vulgar, even obscene, but his major poems, notably *The Hind and the Panther* (1687), are noted for idealism and meditative thought.

His critical prose is of great beauty and distinction. The selection is from the "Preface to the Fables."

Du Bos, Jean Baptiste (1670–1742), was a notable writer on music and literary history. His major work, *Critical Reflections on Poetry, Painting and Music,* was translated into English by Thomas Nugent (1748). From it the selection has been taken.

Eginhard (Einhard) died in 840. He was a friend of Charlemagne, served as imperial architect, and became abbot of the monastery at Seligenstadt. The selection is from the *Vita Caroli Magni,* as translated by S. E. Turner.

Eichendorff, Joseph von (1788–1857), was born and died in Silesia, Germany. He was, perhaps, the most charming of the German Romantic writers, successful in poetry, fiction and criticism. During many years he was a civil servant. The selection is from *Ahnung und Gegenwart* (1815).

England, John, Bishop (1788–1842), was born in Cork and died in Charleston, S.C. Raised to the see of Charleston in 1820, he was enthusiastically committed to the American way of life. His broad tolerance, his interest in the negro, and his indefatigable missionary zeal are all memorable. The selection is from one of his sermons.

Epistle to Diognetus, The, was written by an anonymous author during the second or the third century. Diognetus was a pagan, whom the writer exhorted to embrace Christianity. The whole document can be found in *The Apostolic Fathers,* edited by Kirsopp Lake (Cambridge: Harvard University Press).

Erasmus, Desiderius (1466–1536), was born in Rotterdam, Holland, and died in Basel, Switzerland. Educated in Gouda and Paris, he traveled considerably, fostered the science of Biblical exegesis, and advocated humanistic studies. Erasmus was a critic of the Schools but also a foe of the Reformation. Perhaps his best known work is the *Enchiridon militis christiani* (1502). The selection is from *Twenty Select Colloquies of Erasmus,* as translated by Sir Roger l'Estrange (1680).

Eusebius, Bishop of Caesaria, died in 339. He is known as the "Father of Church History," his writing being notable for the careful use of sources. Unfortunately he was not free of leanings toward Arianism. The selection is from the *Ecclesiastical History,* as translated by Kirsopp Lake (Cambridge: Harvard University Press. Loeb Classical Library. 1926).

Faber, Frederick William, priest of the Oratory (1814–1863), was a poet, an orator and a writer of spiritual treatises. *At the Foot of the Cross* is no doubt one of the most notable of the last. The selection is from *The Creator and the Creature.*

Fénelon, François de Salignac de la Mothe, Archbishop of Cambrai (1651–1715), gained educational experience as a tutor of the Royal Nephew and as the spiritual director of notable women. Few churchmen in the history of France have had so widespread or so beneficent an influence. He resisted both Gallicanism and Jansenism, but certain of the theses in his *Maximes des Saints* were censured by Pope Innocent XII. The selection is from an essay on the education of girls written in 1681, and follows a translation in *Great Pedagogical Essays,* edited by F. V. N. Painter (New York: American Book Company. 1905).

Fisher, John, Saint (c. 1569–1635), was Bishop of Rochester and an antagonist of the Lutheran reform. He was put to death for opposing the divorce sought by King Henry VIII. The selection is from *The English Works of John Fisher* (London, 1876).

Fitzstephen, a contemporary of Saint Thomas à Becket, Archbishop of Canterbury, was the Saint's biographer. The selection is quoted from *Materials for the History of Thomas Becket,* by J. C. Robertson (1875–1885).

Foch, Ferdinand, Marshal of France (1851–1929), was born at Tarbes and died in Paris. He was the victor of the battle of the Marne, and eventually of the series of conflicts which ended the First World War. Foch's best known works are *Les Principes de la guerre* (1918), and *Mémoires pour servir a l'histoire de la Grande Guerre* (1930). The selection is from *For Joan of Arc: an Act of Homage,* edited by Gabriel Hanotaux (New York: Sheed and Ward).

Fogazzaro, Antonio (1842–1911), was an Italian novelist and religious thinker who spent nearly the whole of his life in Vicenza. Such novels as *Piccolo mondo antico* are admirable studies of traditional Italian life. But other books, notably *Il Santo,* have religious and philosophical implications which were held to savour of Modernism. The selection is from an essay contributed to *Hochland,* Munich, Vol. IV, 1.

Francis, of Assisi, Saint (1182–1226), was the son of a wealthy cloth merchant. Having renounced all earthly goods and pleasures, he dedicated himself to a life of monastic seclusion and to the rebuilding of neglected churches. To his first "brethren" he gave (1210) a Rule of the utmost simplicity. The date on which he received the Stigmata was September

14, 1224. His writings were edited by his disciple, Thomas of Celano. The selections are from the Rule, and from the *Fioretti,* a collection of legends compiled during the fourteenth century. Here the translation by W. Heywood (London: Methuen and Company) is used.

Francis de Sales, Saint (1567–1622) was Bishop of Geneva during the years from 1602 to 1622. He is the patron saint of writers. With Saint Jane Frances de Chantal he founded the Order of the Visitation (1610). The selections are from *On the Love of God,* as translated by Dom Henry Mackey (London: Burns, Oates and Washbourne. 1884), and *Introduction to a Devout Life,* as translated by the Rev. Thomas Barns (London: Methuen and Company).

Froissart, John, priest and secretary at the English Court (1338–c. 1410), was the author of *Chronicles of England, France, Spain and the Adjoining Countries.* The text used here is that of the version by Thomas Johnes (London: George Routledge. 1874).

Gerson, John, priest and chancellor of the University of Paris (1363–1429), is known as "Doctor Christianissimus" for his efforts to end the Great Schism of 1378–1417 and for his conciliatory writings on theological and philosophical subjects. Gerson's theory that a Council takes precedence over a Pope has, however, been repudiated. The selection is from the *Dialogue of the Heart,* and has been quoted in *John Gerson Reformer and Mystic,* by James L. Connolly (Louvain. 1928).

Gibbons, James, Cardinal and Archbishop of Baltimore (1834–1921), was the author of *Faith of Our Fathers,* perhaps the most widely read popular exposition of the Catholic faith. The selection is from "Address Delivered on the Occasion of the Silver Jubilee of the Catholic University of America," as reprinted in *A Retrospect of Fifty Years* (Baltimore: John Murphy Company. 1916).

Gorce, Pierre de la (1875–1933), was an eminent French historian and contributor to important periodicals. His principal work, from which the extract quoted is taken, is *Histoire religieuse de la Revolution française* (Vol. III. Paris: Plon-Nourrit et Cie. 1919).

Goyau, Georges (1869–1934), was one of the most learned and highly respected French Catholic writers of his time. His most influential books include *l'Allemagne religieuse* (1898–1908) and *F. Ozanam* (1925). The selection is from *Histoire religieuse de la nation française* (Paris: Plon-Nourrit et Cie. 1922).

Griffin, Gerald (1803–1940), earned fame as a novelist, playwright and poet. Then he became a Christian Brother. The selection is from *The Collegians* (1829).

Guibert, of Nogent-sous-Coucy, Abbot (1053–1124), was the author of numerous works, all of which are reprinted in Migne's *Patrologia Latina.* His *Gesta Dei per Francos* has been edited several times. The selection is from *The Autobiography of Guibert,* translated by C. C. Swinton-Bland (London: J. E. Dent).

Guiney, Louise Imogen (1861–1920), was born in Boston. After 1901 she lived in England, working almost without interruption in the Bodleian Library, Oxford, on such subjects as the Recusant Poets. Her works include *Happy Ending* (1920), a volume of collected verse, *Monsieur Henri,* and *A Little English Gallery.* The selection is from *Hurrell Froude* (London: Methuen and Company. 1904).

Habington, William (1605–1654), was an English poet whose major work is *Castara* (1634), a volume of lyrics in honor of his wife. The selection is from the preface to that book.

Haimon, Abbot of Saint-Pierre-sur Dives, was the author of a letter which, intended as a means of acquainting monks in England with the glories of Mary in France, is our best source of information concerning the spirit which produced the cathedral of Chartres and other mediaeval shrines. It is quoted in *Mont-Saint-Michel and Chartres,* by Henry Adams (Boston: Houghton Mifflin Company. 1905).

Handel-Mazzetti, Enrica von (1871–1939), was an Austrian novelist of great verve and dramatic feeling. Her books include *Meinrad Helmpergers denkwuerdiges Jahr* and *Die arme Margaret.* The selection is from *Jesse und Maria.* An English translation was published by Henry Holt and Company (New York. 1931).

Hawthorne, Nathaniel (1804–1864), began his literary career in Salem. His fame was established with *The Scarlet Letter,* published in 1850, and led eventually to his appointment to a consulship in Liverpool. *The Marble Faun,* from which the selection is taken, was based on experiences attendant upon a trip to Italy.

Hecker, Isaac Thomas (1819–1888), priest, was the founder of the Congregation of St. Paul. He came into the Catholic Church during 1845. Deeply interested in the power of the spoken and the written word, he founded the *Catholic World.* The selection is from his *Diary,* as quoted in *The Student's Handbook to British and American Literature,* by the Rev. C. L. Jenkins (Baltimore: John Murphy Company).

Hello, Ernest (1828–1885), was a forerunner of the modern Catholic revival in French literature. He was an incisive critic of art and also a competent student of theology. *L'homme* (1872) is probably his greatest book. The selection is from *Le style* (1861).

Herran, Jerome, of the Society of Jesus. The selection is from the *Letter on the New Missions in the Province of Paraguay, Derived from the Account of Father Jean-Patrice Fernandez, S.J. Directed to the Serene Prince of the Asturias, in the Year 1726.* Translated by William Ingraham Kip (New York. 1875).

Hinkson, Katharine Tynan (1861–1931), was an Irish novelist and poet whose works include *Ballads and Lyrics* and *Flower of Youth.* The selection is from *Twenty-five Years: Reminiscences* (New York: Devin-Adair Company. 1913).

Hollanda, Francisco de (1517–1584), is one of the sources of information concerning the life and work of Michaelangelo. The selection is from *Four Dialogues on Painting,* translated by Aubrey F. G. Bell (New York: Oxford University Press. 1928).

Hopkins, Gerard Manley, of the Society of Jesus (1844–1889), was received into the Catholic Church during 1866, and was ordained a priest in 1877. His *Poems* were edited by Robert Bridges and published, with an introduction, in 1918. They are distinguished for great originality and beauty. The selection is from *The Note-Books and Papers of Gerard Manley Hopkins,* edited by Humphrey House (New York: Oxford University Press. 1937).

Hügel, Friedrich von, Baron (1852–1925), was an eminent philosopher of religion who, despite certain sympathies with Modernism, remained deeply attached to the Catholic faith. His greatest book is doubtless *The Mystical Element in Religion* (1908). The selection is from *Essays and Addresses on the Philosophy of Religion* (New York: E. P. Dutton and Company. 1925).

Huysmans, Joris-Karl (1848–1917), had the blood of Flemish artists in his veins, but was heart and soul a Parisian. His early novels and short stories were studies in ennui and vice, written in an exotic style but noteworthy by reason of careful observation and mordant irony. Then Catholicism became his chief concern. *A Rebours* (1884) may be called a study in evil leading to the conclusion that man's only escape from the bottomless pit of his own filth is recourse to the grace of God. Huysmans' retreat to a Trappist monastery and his conversion are described in *En Route* (*On the Way*). Two subsequent novels derived from his own religious experience are still widely read—*La Cathedrale* (*The Cathedral*), and *l'Oblat* (*The Oblate*). The selection is from *En Route,* translated by C. Kegan Paul (London. Kegan Paul. 1897).

Ignatius, Saint, Bishop and Martyr, died during the opening years of the second century. His journey as a Christian captive from the Near East to Rome was a veritable triumph. The selection is from the letter "To the Romans," as translated by Kirsopp Lake in his edition of *The Apostolic Fathers* (Cambridge: Harvard University Press).

Ignatius Loyola, Saint (1491–1556), was born in Loyola Castle, near Azpeitia, Spain, and died in Rome. He adopted a military career and was wounded in battle. His decision to live a religious life followed reading done during a period of convalescence from wounds received in battle. After periods of retreat at Montserrat and Manresa, he traveled to the Holy Land. Upon his return, he joined with six companions to found the Society of Jesus. The Pope persuaded the little band to reside in Rome; and thus there was inaugurated a time of activity which had an incalculable effect upon modern Catholic life. The selection is from the *Spiritual Exercises,* a book of preparation for the spiritual life which has since been translated into nearly every language.

Isla, Joseph Francis, of the Society of Jesus, was a Spanish writer. The selection is from *The History of the Famous Preacher, Friar Gerund de Campazas,* as translated by Thomas Davies (London, 1772).

Jacobus, de Voragine, Dominican and Bishop of Genoa (c. 1230–1298), was the author of the *Golden Legend* (*Aurea Legenda*), a volume of lives of the Saints which became one of the most influential books of the Middle Ages. The selections are from the excellent edition by Granger Ryan and Helmut Ripperger (New York: Longmans, Green and Company. 1941).

Jammes, Francis (1868–1938), was preeminently the poet of the Pyrenees. His portrait, showing a long beard, a pair of spectacles, and a Basque beret, was one of the best-known recent literary likenesses. In 1905 he returned to the Catholic Church. Perhaps the most rewarding of his books are *De l'Angelus de l'aube a l'Angelus du soir* (1895), *Les georgiques chrètiennes* (1911) and *Les nuits qui me chantent.* The present selection is from *Le roman du lièvre,* translated as *The Romance of the Rabbit,* by Gladys Edgerton (New York: Nicholas L. Brown. 1920).

Jerome, Saint (340–420), was born in Dalmatia. He studied in Rome, was baptized by Pope Liberius, and was persuaded to lead an ascetic life by Our Lord, who appeared to him in a dream. The "Ciceronian" now became a "Christian," was ordained a priest, and served in Rome as spiritual adviser to many persons. Together with Saint Paula, one of his penitents, Saint Jerome then departed for the Holy Land to establish monasteries and convents. Having been requested by the Holy See to translate the Scriptures, he devoted more than thirty years to the task. The version is known as the Vulgate. Meanwhile he took a part in numerous controversies, expressing his views in brilliantly written but sometimes violent letters. More than a hundred of these have survived. The reader may consult *Selected Letters,* translated by F. A. Wright (Cambridge: Harvard University Press).

John, Saint, was the "beloved disciple." He is believed to have died on the Island of Patmos, and to have been the author of the Fourth Gospel and the Apocalypse. The Gospel according to Saint John is notable for its mystical fervor and its philosophical tone.

Johnson, Lionel (1867–1902), was a poet and critic. The selection is from *The Art of Thomas Hardy.*

Joinville, Jean, Sieur de (c. 1225–c. 1317), accompanied Saint Louis on the Crusade of 1248. He is a representative historian of the thirteenth century. The selection is from *Chronicle of the Crusade of Saint Louis,* as quoted in *Civilization in Mediaeval England,* by R. Trevor Davis (New York: E. P. Dutton and Company).

Juliana, of Norwich, Blessed (c. 1342–c. 1420), appears to have been a Benedictine nun of Norwich, England, and to have lived during the fourteenth century. The selection is from the beautiful and profound *Revelations of Divine Love,* edited by George Tyrell, S.J. (London. 1902).

Justin Martyr, Saint (c. 100–c. 165), devoted most of his youth to the study of the Stoic and Platonic philosophers. He was converted to Christianity at the age of thirty, and thereafter traveled as an apologist, using heathen philosophy to persuade men of the validity of Christian doctrine. A persecution broke out while he was in Rome, and there he suffered death as a martyr. Saint Justin's writings are interesting particularly because they reveal the attitude of an educated early Christian towards Judaism and the Gospels. The *Apology* is a priceless record of many ecclesiastical practices and events. The *Dialogue,* from which the passage here quoted is taken, assumes the form of an argument with Trypho, a learned Jew.

Kilmer, Aline Murray (1888–1941), was born in Norfolk, Va., and died in Stillwater, N.J. She married Joyce Kilmer in 1908. Two books of verse, *Candles That Burn* (1919) and *Vigils* (1921) received considerable attention. The selection is from *Hunting a Hair Shirt and Other Spiritual Adventures* (New York: George H. Doran. 1923).

Kilmer, Joyce (1886–1918), was a journalist, poet and editor. His volumes of verse include *Trees and Other Poems* (1914), and *Main Street and Other Poems* (1917). Though he might have claimed exemption, he enlisted as a private in the "Fighting Sixty-Ninth" and was killed in France during the final months of the war. The selection is from *Joyce Kilmer: Poems, Essays and Letters,* edited by Robert Cortes Holliday (New York: Doubleday Doran and Company. 1940).

Lamartine, Alphonse Louis de (1790–1869), was a French statesman, poet and historian. His most famous lyric is *"Le Crucifix."* The selection is from an English translation (New York, 1854) of one of his works, under the title of *Memoirs of Celebrated Characters.*

Lathrop, Rose Hawthorne (Mother Mary Alphonsa, O.S.D.), was born (1851) the daughter of Nathaniel Hawthorne, and died the superior of Rosary Hill Home, Hawthorne, N.Y., a place of refuge for the cancerous poor. The selection is from *Memories of Hawthorne* (Boston: Riverside Press. 1897).

Lawrence, Brother (d.1691), was the name in religion of Nicholas Herman of Lorraine, who entered the Carmelite Order after a career as a soldier. The selection is from *The Practice of the Presence of God,* by Brother Lawrence (London: Methuen and Company). The conversations were written down by M. Beaufort.

Leo XIII, Pope (1810–1903), was born in Carpineto, Italy, as Gioacchino Pecci. In 1646 he was consecrated bishop of Perugia, and in 1853 he was created a cardinal. In 1878 he was elected to the See of Peter. One of his most important Encyclicals was *Rerum Novarum* (1891), which outlined the doctrine of social reform which has since shaped Catholic discussion of this subject. His Pontificate is considered one of the most brilliant in the history of the Church. The selection is from *Sapientiae Christianae* (1890).

Liber Exemplorum, a mediaeval volume of illustrations deemed useful for sermons, dates from the thirteenth century. It has been edited by A. G. Little. The selection follows the text in G. G. Coulton (*Op. cit.* New York: The Macmillan Company).

Lingard, John, priest (1771–1851), was for many years professor of philosophy in Douai College. His fairness as a historian has been generally recognized. The selection is from his major work, *A History of England from the Invasion of the Romans to the Accession of William and Mary,* which was completed during the years between 1819 and 1830.

Lippert, Peter, of the Society of Jesus (1879–1938), was notable both for his radio addresses and his writings on spiritual subjects. The selection is from *Job the Man Speaks with God* (New York: Longmans, Green and Company. 1936).

Litany of the Saints, The, is the original litany, and is an integral part of the sacred liturgy of the Church. It is one of the oldest of Catholic prayers.

Little Flowers of Saint Francis, The (*Fioretti*), are legends which date from the fourteenth century. The book is one of the most popular in Catholic literature. Here the translation by W. Heywood (London: Methuen and Company, 1906) has been used.

Lodge, Thomas (c. 1558–1625), was an Elizabethan poet, playwright and essayist. The selection is from *Rosalynd* (London, 1590), the source of Shakespeare's *As You Like It.*

Luitprand, of Cremona, Bishop (d.c. 980), served as envoy to Constantinople and then as a courtier at the Court of Otto I. The selection is from *The Works of Luitprand of Cremona,* and follows the translation of F. A. Wright (New York: E. P. Dutton and Company. 1930).

Luke, Saint, was the author of the Third Gospel. He is said to have been a physician and a painter. His is the longest and the most beautifully written of the Gospels. It tells the story of the Nativity in detail; and tradition holds that Saint Luke's information came directly from the Blessed Virgin herself.

Lull, Rámon, Franciscan (1235–1315), is termed the "father of Catalan literature." He was a missionary among the Mohammedans and an enemy of the Averroestic movement. The selection is from *The Book of the Lover and the Beloved,* translated by E. Allison Peers (New York: The Macmillan Company. 1923, London: Society for Promoting Christian Knowledge).

Macaulay, Thomas Babington (1800–1859), was a Cambridge man who became an essayist, a government official, a historian and a member of

Parliament. He was a regular contributor to the *Edinburgh Review* and the author of a brilliantly written *History of England* which is, however, not free from bias. The selection, a famous Protestant's tribute to Rome, is quoted from the essay on Ranke's *History of the Popes,* as originally published in the *Edinburgh Review* for October, 1840.

Mallock, William Hurrell (1849–1923), was an English sociologist, remembered above all as the author of *The New Republic.* The selection is cited from *The Emancipation of a Freethinker,* by Robert Ellsworth Cory (Milwaukee: Bruce Publishing Company. 1941).

Malory, Sir Thomas, lived during the fifteenth century. He was the author of the *Morte d'Arthur,* in which the Arthurian Legend found perfect expression in English. This book throws much light on the gradual conquest of paganism by Christianity. It was printed by William Caxton in 1485.

Mandeville, Sir John, was probably Jean de Bourgogne, a physician of Liège. He was the author of a work written in French toward the close of the fourteenth century and translated into English as *The Voiage and Travaile of Sir John Mandeville.* From this the selection is taken.

Manning, Henry Edward Cardinal (1808–1892), was made archbishop of Westminster in 1865, succeeding Cardinal Wiseman. He had been educated at Harrow and Baliol College, Oxford, and subsequently had taken orders in the Anglican communion. In 1851, he entered the Catholic Church, and soon thereafter was ordained to the priesthood. He was deeply interested in social reform, and supported the workers during the dock strike of 1889. *The Eternal Priesthood* is probably his best known book. The selection is from an essay in *Pastime Papers* (London: Burns, Oates and Washbourne). It has been reprinted in *The Catholic Tradition in English Literature,* by George Carver (Garden City: Doubleday, Page and Company. 1926).

Manzoni, Alessandro (1785–1873), wrote prose fiction and poetry. His odes are justly esteemed, but his fame rests primarily on *Il promessi sposi* (*The Betrothed*) published in 1827. It reflects the influence of Sir Walter Scott, but is probably the first authentic Catholic romance. Manzoni was a favorite with Pope Pius XI, who referred to him on several important occasions. The selection is from *Il promessi sposi.*

Mark, Saint, was an intimate friend of Saint Peter. He is believed to have been the son of the woman whose house was the scene of the Last Supper, to have founded the Church in Alexandria, and to have suffered martyrdom in that city. Most critics hold that the Gospel according to

Saint Mark is based upon the author's conversations with Saint Peter, and that it is the earliest of the written Gospels.

Matthew, Saint, was a publican of Capharnaum before he became an apostle. He is said to have suffered martyrdom in the Near East. The Catholic Church holds him to have been the author of the First Gospel, and places the date of composition at about 70 A. D. Saint Matthew's text incorporates more of Jewish teaching and tradition than do the other Gospels.

Mercier, Desiré, Cardinal (1851–1926), was made archbishop of Malines in 1906. Previously he had been professor of philosophy in the University of Louvain, and abettor of the plans of Pope Leo XIII to bring about a revival of Thomism. During the first World War he was the spokesman for Belgium. The selection is from *Voix de la Guerre: Cardinal Mercier,* edited by Georges Thone (Liège, 1937).

Meynell, Alice Thompson (1850–1922), was the wife of Wilfrid Meynell, editor of *Merrie England.* A convert to the Catholic faith, she befriended Francis Thompson. She was a distinguished poet and a careful essayist. The selection is from *The Children* (London: John Lane. 1897).

Missale Romanum, the Mass-book of the Catholic Church, is the official version sanctioned for general use. The first codification dates from 1570. Other forms of the Missal, notably those employed by the Dominicans and the Carthusians, are older and, of course, approved.

Montalembert, Charles René, Count de (1810–1870), was born in London and died in Paris. He was one of the first great Christian democrats of France, a public figure, an editor (*Le Correspondant*), and an enthusiastic student of the Middle Ages. The selection is from the English translation of his *Moines d'Occident* (*Monks of the West*), completed in 1877.

More, Saint Thomas (1478–1535), was Chancellor of England during the reign of King Henry VIII. He opposed the King's repudiation of Queen Catherine and his marriage with Anne Boleyn. Therefore he was imprisoned in the Tower and eventually executed. His most famous work is *Utopia* (1516). The selection, other than the letter, is from *Dialogue of Comfort against Tribulation.*

Munday, Anthony (1553–1633), was an English dramatist and actor who was befriended by the Earl of Oxford. The selection is from *The English Roman Life* (1562).

Newman, John Henry, Cardinal (1801–1890) was born in London and died in Birmingham. After taking orders in the Anglican Church, he preached at St. Mary's Church, Oxford, took a leading part in the development of the Oxford Movement, and wrote a number of tracts, the most important of which was *Tract 90* (1841). When the Movement encountered opposition on the part of the Anglican bishops, Newman retired to Littlemore and was subsequently received into the Catholic Church (1845). He was ordained a priest in Rome, and almost immediately founded the English Oratory. He was the Rector of the Catholic University of Dublin between 1851 and 1858. In 1878 Pope Leo XIII made him a Cardinal. Newman is the greatest of modern Catholic writers on theological subjects, and is in addition remembered as a creative artist, author of *Lead, Kindly Light, The Dream of Gerontius,* and *Callista.* His doctrine is expounded most effectively in *An Essay in Aid of a Grammar of Assent* (1870); *Apologia pro vita sua* (1864); and *An Essay on the Development of Christian Doctrine* (1845). The very interesting and important *Letters and Correspondence of John Henry Newman* was edited by Anne Mozley and published in 1892. Two selections are from the *Apologia* (New York: Longmans, Green and Company). The third is from *Idea of a University* (*idem*).

Novalis, pseudonym of Georg Friedrich Philip von Hardenberg (1772–1801), was a German Romantic poet whose major work is the unfinished romance, *Heinrich von Ofterdingen.* The selection is from *Die Christenheit oder Europa.*

O'Donnell, Manus, later Lord of Tirconaill, wrote his *Life of Columcille* in 1552. The selection is quoted from *Gaelic Literature Surveyed,* by Aodh de Blácam (Dublin: The Talbot Press. 1929).

Oviedo y Valdés, Gonzalo Fernandez de (1478–1557), was a prolific writer on historical subjects and on the New World in particular. The selection is from the *Historia General* and is based on the diary account of Rodrigo Ranjel. The translation is by Edward Gaylord Bourne, in *A Narrative of De Soto's Expedition* (New York: Allerton Book Company. 1922).

Paradise or Garden of the Fathers, The, is an absorbing series of stories about saints, edited from Coptic manuscripts by Ernest A. Wallis Budge (London: Chatto and Windus. 1927).

Parkman, Francis (1823–1893), was born in Boston and died near that city. During many years he was an invalid, suffering from anemia and super-sensitiveness of the eyes. Nevertheless he made himself the great historian of the struggle between France and England for dominion in the New World. Parkman is not always friendly to the Catholic Church, but the selection is a splendid and characteristic tribute to a Jesuit missionary. It is from *The Jesuits in North America* (Boston: Little, Brown and Company. 1880).

Pascal, Blaise (1623–1662), showed unusual mathematical talent at an early age. After his sister Jacqueline entered the Convent of Port-Royal, he visited that institution in quest of interior peace. In 1623 he experienced a religious conversion. His *Provincial Letters,* attacking the Jesuits in the spirit of Port-Royal and the Jansenists, enjoyed a very considerable success. The book has, however, been overshadowed by the *Pensées,* first published in a much garbled edition in 1670, after the author's death. Many editions appeared subsequently, the best being that of 1884. The selection follows the translation by W. F. Trotter.

Pastor, Ludwig von (1854–1928), was a professor and historian who also served for a time as Austrian ambassador to the Vatican. His *Geschichte der Paepste* (*History of the Popes*) has been translated into all important languages and is a monument of erudition and scholarly objectivity. In writing it Pastor was aided immeasurably by the decision of Pope Leo XIII to give him unrestricted adit to the Vatican archives. The selection is from Vol. I of the English translation by Frederick I. Antrobus (London, 1899). The American publishers are the B. Herder Book Company, St. Louis, Mo.

Pater, Walter Horatio (1839–1894), was elected a fellow of Brasenose College, Oxford, in 1864. His early literary reputation rested on his Studies in the *History of the Renaissance.* The selection is from *Marius the Epicurean,* a novel of the intellectual life in Rome during the days of Early Christianity. Pater's family had in part been Catholic, but he at no time belonged to the Church. Originally the novel was published (1885) by the Macmillan Company.

Patmore, Coventry (1823–1896), was a poet who belonged to the Pre-Raphaelite Movement and contributed to *The German.* Converted to the Catholic Church in 1864, after he had gained a reputation as the author of *The Angel in the House,* he wrote several volumes of prose and verse to give expression to his faith. The selection is from *The Rod, the Root and the Flower* (London: George Bell and Sons. 1923).

Patrologia Latina is the name given to the collection of documents in Latin relating to the doctrine and history of the Church, published in 221 volumes by J. P. Migne (1800–1875). The selections are taken from Coulton, *Life in the Middle Ages* (New York: The Macmillan Company).

Paul, Saint, of Tarsus in Cilicia, probably died as a martyr to Christianity in Rome during the year 67. Born into a Jewish family which lived according to the code of the Pharisees, he was also a Roman citizen. He was educated in Jerusalem, and spoke both Aramaic and Greek. After his conversion (thitherto he had been called Saul) he rendered those extraordinary services to the Christian faith which are recounted both in the Acts of the Apostles and in his own Epistles. The selection is from the Second Epistle to the Corinthians and follows the text in the Douai Version.

Péguy, Charles, was born at Orleans in 1873 and died on the field of battle in 1914. His fame was based during his lifetime on the *Cahiers de la Quinzaine,* which he edited after 1900. Since his death he has been remembered chiefly because of his writings on St. Jeanne d'Arc, especially *Le mystère de la charité de Jeanne d'Arc* (publ. 1910 and 1926). Notable also are *Notre Patrie* (1905) and *Le mystère des Saints Innocents* (1914). The selection is translated from *Le Mystère de la charité de Jeanne d'Arc.*

Peter, Abbot of Cluny, was elected in 1122. He was otherwise known as Pierre Maurice de Montbossier, and was unquestionably a man of wisdom and charm. The selection is a letter to Heloise, and is quoted from *Monastic Life at Cluny,* by Joan Evans (New York: Oxford University Press, 1913).

Petrarca, Francesco (1304–1374), was born in Florence and went thence with his family into political exile. He was educated for the bar, but chose a literary life instead and received minor orders. During a number of years he was in the service of Cardinal Colonna, at Avignon; and there he met "Madonna Laura," the woman whom he loved with a platonic affection and celebrated in his Italian poems. Petrarch was doubtless the greatest classical scholar of his time. As he grew older he became more devout and held the works of Saint Augustine in high esteem. He was also one of the first to describe the delights of mountain climbing, and this was the theme of many letters addressed to friends and famous men. The selection is translated from *Epistolae de rebus familiaribus et variae,* edited by G. Frocassetti (Florence, 1863).

Pius XI, Pope (1857–1938), was born in Desio, Italy, as Ambrogio Domiano Achille Ratti. He was ordained a priest in 1879, became a professor in the Seminary of Milan shortly thereafter, and was named librarian of the Ambrosian Library in 1888. In 1914 he became prefect of the Vatican Library. During 1918 he was sent on a diplomatic mission to Poland, and a year later became Papal Nuncio in Warsaw. Pope Benedict XV named him Archbishop of Milan and Cardinal in 1921. The following year he was elected to the Holy See. His reign is undoubtedly one of the most distinguished in the history of the Papacy, though the promise of the early years gave way to stark tragedy at the end. The selections are from two very famous Encyclical Letters—*Quadragesimo Anno* and *Mit Brennender Sorge.*

Polycarp, Saint, suffered death as a martyr in Smyrna on February 22, 156. The selection is from his letter to the Philippians, and follows the version of Kirsopp Lake, in his edition of *The Apostolic Fathers* (Cambridge: Harvard University Press).

Pope, Alexander (1688–1744), was born in London and educated in part by a Catholic priest. Subsequently he became a famous satirical poet and an exponent of classicism. The *Essay on Man* (1773–1774) shows that Pope was influenced by Deism, but it should be remembered that his rationalism was to a considerable extent typical of Catholic thought in his time. The selection is that given by Sir Arthur Quiller-Couch in *The Oxford Book of English Prose.*

Reymont, Ladislas (1867–1925), was a Polish novelist who received the Nobel Prize in 1924. His principal works are *The Peasants* and *The Promised Land.* The selection is from *The Promised Land,* as translated by M. H. Dziewicki (New York: Alfred A. Knopf. 1927).

Richard de Bury (Aungervyle) (1287–1345), was for many years at the Court of King Edward III, who sent him on several diplomatic missions. The selection is from his *Philobiblon,* one of the first and best books written in praise of book collecting.

Rolle, Richard, of Hampole (d. 1349), is reputed to have been a hermit in Yorkshire, England. A considerable number of works in both verse and prose have been ascribed to him, but scholars agree only about the prose. The present selection is from *The Selected Works of Richard Rolle,* edited by G. C. Heseltine (New York: Longmans, Green and Company. 1930).

Roper, William (1496–1578), was the husband of Margaret, daughter of Saint Thomas More. He is the author of *The Life, Arraingement and Death of That Mirrour of All True Honour and Vertue, Syr Thomas More* (1626). There are many editions of the text, the most recent and probably the best being that edited by Elsie Vaughan Hitchcock.

Roux, Joseph, Abbé (1834–1892), was a learned priest interested in the lore and language of Limousin. He wrote much verse, but his principal book is that translated by Isabel F. Hapgood under the title *Meditations of a Parish Priest. Thoughts* (New York, 1886).

Ruysbroeck, John (Jan Van) (1293–1381) was born near Brussels. He died at Groenendael, a monastery to which he had retired at the age of sixty, after many years of service in the priesthood. His mystical writings stress the lofty virtues of the contemplative life. The selection is taken from *Love's Gradatory,* as translated by Mother St. Jerome (New York: Benziger Brothers).

R. W. was the author of *Mount Tabor, or Private Exercises of a Penitential Sinner* (London, 1639). The selection is from this book and appears under the heading, "Upon a stage-play which I saw when I was a child." The author was seventy-five at the time.

Savonarola, Girolamo, Dominican friar (1452–1498), entered the monastery of San Marco, Florence, in 1481 and became its prior ten years later. His sermons, delivered in the vernacular, assailed corruption in Church and State. Savonarola clashed with Pope Alexander VI over a political issue and was excommunicated. His execution (May 22, 1498), must, however, be placed to the discredit of the Florentine government. Savonarola was always wholly orthodox and in no sense heretical. He was the author of poems, religious treatises and political tracts.

Scheler, Max (1874–1928) was a professor of philosophy at the Universities of Munich, Cologne and Frankfurt. He was one of the most influential German thinkers of his time, making notable contributions to the analysis of ethical concepts and to the sociology of knowledge. The selection is from *Von Ewigen im Menschen* (Leipzig: Neue Geist Verlag, 1921). This book is written in full accord with the Catholic tradition. Not all of Scheler's books are, notably *Stellung des Menschen im Kosmos* (1928).

Schlegel, Friedrich (1772–1829), was born in Hanover and died in Dresden. After a period of study at German universities, he became one of the founders of the German Romantic School of writers. During 1808 he came into the Catholic Church and transferred his residence to Vienna. *Lucinde,* an earlier work (1799), is the representative Romantic novel. His *Geschichte der alten und neuen Literatur* (1815) was an attempt to develop the study of world literature. The selection is from *Philosophie der*

Geschichte (*Philosophy of History*), originally published in 1829. The translation is adapted from that by James Burton in the Bohn Library edition.

Scupoli, Lorenzo (1530–1610) was a Theatine monk and ascetical writer. The selection is from *The Spiritual Combat,* as translated and edited by Thomas Barns (London: Methuen and Co., 1909). This great treatise, written in Venice, was a favorite with St. Francis de Sales and has had more generally a wide influence in France.

Sheehan, Patrick Augustine, Canon (1852–1913), was a novelist, a critic and an observer of events. *My New Curate* (1899) was one of the first novels to treat of the life of a village priest. The selection is from *The Literary Life and Other Essays* (New York: P. J. Kenedy and Sons. 1922).

Sienkiewicz, Henryk (1846–1916), was a native of what was then Russian Poland. The three volumes of his great trilogy concerned with Polish history were published in English translation after 1890—*With Fire and Sword, The Deluge,* and *Pan Michael.* The selection is from *Pan Michael,* as translated by Jeremiah Curtin (Boston: Little, Brown and Co.). Sienkiewicz's other works include *Quo Vadis?* a story of Rome under the Emperor Nero, first published in 1895.

Skinner, Richard Dana (1893–1941), was during many years dramatic critic for *The Commonweal,* and the selection is part of a critical essay contributed to that periodical (Vol. VI, 1927).

Sonnenschein, Carl (1876–1929), one of the great modern apostles of the social conscience, was born in Dusseldorf and died in Berlin. Ordained to the priesthood after studying in Rome, he worked with Catholic organizations (*Volksverein*) until the First World War. When that struggle ended, he carried on indefatigable relief and rehabilitation work. The selection is from *Notizen* (Berlin, 1925).

Southwell, Robert, Blessed (c. 1501–1595), was an English Jesuit who suffered martyrdom under Queen Elizabeth. He was the finest religious poet of his time, his most popular lyric being "The Burning Babe." Father Southwell also wrote much in prose. The selection is from *The Triumphs Over Death,* written in memory of Lady Margaret, wife of Robert Sackville and daughter of Thomas Howard, Duke of Norfolk. This same gracious lady was the theme of the selection by Saint John Fisher.

Spalding, John Lancaster (1840–1916), was Bishop of Peoria from 1877 to 1908. His sermons and essays made him one of the most influential Catholic writers of his time in the United States. The selection is from an essay on "Books," and is quoted from *The Catholic Tradition in English Literature,* edited by George Carver (New York: Doubleday, Page and Co., 1926).

Stevenson, Robert Louis (1850–1894), triumphed over delicate health to become one of the most beloved writers of his time. His books include *Treasure Island* (1883), *Dr. Jekyll and Mr. Hyde* (1886), *The Weir of Hermiston* (1896), and *Travels with a Donkey* (1879). The selection is from *A Footnote to History,* which defended Father Damien against the attacks of one Rev. Dr. Hyde. It was originally published in 1893.

Stoddard, Charles Warren (1843–1909), was one of the discoverers of the literary appeal of life in the Hawaiian Islands. *South-Sea Idyls,* from which the selection is taken, was published in Boston during 1873. Stoddard was a member of the California literary colony which included Kipling and Stevenson; and this he described in *The Island of Tranquil Delights.* Later he taught English literature at Notre Dame University and the Catholic University of America. His other writings include *The Lepers of Molokai* and *Poems.*

Stuart, Henry Longan (1875–1928), was one of the founders and first editors of *The Commonweal,* to which he contributed the essay from which the selection is quoted (July 15, 1925). He was the author of *The Weeping Cross* and *Fenella,* both novels, and the translator of many books by such authors as Paul Claudel and Julian Green.

Teresa, Saint (1515–1582), was born at Avila, Spain, and entered a convent of the Carmelites during her eighteenth year. She was not only a fervent mystic, knowing all the raptures and sorrows of the interior life, but a masterly religious superior. The selection is from her *Autobiography,* one of the noblest books in Spanish literature. The version edited by Benedict Williamson (London: Burns, Oates and Washbourne, 1910) has been followed.

Tertullian (c. 155–222), was a brilliant apologist for Christianity. His full name was Quintus Septimus Florens Tertullianus. He enjoyed a reputation as a jurist prior to his conversion (c. 190), and he eventually sided with the Montanists against Rome. But at the height of his powers he was the most brilliant exponent of the Christian position. To him we owe some of the great paradoxes of Christian literature, as for instance the *Credo quia absurdum* ("I believe because it is absurd") round which much ancient and modern commentary has been written. For information see *The Conflict of Religions in the Early Roman Empire,* by R. R. Glover (London, 1909). English versions of Tertullian's most important writings are to be found in the collections known as *The Ante-Nicene Fathers* and *The Library of the Fathers.* The present selection is from the famous "Testimony of the Christian Soul," as translated in the edition of the Rev. H. Roberts and James Donaldson (Edinburgh: T. and T. Clark, 1869).

Thérèse of Lisieux, Saint (1873–1897), was a Carmelite nun who is reverenced as the "Little Flower," though her name in religion—Soeur Thérèse de l'Enfant Jesu—is also sometimes used. The selection is from the *Autobiography* written at the request of the Prioress of the Convent at Lisieux. The translation by the Rev. T. N. Taylor (New York: Benziger Brothers) has been used.

Thomas à Kempis (c. 1379–1471) lived according to the rule of the Brethren of the Common Life, and spent most of his mature years in the monastery of St. Agnes, near Zwolle, in the Netherlands. He is customarily designated the author of one of the most beautiful books in religious literature—*The Imitation of Christ,* from which the selections are taken. Scholars have, however, sometimes argued in favor of attributing the work to another writer. The translation used here is that of Canon C. Bigg (London: Methuen and Company, 1898). Recently a magnificent older version has been published by E. Klein (New York: Harper and Brothers. 1941).

Thomas Aquinas, Saint (1225–1274), was born near Naples and died at Fossanuova, on the way to the Council of Lyons. He entered the Order of St. Dominic about 1244 and began to study under St. Albertus Magnus. After four years spent in Cologne, he went to Paris and there gained a wide reputation as a teacher and thinker. Popularly he was nicknamed the "Dumb Ox," because of his resolute adherence to the Socratic method, but his title in the Church is *Doctor Angelicus*—the Angelic Doctor. St. Thomas's system of philosophy finds its most nearly complete exposition in the *Summa Theologica,* but other books (notably the *Summa contra Gentiles* and *Questiones disputatae*) are likewise important. In addition he was a great poet, as witness the hymns written, at the behest of Pope Urban IV, for the Mass and Office of Corpus Christi. The selection is from the *Summa Theologica.*

Thomas, Brother, of Eccleston, was the author of the Chronicle *De adventu FF. Minorum in Angliam,* which describes the coming of the Franciscans to England. This has been translated by Father Cuthbert (St. Louis, 1909) and by E. G. Salter (London: Burns, Oates and Washbourne. 1926).

Thomas of Ely, chronicler, is reputed to be the author of the *Historia Eliensis.* The selection is quoted from a translation by Percy V. O. Shelly in *English Prose and Verse,* edited by Henry S. Pancoast (New York: Henry Holt and Company).

Thompson, Francis (1859–1907), was educated at Ushaw College and Owens College, but decided upon a literary career and went to London. There he was reduced to utter poverty, from which he was rescued by Wilfrid Meynell, then editor of *Merrie England.* His fame as a poet rests on three illustrious volumes—*Poems* (1893); *Sister Songs* (1895) and *New Poems* (1897). Thompson's prose essays have been collected by E. Meynell. The selection is from *Shelley,* an essay which originally appeared in the *Dublin Review.*

Ullathorne, William, Archbishop (1806–1889), belonged to the Order of St. Benedict. In 1833 he became vicar-general for Australia, which was at that time primarily a penal colony. His *Autobiography,* from which the selection is taken, is chiefly concerned with the Australian experience. It has not only real historical value but great literary charm. As Bishop of Birmingham, Ullathorne was Newman's superior. The *Autobiography* was originally edited by Mother Augusta Theodosia Drane.

Vallery-Radot, René, is cited here as the author of the *Life of Pasteur,* from which some remarks by the great scientist are quoted. This work was translated into English by Mrs. R. L. Devonshire (New York: Doubleday Doran. 1923), but the version here used is new. Louis Pasteur (1822–1895) was a pioneer in the study of bacteriology, and to him are due discoveries of the very greatest importance, for example the control of fermentation and the treatment of hydrophobia.

Vasari, Giorgio (1511–1574), was an Italian architect and painter who is remembered primarily for his *Lives of the Painters,* originally entitled *Vite de' piu eccelenti architecti, pittori, e scultori italiani* and published in 1550. The standard translation, by Mrs. Jonathan Foster, was published in 1850.

Ward, Wilfrid (1856–1916), was the son of William George Ward, and editor of the *Dublin Review* after 1906. He was a learned man, had a wide range of intellectual interests, and possessed a considerable knowledge of the United States. His books include *William George Ward* and *Last Lectures.* The selection is quoted from *The Life of John Henry, Cardinal Newman,* where it forms part of a document cited (New York: Longmans, Green and Co. 1912).

Ward, William George (1812–1882), was converted from Anglicanism in 1845 and became the first notable English lay theologian. After 1868 he was the editor of the *Dublin Review* and the advocate of highly centralized ecclesiastical government. Ward's books include *Essays on the Church's Doctrinal Authority* (London, 1880) and *Essays on the Philosophy of Theism* (London: Kegan Paul. 1884). The selection is from the second.

Wiseman, Nicholas Patrick Cardinal (1802–1865), was born in Spain and educated in part in Rome. He went (1840) from the English Seminary in the Eternal City to England as vicar apostolic of the central district. When the hierarchy was reestablished in England (1850), Wiseman became first a cardinal and then archbishop of Westminster. He was conciliatory by nature and so able to cope with the difficulties encountered by the Catholic revival. *Fabiola,* a novel dealing with the persecutions suffered by the early Christians, was published in 1854. From it the selection is taken.

Wust, Peter (1884–1937), was a Catholic philosopher who taught at the University of Muenster, Germany. His works include *Die Auferstehung der Metaphysik* (1920) and *Die Dialektik des Geistes* (1928). The selection is taken from an essay entitled "Crisis in the West," which appeared in *Essays in Order,* edited by Christopher Dawson and J. F. Burns (New York: Sheed and Ward).

INDEX OF AUTHORS

The World's Great Catholic Literature

Edited by
GEORGE N. SHUSTER

Here is a superb anthology of the world's great Catholic *prose* literature. It offers a multitude of choice selections from the living literature of outstanding writers during the past nineteen centuries. No living authors are represented. The collection ranges from Biblical passages down to recent works.

Among the writings to be found in this anthology is a choice and varied selection from both English and American literature as well as outstanding translations of noted Continental works. Short stories, essays and biographies are included as well as extracts from famous longer books. Noted letters of interest are included.

THE WORLD'S GREAT CATHOLIC LITERATURE offers the modern reader the heritage of the great writings of over nineteen hundred years, carefully selected for their importance, beauty, and interest. Among the writers represented are both saints and sinners; men who lived happily in their world of everyday and others who found their joy in the heights of mystical experience. Among a host of others, we find St. Augustine, St. Thomas Aquinas, Dante, Petrarch, Cervantes, Cardinal Newman, Huysmans and Chesterton.

This book reflects the effect of Catholic life upon human thought and history and its contribution to Western culture. Readable and interesting in its wealth of selections, it offers an unusual and delightful introduction to a vast and varied literature. Including a convenient index of authors and comprehensive biographical notes, this book is the perfect gift, a "must" volume for every library, and an invaluable reference work.